→ The third part for
  — w/ respect to
   varying scale growth

→ Helpful filmson mystics

Teaching Mysticism

AMERICAN ACADEMY OF RELIGION

TEACHING RELIGIOUS STUDIES

SERIES EDITOR
Karen Y. Jackson-Weaver, Princeton University

A Publication Series of
The American Academy of Religion
and
Oxford University Press

TEACHING LÉVI-STRAUSS
Edited by Hans H. Penner

TEACHING ISLAM
Edited by Brannon M. Wheeler

TEACHING FREUD
Edited by Diane Jonte-Pace

TEACHING DURKHEIM
Edited by Terry F. Godlove, Jr.

TEACHING AFRICAN AMERICAN RELIGIONS
Edited by Carolyn M. Jones and Theodore Louis Trost

TEACHING RELIGION AND HEALING
Edited by Linda L. Barnes and Inés Talamantez

TEACHING NEW RELIGIOUS MOVEMENTS
Edited by David G. Bromley

TEACHING RITUAL
Edited by Catherine Bell

TEACHING CONFUCIANISM
Edited by Jeffrey L. Richey

TEACHING THE DAODE JING
Edited by Gary Delaney DeAngelis and Warren G. Frisina

TEACHING RELIGION AND FILM
Edited by Gregory J. Watkins

TEACHING DEATH AND DYING
Edited by Christopher M. Moreman

TEACHING UNDERGRADUATE RESEARCH IN RELIGIOUS STUDIES
Edited by Bernadette McNary-Zak and Rebecca Todd Peters

TEACHING JUNG
Edited by Kelly Bulkeley and Clodagh Weldon

TEACHING MYSTICISM
Edited by William B. Parsons

Teaching Mysticism

Edited by William B. Parsons

OXFORD
UNIVERSITY PRESS

OXFORD

UNIVERSITY PRESS

Oxford University Press, Inc., publishes works that further
Oxford University's objective of excellence
in research, scholarship, and education.

Oxford   New York
Auckland   Cape Town   Dar es Salaam   Hong Kong   Karachi
Kuala Lumpur   Madrid   Melbourne   Mexico City   Nairobi
New Delhi   Shanghai   Taipei   Toronto

With offices in
Argentina   Austria   Brazil   Chile   Czech Republic   France   Greece
Guatemala   Hungary   Italy   Japan   Poland   Portugal   Singapore
South Korea   Switzerland   Thailand   Turkey   Ukraine   Vietnam

Published by Oxford University Press, Inc.
198 Madison Avenue, New York, New York 10016

www.oup.com

Library of Congress Cataloging-in-Publication Data
Teaching mysticism / edited by William B. Parsons.
p.   cm. — (Teaching religious studies series)
ISBN 978-0-19-975119-8
1. Mysticism—Study and teaching.   I. Parsons, William Barclay, 1955–
BL625.T38   2011
204'.22—dc22   2010050578

9 8 7 6 5 4 3 2 1
Printed in the United States of America
on acid-free paper

{ CONTENTS }

{ CONTRIBUTORS }

Joy R. Bostic is an assistant professor in the Department of Religious Studies at Case Western Reserve University in Cleveland, Ohio. She teaches in the areas of African American religions, religion and healing, women's spiritualities, and issues in social justice and urban religion. Her scholarship focuses on mysticism and social transformation, sacred geography and activist traditions, and womanist/feminist perspectives in religion. She is currently working on a book about mysticism, activism, and nineteenth-century African American women.

David Cook is associate professor of Religious Studies at Rice University specializing in Islam. He did his undergraduate degrees at the Hebrew University in Jerusalem and received his PhD from the University of Chicago in 2001. His areas of specialization include early Islamic history and development, Muslim apocalyptic literature and movements (classical and contemporary), radical Islam, historical astronomy and Judeo-Arabic literature. His first book, *Studies in Muslim Apocalyptic*, was published by Darwin Press in the series Studies in Late Antiquity and Early Islam. Two further books, *Understanding Jihad* and *Contemporary Muslim Apocalyptic Literature* were published during 2005, and *Martyrdom in Islam*, as well as *Understanding and Addressing Suicide Attacks* (with Olivia Allison) were published in 2007. Cook is continuing to work on contemporary Muslim apocalyptic literature, with a focus upon Shi`ite materials, as well as preparing manuscripts on jihadi groups and Western African Muslim history.

April DeConick is the Isla Carroll and Percy E. Turner Professor of Biblical Studies at Rice University. She is a historian of early Jewish and Christian thought. What fascinates her is mapping the many ways that the Jesus tradition emerges across the literature, traditions that have left behind echoes of bitter controversies and competing memories. She has a deep love for exploring the various expressions of ante-Nicene mysticism, including the spirituality of classic Gnostic thinkers. Her work has been called "revisionist," challenging us to seek answers beyond the conventional. She is the author of *Seek to See Him: Ascent and Vision Mysticism in the Gospel of Thomas* (1996); *Voices of the Mystics: Early Christian Discourse in the Gospels of John, Thomas and Other Ancient Christian Literature* (2001); *Recovering the Original Gospel of Thomas: A History of the Gospel and Its Growth* (2005); *The Original Gospel* *of Thomas in Translation: With a Commentary and New English Translation of the Complete Gospel* (2006). She edited a volume of papers, *Paradise Now: Essays on Early Jewish and Christian Mysticism* (2006) and coedited *Thomasine Traditions in Antiquity: The Social and Cultural World of the Gospel of Thomas* (2005). Her book *The Thirteenth Apostle: What the Gospel of Judas Really Says* (2007), which is about the Gospel of Judas, is the first to seriously challenge the interpretation and translation published by National Geographic (2006). She is currently writing a book called *Sex and the Serpent*, and editing a volume on mysticism in the New Testament Gospels for the New Testament Mysticism Project. She is an active member of the Society of Biblical Literature where she serves as Cochair of the New Testament Mysticism Project. She also organized and chaired for many years the Early Jewish and Christian Mysticism Group. She is affiliated with the North American Patristics Society, and the International Association for Coptic Studies as well.

Jorge N. Ferrer is Chair of the Department of East-West Psychology at the California Institute of Integral Studies (CIIS), San Francisco. He is the author of *Revisioning Transpersonal Theory: A Participatory Vision of Human Spirituality* (2002) and coeditor (with Jacob H. Sherman) of *The Participatory Turn: Spirituality, Mysticism, Religious Studies* (2008). He is a distinguished scholar at the Esalen Center for Theory and Research, Big Sur, California, and in 2000, he received the Fetzer Institute's Presidential Award for his seminal work on consciousness studies. In 2009, he became an advisor to the organization Religions for Peace at the United Nations on a research project aimed at solving global interreligious conflict. Featured in *Journal of Transformative Education, Religion, and Education* and *Journal of Holistic Education*, his integral pedagogy is the focus of *Transformative Inquiry: An Integral Approach* (2010), an anthology of writings coedited by Professor Yoshiharu Nakagawa and Yoshiko Matsuda based on Ferrer's recent visit to Ritsumekian University, Kyoto. Professor Ferrer offers presentations, seminars, and workshops on integral spirituality and education both nationally and internationally.

Stephanie Ford is currently teaching part time at the Earlham School of Religion, after serving for ten years as associate professor of Christian Spirituality at ESR, a seminary of the Religious Society of Friends in Richmond, Indiana. After receiving an MA in English and teaching English as a Foreign Language on the college level for several years, Stephanie completed seminary studies at the Baptist Theological Seminary at Richmond (Virginia) in 1996. That fall, she began PhD studies in Christian Spirituality at The Catholic University of America in Washington, D.C., focusing her scholarship on women mystics, Quaker spirituality, and spirituality and suffering. Her dissertation project assessed Evelyn Underhill's contribution to mysticism and to women's spirituality in light of the feminist critique of theologian Grace Jantzen. Stephanie was awarded her doctorate in May 2003. Her teaching at the seminary has ranged from spiritual formation and direction to topical courses such as "Spirituality and the Body." Her ongoing scholarly interests include medieval women mystics, feminist spirituality, and questions related to spirituality and embodiment. Spiritual direction and lay renewal are also key interests. In 2006, she published *Kindred Souls: Connecting Through Spiritual Friendship*. Stephanie has also been a regular faculty presenter with the Upper Room Academy of Spiritual Formation, Protestant spirituality, spiritual disciplines, and depth psychology. She has also written for the devotional journal *Weavings*, and contributed to two dictionaries.

David B. Gray is associate professor of Religious Studies at Santa Clara University, in Santa Clara, California, where he teaches a wide range of Asian religions courses. His research focuses on the development of Tantric Buddhist traditions in South Asia, and their dissemination in Tibet and East Asia. His publications include numerous journal articles and book chapters, as well as *The Cakrasamvara Tantra: A Study and Annotated Translation* (2007).

Wouter J. Hanegraaff is professor of History of Hermetic Philosophy and related currents at the University of Amsterdam, the Netherlands, president of the European Society for the Study of Western Esotericism (ESSWE; see www.esswe.org), and a member of the Royal Dutch Academy of Sciences. He is the author of *New Age Religion and Western Culture: Esotericism in the Mirror of Secular Thought* (1998), *Lodovico Lazzarelli (1447–1500): The Hermetic Writings and Related Documents* (2005, with Ruud M. Bouthoorn), *Swedenborg, Oetinger, Kant: Three Perspectives on the Secrets of Heaven* (2007), and numerous articles in academic journals and collective volumes. He is the main editor of the *Dictionary of Gnosis and Western Esotericism* (2005), editor of *Aries: Journal for the Study of Western Esotericism* and the "Aries Book Series: Texts and Studies in Western Esotericism," as well as of five collective volumes on the study of religions and the history Western esotericism.

Lee Irwin has two MA degrees (Religion and English) and an interdisciplinary PhD (1989) from Indiana University, with specialization in religion, folklore, and anthropology. He has been an assistant editor and contributing author to volume thirteen (*Plains*) of the Smithsonian encyclopedic *Handbook of North American Indians*. He has published fifteen articles on Native American religion and three books: *The Dream Seekers: Native American Visionary Traditions of the Great Plains* (1994), *Native American Spirituality: A Critical Reader* (2000), and *Coming Down from Above: Prophecy, Renewal and Resistance in Native American Religions* (2008). His specialization is in the hermeneutics of dreams, visions, and prophecy among native peoples of North America as well as shamanism more generally. He has also published additional books and many articles in the area of esotericism and contemporary spirituality. He is currently professor and Chair of the Religious Studies Department at the

College of Charleston, the vice president of the Association for the Study of Esotericism (ASE), and an Advisory Board member for the Sophia Institute and for the Institute for Dream Studies.

Livia Kohn graduated from Bonn University, Germany, in 1980. She then spent six years doing research at the Institute for Research in Humanities of Kyoto University in Japan, after which she joined Boston University as Professor of Religion and East Asian Studies. She has also worked variously as visiting professor and adjunct faculty at Eötvös Lorand University in Budapest; the Stanford Center for Japanese Studies in Kyoto; Union Institute in Cincinnati, Ohio; and San Francisco State University. She has served on numerous committees and editorial boards and organized a series of major international conferences on Daoism. Her specialty is the study of the Daoist religion and Chinese long-life practices. She has written and edited over twenty books in this field, such as *Taoist Meditation and Longevity Techniques* (1989), *Daoism and Chinese Culture* (2001), *Monastic Life in Medieval Daoism* (2003), and will soon publish *Chinese Healing Exercises*. Besides English, she is fluent in German, Chinese, and Japanese.

Jeffrey J. Kripal holds the J. Newton Rayzor Chair in Philosophy and Religious Thought at Rice University, where he is also the Chair of the Department of Religious Studies. He is the author of *Esalen: America and the Religion of No Religion* (2007); *The Serpent's Gift: Gnostic Reflections on the Study of Religion* (2006); *Roads of Excess, Palaces of Wisdom: Eroticism and Reflexivity in the Study of Mysticism* (2001); and *Kali's Child: The Mystical and the Erotic in the Life and Teachings of Ramakrishna* (1995). He has also coedited volumes with Wouter Hanegraaff on eroticism and esotericism, *Hidden Intercourse: Eros and Sexuality in the History of Western Esotericism* (2010); Glenn W. Shuck on the history of Esalen and the American counterculture, *On the Edge of the Future: Esalen and the Evolution of American Culture* (2005); with Rachel Fell McDermott on a popular Hindu goddess, *Encountering Kali: In the Margins, at the Center, in the West* (2003); with G. William Barnard on the ethical critique of mystical traditions, *Crossing Boundaries: Essays on the Ethical Status of Mysticism* (2002); and with T. G. Vaidyanathan of Bangalore, India, on the dialogue between psychoanalysis and Hinduism, *Vishnu on Freud's Desk: A Reader in Psychoanalysis and Hinduism* (1999). His areas of interest include the comparative erotics of mystical literature, American countercultural translations of Asian religious traditions, and the history of Western esotericism from ancient Gnosticism to the new age.

William B. Parsons is associate professor of Religious Studies at Rice University. His publications include *The Enigma of the Oceanic Feeling* (1999), *Religion and Psychology: Mapping the Terrain* (2001), *Mourning Religion* (2008), *Disciplining Freud on Religion* (2010), and dozens of essays in multiple journals and edited books. He has served as Chair of the Department of Religious Studies (Rice University), director of the Humanities Research Center (Rice University), editor (the psychology of religion section) with *Religious Studies Review*, and has been a Fellow at the Institute for Advanced Studies (IAS) at Hebrew University.

Michael Stoeber studied philosophy of religion at the University of Calgary (MA, 1986) and the University of Toronto (PhD, 1990). He is currently professor of Spirituality at Regis College, University of Toronto, and cross-appointed to the Centre for the Study of Religion, University of Toronto. His main general area of interest is the nature of religious experience. Among other writings, his publications include *Reclaiming Theodicy: Reflections on Suffering, Compassion and Spiritual Transformation* (2005); *Theo-Monistic Mysticism: A Hindu-Christian Comparison* (1994); and *Evil and the Mystics' God: Towards a Mystical Theodicy* (1992).

Steven J. Sutcliffe is senior lecturer in the Study of Religion in the Religious Studies subject area in the School of Divinity, New College, University of Edinburgh. He is the author of *Children of the New Age: A History of Spiritual Practices* (2003) and editor of *Religion: Empirical Studies* (2004). He has published articles on new age and the history of the study of religion in various international journals including *Culture and Religion, Method and Theory in the Study of Religion, Religion,* and *Temenos*. He is currently working on an edited collection called *What Is Religious Studies? A Reader in Disciplinary Formation* for the Equinox series Critical Categories in the Study of Religion.

Hugh B. Urban is professor of Religious Studies in the Department of Comparative Studies at Ohio State University. He is primarily interested in the study of religion and secrecy, particularly in relation to questions of knowledge and power. The majority of his research has focused on Hindu Tantra in northeast India, but he has also written on the subject of religious secrecy in a variety of other contexts, such as new religious movements, contemporary neopaganism, and American politics. He is the author of five books, including *Tantra: Sex, Secrecy Politics and Power in the Study of Religion* (2003); *Magia Sexualis: Sex, Magic and Liberation in Modern Western Esotericism* (2006); and *The Secrets of the Kingdom: Religion and Concealment in the Bush Administration* (2007).

Philip Wexler is professor of Sociology of Education and holds the Bella and Israel Unterberg Chair in Jewish Social and Educational History at the Hebrew University of Jerusalem. He is the former editor of the American Sociological Association Journal, Sociology of Education, and author of a number of books that relate to education, society, and spirituality, including: *Social Analysis of Education* (1990); *Critical Social Psychology* (1996); *Becoming Somebody: Toward a Social Psychology of School* (1992); *Holy Sparks* (1996); *Mystical*

Society (2000); and, most recently, *Mystical Interactions: Sociology, Jewish Mysticism and Education* (2007) and *Symbolic Movement: Critique and Spirituality in Sociology of Education* (2008).

Elliot R. Wolfson is the Abraham Lieberman Professor of Hebrew and Judaic Studies at New York University. His main area of scholarly research is the history of Jewish mysticism but he has brought to bear on that field training in philosophy, literary criticism, feminist theory, postmodern hermeneutics, and the phenomenology of religion. His publications include *Through the Speculum That Shines: Vision and Imagination in Medieval Jewish Mysticism* (1994), which won the American Academy of Religion's Award for Excellence in the Study of Religion in the Category of Historical Studies (1995) and the National Jewish Book Award for Excellence in Scholarship (1995); *Along the Path: Studies in Kabbalistic Hermeneutics, Myth, and Symbolism* (1995); *Circle in the Square: Studies in the Use of Gender in Kabbalistic Symbolism* (1995); *Abraham Abulafia—Kabbalist and Prophet: Hermeneutics, Theosophy, and Theurgy* (2000); *Language, Eros, and Being: Kabbalistic Hermeneutics and the Poetic Imagination* (2005), which won the National Jewish Book Award for Excellence in Scholarship (2006); *Alef, Mem, Tau: Kabbalistic Musings on Time, Truth, and Death* (2006); *Venturing Beyond—Law and Morality in Kabbalistic Mysticism* (2006); *Luminal Darkness: Imaginal Gleanings From Zoharic Literature* (2007). Wolfson has also published two collections of poetry: *Pathwings: Poetic-Philosophic Reflections on the Hermeneutics of Time and Language* (2004), and *Footdreams and Treetales: 92 Poems* (2007).

Teaching Mysticism

Introduction

TEACHING MYSTICISM: FRAME AND CONTENT

Mysticism. At first glance, the meaning of the term seems readily apparent. With respect to etymology, the term is of Greek origin. Initially *mystikos*, derived from the verb *muo* (to close), lacked any direct reference to the transcendent, referring only to the hidden or secret dimensions of ritualistic activities. As Louis Bouyer (1980) notes, the link between mysticism and the vision of the Divine was introduced by the early church fathers, who used the term as an adjective (mystical theology, mystical contemplation) and defined it with respect to three interrelated contexts: biblical, liturgical, and spiritual. Importantly, access to God was always understood as taking place within a total religious matrix. It was not until the sixteenth and seventeenth centuries that one finds the term *mysticism* (*la mystique*) used as a substantive. Michel de Certeau (1992) reminds us that this shift was linked to a new discourse that framed contemplative figures as social types ("the mystics") and the emergence of a new understanding of the Divine as existing within human beings, a universal dimension of the deepest recesses of the mind hidden beneath the variety of religious traditions and their doctrines. These shifts paved the way for mysticism to be investigated comparatively and with respect to secular social spaces, which is to say both academically and scientifically. Thus it is that, at least in a conversational sense, one could point to St. Teresa of Avila, the Zen master Dogen, the Sufi al-Hallaj, or the Hindu sage Sri Aurobindo as "mystics"; the *Enneads*, the *Upaniṣads*, or the *Zohar* as classic "mystical texts"; and Ramakrishna's vision of Kali, St. Paul's ascent to Paradise, and Buddha's attainment of Nirvana as examples of "mystical experiences."

Yet what might at times seem to be a straightforward phenomenon exhibiting an unambiguous commonality has become, at least within the academic study of religion, opaque and controversial on multiple levels. For example, a cursory perusal of the literature reveals that different religious traditions use the term in different ways, whereas others do not use it at all. Some also call attention to the conflation of mysticism and linked terms (e.g., shamanism, Gnosticism, spirituality, esotericism), stressing the need to carefully sift out the meaning of such terms with respect to their historical trajectories and communal renderings. Further, extant academic scholarship on mysticism reveals a rich diversity of definitional strategies, controversial theoretical agendas, and methodological concerns, many of which have quite different perspectives on its interpretation and meaning. Indeed, the critical study of mysticism has become linked to a spectrum of contemporary issues that continue to be debated in the scholarly and public arenas.

Despite such controversy, many acknowledge that it is difficult to avoid not only the term but also the attendant theories and debates that have accrued as a result of the modern, academic study of mysticism. Bernard McGinn (1991, 265), in speaking to the relation between the study of mysticism and the self-understanding of a particular religious tradition, refers to the comic novel *Small World,* in which the hero, explaining why he wrote a thesis on the influence of T. S. Eliot on Shakespeare, notes: "Well, what I try to show...is that we can't avoid reading Shakespeare through the lens of T. S. Eliot's poetry. I mean, who can read Hamlet today without thinking of Prufrock." Although one must be aware of the potential problems associated with the academic study of mysticism, the hermeneutical strategies found within it have been generally beneficial to informing the insider perspective. At the same time, it is also fair to say that the controversies that have erupted over the use of the term, as well as the attendant attempts at theorizing, behoove those who attempt to teach mysticism to do so with an eye to presenting and unpacking its many problematic features. For example the Buddhologist Robert Gimello, in speaking to the etymology of the term, notes the implicit ways culture has crept into its supposed value-neutral formulation, complaining that "it is difficult to apply any of the widely accepted definitions or descriptions of mysticism to Buddhist praxis without the most serious reservations" (1979, 173). Indeed, even those within western traditions have raised their voices: Carl Ernst (2003, 121), warning that "not enough has been done to historicize and problematize the category of mysticism," notes that Sufi forms of mysticism cannot be properly understood absent some relation to Islam's focus on political, economic, and social issues; McGinn (1991) argues for his preferred use, with respect to Christian mysticism, of the term "Presence of God" which, as an umbrella concept, admits of not only the more familiar unitive encounters but a host of visionary, auditory, and related sensory and nonsensory encounters whose meaning depends on mystic, text, and context. Many also decry the misleading modernist assumptions linked with mysticism: the invariable focus away from the shared life of the community in favor of the atomistic individual and episodic "experience" (some going further to question the wisdom of the term *experience,* citing its epistemologically dubious and assumed import), as well as the failure to distinguish between episodic experience and mysticism as a *process* that, though surely punctuated by moments of visionary, unitive, and transformative encounters, is ultimately inseparable from its embodied relation to a total religious matrix: liturgy, scripture, worship, virtues, theology, rituals, practice, and the arts.[1]

These initial concerns are but preludes, having been amplified over the last few decades by a host of theoretical issues (e.g., the constructivist/perennialist controversy, comparativist dialogue, sexuality and gender issues, mysticism and ethics, mysticism and postcolonialist/postmodern discourse, mysticism and politics, mysticism and entheogens, typologies) all played out with respect to multiple methodological perspectives and varying institutional spaces. The academic study of mysticism has become rich and complex, mysterious and compelling, dense and troubling but, above all, of immense cultural relevance.

Structure

The contributors to this volume engage many of these concerns. Their primary aim, however, involves not simply the delineation and analysis of the various perspectives and debates spawned by the study of mysticism (although that can hardly be avoided in a book such as this) so much as it does the complexities of pedagogy. This is a book directed not simply at the educated layperson but also, and especially, at teachers: those invested in learning not only about the *what* of mysticism but also about the *how* to communicate its complex features.

To render intelligible the diverse literature surrounding this topic, and to ensure the best pedagogical results, this volume is organized with respect to four interrelated parts: (I) *Presenting the Mystical Element: Tradition and Context;* (II) *Negotiating Mysticism: Expanding the Map;* (III) *Investigating Mysticism: Perspectives, Theories, and Institutional Spaces;* and (IV) *Tracking Mysticism: Pedagogy and Contemporary Culture.* The contributors to this volume offer multiple pedagogical strategies from a variety of institutional spaces, the latter targeted with the understanding that different dynamics may accrue when faced with teaching in secular and religiously plural as opposed to specifically religious or theological social spaces. Taken together, the essays present pedagogical reflections on how best to communicate the broad range of the meanings of mysticism, its utilization in the traditions, the theories and methods used to understand it, and the multiple controversies that have ensued as a result.

In acknowledging the integrity and diversity of religious traditions, and the important fact that many who teach courses in mysticism concentrate on single religious traditions or a combination of traditions, part I, *Presenting the Mystical Element: Tradition and Context,* is devoted to unpacking the mystical element found in multiple religious traditions. The choice of the term *mystical element* is designed to emphasize that mysticism is to be understood as part of a religious matrix. The point here is not a simple affirmation of the "insider" perspective. Rather, it acknowledges that the term *mysticism* is ambiguous and problematic and must be qualified and allowed to accrue specificity within the context of individual traditions. Put simply, teaching Christian mysticism can be a radically different project than teaching Daoist mysticism. To allow for this diversity, part I contains essays from contributors (Hugh Urban, April De-Conick, Livia Kohn, David Gray, David Cook, and Elliot Wolfson) who canvass six major traditions: Hinduism, Christianity, Chinese religions, Buddhism, Islam, and Judaism. Part II, *Negotiating Mysticism: Expanding the Map*, adopts a similar strategy, offering contributions from scholars (Lee Irwin, Joy Bostic, and Wouter Hanegraaff) engaging those traditions and religio-cultural strands (Native American, African American, and Western Esotericism) where mysticism meets linked terms and widens its purview.

Parts I and II do not neglect reflections on comparative work and method or, for that matter, on the substantial theoretical issues animating the contemporary state of the field. However, and generally speaking, whereas the essays in parts I and II focus more on teaching the meaning of mysticism within individual traditions, the essays of parts III and IV center more on methodological perspectives, theoretical issues, social spaces, and contemporary trends. As indicated, it was not until the introduction of *mysticism* as a substantive, the mystics as a distinct category of religious types, and the rise of the academic study of religion that one began to see what in contemporary academia has become the study of mysticism. *Mysticism* and related "terms of art" have been defined (and often redefined) to serve as constructive conceptual lenses through which scholars and their multiple methodological tools understand, interpret, and analyze the mystical element within the traditions. The modern study of mysticism may well start with the data available within mystical traditions. However, its use of critical lenses is also designed to uncover the kind of complications, consequences, and contradictions that have at times gone unacknowledged by a given tradition.

The essays of part III, *Investigating Mysticism: Perspectives, Theories, and Institutional Spaces* (penned by Jorge Ferrer, Stephanie Ford, William Parsons, and Michael Stoeber), though hardly neglecting individual traditions, focus on multiple definitional strategies, perspectives, and methodological approaches (e.g., comparative, theological/philosophical, social scientific, feminist), as well as multiple theoretical debates played out with respect to varying social spaces (e.g., institutes, seminaries, universities). In part IV, *Tracking Mysticism: Pedagogy and Contemporary Culture*, Steven Sutcliffe, Philip Wexler, and Jeffrey Kripal acknowledge that contemporary social issues and movements have influenced the meaning, study, and pedagogy of mysticism. Sutcliffe, for example, in surveying the contemporary social surround, offers pedagogical insights on how to understand and communicate those mystical phenomena that have been subsumed under the umbrella term *the New Age*. Wexler is concerned with the sociological impact of a mystical society on educational theory and pedagogical strategy, the desirability of bringing mystical practices into religiously neutral or religiously diverse social spaces, and the challenges that a pedagogical strategy emphasizing an ethnography of being and mysticism brings to standard, traditional models of education. Kripal concludes the proceedings by suggesting that the pedagogical task cannot dispense with how issues concerning eroticism, anomalous phenomena, pluralism, the secular/religious divide, a heterogeneous student population, and the search for existential immediacy and healing influence the sense of identity of the participants in the classroom setting.

On Use

All essays offer a multitude of pedagogical strategies for teaching mysticism ranging from those based on the text, on fieldwork, and with respect to multiple forms of media to those based in the dynamics of the classroom, diverse forms of knowing, being, expression (e.g., somatic, emotional, artistic) and even the integration of contemplative exercises. In perusing the totality of essays, it is important to keep in mind that whereas each of the parts and the essays that compose them has an integrity all its own, they are hardly mutually exclusive. For example, it is evident that those interested in particular traditions would do well to focus on the essays that compose the first two parts, being that they offer strategies for defining mysticism and linked terms while pointing to indispensable texts and issues, extensive bibliographies, and even detailed syllabi. At the same time, one could, in the effort to construct such a course, also use any number of the reflections on methodological approaches and the delineation of major issues and debates in the field as contained in parts III and IV. In other words, the essays are constructed in such a manner so as to admit of selective appropriation and mixing. Along these lines, one could point to how the issues of mysticism, sexuality, and gender are tackled by a number of scholars in all sections, as are the problems of mysticism and society. Indeed, there are many such issues (e.g., the "definitional" problem, the question of a common-core) shared by contributors to all sections.

Finally, to advance the continuation of the dialogue between the members of a community of scholars interested in teaching mysticism, this volume is linked to an interactive website. Respondents can mix and match syllabi, post comments, ask questions, and engage in fruitful dialogue. Rice University has agreed to house and maintain this website on the webpage of the Rice University Religious Studies Department and its doctoral program in Gnosticism, Esotericism, and Mysticism (or GEM). The site is designed to grow organically once initial discussions and syllabi have been posted. Other avenues for enhancing teaching and scholarship (e.g., resources for graduate students, planning for conferences, possible edited projects) are also encouraged. In this regard I would like to thank Chad Pevateaux, my research assistant and colleague, who will help maintain the site and who has been a resourceful and steady hand throughout the formation of this volume.

Notes

1. For an especially cogent critique of the use of *experience,* see Sharf (1998).

References

Bouyer, L. 1980. "Mysticism: An Essay on the History of the Word." In *Understanding Mysticism,* edited by R. Woods, 42–56. Garden City, NJ: Inage Books.

de Certeau, M. 1992. "Mysticism," *Diacritics* 22 (2): 11–25.

Ernst, C. 2003. "Between Orientalism and Fundamentalism: Problematizing the Teaching of Sufism." In *Teaching Islam*, edited by B. Wheeler, 108–123. New York: Oxford University Press.

Gimello, R. 1979. "Mysticism and Meditation." In *Mysticism and Philosophical Analysis*, edited by S. Katz, 170–199. New York: Oxford University Press.

McGinn, B. 1991. *The Foundations of Mysticism.* New York: Crossroad.

Sharf, R. 1998. "Experience." In *Critical Terms for Religious Studies*, edited by Mark C. Taylor, 94–116. Chicago: University of Chicago Press.

PART I

Presenting the Mystical Element

TRADITION AND CONTEXT

Teaching "Hindu Mysticism"

Hugh B. Urban

"Hindu Mysticism" is arguably among the most challenging—but also most pedagogically fruitful—topics one might teach in a religious studies or any other classroom. I say this for three reasons. First, the material that could be placed under the category Hindu mysticism is vast and extremely diverse, spanning roughly 3500 years and encompassing literally thousands of different texts, sectarian traditions, philosophical schools, meditative practices, and physical techniques. Second, Hindu mystical traditions often include highly sophisticated philosophical debates that are difficult, confusing, and often bewildering to most students. Third, and perhaps most important, both terms in the phrase *Hindu mysticism* are extremely problematic for historical, political, and linguistic reasons and, therefore, require some critical unpacking. *Hindu* is itself not an indigenous term, but rather one derived from the Persian adaption of *sindhu*, the Sanskrit term for the Indus river. The terms *Hindu* and *Hinduism* were not adopted by South Asians to describe themselves until the nineteenth century, and even then, their use was tied to the complex politics of nationalism and Indian responses to colonial power (see Frykenberg 1991; King 1999, 82–142; Flood 1996, 6). Likewise, *mysticism* has no exact counterpart in any Indian language and has in fact historically been part of the Western imagining of the "mystic Orient." Indeed, the stereotype of the Hindu as the irrational, passive, otherworldly, navel-gazing mystic is one of the most enduring tropes in Western Orientalist literature and, not surprisingly, went hand in hand with the colonialism and imperialism that accompanied such stereotypes (see King 1999b, 82–142; Urban 2003, 1–72).

But all of these challenges can also be extremely productive for pedagogical reasons in the classroom. Indeed, they can be effective ways to help students challenge their own preconceptions about South Asian religions, the very nature of mysticism, and the complex historical encounters between European and Asian cultures in precolonial, colonial and postcolonial contexts.

This chapter will present some of the basic issues, methods, and materials for the teaching of Hindu mysticism. With some modifications, these could be adapted to either an undergraduate or graduate classroom, to a single class devoted to Hindu mysticism, to an introductory class on world religions, or to a seminar on mysticism more generally. I will begin with a discussion of the problems with both the terms *Hindu* and *mysticism* in the South Asian context as a part of a larger project of critical and engaged pedagogy; I will then suggest a possible outline for a syllabus on "Hindu Mysticism," organized both historically and thematically; and finally, I will conclude with some pedagogical techniques and devices that I have found especially useful in teaching the subject, ranging from analysis of film, to in-class debates, to local ethnographic projects, to theoretical workshops on comparative themes such as the body, gender, and sexuality in mystical experience.

Orientalism, Hinduism, and the Stereotype of the "Mystic East"

From the outset of any intelligent discussion of Hindu mysticism, I would argue, one first needs to help students critically interrogate both the terms *Hindu* and *mysticism*. The approach to teaching that I find most useful is a form of critical, engaged, and participatory pedagogy suggested by authors such as bell hooks (1994), Henry Giroux, and Peter McLaren. The basic aim of critical pedagogy is to transform students from passive recipients of information into active, engaged, and critical participants in the creation of knowledge. As McLaren observes, a critical approach requires that we ask students not simply to memorize an array of facts, but rather that we help them to think carefully about the ways in which knowledge is constructed and the ways in which knowledge is inevitably tied to real relations of power: "Critical pedagogy asks how and why knowledge gets constructed the way it does, and how and why some constructions of reality are legitimated and celebrated by the dominant culture" (2003, 72).

In this case of teaching "Hindu Mysticism," this would mean first analyzing these two terms and asking students to look critically at the ways in which their construction was also historically tied to relations of power. After all, neither Hinduism nor mysticism are indigenous South Asian categories, and both have complex genealogies and tangled political implications. The terms *Hindu, Hindoo,* and *Hinduism* first begin to be used by Indian reformers and British Orientalist scholars writing in the early nineteenth century. And for the next two hundred years, these terms would be intimately tied to the politics of colonialism, imperialism, and nationalism. For British missionaries and Orientalists, such as Reverend William Ward, the wild diversity of "Hindoo" idolatry and polytheism presented the surest evidence of India's need to be ruled by a more civilized power and converted to the guiding light of Christ (see

Ward 1822; Inden 1990; Urban 2003, chap. 1). For Indian authors such as Rāmmohun Roy, Swāmī Vivekānanda and many others, conversely, defining a coherent, respectable "Hindu religion" was a key part of the defense of Indian identity in the face of foreign rule. The ongoing redefinition of Hinduism remains a key part of Indian national identity today, both in South Asia and in a diasporic context (see King 1999b, 82–142; Larson 1995).

Mysticism, meanwhile, is a term with an equally complex genealogy in European literature and is likewise tied to very real relations power. As Grace Jantzen has persuasively shown, the category of mysticism in Christianity has historically been closely tied to questions of power, authority, and gender—that is, who gets to claim the authority of mystical experience, and who is branded a heretic or a witch? What sorts of power and risks come with the claim to mystical experience? And how is mystical experience imagined differently for males and females? "'[M]ysticism' is a social construction, and it has been constructed in different ways at different times.... The current philosophical construction of mysticism is therefore only one in a series of social constructions of mysticism; and, like the others, is implicitly bound up with issues of authority and gender" (1995, 1).

In the case of Orientalist literature on India, as Richard King (1999b) argues, the category of mysticism was also closely tied to the power relations between East and West and to the definition of Hinduism. There is no Sanskrit or any South Asian vernacular term that precisely corresponds to the abstract category "mysticism" (though there are terms that come close to the English words *mystery* and *secret,* such as *rahasya, gupta, guhya, gūdha, marman*). Yet from the early nineteenth century onward, Western literature on Hinduism has consistently portrayed this as a land of exotic mysticism, otherworldly introspection, and impractical irrationality. As such, King suggests, the Western imagining of the mystical Hindu both helped justify the need for rational, strong, practical imperial rule and helped construct the modern category of "religion." Even as Hinduism was increasingly imagined as the irrational, passionate, exotic, effeminate realm of the mystical, so too, Western European (and particularly Protestant) Christianity was reimagined as the realm of rational, orderly, civilized, masculine religion.

> The association of the religions such as Hinduism and Buddhism with mysticism and the stereotype of the navel-gazing, antisocial and otherworldly mystic has come to function as one of the most prevailing cultural representations of Indian religion and culture in the last few centuries.
>
> The privatization of mysticism, when coupled with the post-Enlightenment association of the mystical with the non-rational... has also led to the characterization of "mystics" as largely uninterested in or antithetical to social, ecclesiastical and religious authority. (King 1999b, 33)

These debates surrounding the Western imagining of Hinduism are by no means relics of the colonial past but are still raging in the twenty-first century (Urban 2003, chaps. 1–3). Indeed, a number of American scholars have been severely criticized by contemporary Hindus, who argue that their tradition continues to be portrayed as an exotic, erotic, mystical "other." Much of the debate began with the publication of Jeffrey J. Kripal's (1998) hugely influential but controversial work on the mystical life and sexuality of the revered Hindu saint Ramakrishna, which triggered a firestorm of criticism in both the United States and India. Shortly thereafter, other American scholars also came under fire, including David Gordon White (2003) for his work on Hindu Tantra and Sarah Caldwell (1999) for her work on goddess worship in Kerala. Indeed, in 2007, Ramaswamy, de Nicholas, and Banerjee, a group of critics, even published a massive tome titled *Invading the Sacred*, which argues that American scholars are perpetuating a form of neocolonialism and cultural imperialism in their ongoing depiction of Hinduism as an exotic other. Ramaswamy et al. are particularly critical of the ways in which Hindu traditions are being taught in undergraduate classrooms, where they see American professors continuing to present a distorted, exotic image of their religion.

As such, a critical interrogation of terms such as *Hindu* and *mysticism* in the South Asian context is by no means a purely scholarly exercise; rather, it can also be an important pedagogical tool in the classroom to help students to interrogate these categories more broadly. Indeed, it raises key questions about how religious categories and identities are formed, what gets to count as "religious" or "mystical," and what are the very real political stakes in these ongoing debates. It also lends itself perfectly to a pedagogical approach based not on passive memorization but rather on engaged questioning and dialogue, as students are challenged to rethink and debate some of our most taken-for-granted categories of knowledge such as Hinduism, mysticism, and religion.

Creating a "Hindu Mysticism" Syllabus: Historical, Thematic, and Historically Thematic Approaches

Because of the vastness and diversity of the materials that could be labeled Hindu mysticism, there is no single right or wrong way to organize them pedagogically. The most common ways of presenting the topic are either: historically (i.e., begin with the Vedas, work through classical yoga, philosophical schools such as Vedānta, bhakti devotional literature, Tantra, and then end with colonial and postcolonial literature); or thematically (i.e., organize the material around major tropes such as the self and ultimate reality, the role of the body, the social position of mysticism in Indian culture, gender, sexuality, politics, and power, etc.).

Both approaches have their advantages and disadvantages. M[
proach is something of a compromise between the two, following
historically framework, while also introducing key themes in the dis
each historical period. One, admittedly somewhat arbitrary, way of c̶.̶ᵧ̶.̶.̶.̶.̶.̶.̶.̶.̶ᵧ̶
the material for a ten-week quarter (or ten units spread over a longer semester)
would be as follows:

I. Introduction: What is *Hindu*, and what is *mysticism?*
II. The Vedas: Early speculations on the nature of the self and ultimate
reality
III. Early yoga literature: The body and meditation
IV. The path of knowledge: Mysticism and Hindu philosophical schools
V. The path of love: Bhakti and devotional mysticism
VI. The path of desire and power: Tantra, gender, and sexuality
VII. Mysticism and social critique: Sants and Bāuls
VIII. Colonialism and nationalism: Constructing the "Mystic Orient"
IX. Postcolonialism and globalization: Gurus, god-men, and goddesses
incarnate
X. Political and theoretical debates in the study of Hindu mysticism
today *everyday mysticism*

The introductory section would thus grapple with the basic questions of defining *Hindu* and *mysticism* in the South Asian context, as discussed in the previous section. Here students would engage the complex questions of how these
two terms have been tied to the politics of colonialism and nationalism, and
how both have been used in problematic ways over the last two hundred years.

The second section would then focus on the earliest Hindu scriptures, the
Vedas (roughly 1500–300 BCE), and the first speculations about the nature of
ultimate reality and the self. Mystical themes can be found in the oldest stratum
of the Vedas, the *Ṛg Veda*, where we find the earliest speculations about the oneness of reality and the manyness of phenomenal experience; but these themes
become progressively more important in later Vedic literature and reach their
full flowering in the body of texts called the *Upaniṣads* (700–300 BCE), which
contain the most elaborate early discourses on the nature of the self (*ātman*)
and its relation to ultimate reality (*brahman*) (Olivelle 2008; Samuel 2008).
Here students would be introduced to both a close reading of mystical literature
and an analysis of the social and institutional structures through which mystical knowledge is transmitted: priesthood and various lineages of priestly authority, the guru-disciple relationship, the relations between priests and kings,
and differential access to mystical literature by social class (Thapar 1994).

The third section of the course would then focus on the early yoga literature
that begins in the *Upaniṣads* and comes to fruition in classic texts such as the
Yoga Sūtras of Patañjali (roughly 100 BCE–500 CE). Here we find increasing
interest in techniques of concentration and meditation, accompanied by

physical postures and the role of the body, the breath and senses in spiritual practice. This can provide an opportunity for students to think about the embodied dimensions of mysticism and the ways in which the physical body can be at once an obstacle to overcome and a tool used in the liberation of the spirit. Students will likely be surprised to discover, for example, that the *āsanas* or physical postures play a very minor role in Patañjali's early system and the final goal is the separation of the spirit from the physical-material realm. This can generate a useful discussion of how yoga finally evolved into its present forms as practiced in modern Indian and in its popularized varieties practiced throughout the United States (see Miller 1998; White 2009).

In the fourth section, the course would engage the more intellectual side of Hindu mysticism that developed with philosophical traditions such as Vedānta, Sāṃkhya, and the other major schools (*darśanas*). Students would encounter the remarkable sophistication of Hindu philosophical debate that gave birth to various positions on the nature of ultimate reality, the self and the material world. This would in turn give them a sense of the extremely subtle distinctions between specific philosophical views of reality and religious experience, such as the debates even among different schools of even one *darśana* such as Vedānta—Advaita (absolute nondualism), Dvaita (dualism), Viśiṣṭādvaita (qualified nondualism), and so on—not to mention the complex distinctions within the other major philosophical schools. In other words, students would quickly realize that mysticism is rarely just a matter of merging directly into the Godhead, but involves incredibly nuanced distinctions between the most minute details of philosophical language (see King 1999a).

The fifth part of the course would then turn to the devotional side of Hindu mysticism, the *bhakti* tradition, whose roots can be traced back to as early as 500 BCE and which flowered for the next 1000 years. This would trace the rise of new forms of affective mysticism that developed in the Sanskrit epics, the *Mahābhārata* and *Rāmāyaṇa*, mythological literature, the *Purāṇas*, and a wide range of vernacular texts, poetry, and drama. Here students would encounter the highly passionate, often erotic mystical themes that emerged in the worship of personal deities such as Viṣṇu (and his incarnations Kṛṣṇa and Rāma), Śiva, and various forms of the goddess (e.g., Kālī, Umā). At the same time, students would explore the wide range of devotional literature that flowered not just in Sanskrit but in Tamil, Hindi, Bangla, and other vernacular languages (see, e.g., McDermott 2001; Ramanujan 1973).

In the sixth section, the course would examine the role of gender, sexuality, and the body in the Hindu Tantric tradition, which begins in roughly the fourth or fifth century CE. While there are many, many ways to try to define the complex body of texts, sectarian traditions, rituals, and meditative techniques that are today lumped under the general category "Tantra" or "Tantrism," I find it most useful to define Tantra as a "path of desire and power." That is to say, Tantra seeks to harness desire (*kāma*) in all its forms—including but not limited to sexual desire—and to transform desire from a source of t into a source of spiritual liberation (see Urban 2009, 19–25; White 2003; 2008; Flood, 2006).[1] At the same time, Tantra is also a path of power that seeks to awaken and harness the tremendous energy (*śakti*) of the goddess that is believed to circulate through all aspects of the cosmos, the social-political order, and the human body alike. Here students can grapple with the complex role of the body and the senses in spiritual practice, the debates over the role of sexual union in Tantric ritual, and the controversies surrounding women's roles in Tantra. Is Tantra a source of authority and empowerment for women, or is it rather a new form of exploitation of women's bodies for male ends? (Or is it perhaps a far more complex, historically diverse and ambiguous tradition in which women might have multiple and multivalent roles?) (See Urban 2009, chap. 5; Biernacki 2007.)

In the seventh part of the course, students would examine the role of mysticism as a form of cultural critique and social resistance, by examining movements such as the Sants (thirteenth century CE onward), Bāuls (nineteenth century to present), and others. Central to both the Sant and the Bāul traditions is the belief that the divine lies within every human heart and that outward religious institutions and social hierarchies are obstacles rather than aids to spiritual realization. Many of the Sant songs contain powerful critiques of class and caste divisions, while the Bāuls engage in even more radical transgressions of traditional laws of purity, class, and sexual relations (see Hess 2002; Salomon 1995). As such, students would encounter forms of Hindu mysticism that are hardly just a matter of "otherworldly navel-gazing," but are in fact also involved in serious critique of society, culture, and religious institutions.

The eighth section of the course would then discuss the impact of colonialism and nationalism on both the category of Hinduism generally and the idea of Indian mysticism, in particular. While mystical currents of various forms can be found throughout Indian literature for the preceding 3500 years, the stereotype of the Hindu mystic became a key part of the discourse of Orientalist scholars, Christian missionaries, and colonial authorities of the nineteenth and early twentieth centuries. In turn, a variety of Indian reformers such as Rāmmohun Roy, Swami Vivekānanda, Śrī Aurobindo, and various others set out to reimagine Hinduism as a major "world religion," comparable to Christianity, Judaism, and the other "great religions" (Halbfass 1988; Masuzawa 2005). As authors such as Vivekānanda argued, the Hindus may be weaker in terms of physical fore and military might than the Europeans, but they are superior in their philosophy, spirituality, and mystical insight. The West may have conquered India politically and economically, but Hindus would rise to "conquer the world with [their] spirituality" (Urban 2003, 154–156). In short, ironically, Vivekānanda and Hindu reformers helped perpetuate the stereotype of the mystical Orient, set in opposition to the materialist Occident, simply by inverting the binary and making the former now superior to the latter (King 1999b, 118–142; Urban 2009, 18). Students would thus be pushed to engage the highly complex cross-cultural dynamics of colonialism, imperialism, and nationalism. Indeed, they would engage the very question of how the categories of both Hinduism and "the mystic Orient" were constructed, in relation to a variety of complex social, historical, and political dynamics.

The ninth section of the course would then examine the rise of a variety of new forms of mysticism, along with new gurus, god-men, and goddesses incarnate, in a twentieth- and twenty-first-century global context. Students would discuss the impact of globalization, new information technologies, and transnational capitalism on Hindu mysticism, by examining a range of modern gurus, both Eastern and Western. Among the more fascinating neo-Hindu gurus one might examine are the self-styled guru of the rich and sex guru, Bhagwan Shree Rajneesh, who made a global circuit from India to Oregon and back to India again (where he was reborn as Osho); Sathya Sai Baba, one of the most influential mega-gurus in contemporary times, known for his ability to miraculously materialize small objects from his hands; and Shree Maa of Kāmākhyā, who is believed to be a living embodiment of the goddess Kāmākhyā, and now resides at a lively temple in Napa Valley, California (see Urban 2003, chap. 6; 2009, chap. 7; McKean 1996). In the process, the students would debate the ways in which Hindu mysticism is being translated, transformed, reinterpreted, and redefined—at times almost unrecognizably—amid the transnational flows of people, ideas, and capital in the twenty-first century.

Finally, the last part of the course would focus on the more complex and volatile debates surrounding the study of Hindu mysticism today, particularly in the United States. Here students could read the critiques of American scholarship on Hinduism, such as *Invading the Sacred* (Ramaswamy, de Nicholas, and Banerjee 2007), along with the equally powerful responses to these critiques by American scholars (see, e.g., Kripal 2001; Courtright 2004). Kripal, for example, has an entire website devoted to the discussion, critique, and defense of *Kālī's Child*, which offers a fine resource for students to engage this complex debate.[2] This debate would bring the discussion of the very category of Hindu mysticism full circle, by asking students to debate whether Orientalist stereotypes of the mystic East have indeed been perpetuated in twenty-first century America, or whether there is a new and more complex transnational dynamic at work (see Urban 2009, intro., concl.).

Some Suggested Pedagogical Methods and Tools

Because of the challenges I mentioned at the beginning of this chapter, teaching Hindu mysticism calls for some creative pedagogical strategies. But again, these challenges can be extremely fruitful in the classroom and can push students to think in new ways about the very nature of religious studies and cross-cultural understanding.

Indeed, the very complexity of Hindu mysticism—as well as the historical and political complexity of the category itself—make it ideally suited to the sort of engaged, participatory, critical pedagogy suggested by hooks, McLaren, Giroux, and others. What follow are a few of the pedagogical tools I have found to be useful in my own classrooms.

CRITICAL ANALYSIS OF THE "MYSTIC ORIENT" STEREOTYPE IN POPULAR CULTURE

One easy and entertaining way to get students to interrogate the stereotype of the mystic Orient is through the analysis of popular cultural forms (such as films, novels, music, the Internet), both American and Indian. Students of the twenty-first century may be less and less skilled at reading texts, but they are arguably more and more skilled at critically analyzing film and other media. One can easily get students to analyze and deconstruct, for example, the imagining of the exotic Orient that begins with the American film *Gunga Din* (1939), continues with the Beatles' *Help!* (1965), and culminates in Stephen Spielberg's *Indiana Jones and the Temple of Doom* (1984). But there are also a variety of Bollywood films one can bring in to show how these stereotypes have permeated Indian cinema as well. Wajib Shaikh's (2000) film, *Shaitan Tantrik*, for example, features a sinister Tantric priest who bears no slight resemblance to the ones in *Gunga Din* and *Indiana Jones* and sets out to kidnap beautiful maidens to sacrifice them to the dark goddess Kālī.

This sort of analysis of popular cultural forms can be one of the easiest and most effective ways to get students to think about the complex questions of how these traditions have been represented and imagined historically. Moreover, students could then be asked to think critically about how these representations of Indian traditions compare to those in more "serious" documentary films. Some of the more useful documentaries I have used in my classes include the classic *Altar of Fire* on the contemporary performance of Vedic ritual; the series *Sadhus: India's Holy Men* (Bedi 1994), which focuses on three fascinating figures from three separate mystical traditions; and Tracy Wares's (2001) documentary *Shakti*, which examines gender roles in contemporary Tantra and goddess worship in Assam. Students could then grapple with the question of whether and to what degree these more serious and "academic" films are more accurate or less laden with Orientalist stereotypes than these popular representations.

THE DEBATE: ARGUING HINDU MYSTICISM FROM MULTIPLE PERSPECTIVES

One pedagogical tool that I have found extremely useful in my classes on South Asian religions is the debate format. I often use this in place of either a midterm exam or a group project. Because there is a long history of philosophical debate within Indian traditions, it seems appropriate to have students engage in their own imaginative debate, by asking them to embody, articulate, and defend the positions of various philosophical schools. In my classes, I often do this as a role-playing exercise, in which I play, for example, the role of Emperor Akbar in the Mughal court and have students play the role of various mystical traditions and philosophical schools which each have to persuade me of the superiority of their respective positions. I ask the students to debate questions such as the nature of mystical experience, the relation between the self and ultimate reality, the most effective techniques of spiritual practice, and the implications of these traditions for social structure, politics, and gender.

Another possible topic for a debate is the critique of American scholarship on Hinduism that has erupted since the 1998 publication of Kripal's *Kālī's Child*. In this scenario, students could embody different groups of Hindu critics such as the authors of *Invading the Sacred;* scholars of Hindu mysticism such as Kripal, White, and Caldwell; South Asians groups in the United States and in India; and other academic and nonacademic parties. This could really give them a sense of both the intellectual and political issues at stake in the study of Hindu mysticism today and, ideally, a greater understanding of the strong emotions on all sides of this debate.

If the students are given adequate guidance and time to prepare serious arguments to pit against one another, this exercise tends to work extremely well and is usually a lot of fun. This can in turn help them understand both the history of philosophical debate in India and the ongoing debates surrounding the politics of Hindu studies today.

CRITICAL AND COMPARATIVE WRITING ASSIGNMENTS

In addition to debate, one of the best tools to help students develop the skills of critical, engaged analysis of Hindu mysticism is to assign writing topics on comparative themes. This asks students not simply to master a body of materials but also to analyze it in a broader historical and comparative context. For example, one could ask them to compare techniques of meditation in the *Yoga Sūtra*, in Kashmir Śaivite Tantra, and in a contemporary Hindu movement such as Transcendental Meditation; or to compare the role of spiritual authority in the Vedas, in Tantra, and in a contemporary Hindu tradition such as ISKCON (International Society for Krishna Consciousness); or to compare the role of social class in the Upaniṣads, in one *bhakti* movement, and in the Bāul tradition. For advanced students in a comparative religion program, one could also ask them to write comparative essays on mystical themes across cultures: for example, the role of gender in Jewish Kabbalah and in Hindu Tantra, or the role of spiritual authority in yogic traditions and Sufi traditions.

LOCAL ETHNOGRAPHY: FROM THE KRISHNA HOUSI
TO THE NEIGHBORHOOD YOGA CENTER

Depending on where one happens to be teaching, another useful exercise is to have students engage in some local ethnography and comparative analysis. Most college towns have some branch of ISKCON, a.k.a. Hare Krishna, which tends to be very open to students. This can provide an excellent opportunity to compare the role of devotional mysticism in Indian historical traditions with its contemporary interpretation in new religious groups such as ISKCON. Similarly, one could ask students to compare the role of bodily practice and mystical experience in a classical text such as the *Yoga Sūtra* or *Haṭha Yoga Pradīpikā* and its contemporary role in American yoga centers. This can generate some very productive discussions of the changing role of mystical traditions in a diasporic context, in the wake of globalization, and amid a vibrant global marketplace of spiritual commodities.

THEORETICAL WORKSHOP, I: THE BODY IN MYSTICAL
PRACTICE AND EXPERIENCE

Once students have a bit of the history and cultural context of Hindu mysticism under their belts, they should be ready for more advanced theoretical discussions of major recurrent themes. In my classes, I often take time to have students engage in a more complex discussion of pervasive tropes in Hindu traditions, such as the role of the human body in mystical practice and experience. One could ask students to compare the role of the body in the *Upaniṣads* and early yoga literature with its rather different role, for example, in Tantra or in the Bāul tradition. One could also examine different physical techniques, ranging from the use of *āsanas* and breath control in the *Yoga Sūtras* to the deliberate consumption of impure substances and practice of sexual rituals in violation of class laws, which one often finds among *tāntrikas* and Bāuls.

Students in more advanced classes could also be asked to read some contemporary theoretical literature on the body and sexuality, and then engage the question of whether and how one can put Hindu mystical traditions and Western theory into dialogue with one another. In my own classes (and in my research), I typically bring in theoretical perspectives from authors such as Michel Foucault, Gilles Deleuze, Georges Bataille, and Judith Butler (Urban 2009, intro.),[3] but one could easily bring in a different theoretical lineage, such as sociological work on the body, cognitive or phenomenological perspectives, and any number of others.

THEORETICAL WORKSHOP, II: GENDER, FEMINISM,
AND HINDU MYSTICISM

A second possible topic for a broader theoretical discussion is the role of gender and the use of feminist theory in the interpretation of Hindu mysticism.

Indeed, some of the most intense debates have centered on the role of women, for example, in Tantra, in devotional worship of the goddess, or in the Bāul tradition, and whether and to what degree contemporary feminist analysis is useful for understanding Hindu traditions. Here students could be asked to compare the role of women (or lack thereof) in early Vedic and Upaniṣadic literature with that in the *Tantras* or in the goddess-oriented *Purāṇas*; they could then engage the key question of whether worship of a female deity or celebration of the female body and powers of reproduction necessarily translates into greater power or status for actual human women (see Hiltebeitel and Erndl, 2000; Biernacki 2007; Urban 2009, chap. 5). They could also examine textual and ethnographic accounts of women's roles as gurus in various lineages (such as Śākta Tantra or the Bāul tradition) and discuss the question of how positions of religious authority might or might not affect women's place in mainstream society. A very useful film on this topic for pedagogical purposes is Tracy Wares's *Shakti*, which looks at a variety of women's roles in the goddess-centered tradition of contemporary Assam, northeast India.

In my own teaching and research, I tend to draw on theoretical literature on gender and sexuality such as Butler, Jantzen, Elizabeth Grosz, Amy Hollywood, and feminist critiques of Foucault and Deleuze (Grosz 1994; Hollywood 2002; Armour and St. Ville 2006). But one could easily bring in any number of other feminist perspectives, ranging from 1970s second-wave and radical feminists such as Mary Daly to third-wave critics of feminist essentialism to postfeminists and postcolonial feminist theorists. The key, it seems to me, would be to impress upon the students *both* the rich diversity of women's roles in Hindu mystical traditions *and* the rich diversity of contemporary feminist perspectives that could be used to interpret the Indian materials.

Conclusions and Comparative Issues

In sum, teaching Hindu mysticism is not only an ideal way to introduce students to a rich, complex religious tradition, but also an opportunity to engage in some of the most challenging issues in the study of comparative religions. Indeed, it raises some of the most difficult and politically volatile issues that are inherent in any attempt at cross-cultural understanding in a postcolonial but still violently contested global context. But for that very reason, teaching Hindu mysticism can also be a remarkably productive and rewarding pedagogical experience.

To close, I would like to suggest that the topic of Hindu mysticism can also generate some important comparative questions for the study of mysticism more broadly. These could be raised either within the context of a course on Hindu mysticism or in a comparative course on mysticism and religion. As Edward C. Dimock (1966) has shown, there are fascinating comparisons to be made between the erotic *bhakti* of groups such as the Vaiṣṇava-Sahajiyās and the devotional mysticism of medieval Christian literature. One could also draw useful comparisons between the role of the human body and sexuality in yoga and Tantra with their role in Jewish Kabbalah, as, for example, Elliot Wolfson (2005) has done. One could ask students to compare the role of women as gurus and religious authorities in Hindu traditions with their role in medieval Christianity or nineteenth-century American Spiritualism, as I (2009, chap. 4) and others have suggested. Of course, students could easily undertake some very entertaining comparisons of contemporary gurus in India with their popular counterparts in California or in cyberspace. In sum, a course on Hindu mysticism should push students toward a much broader comparative and critical inquiry into the category of mysticism itself, and ultimately into the complex, shifting nature of religion itself in an increasingly interconnected but no less volatile global context.

Notes

1. I adapt this definition from Biardeau (1991), pp.149–150.
2. Kripal, "Kālī's Child." http://www.ruf.rice.edu/~kalischi/.
3. Basic readings here could include: Carrette (2000), Bryden (2001), Armour and St. Ville (2006).

References

Armour, Ellen T., and Susan M. St. Ville. 2006. *Bodily Citations: Religion and Judith Butler.* New York: Columbia University Press.

Bedi, Rajesh and Denis Whyte, dirs. 1994. *Sadhus: India's Holy Men.* Film. Princeton, NJ: Films for the Humanities and Sciences.

Biardeau, Madeline. 1991. *Hinduism: The Anthropology of a Civilization.* Paris: Flammarion.

Biernacki, Loriliai. 2007. *Renowned Goddess of Desire: Women, Sex and Speech in Tantra.* New York: Oxford University Press.

Bryden, Mary ed. 2001. *Deleuze and Religion.* New York: Routledge.

Caldwell, Sarah. 1999. *Oh Terrifying Mother: Sexuality, Violence and Worship of the Goddess Kālī.* New York: Oxford University Press.

Carrette, Jeremy. 2000. *Foucault and Religion: Spiritual Corporality and Political Spirituality.* New York: Routledge.

Courtright, Paul. 2004. "Studying Religion in an Age of Terror," *The Academic Exchange* (April–May). [Online]. Available: http://www.emory.edu/ACAD_EXCHANGE/2004/ aprmay/courtright.html

Dimock, Edward C. 1966. *The Place of the Hidden Moon: Erotic Mysticism in the Vaiṣṇava-Sahajiyā Cult of Bengal.* Chicago: University of Chicago Press.

Flood, Gavin. 1996. *An Introduction to Hinduism*. Cambridge: Cambridge University Press.

———. 2006. *The Tantric Body: The Secret Tradition of Hindu Religion*. London: I. B. Tauris.

Frykenberg, R. E. 1991. "The Emergence of Modern 'Hinduism' as a Concept and an Institution." In *Hinduism Reconsidered*, edited by Gunter D. Sontheimer and Hermann Kulke, 29–50. New Delhi: Manohar.

Gardner, Robert, and J. F. Staal, dirs. 1976. *Altar of Fire*. Film. Harvard University: Film Study Center.

Grosz, Elizabeth. 1994. *Volatile Bodies: Toward a Corporeal Feminism*. Bloomington: University of Indiana Press.

Halbfass, Wilhelm. 1988. *India and Europe: An Essay in Understanding*. New York: State University of New York Press.

Hess, Linda, trans. 2002. *The Bijak of Kabir*. Boston: Beacon Press.

Hiltebeitel, Alf, and Kathleen Erndl, eds. 2000. *Is the Goddess a Feminist? The Politics of South Asian Goddesses*. New York: New York University Press.

Hollywood, Amy. 2002. *Sensible Ecstasy: Mysticism, Sexual Difference and the Demands of History*. Chicago: University of Chicago Press.

hooks, bell. 1994. *Teaching to Transgress: Education as a Practice of Freedom*. New York: Routledge.

Inden, Ronald. 1990. *Imagining India*. Oxford: Basil Blackwell.

Jantzen, Grace. 1995. *Power, Gender and Christian Mysticism*. Cambridge: Cambridge University Press.

King, Richard. 1999a. *Indian Philosophy*. Washington: Georgetown University Press.

———. 1999b. *Orientalism and Religion: Postcolonial Theory, India and the "Mystic East."* New York: Routledge.

Kripal, Jeffrey J. 1998. *Kali's Child: The Mystical and the Erotic in the Life and Teachings of Ramakrishna*. Chicago: University of Chicago Press.

———. 2001. "Secret Talk: Sexual Identity and the Politics of the Study of Hindu Tantrism," *Harvard Divinity Bulletin* 29 (4): 14–17.

Larson, Gerald James. 1995. *India's Agony Over Religion*. New York: State University of New York Press.

Masuzawa, Tomoko. 2005. *The Invention of World Religions: or, How European Universalism Was Preserved in the Language of Pluralism*. Chicago: University of Chicago Press.

McDermott, Rachel Fell. 2001. *Singing to the Goddess: Poems to Kālī and Umā from Bengal*. New York: Oxford University Press.

McKean, Lise. 1996. *Divine Enterprise: Gurus and the Hindu Nationalism Movement*. Chicago: University of Chicago Press.

McLaren, Peter. 2003. "Critical Pedagogy: A Look at the Major Concepts." In *The Critical Pedagogy Reader*, edited by Antonia Darder, Marta Baltadano, and Rodolfo Torres, 72. New York: RoutledgeFalmer.

Miller, Barbara Stoler, trans. 1998. *Yoga: Discipline of Freedom*. New York: Bantam Books.

Olivelle, Patrick, trans. 2008. *Upaniṣads*. New York: Oxford University Press.

Ramanujan, A. K. 1973. *Speaking of Śiva*. Baltimore: Penguin.

Ramaswamy, Krishnan, Antony de Nicholas, and Aditi Banerjee, eds. 2007. *Invading the Sacred: An Analysis of Hinduism Studies in America*. New Delhi: Rupa and Co.

Salomon, Carol. 1995. "Bāul Songs." In *Religions of India in Practice*, edited by Donald S. Lopez, 187–208. Princeton: Princeton University Press.

Samuel, Geoffrey. 2008. *The Origins of Yoga and Tantra: Indic Religions to the Thirteenth Century*. New York: Cambridge University Press.

Shaikh, Wajib, dir. 1999. *Shaitan Tantrik*. Film. Mumbai: Shri Film Production.

Thapar, Romila. 1994. "Sacrifice, Surplus and the Soul," *History of Religions* 33 (4): 304–324.

Urban, Hugh B. 2003. *Tantra: Sex, Secrecy, Politics and Power in the Study of Religion*. Berkeley: University of California Press.

———. 2009. *The Power of Tantra: Religion, Sexuality and the Politics of South Asian Studies*. London: I. B. Tauris.

Ward, William. 1822. *A View of the History, Literature and Mythology of the Hindoos*. London: Kingsbury, Parbury and Allen.

Wares, Tracy, dir. 2001. *Shakti: The Performance of Gender Roles at Kamakhya, Assam*. Film. Department of Anthropology: University of California, Berkeley.

White, David Gordon. 2003. *Kiss of the Yoginī: "Tantric Sex" in its South Asian Contexts*. Chicago: University of Chicago Press.

———. 2009. *Sinister Yogis*. Chicago: University of Chicago Press.

Wolfson, Elliott. 2005. *Language, Eros, Being: Kabbalistic Hermeneutics and Poetic Imagination*. New York: Fordham University Press.

2

Mysticism Before Mysticism

TEACHING CHRISTIAN MYSTICISM
AS A HISTORIAN OF RELIGION

April DeConick

Where does mysticism begin in the Christian tradition? Traditionally it has been conceived to begin in the fifth century with (Pseudo)-Dionysius the Areopagite who taught the *apophatic* way, where the soul escapes the created order to unite with the unknowable God (Louth 1981, 159). So conventional courses in Christian mysticism and the books on which they are based foster the idea that Christian mysticism is a relatively late Platonic and philosophical product of patristic theology. The first generations of Christianity and their foundational memories and narratives are casually brushed aside as "background" to a mysticism arising later, from Christianity's fusion with neo-Platonism (Louth 1981; Cohn-Sherbock and Cohn-Sherbock 1994).[1]

My pedagogical goal is to challenge this understanding of Christian mysticism by tracing the growth of mysticism in early Christianity as a distinctive expression of an already developed tradition of Jewish mysticism. I have named the course appropriately, "Mysticism Before Mysticism." It is a seminar for upper-class undergraduates and graduate students in Religious Studies at Rice University. It meets once a week for fifteen weeks in three-hour sessions.

The seminar progresses diachronically and dialogically, exploring mysticism in Second Temple Judaism and early Christianity, a period prior to the Kabbalah and Dionysius the Areopagite. Materials covered include Jewish and Christian scriptures; pseudepigrapha; Dead Sea Scrolls; and Gnostic, Hermetic, Patristic, neo-Platonic, and Hekhalot literature. Ancient astrological and magical traditions are also discussed.

Primary and secondary readings are assigned for each session. Each week, one student is responsible for leading the discussion by covering the primary materials in review. The other students are responsible for providing an oral overview of one book or set of articles from the required readings for that particular session. This generates a fascinating discussion and interchange among the members of the seminar about the history of Christian mysticism and its relationship to Jewish, Egyptian, and Greek expressions of mysticism.

A Contextual-Comparative Approach

The traditional definition of *mysticism* as it is applied to Christianity (and other religious traditions!) was fashioned from medieval monastic sources. Mysticism within the Christian tradition was identified with the spiritual life of the monk and nun who worked to purify their souls of darkness. Eventually, they undergo a spiritual death and upward journey to unite with a god who is described as "love" (cf. Underhill 1911; Egan 1991, xvi–xxv). This framing of the subject has resulted in privileging the monastic devotional experiences and practices, at the expense of other forms of mysticism.

Consequently, the problem of definition does not just involve semantics. It also involves comparativism and the distortion of history that can result when the point of comparison is not selected carefully. When historians of Christianity developed the language of mysticism, it was done with the medieval Christian monastic descriptions of immediate and direct contact with the divine as the yardstick. So mysticism became analogous to the experience of the monastic devotee. If this later developed concept becomes the point of comparison for the earlier period, then the earlier period becomes "background" with no mysticism to be found within it. This approach values and privileges the Christian monastic experience while failing to recognize the existence of mysticism in the earlier period.

So the problem of definition is not simply an academic exercise that I discuss with my students to launch my course. It is a question with profound implications, because the definitions we impose on our subject ultimately determine what we see and what we take away with us from that experience. If our definition of Christian mysticism is what medieval Christian mystics relate, involving a *unio mystica*, then Paul was not a mystic, nor was Jesus or any of Jesus's Jewish contemporaries. Christian mysticism, in fact, would begin with (Pseudo-)Dionysius the Areopagite, as the historical introductions to Christian mysticism suggest. The same problem can be tracked in the secondary literature about Jewish mysticism, which is conventionally defined from the point of view of the later Kabbalah, so that in the earlier centuries, Judaism is devoid of mysticism.

Yet, from the beginning, Christianity understood itself as a "revealed" religion, as a religion that was not only disclosed through direct and immediate divine-to-human communication, but whose dogma reveals to humans the hidden God and his will. With this self-identity, mysticism can scarcely be far away. Although it is true that a particular strand of Christianity fused with neo-Platonism produced the type of mysticism taught and practiced by

(Pseudo)-Dionysius, it is also true that long before (Pseudo)-Dionysius lived, there was a rich tradition of Christian mysticism already in place, a mysticism that grew out of even older Jewish mystical traditions as I have described elsewhere.[2] It was this Christian brand of early Jewish mysticism that eventually yielded a pliable branch for a neo-Platonic graft to take hold, such as it did in the teachings of (Pseudo-)Dionysius.

So what are we to do? I suggest a three-fold solution. By making these three shifts in approach, the discussion will no longer privilege the later monastic sacred experiences and route to the divine, but it will open up the exploration so that the texts of the early Christian period, rather than the conventional definition, will be allowed to circumscribe the specifics of the phenomenon.

First, I recommend beginning by working from a flexible understanding of mysticism that transcends cultural and historical relativism, such as *mysticism is the solicitation and participation in a direct immediate experience of the ultimate reality*. I would distinguish mysticism from *the mystical experience itself, which is the direct immediate experience of the ultimate reality solicited or not*. Working with this type of definition as a starting point has the advantage of controlling the problem of privileging certain religious traditions and their practices over others.

Second, to avoid the imposition of later developed views of mysticism on the earlier period, I suggest that we shift our point of comparison to the study of traditions closest to the early Christian texts, to move the discussion of mysticism to the materials that were produced by the Jews and Christians during the formative years of their religions. Christianity in this period is a form of Judaism that is beginning to self-identify as an entity distinct from Judaism. Even more complicated is the fact that Judaism is in its own process of self-definition in this same period. What we have is a situation in which two competing religions are emerging simultaneously, while claiming allegiance to a common scripture and history. Although Christianity eventually self-identifies as a distinct religion, its scripture, ideologies, and practices remain connected to its sibling through its common scripture and history. So to speak about early Christian mysticism means that it is impossible to talk about it without reference to Jewish traditions. Jewish mysticism and Christian mysticism are two sides of a single coin.

I have found that to study early Christian mysticism successfully, the Christian story needs to be integrated with the Jewish story. It is most enlightening when the course includes the study of Jewish and Christian materials simultaneously so that the one informs the other. This approach will not only identify certain characteristics of early mysticism held in common by the Jews and Christians, but it will also allow the students to identify those characteristics that are unique to Christian mysticism. Common features include a priestly cosmology based on foundational Jewish texts, particularly but not exclusively Genesis 1–3, Exodus 24, 33, Ezekiel 1, 8, 10, 40–48, Daniel 7, and Isaiah 6.[3] The centerpiece of this cosmology is the belief that God has a "body," called the "Glory" or *Kavod* of YHWH that could be viewed. The celestial realm was perceived to be the heavenly equivalent of the Jerusalem temple (and vice versa). The heavens themselves are *hekhalot*, shrine rooms or sanctuaries within the temple. The highest heaven is the holy of holies where the Glory resides, seated on the *merkavah*, the throne-chariot. Certain communities of Jews and Christians thought that it was possible for "prepared" humans to enter these sacred zones even before their deaths in order to participate in heavenly worship or to glance upon the Glory. This process often resulted in their transformation, for instance, when they would become "glorified," "exalted," or "angelic." These journeys were often solicited through "ritual" speech, hymning, asceticism, dream incubation, or participation in special liturgies.

In terms of distinct features of early Christian mysticism, the Glory is identified with Jesus Christ.[4] Because of this, the mysticism of early Christianity is strikingly Christocentric. It focuses on the "revelation of Jesus Christ," which is understood to be the disclosure of the mystery that has been hidden with God for the ages. This mystery is Jesus Christ as the Power and the Glory of God. The other unique feature of early Christian mysticism is the belief that *all* Christians experience this revelation. The experience was made "democratic" through a series of initiation and communal rituals, beginning with baptism when the Christ indwelled the initiate as the Spirit. The Christ/Spirit is regularly experienced in the life of the community and the other sacraments, particularly the Eucharist, where Jesus Christ is consumed by the faithful and thus taken directly into their bodies. This revelation of Jesus Christ results in (*apo*)*theosis*, where the believer morphs into Christ as God's image and (eventually) achieves the "lot" of immortality.

Third, I use a second point of comparison, carefully chosen, to provide further context and dialogical insight: contemporaneous non-Jewish and non-Christian traditions within the same cultural and historical locations, such as Greek mystery religions and neo-Platonic traditions. This comparative group helps us distinguish unique features of Jewish and Christian mysticism. At the same time, studying this data set allows us to see how the Greek ideas and practices become integrated into the Christian mystical tradition. From this, the integration can be mapped.

The Social Dynamic

Mysticism even within the "same" religious tradition may look very different in different social contexts. For example, the liturgies and mystical practices put into place by the Dead Sea Jews who "imaginatively" entered the heavenly tabernacle as a community of "angels" through the verbalization of Sabbath liturgies are quite distinct from the shamanistic practices of the Hekhalot Jews who individually descended to the chariot. The Gnostic Christian who rehearsed the names of the archons and underwent multiple baptisms and anointings in order to ascend out of this universe is doing something different from the Catholic Christian who undergoes a one-time initiatory baptism for his or her redemption. Even though all these groups reference similar themes (e.g., temple, glorification, gods of light, celestial beings, visions, ascents, angelification, spirit possession) and practices (e.g., water and anointing rituals, scriptural study, prayers, liturgies, incantations, hymning), the way in which these themes and practices emerge and develop within specific social contexts are strikingly different and idiosyncratic. When examining the historical development of mysticism, the social dimension and group dynamics cannot be overemphasized.

This appears to me to be a straightforward historical observation that does not require extensive philosophical discussion. So I am consistently asking my students to be aware of geographical, chronological, social, and cultural contexts of the historical and literary data and to map these as the course unfolds. I probe my students to consider the history of a specific group and to try to reconstruct group dynamics whenever possible. How do particular social dynamics affect the development of mysticism within that context? Who are the author's dialogue partners? What do we discover when we read the text against the grain?

In this way, the course challenges students to think not only in dialogical terms, but it asks students to read texts as a repository of a group's memory of the growth of its traditions. Students are made aware of the interactive and responsive nature of religious traditions. As they study different texts and the groups that created them, they begin to see that hermeneutics shift, meanings flip, and ideas invert as memories and traditions are passed along generationally and become part of a "new" group's cognitive reservoir.[5]

I have found that mysticism in the early Christian period develops a common "core." It is Christocentric, understanding the goal to be a vision of Christ or an experience of possession where Christ's spirit enters the person and "abides" within. Christ is perceived to be the Glory of God, the manifestation of the father God. This is the hidden secret of the eternal ages. The Christian mystical praxis involves water, oil, and eating rituals, as well as hymning, prayers, incantations, studying scriptures, and participating in liturgies. I cannot emphasize enough how central the Temple is to the mysticism that the early Christians develop. They understand their invasion of the celestial realms to be the journey of a priest into the sacred rooms of the Temple.

Clearly the mysticism that the early Christians develop is part of a coherent conversation that engages Judaism and certain Egyptian and Hellenistic traditions from the same period. Whether this identifiable "core" is comparable across a wider religious and chronological data set is beyond the scope of this course. Whether there is "something" perennial about mysticism, something

that transcends culture, is a question that requires a more thorough philosophical discussion, should this become one of the goals of the course.

Empathic Reading

The contextual-comparative approach means that the students ought to be
made aware of the necessity placed on historians to consciously distance ourselves from *etic* definitions. *Etic* definitions are those that we impose on our
subject. Because they are secondary and can grossly distort the subject by misunderstanding and misrepresenting it, we must continually evaluate those *etic*
definitions that do inform our thinking. Whenever possible, students ought to
read the ancient texts on their own grounds and dialogically, that is, in relation
to each other. They should attempt to assume the worldview of the ancient Jew
and Christian, and read out the ancient *emic* understandings of the mystical
whenever possible. What do the ancient people tell us about their own framings
of the mystical?

Such an approach means that I am asking students to no longer be complete
strangers to the old textual traditions, but to enter into them, to assume them
for a moment, and to look at the world through the author's eyes. This is a
precarious position for the historian, to be neither an insider nor an outsider,
but to adopt a liminal view as an interloper. It is the position that emerges from
empathy, rather than sympathy or antipathy. This position, however, should
not be perceived as one that collapses critical distance. The historian should
never be an apologist. Nevertheless, it is necessary to enter the "mind" of the
authors in order to appreciate and understand what these texts have to say
about the subject. To accomplish this successfully, students will need to be
trained in ancient worldviews and belief systems as different texts are assigned
and discussed.

What the student discovers from empathic reading is that the ancient Christians do not favor the word *mysticism* and its cognates, which derive from the
Greek word *myeô*, "to be initiated." Although they do sometimes speak of the
revelation of "mysteries" or "divine secrets" (*mystêria*), the first Christians call
their direct immediate pre-mortem experiences of God "apocalypses" (*apoca-
lypseis*) or "revelations." They write about these revelations as "rapture" events
as well as "solicited" events for which they prepare through a prescribed praxis.
They speak of the events as waking visions, dreams, trances, and auditions,
conceiving of them as events that often involved spirit possession and ascent
journeys. The development of the sacraments (*mystêria*), baptism, and the Eucharist resulted in the democratization of the mystical. They were the moments
in the life of the faithful when Christ and/or the Spirit were encountered and
embodied, and (progressive) transfiguration resulted. But in this early period,
the transfiguration is not described by them in terms of the *unio mystica* of

medieval mysticism. Rather it is perceived to be a transformative event, which, for example, delivered heavenly knowledge, or resulted in membership in the angelic choir, or enthronement, or a shining glorified body. In this way, the mystic's sacred transformation reflects the hopes and promises of the Eschaton, the conventional moment of bodily transfiguration and paradisial rewards. This is a Jewish story, not the Platonic one in which the hope was very different: the reunification of the immortal soul with the One, the Good.

What about Religious Experience?

As historians who study mysticism, we are plagued with the problem of religious experience. Put simply, in-and-of-itself religious experience cannot be studied from a historical-critical perspective. This problem has led to a disturbing undercurrent in our discussions, an undercurrent that hinders our investigation. Scholars have become divided over whether texts that relate stories of mystical experiences and practices assume genuine mystical experiences and practices or not. If not, what do they represent? Creative imagination? Hallucination? Trickery? Exegetical gymnastics?

It is unfortunate that scholars have structured their analyses along these lines. By doing so, the veracity of religious experience (something that cannot be empirically observed or described) has overwhelmed and impeded our otherwise critical conversation. I imagine that this argument was originally generated to offer a rational explanation for the irrational. Because the supernatural does not exist in modernity, some scholars tried to account for the ancient descriptions of mystical experience in rational ways, as hallucinations or exegetical enterprise. But this move to dismiss the "supernatural" conversation by rationalizing it has not increased our knowledge of ancient mysticism, although it does speak to modern perceptions that mysticism cannot exist.

The problem of modern mysticism—that the mystical experience cannot exist—appears to me to factor into the philosophical discussions and the contemporary constructivist approaches of Steven Katz (1978) and Wayne Proudfoot (1985) who take issue with the classical view that there is some pure ineffable experience that is described in a variety of fashions by a variety of mystics. Katz argues that there is no pure unmediated experiences because all our experiences are processed and shaped by our ways of knowing, and these are culturally derivative and dependent. Even similarly described experiences may reflect very different experiences. Proudfoot argues that the prevailing religious traditions create and simultaneously interpret the religious experiences of the mystics. The ineffable, he says, cannot be communicated (1985, 126). I wonder about these approaches. Should the different cultural manifestations of mysticism be used to challenge the veracity of the mystical experience itself? Certainly they offer an explanation for the modern dilemma, which does not recognize the veracity of mystical experience due to its connection to the supernatural. Although we might be able to plainly see that mysticism looks the same and different across cultures and times, and that all experiences are processed or perceived, it is quite another to conclude from this that pure mystical experience does not exist or cannot be communicated.

My historical solution to the problem is simple. It involves two straightforward observations. First, because the ancient people we are studying had a profound belief in the reality of the supernatural, we will learn more about their understandings of mysticism if we allow the supernatural to continue to exist for them. In other words, whether or not any of their claims to religious experience represent genuine encounters with God is a discussion that misses the historical-critical point. Our prime observation ought to concern the perceptions of the ancient people themselves, something that we can empirically recover from the literature.

The ancient people who read the scriptures and para-biblical texts that described the mystical journeys and experiences of the ancestors and heroes believed that these texts reported actual experiences with God. The same can be said about those who, such as Paul or John of Patmos or Hermas, wrote about their mystical experiences. The scriptures and para-biblical texts served as templates for their own mystical hopes, dreams, and practices. Study of the texts and their exegesis became integral to the development of their mystical practices. The images in these texts deeply affected the way in which the early Christians described and interpreted their own experiences.

This takes us to my second observation that a distinction ought to be made between "religious experience" and "religiously interpreted experience" (Segal 2006, 27–40). The former cannot be empirically known or observed. The latter can. I can never know whether or not John of Patmos saw a glorious angel, one like a son of man, with hair white as wool and eyes like fire, and if he did, whether or not Daniel 7 influenced his vision (Revelation 1:12–16). What I can discuss, however, is how and why John of Patmos interpreted his experience (whatever it may have been) to be an experience with great religious significance, even comparable to the vision of Daniel related in the scripture. I can discuss how this frame served John's purposes and what it might tell me about John's religious location, ideology, and expectations.

When the problem of religious experience is reframed in terms of "religiously interpreted experience," the door swings open for critical analysis, especially given the fact that it is the religious community that controls the hermeneutical process rather than the individual. It is the community that ultimately decides whether an individual's experience represents an "authentic" mystical encounter or not. If so, the community will shape the retelling of the experience to meet its criteria for authenticity and religious legitimacy. If not, the experience is cast as a demonic encounter or one with no religious relevance.

Course Delivery and Syllabus

course description [handwritten annotation]

.৩n the way in which I have schematized the subject, I have found that the most successful approach is the adoption of a chronological approach. This allows the Jewish, Christian, and other ancient religious materials to overlap in terms of content delivery and hermeneutic. This provides an optimal comparative lens as well as historical contextualization and localization. Jewish and Christian forms of mysticism can be discussed in relationship to each other and successfully compared with other contemporaneous religious traditions. The following syllabus represents a generic syllabus along with some suggestions for readings. Although the primary readings are stable, the secondary readings are more flexible and should be altered to fit the goals of the particular course. I include in the syllabus those secondary readings that I consider essential or classic, references that students will come across consistently in the scholarly discussions of the subject.

Christian mysticism can be studied from a historical-critical perspective and successfully taught from the point of view of the historian of religion. It is a rich and rewarding field, and an emerging field at that. Reframing the definition of mysticism with an eye toward the *emic*, shifting the point of comparison to literature contemporaneous with the early Christian, and reading empathically with a social orientation reveals a rich tradition of Christian mysticism in the foundational period. This mysticism reflects the Jewish story, not the Greek one. It becomes the ground for Platonic ideas about a union with the One to take root and develop later into the more familiar monastic expression of Christian mysticism. But that is a story for another class.

Syllabus

Week 1: What Is Mysticism?

1.1 Primary literature: Genesis 1–3; Exodus 24 and 33; Ezekiel 1, 8, 10, and 40–48; Isaiah 6; Daniel 7; 1 Chronicles 28:18.

1.2 Secondary literature: DeConick (2006), 1–24; Segal (2006), 27–40; Rowland, Gibbons, and Dobroruka (2006), 41–56; Sanders (2006), 57–79.

Week 2: Early Jewish Pseudepigrapha

2.1 Primary literature: Charlesworth (1983–1985): 1 Enoch, 2 Enoch, Ezekiel the Tragedian, Ascension of Isaiah, Joseph and Aseneth, Life of Adam and Eve, History of the Rechabites, Apocalypse of Abraham, Apocalypse of Adam, Testament of Levi, Apocalypse of Zephaniah, 3 Baruch

2.2 Secondary literature: Boustan and Reed (2004); Davila (2006), 105–126; Dean-Otting (1984); Flannery-Dailey (2006), 231–248; Fossum (1999), 348–352; Halperin (1988a), 47–67; Himmelfarb (1993); Morray-Jones (1992), 1–31; Orlov (2007); Rowland (1979), 145–150, and (1982); Segal (1980), 1333–1394; Stone (1976), 414–451.

Week 3: Philo of Alexandria

3.1 Primary literature: Winston (1981): *On the Contemplative Life*, the *Giants*, and "selections" from Philo.

3.2 Secondary Literature: Borgen (1997); Chadwick (1966), 286–307; Deutsch (2006), 287–312; Goodenough (1969); Smith (1968), 315–326; Winston (1981), 1–37, and (1982), 15–39.

Week 4: Hermetic Literature, Magic, and Astrology

4.1 Primary literature: Copenhaver (1992), Corpus Hermeticum, Asclepius; Scott (1993), Extracts of Stobaeus; Robinson (1988), Discourse on the Eigth and Ninth, Prayer of Thanksgiving, Asclepius fragment; Meyer andSmith (1994); Salaman et al. (2000), The Definitions of Hermes Trismegistus to Asclepius; Betz (1992).

4.2 Secondary literature: Barton (1994); Bohak (2008); Van den Broek and Van Heertum (2000); Van den Broek and Hanegraaff (1998); Fowden (1986); Segal (1981), 349–375; Von Stuckrad (2000a) and (2000b), 1–40; Trachtenberg (1974).

Week 5: Dead Sea Scrolls

5.1 Primary literature: García Martínez (1994).

5.2 Secondary literature: Davila (2000), 249–264; Dimant (1996), 93–103; Dimant and Strugnell (1990), 331–348; Elior (2006), 83–104; Fletcher-Louis (2002); Morray-Jones (2006), 145–178; Newsom (1985), 1–83; Popovic (2007); Schiffman (1982), 14–47; Smith (1990); Schäfer (2006), 37–66; Strugnell (1960), 318–345; Wolfson (1994a), 185–202, and (2003), 177–215.

Week 6: Synoptic Gospels, Acts, Johannine Literature, Thomasine literature

6.1 Primary literature: Mark, Matthew, Luke-Acts, John, 1and 2 John; Robinson (1988), Gospel of Thomas, Dialogue of the Savior, Book of Thomas the Contender; Elliott (1993), Acts of Thomas.

6.2 Secondary literature: Barker (1995a) and (1995b), 31–67; Daniélou (1962); DeConick (1996,, 2005, 2011); Fletcher-Louis (1997); Fossum (1995); Hurtado (2000), 183–205; Johnson (1998); Kanagaraj (1998); Odeberg (1974); Rowland and Morray-Jones (2009); Smith (1981), 403–429.

Week 7: Pauline and Deutro-Pauline Literature

    7.1 Primary literature: Paul's letters, Colossians, and Ephesians.

    7.2 Secondary literature: Ashton (2000); Bowker (1971), 157–173; Francis (1975), 163–195; Gieschen (1998); Morray-Jones (1993a), 177–217, and (1993b), 265–292; Segal (1990), 34–71; Schäfer (1984), 19–35; Schweitzer (1998); Tabor (1986).

Week 8: Hebrews, Revelation, Shepherd of Hermas, Montanists

    8.1 Primary literature: Hebrews, Revelation, Shepherd of Hermas

    8.2 Secondary literature: Afzael (2006), 195–210, and (2008); Aune (1983); Barker (2007); Bauckham (1993); Draper (1983), 113–147; Gieschen (2003), 115–158, and (2006), 341–354; Rowland (1980), 1–11; Tabbernee (2007).

Week 9: The Mystery Religions

    9.1 Primary Literature: Grant (1953); Meyer (1987).

    9.2 Secondary Literature: Beck (2006); Burkert (1987); Kerényi (1976); Mylonas (1969); Reitzenstein (1978); Ulansey (1989); Witt (1971).

Week 10: Second and Early Third Century Gnostics

    10.1 Primary literature: Robinson (1988), Valentinian (Prayer of the Apostle Paul, Gospel of Truth, Treatise on the Resurrection, Tripartite Tractate, Gospel of Philip, 1 Apocalypse of James, Exegesis on the Soul, Interpretation of Knowledge, A Valentinian Exposition, Gospel of Mary), and Sethian (Apocryphon of John, Hypostasis of the Archons, Gospel of the Egyptians, Apocalypse of Adam, Three Steles of Seth, Zostrianos, Melchizedek, Thought of Norea, Marsanes, Allogenes, Hypsiphrone, Trimorphic Protennoia). DeConick (2007), translation of the Gospel of the Judas.

    10.2 Secondary literature: DeConick (2007), 26–46, (2001a), 225–261, and (2003), 307–342; Deutsch (1995, 1999); Fossum (1985); Gruenwald (1988); Mastrocinque (2005); Morray-Jones (2002), 138–172; Quispel (1980), 1–13, and (1992), 1–19; Stroumsa (1996), 46–62; Wolfson (2007), 234–271.

Week 11: Alexandrian Fathers: Clement and Origen

    11.1 Primary literature: *Anti-Nicene Fathers*, writings of Clement of Alexandria and Origen

    11.2 Secondary literature: Barker (2003); Bucur (2006), 251–268; Chadwick (1954), 15–39; Christman (2005); Dillon (1996); Halperin (1981), 261–275; Lilla (1971); Roberts (1979); Stroumsa (1996), 27–46, 92–131, 147–168; (Trigg) 1983.

Week 12: Plotinus and Neo-Platonism

    12.1 Primary literature: Enneads

    12.2 Secondary Literature: Bussanich (1988), (1994), 5300–5330, and (1997), 339–365; Dillon (1986), 55–70, and (2002), 278–295; Dodds (1986), 230–249; Jonas (1969), 315–329; Kenney (1997), 315–337; Meijer (1992), 294–333; Rist (1964); Majercik (1995), 38–61; Thesleff (1980), 101–114; Wallis, (1976), 121–153, and (1986), 460–480.

Week 13: Hekhalot Literature

    13.1 Primary literature: Charlesworth 1983–1985, 3 Enoch; Janowitz 1989, Maaseh Merkavah; Smith 1963, 142–160, Hekhalot Rabbati; Schäfer 1991–1995, German translation of Hekhalot literature.

    13.2 Secondary literature: Arbel (2003); Chernus (1982), 123–146; Dan (1986), 289–307; Elior (1993/1994), 3–53, and (1997), 217–267; Gruenwald (1973), 63–107, and (1980); Halperin (1988a); Himmelfarb (1988), 73–100; Lesses (1988); Morray-Jones (2002); Orlov (2005); Schäfer (1992) and (2009); Scholem (1955), 1–79, and (1960); Swartz (1996); Wolfson (1994b), 13–187.

Weeks 14–15: Student Research Presentations

Notes

1. Although McGinn does not wish to neglect the Jewish origins of Christian mysticism, his treatment of the Jewish materials hinges on fourteen pages before turning to a discussion of the Greek materials and never looking back: McGinn (1992, 9–22). In part, this minimal treatment may be due to the definition of mysticism generated by McGinn, which views mysticism as a "part" of a religion (following Friedrick Baron von Hügel). It reflects a "way of life" as well as the mystical experience of God's presence, abandoning the idea of "union" in favor of "presence" (following Joseph Maréchal). McGinn states that his definition was borne from close readings of the texts that have been accepted as mystical classics in the history of Christianity (McGinn 1992, xv–xx).

2. For a treatment of the major characteristics of early Jewish and Christian mysticism, see DeConick (2006, 1–24).

3. For an overview of common features, see DeConick (2006, 1–24).

4. On these unique features, see DeConick (2011).

5. On this approach to tradition-history, see DeConick (2005, 3–37).

Bibliography

Afzael, Cameron C. 2006. "Wheels of Time in the Apocalypse of Jesus Christ." In DeConick (2006), 195–210.

————. 2008. *The Mystery of the Book of Revelation: Reenvisioning the End of Time*. Lewiston: Mellon.

Arbel, Daphna. 2003. *Beholders of Divine Secrets: Mysticism and Myth in the Hekhalot and Merkavah Literature*. Albany: State University of New York Press.

Ashton, John. 2000. *The Religion of Paul the Apostle*. New Haven, CT: Yale University.

Aune, David E. 1983. *Prophecy in Early Christianity and the Ancient Mediterranean World*. Grand Rapids, MI: Eerdmans.

Barker, Margaret. 1995a. *On Earth as It Is in Heaven: Temple Symbolism in the New Testament*. Edinburgh: T&T Clark.

————. 1995b. "The Secret Tradition," *Journal of Higher Criticism* 2/1 (Spring, 1995), 31–67.

————. 2003. *The Great High Priest: The Temple Roots of Christian Liturgy*. London: T&T Clark.

————. 2007. *The Hidden Tradition of the Kingdom of God*. London: SPCK Publishing.

Barton, Tamsyn. 1994. *Ancient Astrology*. New York: Routledge.

Bauckham, Richard. 1993. *The Climax of Prophecy: Studies on the Book of Revelation*. Edinburgh: T&T Clark.

Beck, Roger. 2006. *The Religion of the Mithras Cult in the Roman Empire: Mysteries of the Unconquered Sun*. Oxford: Oxford University Press.

Betz, Hans Dieter, ed. 1992. *The Greek Magical Papyri in Translation*. Vol. 1. Rev. ed. Chicago: University of Chicago.

Bohak, Gideon. 2008. *Ancient Jewish Magic*. Cambridge: Cambridge University Press.

Borgen, Peder. 1997. *Philo of Alexandria: An Exegete for His Time*. Novum Testamentum Supplement 86. Leiden: Brill.

Boustan, Ra`anan, and Annette Yoshiko Reed. 2004. *Heavenly Realms and Earthly Realities in Late Antique Religions*. Cambridge: Cambridge University Press.

Bowker, J. W. 1971. " 'Merkavah' Visions and the Visions of Paul," *Journal of Semitic Studies* 16: 157–173.

Broek, Roelof van den, and Wouter J. Hanegraaff, eds. 1998. *Gnosis and Hermeticism from Antiquity to Modern Times*. Albany: State University of New York Press.

Broek, Roelof van den, and Cis van Heertum. Editors. 2000. *From Poimandres to Jacob Böhme: Gnosis, Hermetism and the Christian Tradition*. Amsterdam: Bibliotheca Philosophica Hermetica.

Bucur, Bogdan G. 2006. "The Other Clement of Alexandria: Cosmic Hierarchy and Interiorized Apocalypticism," *Vigiliae Christianae* 60: 251–268.

Burkert, Walter. 1987. *Ancient Mystery Cults*. Cambridge, MA: Harvard University Press.

Bussanich, J. 1988. *The One and Its Relation to Intellect in Plotinus*. Leiden: Brill.

————. 1994. "Mystical Elements in the Thought of Plotinus," *Aufstieg und Niedergang der römischen Welt* 2 (36.7): 5300–5330.

————. 1997. "Plotinian Mysticism in Theoretical and Comparative Perspective," *American Catholic Philosophical Quarterly* 71 (3): 339–365.

Chadwick, Henry, ed. 1954. *Alexandrian Christianity*. Philadelphia: Westminster.

————. 1966. "St. Paul and Philo of Alexandria," *Bulletin of the John Rylands Library* 48: 286–307.

Charlesworth, James H., ed. 1983–1985. *The Old Testament Pseudepigrapha.* 2 vol. Garden City, NJ: Doubleday.

Chernus, Ira. 1982. "Visions of God in Merkavah Mysticism," *Journal for the Study of Judaism* 8: 123–146.

Christman, Angela Russell. 2005. *"What Did Ezekiel See?" Christian Exegesis of Ezekiel's Vision of the Chariot from Irenaeus to Gregory the Great.* Leiden: Brill.

Cohn-Sherbok, Dan, and Lavinia Cohn-Sherbok. 1994. *Jewish and Christian Mysticism: An Introduction.* New York: Continuum.

Copenhaver, Brian P., ed. 1992. *Hermetica.* Cambridge: Cambridge University Press.

Dan, Joseph. 1986. "The Religious Experience of the Merkavah." In *Jewish Spirituality from the Bible through the Middle Ages,* edited by Arthur Green, 289–307. New York: Crossroad.

Daniélou, J. 1962. "Les Traditions Secretes des Apôtres," *Eranos-Jahrbuch* 31: 199–215.

Davila, James R. 2000. "The Dead Sea Scrolls and Merkavah Mysticism." In *The Dead Sea Scrolls in Their Historical Context,* edited by Timothy H. Lim, Larry W. Hurtado, and A. Graeme Auld, 249–264. Edinburgh: T&T Clark.

———. 2006. "The Ancient Jewish Apocalypses and the Hekhalot Literature." In DeConick (2006), 105–126.

Dean-Otting, Mary. 1984. *Heavenly Journeys: A Study of the Motif in Hellenistic Jewish Literature.* Judentum und Umwelt 8. Frankfurt am Main: Peter Lang.

DeConick, April D. 1996. *Seek to See Him: Ascent and Vision Mysticism in the Gospel of Thomas.* Leiden: Brill.

———. 2001a. "The True Mysteries: Sacramentalism in the Gospel of Philip," *Vigiliae Christianae* 55: 225–261.

———. 2001b. *Voices of the Mystics: Early Christian Discourse in the Gospels of John and Thomas and Other Ancient Christian Literature.* Sheffield: Sheffield University Press.

———. 2003. "The Great Mystery of Marriage: Sex and Conception in Ancient Valentinian Traditions," *Vigiliae Christianae* 57: 307–342.

———. 2005. *Recovering the Original Gospel of Thomas.* London: T&T Clark.

———. 2006. "What Is Early Jewish and Christian Mysticism?" In *Paradise Now: Essays on Early Jewish and Christian Mysticism,* edited by April D. DeConick. Symposium 11, 1–24. Atlanta: Society of Biblical Literature.

———. 2007. *The Thirteenth Apostle: What the Gospel of Judas Really Says.* New York: Continuum.

———. 2011. "Jesus Revealed: The Dynamics of Early Christian Mysticism." In *With Letter of Light: Studies in the Dead Sea Scrolls, Early Jewish Apocalypticism, Magic, and Mysticism in Honor of Rachel Elior,* edited by Daphna Arbel and Andrei Orlov, 299–324. Berlin: Walter de Gruyter.

Deutsch, Celia. 2006. "The Therapeutae, Text Work, Ritual, and Mystical Experience." In DeConick (2006), 287–312.

Deutsch, Nathaniel. 1995. *The Gnostic Imagination: Gnosticism, Mandaeism, and Merkabah Mysticism.* Leiden: Brill.

———. 1999. *Guardians of the Gate: Angelic Vice Regency in Late Antiquity.* Leiden: Brill.

Dillon, J. 1986. "Plotinus and the Transcendental Imagination." In *Religious Imagination,* edited by J. P. Mackey, 55–70. Edinburgh: University of Edinburgh Press.

————. 1996. *The Middle Platonists, 80 B.C. to A.D. 220*. Rev. ed. Ithaca, NY: Cornell University Press.

————. 2002. "The Platonic Philosopher at Prayer." In *Metaphysik und Religion: zur Signatur des spätantiken Denkens. Akten des internationalen Kongresses vom 13.-17. März 2001 in Würzburg*, edited by T. Kobusch and M. Erler, 278–295. Munich: K. G. Saur.

Dimant, Devorah, and John Strugnell. 1990. "The Merkavah Vision in Second Ezekiel (4Q385 4)," *Revue de Qumrân* 4: 331–348.

Dimant, Devorah. 1996. "Men as Angels: The Self-Image of the Qumran Community." In *Religion and Politics in the Ancient Near East*, edited by Adele Berlin, 93–103. Potomac: University Press of Maryland.

Dodds, E. R. 1986. "Neoplatonist Spirituality I: Plotinus and Porphyry." In *Classical Mediterranean Spirituality: Egyptian, Greek, Roman*, edited by A. H. Armstrong, 230–249. New York: Crossroad.

Draper, Jonathan. 1983. "The Heavenly Feast of Tabernacles: Revelation 7.1–17," *Journal of the Study of the New Testament* 9: 113–147.

Egan, Harvey D. 1991. *An Anthology of Christian Mysticism*. Collegeville, MN: The Liturgical Press.

Elior, Rachel. 1993/1994. "Mysticism, Magic, and Angelology: The Perception of Angels in Hekhalot Literature," *Jewish Studies Quarterly* 1: 3–53.

————. 1997. "From Earthly Temple to Heavenly Shrines," *Jewish Studies Quarterly* 4: 217–267.

————. 2006. "The Emergence of the Mystical Traditions of the Merkavah." In DeConick (2006), 83–104.

Elliott, J. K., ed. 1993. *The Apocryphal New Testament*. Oxford: Clarendon.

Flannery-Dailey, Frances. 2006. "Lessons on Early Jewish Apocalypticism and Mysticism from Dream Literature." In DeConick (2006), 231–248.

Fletcher-Louis, Crispin H. T. 1997. *Luke-Acts: Angels, Christology and Soteriology*. Wissenschaftliche Untersuchungen zum Neuen Testament 2: 94. Tübingen: Mohr Siebeck.

————. 2002. *All the Glory of Adam: Liturgical Anthropology in the Dead Sea Scrolls*. Studies of the Texts of the Desert of Judah 42. Leiden: Brill.

Fossum, Jarl E. 1985. *The Name of God and the Angel of the Lord*. Wissenschaftliche Untersuchungen zum Neuen Testament 36. Tübingen: Mohr Siebeck.

————. 1995. *The Image of the Invisible God: Essays on the Influence of Jewish Mysticism on Early Christology*. Göttingen: Vandenhoeck & Ruprecht.

————. 1999. "Glory." In *Dictionary of Deities and Demons in the Bible*, 2nd ed., edited by Karel van der Toorn, Bob Becking, Pieter W. van der Horst, 348–352. Leiden: Brill.

Fowden, Garth. 1986. *The Egyptian Hermes: A Historical Approach to the Late Pagan Mind*. Princeton: Princeton University Press.

Francis, Fred O. 1975. "Humility and Angelic Veneration in Col 2:18." In *Conflict at Colossae*, edited by Fred. O. Francis and Wayne A. Meeks, 163–195. Missoula: Scholars Press.

García Martínez, Florentino, ed. 1994. *The Dead Sea Scrolls Translated: The Qumran Texts in English*. Leiden: Brill.

Gieschen, Charles. 1998. *Angelomorphic Christology: Antecedents and Early Evidence*. Arbeiten zur Geschichte des antiken Judentums und des Urchristentums (AGJU) 42. Leiden: Brill.

————. 2003. "The Divine Name in Ante-Nicene Christology," *Vigiliae Christianae* 57: 115–158.

————. 2006. "Baptismal Praxis and Mystical Experience in the Book of Revelation." In De-Conick (2006), 341–354.

Goodenough, Erwin R. 1969. *By Light, Light: The Mystic Gospel of Hellenistic Judaism.* Amsterdam: Philo Press.

Grant, Frederick C., ed. 1953. *Hellenistic Religions: The Age of Sycretism.* New York: TheWW Liberal Arts Press.

Gruenwald, Ithamar. 1973. "Knowledge and Vision: Towards a Clarification of Two 'Gnostic' Concepts in the Light of Their Alleged Origins," *Israel Oriental Studies* 3: 63–107.

————. 1980. *Apocalyptic and Merkavah Mysticism.* AGJU 14. Leiden: Brill.

————. 1988. *From Apocalyptic to Gnosticism.* Beitrage zur Erfarschung des Alten Testaments und des antiken Judentums 14. Frankfurt am Main: Peter Lang.

Halperin, David. 1981. "Origen, Ezekiel's Merkabah and the Ascension of Moses," *Church History* 50: 261–275.

————. 1988a. "Ascension or Invasion: Implications of the Heavenly Journey in Ancient Judaism," *Religion* 18: 47–67.

————. 1988b. *Faces of the Chariot: Early Jewish Responses to Ezekiel's Vision.* Texte und Studien zum Antiken Judentum 6. Tübingen: Mohr Siebeck.

Himmelfarb, Martha. 1988. "Heavenly Ascent and the Relationship of the Apocalypses and the Hekhalot Literature," *Hebrew Union College Annual* 59: 73–100.

————. 1993. *Ascent to Heaven in Jewish and Christian Apocalypses.* Oxford: Oxford University Press.

Hurtado, L. W. 2000. "Religious Experience and Religious Innovation in the New Testament," *Journal of Religion* 80: 183–205.

Janowitz, Naomi. 1989. *The Poetics of Ascent: Theories of Language in a Rabbinic Ascent Text.* Albany: State University of New York Press.

Johnson, Timothy Luke. 1998. *Religious Experience in Earliest Christianity: A Missing Dimension in New Testament Studies.* Minneapolis: Fortress.

Jonas, H. 1969. "Myth and Mysticism: A Study of Objectivization and Interiorization in Religious Thought," *Journal of Religion* 49 (4): 315–329.

Kanagaraj, Jey J. 1998. *"Mysticism" in the Gospel of John: An Inquiry into Its Background.* Journal of the Study of the New Testament Supplement 158. Sheffield: Sheffield Academic Press.

Katz, Steven K. 1978. "Language, Epistemology, and Mysticism." In *Mysticism and Philosophical Analysis,* edited by Steven K. Katz, 22–74. New York: Oxford University Press.

Kenney, J. P. 1997. "Mysticism and Contemplation in the *Enneads,*" *American Catholic Philosophical Quarterly* 71 (3): 315–337.

Kerényi, Carl. 1976. *Dionysus: Archetypal Image of Indestructible Life,* translated by Ralph Manheim. Princeton, NJ: Princeton University Press.

Lesses, Rebecca Macy. 1988. *Ritual Practices to Gain Power: Angels, Incantations, and Revelation in Early Jewish Mysticism.* Harrisburg, PA: Trinity Press.

Lilla, Salvatore R. C. 1971. *Clement of Alexandria: A Study in Christian Platonism and Gnosticism.* Oxford: Oxford University Press.

Louth, Andrew. 1981. *Origins of the Christian Mystical Tradition: From Plato to Denys.* Oxford: Clarendon.

Majercik, R. 1995. "Plotinus and Greek Mysticism." In *Mysticism and the Mystical Experience East and West,* edited by D. Bishop, 38–61. Selinsgrove: Susquehanna University Press.

Mastrocinque, Attilio. 2005. *From Jewish Magic to Gnosticism*. Studies and Texts in Antiquity and Christianity 24. Tübingen: Mohr Siebeck.

McGinn, Bernard. 1992. *The Foundations of Mysticism: Origins to the Fifth Century*. New York: Crossroad-Herder.

Meijer, P. 1992. *Plotinus on the Good or the One (Enneads VI.9): an Analytical Commentary*. Amsterdam: Gieben.

Meyer, Marvin. 1987. *The Ancient Mysteries: A Sourcebook*. San Francisco: Harper.

Meyer, Marvin, and Richard Smith, eds. 1994. *Ancient Christian Magic: Coptic Texts of Ritual Power*. San Francisco: Harper.

Morray-Jones, Christopher. 1992. "Transformational Mysticism in the Apocalyptic-Merkavah Tradition," *Journal of Jewish Studies* 43: 1–31.

———. 1993a. "Paradise Revisited (2 Cor 12:1–2): The Jewish Mystical Background of Paul's Apostolate, Part 1: The Jewish Sources," *Harvard Theological Review* 86: 177–217.

———. 1993b. "Paradise Revisited (2 Cor 12:1–2): The Jewish Mystical Background of Paul's Apostolate, Part 2: Paul's Heavenly Ascent and Its Significance," *Harvard Theological Review* 86: 265–292.

———. 2002. *A Transparent Illusion: The Dangerous Vision of Water in Hekhalot Mysticism, A Source-Critical and Tradition-Historical Inquiry*. Supplements to the *Journal for the Study of Judaism* 59. Leiden: Brill.

———. 2006. "The Temple Within." In DeConick (2006), 145–178.

Mylonas, George E. 1969. *Eleusis and the Eleusinian Mysteries*. Princeton, NJ: Princeton University Press.

Newsom, Carol A. 1985. *Songs of the Sabbath Sacrifice: A Critical Edition*. Cambridge, MA: Harvard University Press.

Odeberg, Hugo. 1973. *3 Enoch or The Hebrew Book of Enoch*. Jersey City, NJ: KTAV Publishing House.

———. 1974. *The Fourth Gospel*. Amsterdam: Grüner.

Orlov, Andrei A. 2005. *The Enoch-Metatron Tradition*. Texts and Studies in Ancient Judaism 107. Tübingen: Mohr Siebeck.

———. 2007. *From Apocalypticism to Merkavah Mysticism: Studies in the Slavonic Pseudepigrapha*. Supplements to the *Journal for the Study of Judaism* 114. Leiden: Brill.

Popovic, Mladen. 2007. *Reading the Human Body, Physiognomics and Astrology in the Dead Sea Scrolls and Hellenistic-Early Roman Period Judaism*. Leiden: Brill.

Proudfoot, Wayne. 1985. *Religious Experience*. Berkeley: University of California.

Quispel, Gilles. 1980. "Ezekiel 1:26 in Jewish Mysticism and Gnosis," *Vigiliae Christianae* 34: 1–13.

———. 1992. "Hermes Trismegistus and the Origins of Gnosticism," *Vigiliae Christianae* 46: 1–19.

Reitzenstein, Richard. 1978. *Hellenistic Mystery-Religions: Their Basic Ideas and Significance*, translated by John E. Steely. Pittsburg: Pickwick.

Rist, J. M. 1964. *Eros and Psyche: Studies in Plato, Plotinus, and Origen*. Toronto: University of Toronto Press.

Roberts, Colin H. 1979. *Manuscript, Society and Belief in Early Christian Egypt*. London: Oxford University Press.

Robinson, James M., ed. 1988. *The Nag Hammadi Library in English*. San Francisco: Harper.

Rowland, Christopher. 1979. "The Visions of God in Apocalyptic Literature," *Journal for the Study of Judaism* 19: 145–150.

———. 1980. "The Vision of the Risen Christ in Rev. 1:13ff: The Debt of Early Christology to an Aspect of Jewish Angelology," *Journal of Theological Studies* 31: 1–11.

———. 1982. *The Open Heaven: A Study of Apocalyptic Judaism and Early Christianity*. New York: Crossroad.

Rowland, Christopher, with Patricia Gibbons and Vicente Dobroruka. 2006. "Visionary Experience in Ancient Judaism and Christianity." In DeConick (2006), 41–56.

Rowland, Christopher, and Christopher Morray-Jones. 2009. *The Mystery of God: Early Jewish Mysticism and the New Testament*. Leiden: Brill.

Salaman, Clement, Dorine van Oyen, William D. Wharton, and Jean-Pierre Mahé, eds. 2000. *The Way of Hermes*. Rochester: Inner Traditions.

Sanders, Seth. 2006. "Performative Exegesis." In DeConick (2006), 57–79.

Schäfer, Peter. 1984. "New Testament and Hekhalot Literature: The Journey into Heaven in Paul and in Merkavah Mysticism," *Journal for Jewish Studies* 35: 19–35.

———., ed. 1991–1995. *Übersetzung der Hekhalot-Literatur*. 4 vols. Tübingen: Mohr Siebeck.

———. 1992. *The Hidden and Manifest God: Some Major Themes in Early Jewish Mysticism*. Albany: State University of New York Press.

———. 2006. "Communion with Angels." In *Wege mystischer Gotteserfahrung: Judentum, Christentum und Islam*. 37–66. München: Oldenbourg.

———. 2009. *The Origins of Jewish Mysticism*. Tübingen: Mohr Siebeck.

Schiffman, L. 1982. "Merkavah Speculation at Qumran." In *Mystics, Philosophers and Politicians,* edited by J. Reinharz and D. Swetschinski, 14–47. Durham: Duke University Press.

Scholem, Gershom G. 1955. *Major Trends in Jewish Mysticism*. London: Thames and Hudson.

———. 1960. *Jewish Gnosticism, Merkabah Mysticism, and Talmudic Tradition*. New York: Jewish Theological Seminary of America.

Schweitzer, Albert. 1998. *The Mysticism of Paul the Apostle,* translated by William Montgomery. Baltimore: John Hopkins University Press.

Scott, Walter, ed. 1993. *Hermetica*. Boston: Shambhala.

Segal, Alan F. 1980. "Heavenly Ascent in Hellenistic Judaism, Early Christianity and Their Environment," *Aufstieg und Niedergang der Roemischen Welt* II (23.2): 1333–1394.

———. 1981. "Hellenistic Magic: Some Questions of Definition." In *Studies in Gnosticism and Hellenistic Religions,* edited by Roelof van den Broek and M. J. Vermaseren, 349–375. Leiden: Brill.

———. 1990. *Paul the Convert: The Apostolate and Apostasy of Saul the Pharisee*. New Haven, CT: Yale University Press.

———. 2006. "Religious Experience and the Construction of the Transcendent Self." In DeConick (2006), 27–40.

Smith, Morton. 1963. "Observations on Hekhalot Rabbati." In *Biblical and Other Studies,* edited by Alexander Altmann, 142–160. Cambridge, MA: Harvard University Press.

———. 1968. "On the Shape of God and the Humanity of Gentiles." In *Religions in Antiquity, Essays in Memory of Erwin Ramsdell Goodenough*. Edited by J. Neusner. Supplememts to Numen (SHR) 14, 315–326. Leiden: Brill.

———. 1981. "Ascent to the Heavens and the Beginning of Christianity," *Eranos-Jahrbuch* 50: 403–429.

———. 1990. "Ascent to the Heavens and Deification in 4QMᵃ." In *Archeology and History: The New York University Conference in Memory of Yigael Yadin,* edited by Lawrence H. Schiffman. Journal for the Study of the Pseudepigrapha Series 8, pp. 181-188. Sheffield: JSOT Press.

Stone, Michael E. 1976. "Lists of Revealed Things in the Apocalyptic Literature." In *Magnalia Dei: The Mighty Acts of God,* edited by Frank Moore Cross, Werner E. Lemke, and Patrick D. Miller Jr., 414–451. Garden City, NJ: Doubleday.

Stroumsa, Guy G. 1996. *Hidden Wisdom: Esoteric Traditions and the Roots of Christian Mysticism.* Leiden: Brill.

Strugnell, J. 1960. "The Angelic Liturgy." In *Supplements to Vetus Testamentum 7,* 318–345. Leiden: Brill.

Stuckrad, Kocku von. 2000a. *Das Ringen um die Astrologie: Jüdische und christliche Beiträge zum antiken Zeitverständnis.* Berlin: de Gruyter.

———. 2000b. "Jewish and Christian Astrology in Late Antiquity—A New Approach," *Numen* 47: 1–40.

Swartz, Michael D. 1996. *Scholastic Magic: Ritual and Revelation in Early Jewish Mysticism.* Princeton, NJ: Princeton University Press.

Tabbernee, William. 2007. *Fake Prophecy and Polluted Sacraments: Ecclesiastical and Imperial Reactions to Montanism. Vigiliae Christianae* Supplement 84. Leiden: Brill.

Tabor, James. 1986. *Things Unutterable: Paul's Ascent to Paradise in its Greco-Roman, Judaic, and Early Christian Contexts.* New York: University Press of America.

Thesleff, H. 1980. "Notes on Unio Mystica in Plotinus," *Arctos [Acta Philologica Fennica]* 14: 101–104.

Trachtenberg, Joshua. 1974. *Jewish Magic and Superstition: A Study in Folk Religion.* New York: Atheneum.

Trigg, Joseph Wilson. 1983. *Origen: The Bible and Philosophy in the Third-Century Church.* Atlanta: John Knox.

Underhill, Evelyn. 1911/1977. *Mysticism: A Study in the Nature and Development of Man's Spiritual Consciousness.* London: Methuen and Company.

Ulansey, David. 1989. *The Origins of the Mithraic Mysteries: Cosmology and Salvation in the Ancient World.* Oxford: Oxford University Press.

Wallis, R. T. 1976. "NOUS as Experience." In *The Significance of Neoplatonism,* edited by R. B. Harris, 121–153. Norfolk: International Society for Neoplatonic Studies.

———. 1986. "The Spiritual Importance of Not Knowing." In *Classical Mediterranean Spirituality: Egyptian, Greek, Roman,* edited by A. H. Armstrong, 460–480. New York: Crossroad.

Winston, David, ed. 1981. *Philo of Alexandria: The Contemplative Life, the Giants, and Selections.* Ramsey, NJ: Paulist Press.

———. 1982. "Was Philo a Mystic?" In *Studies in Jewish Mysticism, Proceedings of Regional Conferences Held at the University of California, Los Angeles and McGill University in April, 1978,* edited by Joseph Dan and F. Talmage, 15–39. Cambridge, UK: Association for Jewish Studies.

Witt, R. E. 1971. *Isis in the Ancient World.* New York: Cornell University Press.

Wolfson, Elliot. 1994a. "Mysticism and the Poetic-Liturgical Compositions from Qumran: A Response to Bilhah Nitzan," *Jewish Quarterly Review* 85: 185–202.

———. 1994b. *Through a Speculum that Shines: Vision and Imagination in Medieval Jewish Mysticism.* Princeton, NJ: Princeton University.

———. 2003. "Seven Mysteries of Knowledge: Qumran E/sotericism Recovered." In *The Idea of Biblical Interpretation: Essays in Honor of James L. Kugel,* edited by Hindy Najman and Judith H. Newman, 177–215. Leiden: Brill.

———. 2007. "Inscribed in the Book of the Living: Gospel of Truth and Jewish Christology," *Journal for the Study of Judaism* 38: 234–271.

3

Teaching Chinese Mysticism

Livia Kohn

Chinese mysticism can be taught r on its own, as a section in a comprehensive class on Chinese religions and/or Daoism, or as part of an introduction to mysticism. The presentation has to deal with certain aspects of the Chinese tradition in contrast to Western assumptions, outline the worldview systems of Confucianism and Daoism, provide an understanding of their historical transformation, and examine key concepts: the ultimate, notions of language, the self, training, ethics, the ideal human, and mystical union. Not all of these dimensions have to be given equal emphasis and some may even be left out altogether. To provide the broadest possible overview, I discuss each area, outlining key concepts and supplying references for further reading.

Main Features

The first fact students need to understand when looking at Chinese religion and the mystical tradition is that the Chinese tradition does not have a single creator deity or focus on a monotheistic god. There is no entity completely beyond the world, no transcendent other, no power that will never cease and never change; the Chinese tradition sees its ultimate in Dao, a divine force so immanent that it is even in the soil and tiles, so much a part of the world that it cannot be separated from it.[1] Oneness or union with Dao is the birthright of every being, not a rare instance of divine grace. It is natural to begin with and becomes more natural as it is realized through practice (Kohn 1992a, 11).

The Chinese mystical experience of oneness with Dao is astounding only in the beginning. It represents a way of being in the world that is different from ordinary perception, which is determined by the senses and the intellect, but is not essentially alien. The longer the mystic lives with the experience, the more it is integrated into his or her life and being and the less extraordinary it becomes. Being at one with Dao, joining Heaven and Earth, is the natural and original state of humanity, which is recovered through mystical practice (Kohn 1992a, 23). Neither is the experience the central feature of the tradition nor is there a desperate search for a glimpse of the transcendent divine. Dao is here and now, residing right within oneself. The main difficulty Chinese mystics face in realizing Dao is the scatterbrained and pleasure-seeking nature of their ego-centered selves. This is discussed in the texts, together with techniques to overcome it.[2]

Still, the Chinese go their own way; they do not envision the ego-centered self in a dualism of body versus divine soul or rational mind. Rather, the human being—body, mind, and spirit, plus everything else that exists in the universe—consists of *qi*, vital cosmic energy, the material aspect of Dao (Kohn 2005, 11).[3] There is only one *qi*, and there is only one Dao; the ancient thinker Zhuangzi emphasizes that human life is the accumulation of *qi*, whereas death is its dispersal. After receiving a core potential of primordial *qi* at birth, people throughout life must sustain it by drawing postnatal *qi* into the body from air and food as well as from other people through social interaction. But they lose *qi* through breathing bad air, overburdening their bodies with food and drink, and getting involved in negative emotions and excessive social interactions. Body, mind, and soul are part of one and the same continuum of *qi* (Kohn 2005, 12).

Rather than by overcoming a body that is a prison or hindrance to the soul, the Chinese find mystical attainment through adapting to the dynamic change of the world, by creating harmony of *qi*-flow: a perfect balance of patterns and forces, a refinement of vital energy. Reaching such a balance, they continue and gradually transform their *qi*, personal and universal at the same time, into a finer cosmic energy known as spirit (*shen*).[4] A subtle dimension of *qi*, this serves as the guiding vitality behind all its other forms; it is the active, organizing force and transformative influence in the individual that connects him or her to Heaven and the underlying oneness with Dao. Within the person it is individual awareness and mental direction; it resides in the heart and is related to the mind and the emotions (Kaptchuk 1983, 58).

As mystics attain their realization of personal *qi* subtlety, they not only gain physical health, mental well-being, and a sense of oneness with Dao; they also contribute to harmony and health in the larger universe: in nature, in society, and in the greater world in the state of Great Peace, the great cosmic harmony of all (Kaltenmark 1979; Lai 2001).

This outflowing dimension of mystical attainment constitutes another major contrast to common Western and Indian notions. It means that the mystic is not one to leave society behind and stay away from all involvement. On the contrary, the accomplished mystic is always a social being who spreads wisdom and radiates mystical calmness throughout. Placed ideally at the pinnacle of society, the mystic is the sage or the perfect ruler, a continuation of the ancient Chinese ideal of the shaman-king as the chief intermediary between humanity and the cosmos.[5] Thus, mysticism in China was never isolated from society but always had a strong political dimension (Kohn 1992a, 172). The tradition is more immanent, body-focused, and socially responsible than what one might expect from Western and Indian models.

Confucianism and Daoism

Two traditions of China that have brought forth active mystical traditions are Confucianism and Daoism. Both arose around 500 BCE with thinkers who formed part of the Axial Age, had their founders divinized under the Han dynasty, underwent transformations under Buddhist influence in the Middle Ages, and have survived in modern forms.

CONFUCIANISM

Confucianism goes back to the thinker Confucius, Kongfuzi or "Master Kong" (551–479 BCE), the illegitimate son of the ruler of Lu, a small state in eastern China (modern Shandong). Trained in elementary feudal arts and taught to read and write, he became a minor functionary in the state's administration, then developed ideas about the causes of his country's problems and their remedy (Fingarette 1972). Wanting to see his ideas put into practice, he left his employment and traveled through China, presenting himself as a potential prime minister to local rulers. However, no ruler employed Confucius, so he returned home and began to teach disciples in private, soon establishing a name for himself and his ideas.[6] The disciples later collected his sayings into a volume known as the *Lunyu* (*Analects*).[7]

The main concept of early Confucianism is the idea of ritual formality or etiquette (*li*) in alignment with the universal power of Heaven (Eno 1990). The character represents the image of a ritual vessel and indicates the proper behavior in social, political, and religious situations among people of different rank and status, defined through hierarchical relationships that include a senior and a junior person, each of whom has obligations toward the other, expressed in the so-called Confucian virtues that foster the positive, heavenly nature in people: benevolence, righteousness, filial piety, and loyalty. According to Confucius and his followers, if everyone knew his or her personal and social position at any given moment and acted in accordance with it, society would be fully harmonious (Hall and Ames 1987).

The same idea also applies to government organizations, which should act in proper accordance with their specific duties and not infringe upon or compete with each other, and to religious rituals, where it is important to honor the ancestors and the local and cosmic deities with proper formalities, offering sacrifices of food and drink. All should participate in this ideal Confucian world of *li* to their best ability; everyone can learn. In fact, learning for the Chinese throughout history has been the key method of attaining the proper feeling for *li* in all given situations, and good behavior that creates social harmony is at first a learned response, which becomes natural after many years of training.[8] Social harmony, moreover, as formulated most expressively in the "Great Learning" (*Daxue*) chapter of the *Liji* (*Book of Rites*), begins with the individual and radiates outward, to create an overarching sense of oneness and balance throughout the world.[9]

During the Song dynasty (960–1260), Confucianism underwent a revival and transformed to include Buddhist elements. Its thinkers began to encourage a more internal realization of "bright virtue," the power of the individual that could make the self one with Heaven and Earth and bring Great Peace to the world. They supported meditation methods such as "quiet-sitting" and lauded a spontaneous connection to Heaven known as "innate knowledge," thus giving rise to their mystical tradition.[10]

DAOISM

Unlike the Confucian preoccupation with society, the proponents of the cosmic "Way" (Dao) proposed a return to naturalness, spontaneity, and organic so-being. Their ideas were first represented in the *Daode jing* (*Book of the Way and Its Virtue*) associated with the thinker Laozi, the Old Master, a legendary figure who allegedly served at the royal Zhou court and instructed Confucius about the rites.[11]

The text consists of about five thousand characters and is commonly divided into eighty-one chapters and two parts: one on Dao (1–37) and one on De (38–81).[12] It is written in nonrhyming verse, a stylized prose that has strong parallels and regular patterns, and contains sections of description contrasted with punch lines.[13]

The *Daode jing* has been transmitted in several editions, three of which are most important today. The first is the so-called standard edition, also known as the transmitted edition. Handed down by Chinese copyists, it is at the root of almost all translations of the text. It goes back to the erudite Wang Bi (226–249 CE), who edited the text and wrote a commentary on it that has shaped the reception of the text's worldview until today.[14]

The second edition is called the Mawangdui edition, named after a place in south China (Hunan) where a tomb was excavated in 1973 that dated from 168 BCE. It contained an undisturbed coffin surrounded by artifacts and manuscripts, mostly dealing with cosmology and medicine (Harper 1998). Among them were two copies of the *Daode jing*. The Mawangdui version differs little from the transmitted edition: there are some character variants, and the two parts are in reversed order, that is, the text begins with the section on De, then adds the section on Dao (Henricks 1989). The manuscripts are important because they show that the *Daode jing* existed in its complete form in the early Han dynasty, and that it was considered essential enough to be placed in someone's grave.

The third edition was discovered in 1993 in Guodian (Hubei). Written on bamboo slips and dated to about 300 BCE, the find presents a collection of philosophical works of the time, including fragments of texts. Among them are thirty-three passages that can be matched with thirty-one chapters of the *Daode jing*, but with lines in different places and variation in characters. Generally they are concerned with self-cultivation and its application to questions of rulership and the pacification of the state; negative attitudes and emotions are criticized.[15] This so-called "Bamboo Laozi" tells us that in the late fourth century BCE, the text existed in rudimentary form and consisted of a collection of sayings not yet edited into a coherent presentation. Another Guodian text, *Taiyi sheng shui* (*Great Unity Creates Water*), gives further insights into the growing and possibly "Daoist" cosmology of the time, as does a contemporaneous work on self-cultivation, the "Inward Training" (*Neiye*) chapter of the *Guanzi* (Roth 1999). It appears that a set of ideas and practices was growing that would eventually develop into something specifically and more religiously Daoist.

DAO AND NONACTION

The *Daode jing* has often been hailed as representing the core of the Daoist worldview and the root of Daoist mysticism. It is, in fact, a multifaceted work that can be, and has been, interpreted in many different ways, not least as a manual of strategy, a political treatise on the recovery of the golden age, a guide to underlying principles, and a metalinguistic inquiry into forms of prescriptive discourse. It can be read in two ways: as a document of early Chinese culture, or as a scripture of universal significance.

It outlines the ultimate power and reality of Dao, the source and power of the universe. Benjamin Schwartz describes it as "organic order"—"organic" because it is part of the world; "order" because it can be felt in the rhythms of the world (Schwartz 1998, 192). Dao is at the root of creation—tight, concentrated, intense, and ultimately unknowable, ineffable, and beyond conscious or sensory human attainment—and also present in the world, in the patterned cycles of life and visible nature. The way to be with Dao is through nonaction (*wuwei*) and naturalness (*ziran*), which means letting go of egotistic concerns, passions, and desires; finding a sense of where life, nature, and the world are headed on the social level; and abstaining from forceful and interfering measures in the political realm. The person who has realized Dao to the utmost is the sage, in the *Daode jing*, ideally the ruler, to whom the treatise was originally addressed (LaFargue 1992).

In the course of history, Laozi was divinized as a personification of Dao and began to appear in ecstatic visions to selected seekers (Seidel 1969; Kohn 1998). These seekers founded organized schools that proposed specific celestial realms to attain, moral rules to follow, rituals to observe, and a plethora of mystical practices to master, from basic physical refinements of *qi* to advanced meditations of all kinds (Kohn 1989b).

Common Points

Of the main common points and unique features of Confucianism and Daoism, the first is the belief in what perennialists call the "Ground," an underlying power or force that creates and supports the universe.[16] Described as Dao or "Way" in both, it is known as the Nonultimate among the Confucians. This is depicted as an empty circle from which the Great Ultimate arises, the classic diagram of yin and yang. The Great Ultimate is the core of the existing universe and, as such, gives rise to the three forces (Heaven, Earth, Humanity) and the five phases (wood, fire, earth, metal, water), which in different combinations appear in everything that exists (see Table 3.1).[17]

In Daoism, Dao is said to give rise to the One, the core of creation and existence that is part of chaos yet also contains the universe in seminal form. This unfolds in a dividing movement to produce the two, the two forces yin and yang, which in their turn unite to form the three, described as yin and yang plus "yin and yang in harmony." These three characterize everything created in the world and are said to "produce the myriad beings" (*Daode jing* 42).

Within this overall cosmogonic framework and common reliance on the universal Ground, Confucian and Daoist mysticism rely heavily on the traditional Chinese cosmology of yin-yang and the five phases and their complex correspondences. All beings actively participate in the cosmic cycles. They have the power either to go along with them smoothly or distort them. The ordinary consciousness of people, typically governed by passions and desires, and their actions in society are then understood as forms of distortion, which cause self and world to be out of balance. The mystical endeavor in both traditions aims not only at the restoration of cosmic harmony but at its conscious

TABLE 3.1 The five phases and their correlates

Yin/Yang	Phase	Direct.	Season	Color	Yin Organ	Yang Organ	Emotion	Sense
Lesser yang	wood	east	spring	green	liver	gall bladder	anger	eyes
Greater yang	fire	south	summer	red	heart	small intestine	euphoria	tongue
Yin-yang	earth	center		yellow	spleen	stomach	worry	lips
Lesser yin	metal	west	fall	white	lungs	large intestine	sadness	nose
Greater yin	water	north	winter	black	kidneys	bladder	fear	ears

and active realization within the individual, who is then able to live as long as Heaven and Earth.

From this arises a third common point: the understanding that every part of the world is closely interrelated with every other part and that the macrocosm and microcosm mirror each other to perfection. The world is seen as a series of concentric circles, which are isomorphic structurally and in their energy makeup. They begin with the body on the microcosmic level, then proceed through the family, the community or society, and the natural world to the cosmos as visible in the movements of the stars and planets. Each level is a replica of the next, and impulses in one have inevitable responses in all others. Mystical realization means the perfection of the whole, beginning with the smallest entity and extending toward the larger universe. The mystic in China, whether Confucian or Daoist, is, therefore, never socially separate and his realization has highest relevance for the perfection of human life.

These points appear in the "Great Learning" chapter and are formulated strongly in the philosophy of resonance or "impulse and response" (*ganying*) in the Han dynasty (see LeBlanc 1992), later taken up vibrantly in Ming dynasty neo-Confucianism, notably in the thought of Wang Yangming (Ching 1976). In Daoism, they form part of the vision of Great Peace but are also present in the understanding of the body and the role of humanity in the universe.

Another aspect both traditions share is their indebtedness to Buddhism: Daoism since the Six Dynasties period (ca. 406–489 CE) and Confucianism since the Song dynasty.[18] To Daoism, Buddhism contributed the monastic setting of its practice, the doctrine of karma and retribution (including punishments in the hells), the belief in popular savior figures, and techniques of insight meditation (Zürcher 1980). Neo-Confucianism owes to the religion its understanding of the difference between principle and affairs, the underlying essence of the world and its manifestation in reality, as well as its meditation of quiet-sitting, which goes back to the practice of *zazen* (Chang 1962; Taylor 1988). Buddhism, a sophisticated system of doctrines, meditations, and monastic organization, thus contributed significantly to the shaping of the Chinese mystical tradition.

Historical Unfolding

These four points common to both Confucianism and Daoism—the belief in the Ground, the application of five-phases cosmology, the correspondence of macro- and microcosms, and the adaptation of Buddhist concepts—have their roots in the historical development of the traditions. Typically, this development is divided into three periods: classical, which reaches from the ancient philosophers to the Han dynasty (206 BCE–220 CE); medieval, which lasts from the Three Kingdoms (221–265) to the Tang (618–907); and modern, which begins with the Song dynasty in 960 and goes through late imperial China (Ming [1368–1644] and Qing [1644–1911] dynasties) to the present.[19]

Each of these periods has its specific tendencies and overall marks. The classical is characterized by a high emphasis on philosophical speculation and the emergence of a systematic cosmological base. The medieval evolves under the strong influence of Buddhism and sees the emergence of sophisticated concepts of body and mind as well as methods of meditation and mystical attainment. The modern recovers the classical models and integrates them in a new synthesis that allows a broader vision of practice and realization.

In the classical period, we have the key thinkers of the two traditions: Confucius and Mencius in Confucianism, and Laozi and Zhuangzi in Daoism. Even though none of them wrote anything, their words were considered important enough to be transmitted through generations of disciples and committed to bamboo and silk around the third century BCE. Even the vagaries of changing dynasties and the notorious book burnings of 214 BCE did not lessen either their intactness or importance for Chinese culture. Classics were used for governmental and personal guidance, cited frequently, and interpreted ever anew, and in both their overall outlook and particular phrasing gave the two traditions their unique foundations. In addition, the classical period saw the emergence of the five-phases cosmology with its complex correspondence system and its vision of the universe as concentric circles of parallel layers and its postulation of an intimate interrelation between all levels of life.

The medieval period of about seven hundred years is divided into an early and a high phase, the boundary set in the sixth century, when the country was reunified after a long division. The early medieval period is characterized by an unprecedented dynamic, especially in Daoism, which saw the emergence of its major schools (Celestial Masters, Highest Clarity, Numinous Treasure) under the influence of Buddhism, which was sponsored particularly by the Central Asians in north China. The period saw the divinization of the philosopher Laozi, who was venerated as a personification of Dao and became increasingly like the Buddha in character. It also saw the formulation of Daoist mystical attainment through ecstatic journeys to the stars and the realization of mental detachment.[20] Confucianism, the more dominant creed of the south, was less affected but still engaged in debates with a growing number of Buddhists and gradually began to incorporate Buddhist ways of thinking. The high medieval phase saw a consolidation of the new forms of thinking, integrating Buddhist visions into indigenous Chinese systems and creating the sophisticated mid-Tang mystical systems. These systems were carried largely by Daoists, Confucianism being relegated to state-supporting doctrine.

This changed in the Song dynasty, when an overall recovery of Chinese roots and the ancient classics took place. This recovery followed two hundred years of confusion and civil war, beginning in 755 with the rebellion of General An Lushan and ending with the founding of the Song dynasty in 960. With much of high culture and social infrastructure in ruins, the new dynasty engaged in the eager collection of lost materials (turning the Song into the great age of Chinese encyclopedias) and in the return to ancient models that were more Chinese and less Central Asian or Indian. As a result, Confucianism was greatly revived and turned, in its neo-Confucian form as formulated by the great Zhu Xi (1130–1200), into a form of mystical self-cultivation, giving rise to a rich tradition that had its own form of meditation (quiet sitting), its own centers of learning (academies), and its own specific vision of the world (as issuing from the Great Ultimate and relying on universal principle) (Chan 1987; 1989).

Daoism, at this time much less important than Confucianism, reformulated its doctrines in the integrated system of internal alchemy, which applies alchemical metaphors and the symbols of the *Yijing* (*Book of Changes*) to express a vision of immortality patterned on the Buddhist attainment of nirvana. In addition, its new leading school of Complete Perfection imitated the Chan (Zen) tradition in many ways, organizationally, doctrinally, and methodologically. Both traditions have continued to the present along the patterns established in the Song dynasty, evolving new forms of interpretation and practice but leaving the framework of worldview and mystical vision unchanged. Even though both suffered under Communist rule in China and are today recovering, Confucianism was also heartily adopted in Korea, Japan, Vietnam, and Singapore and has an extended environment for its modern unfolding.

Unique Characteristics

We now turn to the distinct characteristics[21] of the two traditions, understanding how they differ. In their vision of the ultimate, Confucians posit a relationship between humanity and the cosmos that is direct and immediate, with harmony and virtuous order the key factors in the attainment of oneness and mystical vision. The same holds true for classical Daoism, the teachings of the ancient thinkers Laozi and Zhuangzi, but is vastly different in the religion, where Dao gives rise to the One, which unfolds into three *qi*, or cosmic energies, called the mysterious, beginning, and primordial. These, then, coagulate to bring forth the first god, Laozi, the personification of Dao.

Coagulating further, the energies also produce a series of nine heavens, a number of other deities (as, for example, the Queen Mother of the West as representative of pure yin), and a canon of sacred scriptures that contain, in essential and celestial form, the teachings the world will need to be created. Before the world ever comes into existence, there is a level of manifest divinity, found in the heavens, the gods, and the scriptures, which is neither beyond sensory experience and verbal expression as is Dao itself nor yet manifest in the world. Mediating chaos and creation, it represents a level of Dao existence from which human life springs and to which it will return. Dao is a willful agent that is no longer a spontaneous "flow of life" but gives a soteriological dimension to the creation. The mystical quest goes beyond the attainment of harmony with the cosmos to the transcendence of the world in a state of immortality in the celestial realm (Kohn 2001, 89–90).

Language in the classical texts and later interpretation of the two traditions appears differently, too. Confucians emphasize language and learning as key factors in the acquisition of wisdom and essential for its practical application in benevolence and social harmony (Ching 1976, 15). They begin with inherent intelligence, whose training through historical study, poetry, and other forms of verbal expression leads to sincerity. Sincerity, in turn, brings forth wisdom, which leads to an equilibrium of all forces, an overarching harmony that radiates from the person to the community and into the world, bringing "happy order" to Heaven and Earth. Daoists, on the contrary, find Heaven and Earth beyond linguistic expression. For them, the five phases of the larger universe are both cosmic powers and spirits in the five yin organs, whose function is to store *qi* (as opposed to the yang organs, which serve to transform outer energy from air and food into internally useful forms). Practicing controlled breathing and using a more right-brain approach through visualization and rhythmic incantations, they balance the different powers on a microcosmic level and find the One in themselves to then reach out to the celestial spheres.[22]

As wisdom and a sense of harmony in Confucianism are acquired through learning, based on the classics, the goals and means of the practice are always described in words. The tradition acknowledges that some words are better than others but never denies their potential or use. Not so the Daoists. They, in both the classical and religious traditions, emphasize the ineffability of Dao. Zhuangzi, in his famous chapter "Making All Things Equal" denies any applicability of words whatsoever (Watson 1968, 41). Words to Daoists are just sounds, made meaningful only by convention. Dependent on opposites, they are eternally relative and therefore nowhere near the truth. Valuing silence highest, Daoists describe their creed as "teaching without words" and follow the statement of the *Daode jing*: "Who speaks does not know, and who knows does not speak" (chap. 81). Thus the state of oneness with Dao is explained in paradoxes and by redefining words in spiraling circles, taking the adept's consciousness to more formless and ineffable levels until it dissolves in utter serenity.[23]

The self in mystical experience is similarly verbalized and conscious in the Confucian tradition and ineffable and formless in Daoism, where mythological figures are called upon to replace words in giving expression to its transformation (Kohn 1992b). An individualized aspect of the Great Ultimate, the self in neo-Confucianism is linked to the origins in its inherent "mind of Heaven," which has to be freed from attachments to externals and focused back on stillness and sincerity. As Confucian autobiographies document, this process is a conscious search that takes place as part of a government career that leaves room for serious practice after hours and between official postings and never necessitates complete withdrawal from society. Inspired by readings and verbal teachings, the conscious mind is led to give certain interpretations to the world and accordingly finds harmony in its social environment (Taylor 1978; 1990).

The Daoist self, on the other hand, is transformed into celestial dimensions after it is first seen as consisting of several contradictory forces—seven material or yin souls matching three spiritual or yang souls, plus various celestial deities of the pure Dao and demonic parasites known as the three worms—which pull it into opposite directions, yin toward instinct satisfaction, sensuality, and darkness; yang toward intellectual endeavors, spirituality, and light (Yü 1987). Through control of the yin impulses and the destruction of inner demons, the adept's inner nature is changed into pure yang. Then the celestials, notably the Three Ones, can come to occupy all thinking and feeling by being constantly visualized in the energy centers of head, chest, and abdomen (Andersen 1994). The body, a microcosm of the created world, is transformed into a replica of the heavens, the gods, and the scriptures that reside before the creation of the material universe. Adepts in the process become denizens of the empyrean, leaving behind the perfection of naturalness in the attainment of celestial purity.

Mystical training differs accordingly. Centered on the five virtues (honesty, propriety, wisdom, benevolence, and righteousness) and their proper feelings, Confucians are guided to see the inherent principle of universal oneness in their body and mind and then expand it into the family, community, and world.[24] As the virtues, with benevolence first, are realized, all selfish impulses are overcome, and the mind becomes identical with the impartiality of Heaven. A harmonious life is possible, and the world itself finds perfect balance (see Ivanhoe 1993).

Daoists, on the other hand, undertake mystical training in a monastic setting. They live in establishments in remote mountain areas, set up to replicate the world of the immortals; wear formalized ritual garments; adapt a simple vegetarian diet combined with regular periods of fasting; and follow a strict ritual schedule that denies normal patterns of waking and sleeping (Kohn 2003, 173–174). They vow to obey sets of precepts that also include Confucian values, but rather than cultivating specific virtues, they strive for an overall harmony with the natural forces. In their practice, moreover, they think less of the social impact and focus on their physical bodies, which they see as the primary residence of the gods, nurturing them with herbal remedies, not rich foods. In place of man-made structures, they engage actively with physical nature, close to mountains and streams, boulders and grottoes, while yet maintaining a strong cosmic awareness and visualizing celestial palaces both in the body and in the stars.

Directly related to this aspect of mystical training is the nature of community and ethics, which are highly hierarchical and family-centered in Confucianism and more egalitarian and universal in Daoism. Confucian specialist communities, preparatory to life in society, are academies where the classics are read and thoughts are developed in active contemplation. Their rules include reverence for elders, awareness of hierarchies, and abstention from harmful social actions. As the neo-Confucian thinker Dai Zhen (1723–1777) says: "When a person is neither selfish nor beclouded, his mind is pure and clear; this is a state of supreme illumination. When a mind is still and does not move, it is pure and attains the perfection of heavenly virtue" (Cheng 1971, 106).[25]

Daoist communities, in comparison, are religious organizations, dedicated under Mahayana influence to the universal salvation of all beings. Community rules here imitate the Buddhist precepts, emphasizing the restraint of baser appetites and often focusing on the purity of the body attained through the retention of the gods within (Kohn 2004). In addition, they guide adepts to give proper veneration to sacred locations and objects and threaten punishments in mythological form as tortures in the various hells.

Confucians, aside from reading the classics and pondering the oneness of the universe, engage in a meditation called quiet-sitting, which is a form of contemplation that aims at stilling the mind and making it a mirror that reflects but does not act.[26] Without cutting off social relationships and responsibilities, practitioners develop a pure and reflecting mind and lose all selfish impulses in favor of a calm and impartial response to the world. Anger and happiness in this context are accepted as part of the natural response and encouraged to occur at the right times.

Daoists, who are more Heaven-oriented, have a much larger variety of practices. They begin with a change in diet and daily habits, then perform physical and breathing exercises to open up the *qi* channels in the body and activate the energy centers in the five organs. These practices combine slow body movements with deep breathing and a keen mental awareness. They are nowadays known under the name of qigong.[27]

Daoists also engage in meditations, visualizing the five cosmic energies as they appear in their characteristic colors in the five organs and thus relating the body to the heavenly spheres. They also imagine in the body deities such as the Three Ones, who, often in the form of infants and clad in luscious brocades, reside in the inner palaces and bestow health, harmony, and celestial empowerment on the practitioner. Externalizing these gods, Daoists visualize them as outside entities from whom they can acquire valuable knowledge or celestial energies. In yet another form of Daoist practice, adepts refine their bodies to heavenly purity in a quasi-alchemical process, seeing the yin and yang energies of the body as the lead and mercury of the crucible and concocting a cinnabar elixir, the pearl of immortality, within. This pearl grows into an immortal embryo, the spirit *alter ego*, allowing the practitioner to leave the body behind and traverse the heavens in freedom. As the body falls away in death, this spirit entity survives, and the practitioner becomes a celestial being, living forever and attaining a celestial form of oneness with Dao.

Anyone having attained the goal of the tradition becomes a master, an ideal human being in the Confucian tradition and a celestial sage or heavenly perfected in the Daoist vision. The Confucian gentleman (*junzi*) is characterized as highly virtuous and eminently learned, a paragon of benevolence and filial piety, who knows all about ceremonies and music and can explain the truth of cosmic harmony with ease and simplicity. As described in a neo-Confucian document, "he is as pure as pure gold, and as mild and lovable as excellent jade. Liberal but not irregular, he maintains harmony with others but does not drift with them. His conscientiousness and sincerity penetrate metal and stone, and his filial piety and brotherly respect influence all beings" (Chan 1967, 299).

The Daoist sage (*shengren*), or perfected (*zhenren*), has similar characteristics but more dominantly is a heavenly being with no explicit teachings who acts in complete nonaction among people. Moving along with the currents of the world gives free rein to the currents of life. The accomplished Daoist floats through in the world as a ray of pure heavenly light, shining widely and transforming all without active intention. As the *Daode jing* says: "The Sage does not act and so does not ruin; he does not grasp and so does not lose" (chap. 64), and: "He always helps people and rejects none; always helps all beings and rejects none" (chap. 27). This is called practicing brightness.

Despite these differences, both traditions emphasize the importance of microcosmic perfection in macrocosmic reality and claim the transformative powers of the accomplished mystic in society. The goal is ultimately the transformation of Earth, seen here as the establishment of a celestial kingdom on Earth, a state that both contains and transcends the happy order of Confucianism.

Mystical union, as celebrated in the traditions, reflects once more their fundamental difference as inherent versus transcendent. Confucians hope to "regard Heaven, Earth, and the myriad things as one body, the world as one family and the country as one person." They come to "form one body with Heaven, Earth, and the myriad beings," seeing "all people as their brothers and sisters, and all things as their companions" (Chan 1963b, 272, 274). The underlying oneness of the cosmos is fully realized in the mystics' minds as they become impartial and pure in their relationships to all. Joining with the family, the community, the world, and the cosmos, they radiate bright virtue, spreading benevolence and goodness wherever they go.

Daoist mystics, on the contrary, after living out an extended lifespan as sages, or perfected, on Earth, find complete realization in a triumphant ascent to the heavens. Having realized the cosmos within, they ride into the empyrean on cloudy chariots drawn by dragons, encountering pure divinities of Dao and joining splendid banquets in the celestial palaces.[28] As the Tang poet Wu Yun (d. 778) expressed it:

> The emperor of the Great One settles in my heart;
> As streaming light pours from my Cinnabar Field.
> The gods, like Nonradiance and the Lord Peach,
> Chant brightly from the chapters of long life.
> My six viscera glow with luminous morning light;
> My hundred joints are like a net of purple mist.
> My whirlwind carriage traverses endless space:
> Slow and steady, I rise on light itself. (Schafer 1981)

Watching phoenixes and unicorns dance to spheric music, mystics as immortals enjoy the eternal freedom of pure spirit; at one with Dao in its first creative stage and partaking of its powers, they can live forever, appear and disappear at will, be in numerous places at once, and reverse the course of nature.[29] Still dedicated to universal salvation, they then use their new power and position to administer celestial justice and, almost in bodhisattva fashion, aid humanity in its plight. Having become gods, Daoist mystics are beyond the world and yet for it, personifications of the purity of Heaven and the creative powers of Dao.

Classroom Adaptation

In whatever setting and context one teaches Chinese mysticism, it is essential to emphasize that it always focuses on the attainment of oneness with Heaven and Earth, is centered on the body-mind of the living individual, has a strong social and political dimension, and relates to an underlying force of potent vital energy that is, in some traditions, seen in multiple divinities rather than a single creator god. In its indigenous mode, it comes in two major traditions: Confucian and Daoist, which have undergone parallel phases of historical development, are deeply indebted to Buddhism, and have served Chinese society widely with their vision.

Classified traditionally in the complementary system of yin and yang, Confucian self-realization is the more outward-going form, achieved through conscious learning and the steadfast practice of essentially communal virtues. Daoist perfection, on the other hand, is more transcendent and steeped in myth. It, too, begins with the individual and encourages ethical conduct and social responsibility, but in its higher stages, it focuses on venerating revealed scriptures, connecting to divine entities, ecstatically traveling to otherworldly realms, and going completely beyond the limitations of human life and world. Both traditions are eager to contribute to a greater sense of wholeness of the person, to peace and harmony in the world, and to a sense of cosmic integration and oneness. They start from a positive outlook and encourage being in the world, making a contribution to society, and finding happiness in this life. Yet they also retain a sense of a connection to higher cosmic realities and express the urge to reach for the ultimate, a life in oneness with Heaven and Earth.

To make these points accessible to students, it is very helpful to have original sources in translation, so that they receive the taste of bygone generations; the contemporary relevance of the teachings is a key factor to engaging students' minds and hearts. For the Confucian way, the works by Tu Wei-ming are most important in this context. He repeatedly places the teachings in a personally relevant and modern political context, creating a new vision of Confucian society that plays an increasing role in the ongoing Chinese debate on harmony and the adaptation of democracy to twenty-first–century technology and non-Western social systems (1979; 1998). In light of the fact that Chinese culture and economic and political power are on the rise, it is essential to understand the ultimate goal of Chinese spirituality and its vision of an integrated personal, social, political, and ultimately cosmic realization.

For the Daoist tradition, Wayne Dyer's meditations on the *Daode jing* are most recent and increasingly popular (2007). Making Daoist ideas relevant, he encourages people to change their basic outlook from fear to curiosity, from control to trust, and from entitlement to humility. He rephrases nonaction as "noninterference" and explains the idea of knowing when to stop as "When your cup is full, stop pouring." Much like other interpreters of the *Daode jing*, he applies Daoist spirituality in four distinct areas of modern life: the Western tendency toward action and progress; the importance of reducing stress; the reversal of common cultural and ethical values; and concerns for the environment and social harmony. Like traditional Daoist mystics, modern interpreters move from personal transformation into greater social contexts, but they all share with their Confucian counterparts the ideal of a harmonious and cosmically sustained world, spearheaded, modeled, and realized by the mystics and their personal practices.

Notes

1. In fact, the entire early philosophy of China focuses on Dao and how best to live in and with it. Thus, A. C. Graham named his discussion of early Chinese thought *Disputers of the Tao* (1989).

2. Some of these techniques involve the conscious reorganization of thinking and perception in a meditation practice known as "observation." Adapted from Buddhist insight meditation, it forms an important part of a seven-step program to Daoist realization. For studies, see Kohn (1987 [expanded edition Kohn 2010]; 1989a).

3. For further discussions of *qi*, see Chang (1976), Kaptchuk (1983), and Kendall (2002).

4. A powerful discussion of *shen* in Chinese medicine is found in Porkert (1974). An examination of the notion in ancient Chinese and Daoist thought appears in Roth (1990).

5. This notion is already a central feature of the thought of the ancient *Daode jing*. See Schwartz (1985; 1998). On the spiritual dimensions of rulership in ancient China, see Ames (1983).

6. Biographical studies of Confucius include Dawson (1982), Kelen (1971), and Liu (1955).

7. For translations of the *Analects*, see Waley (1989), Lau (1979), and Ames (1998).

8. For the development and role of Confucianism in Chinese society, see Berthrong (1998) and Oldstone-Moore (2002).

9. A translation of this chapter, together with other Confucian documents, is found in Chan (1963b). For a complete rendition of the *Liji*, see Legge (1968). A discussion of the role of ritual in ancient China is found in McDermott (1999).

10. On the development of Confucianism in its modern form since the Song dynasty, see DeBary (1975; 1981). For its modern vision and relevance, see Tu (1979).

11. As A. C. Graham has shown, the early legend of Laozi arose as part of the Confucian effort to show the humility and continuous learning of their master. He was associated with a growing "Daoist" community in the fourth century BCE and credited with longevity and even immortality under the Qin. See Graham (1990).

12. The *Daode jing* is among the most frequently translated books. For a discussion of the intricacies of its translation and a guide to the most commonly used ones, see LaFargue and Pas (1998).

13. The particular style of *Daode jing* poetry is closely related to that of the *Shijing* (*Book of Songs*), a collection of ancient local songs and poems that date back to around 500 BCE. For a discussion, see Baxter (1998).

14. On the creation of the standard edition and the commentary by Wang Bi, see Chan (1991). A translation of the commentary appears in Lin (1977) and Rump and Chan (1979).

15. A translation of the various manuscripts unearthed at Guodian appears in Henricks (2000). A collection of essays on the texts is found in Allan and Williams (2000).

16. The notion of the Ground appears in discussions of the perennial philosophy, a term coined by the German philosopher Leibniz and more extensively formulated by Aldous Huxley (1946). Among mysticism studies, it is most clearly present in Happold (1970).

17. Although this cosmology is already part of the ancient *Yijing* and appears in Han-dynasty commentaries to the text, it is most explicitly formulated in early neo-Confucian documents, notably the works of Zhou Dunyi (1017–1073). A translation of the complete document is found in Chan (1963b, 463–464).

18. On the transmission and adaptation of Buddhism in China, see Ch'en (1973), Zürcher (1959), and Tsukamoto and Hurvitz (1985).

19. For a discussion of periodization issues in Chinese religion and Daoism, see Kirkland (1997).

20. For an overview of Daoist history, see Kohn (2001; 2008b).

21. Translations of original Daoist sources suitable for students' appear in Kohn (1993). Texts specifically on mysticism presented in the same order as the topics here are found in Kohn (2009); they are available both in printed form and as an electronic publication (www.

threepinespress.com). The work also contains a bibliographical list of Confucian resources.

22. For the complexities of inner landscape and gods in the Daoist body, see Kohn (1991b), Andersen (1994), Kroll (1996), Saso (1997), Bumbacher (2001), Komjathy (2008; 2009), and Neswald (2009).

23. A good example of the mystical use of language in Daoism is found in the medieval *Xisheng jing* (*Scripture of Western Ascension*), which purports to contain Laozi's oral instructions at the time of *Daode jing* transmission. For a translation and study, see Kohn (1991a).

24. A discussion of the virtues and their role in Confucian self-cultivation is found in Chan (1986, 177–179).

25. For more details on Confucian rules for mystical training, see the Korean interpretation of Zhu Xi's guidelines translated in Kalton (1989).

26. For an outline of traditional Confucian practice, see Chan (1986). For contemporary forms of Confucian meditation, see Taylor (1988).

27. A good overview of qigong as practiced today is found in Cohen (1997). Traditionally it goes back to a practice called *daoyin* (lit. "guiding the *qi* and stretching the body"), for which see Kohn (2008a). The martial art of *taiji quan* is often also practiced in a similar healing and self-awareness manner and has been adopted in many Daoist establishments today. For a discussion, see Kohn (2005, 191–202).

28. Poetic descriptions of the ecstatic flight of the Daoist mystic are first found in ancient shamanic songs, then in medieval poetry. See Hawkes (1959) and Holzman (1976).

29. Detailed descriptions of ideal Daoists, their activities, and their powers are found in a collection of immortals' biographies from the fourth century and translated in Campany (2002).

References

Allan, Sarah, and Crispin Williams, eds. 2000. *The Guodian Laozi*. Berkeley, CA: Institute of East Asian Studies.

Ames, Roger T. 1983. *The Art of Rulership: A Study in Ancient Chinese Political Thought*. Honolulu: University of Hawai'i Press.

———. 1998. *The Analects of Confucius: A Philosophical Translation*. New York: Ballentine.

Andersen, Poul. 1994. "The Transformation of the Body in Taoist Ritual." In *Religious Reflections on the Human Body*, edited by Jane Marie Law, 181–202. Bloomington: Indiana University Press.

Baxter, William H. 1998. "Situating the Language of the *Lao-tzu*: The Probable Date of the *Tao-te-ching*." In *Lao-tzu and the Tao-te-ching*, edited by Livia Kohn and Michael LaFargue, 231–254. Albany: State University of New York Press.

Berthrong, John H. 1998. *Transformations of the Confucian Way*. Boulder: Westview Press.

Bumbacher, Stephan Peter. 2001. "Zu den Körpergottheiten im chinesischen Taoismus." In *Noch eine Chance für die Religionsphänomenologie?*, edited by D. Peoli-Olgiati, A. Michaels, and F. Stolz, 151–172. Frankfurt: Peter Lang.

Campany, Robert F. 2002. *To Live as Long as Heaven and Earth: A Translation and Study of Ge Hong's Traditions of Divine Transcendents*. Berkeley: University of California Press.

Chan, Alan K. L. 1991. *Two Visions of the Way: A Study of the Wang Pi and the Ho-shang-kung Commentaries on the Laozi*. Albany: State University of New York Press.

Chan, Wing-tsit. 1963a. *Instructions for Practical Living and Other Neo-Confucian Writings by Wang Yang-ming*. New York: Columbia University Press.

———. 1963a. *A Source Book in Chinese Philosophy*. Princeton, NJ: Princeton University Press.

———. 1967. *Reflections on Things at Hand: The Neo-Confucian Anthology Compiled by Chu Hsi and Lü Tsu-ch'ien*. New York: Columbia University Press.

———. 1986. *Neo-Confucian Terms Explained: The Pei-hsi tzu-i by Ch'en Ch'un (1159–1223)*. New York: Columbia University Press.

———. 1987. *Chu Hsi: Life and Thought*. Hong Kong: Chinese University Press.

———. 1989. *Chu Hsi: New Studies*. Honolulu: University of Hawai'i Press.

Chang, Carsun. 1962. *The Development of Neo-Confucian Thought*. New York: Bookman Associates.

Chang, Stephen. 1976. *The Complete Book of Acupuncture*. Berkeley, CA: Celestial Arts.

Ch'en, Kenneth. 1973. *The Chinese Transformation of Buddhism*. Princeton, NJ: Princeton University Press.

Cheng, Chung-ying. 1971. *Tai Chen's Inquiry into Goodness: A Translation of the Yuan Shan, with an Introductory Essay*. Honolulu: East-West Center Press.

Ching, Julia. 1976. *To Accumulate Wisdom: The Way of Wang Yang-ming*. New York: Columbia University Press.

Cohen, Kenneth S. 1997. *The Way of Qigong: The Art and Science of Chinese Energy Healing*. New York: Ballantine.

Dawson, Raymond. 1982. *Confucius*. New York: Hill and Wang.

DeBary, Wm. Th. 1975. *The Unfolding of Neo-Confucianism*. New York: Columbia University Press.

———. 1981. *Neo-Confucian Orthodoxy and the Learning of the Mind-and-Heart*. New York: Columbia University Press.

Dyer, Wayne W. 2007. *Change Your Thoughts—Change Your Life: Living the Wisdom of the Tao*. Carlsbad, CA: Hay House.

Eno, Robert. 1990. *The Confucian Creation of Heaven. Philosophy and the Defense of Ritual Mastery*. Albany: State University of New York Press.

Fingarette, Herbert. 1972. *Confucius—The Secular as Sacred*. New York: Harper & Row.

Graham, A. C. 1989. *Disputers of the Tao: Philosophical Argument in Ancient China*. La Salle, IL: Open Court Publishing Company.

———. 1990. "The Origins of the Legend of Lao Tan." In *Studies in Chinese Philosophy and Philosophical Literature*, edited by A. C. Graham, 111–124. Albany: State University of New York Press.

Hall, David, and Roger T. Ames. 1987. *Thinking Through Confucius*. Albany: State University of New York Press.

Happold, F. C. 1970. *Mysticism: A Study and an Anthology*. Baltimore: Penguin

Harper, Donald. 1998. *Early Chinese Medical Manuscripts: The Mawangdui Medical Manuscripts*. London: Wellcome Asian Medical Monographs.

Hawkes, David. 1959. *Ch'u Tz'u: The Songs of the South*. Oxford: Clarendon Press.

Henricks, Robert. 1989. *Lao-Tzu: Te-Tao ching*. New York: Ballantine.

———. 2000. *Lau Tzu's Tao Te Ching: A Translation of the Startling New Documents Found at Guodian*. New York: Columbia University Press.

Holzman, Donald. 1976. *Poetry and Politics: The Life and Works of Juan Chi (210–263)*. Cambridge: Cambridge University Press.

Huxley, Aldous. 1946. *The Perennial Philosophy*. New York: Harper and Brothers

Ivanhoe, Philip J. 1993. *Confucian Moral Self-Cultivation*. New York: Peter Lang.

Kaltenmark, Max. 1979. "The Ideology of the *T'ai-p'ing-ching*." In *Facets of Taoism*, edited by Holmes Welch and Anna Seidel, 19–52. New Haven, CT: Yale University Press.

Kalton, Michael. 1989. *To Become a Sage: The Ten Diagrams of Sage Learning by Yi T'oegye*. New York: Columbia University Press.

Kaptchuk, Ted J. 1983. *The Web That Has No Weaver: Understanding Chinese Medicine*. New York: Congdon and Weed.

Kelen, Betty. 1971. *Confucius in Life and Legend*. New York: T. Nelson.

Kendall, Donald E. 2002. *Dao of Chinese Medicine: Understanding an Ancient Healing Art*. New York: Oxford University Press.

Kirkland, J. Russell. 1997. "The Historical Contours of Taoism in China: Thoughts on Issues of Classification and Terminology," *Journal of Chinese Religions* 25:57–82.

Kohn, Livia. 1987. *Seven Steps to the Tao: Sima Chengzhen's Zuowanglun*. Monumenta Serica Monograph 20. St. Augustin/Nettetal: Steyler Verlag.

———. 1989a. "Taoist Insight Meditation: The Tang Practice of *Neiguan*." In *Taoist Meditation and Longevity Techniques*, edited by Livia Kohn, 191–222. Ann Arbor: University of Michigan, Center for Chinese Studies Publications.

———, ed. 1989b. *Taoist Meditation and Longevity Techniques*. Ann Arbor: University of Michigan, Center for Chinese Studies Publications.

———. 1991a. *Taoist Mystical Philosophy: The Scripture of Western Ascension*. Albany: State University of New York Press.

———. 1991b. "Taoist Visions of the Body." *Journal of Chinese Philosophy* 18:227–252.

———. 1992a. *Early Chinese Mysticism: Philosophy and Soteriology in the Taoist Tradition*. Princeton, NJ: Princeton University Press.

———. 1992b. "Selfhood and Spontaneity in Ancient Chinese Thought." In *Selves, People, and Persons*, edited by Leroy Rouner, 123–138. South Bend, IN: University of Notre Dame Press.

———. 1993. *The Taoist Experience: An Anthology*. Albany: State University of New York Press.

———. 1998. *God of the Dao: Lord Lao in History and Myth*. Ann Arbor: University of Michigan, Center for Chinese Studies.

———. 2001. *Daoism and Chinese Culture*. Cambridge, MA: Three Pines Press.

———. 2003. *Monastic Life in Medieval Daoism: A Cross-Cultural Perspective*. Honolulu: University of Hawai'i Press.

———. 2004. *Cosmos and Community: The Ethical Dimension of Daoism*. Cambridge, MA: Three Pines Press.

———. 2005. *Health and Long Life: The Chinese Way*. Cambridge, MA: Three Pines Press.

———. 2008a. *Chinese Healing Exercises: The Tradition of Daoyin*. Honolulu: University of Hawai'i Press.

———. 2008b. *Introducing Daoism*. London: Routledge.

———. 2009. *Readings in Daoist Mysticism*. Dunedin, FL: Three Pines Press.

———. 2010. *Sitting in Oblivion: The Heart of Daoist Meditation*. Dunedin, FL: Three Pines Press.

Komjathy, Louis. 2008. "Mapping the Daoist Body (1): The *Neijing tu* in History." *Journal of Daoist Studies* 1: 67–92.

———. 2009. "Mapping the Daoist Body (2): The Text of the *Neijing tu*." *Journal of Daoist Studies* 2: 64–108.

Kroll, Paul W. 1996. "Body Gods and Inner Vision: *The Scripture of the Yellow Court*. In *Religions of China in Practice*, edited by Donald S. Lopez Jr., 149–155. Princeton, NJ: Princeton University Press.

LaFargue, Michael. 1992. *The Tao of the Tao-te-ching*. Albany: State University of New York Press.

LaFargue, Michael, and Julian Pas. 1998. "On Translating the *Tao-te-ching*. In *Lao-tzu and the Tao-te-ching*, edited by Livia Kohn and Michael LaFargue, 277–302. Albany: State University of New York Press.

Lai, Chi-tim. 2001. "The Daoist Concept of Central Harmony in the *Scripture of Great Peace*: Human Responsibility for the Maladies of Nature." In *Daoism and Ecology: Ways Within a Cosmic Landscape*, edited by Norman Girardot, James Miller, and Liu Xiaogan, 95–112. Cambridge, MA: Harvard University Press, Center for the Study of World Religions.

Lau, D. C. 1979. *The Analects*. New York: Penguin.

LeBlanc, Charles. 1992. "Resonance: Une interpretation chinoise de la réalite." In *Mythe et philosophie a l'aube de la Chine imperial: Etudes sur le Huainan zi*, edited by Charles Le Blanc and Remi Mathieu, 91–111. Montreal: Presses de l'Université de Montréal.

Legge, James. 1968 [1885]. *The Li Ki—Book of Rites*. Delhi: Motilal Bernasidass.

Lin, Paul J. 1977. *A Translation of Lao-tzu's Tao-te-ching and Wang Pi's Commentary*. Ann Arbor: University of Michigan, Center for Chinese Studies Publications.

Liu, Wu-chi. 1955. *Confucius, His Life and Time*. New York: Philosophical Library.

McDermott, Joseph P. 1999. *State and Court Ritual in China*. Cambridge: Cambridge University Press.

Neswald, Sara Elaine. 2009. "Internal Landscapes." In *Internal Alchemy: Self, Society, and the Quest for Immortality*, edited by Livia Kohn and Robin R. Wang, 27–53. Magdalena, NM: Three Pines Press.

Oldstone-Moore, Jennifer. 2002. *Confucianism: Origins, Beliefs, Practices, Holy Texts, Sacred Places*. New York: Oxford University Press.

Porkert, Manfred. 1974. *The Theoretical Foundations of Chinese Medicine*. Cambridge, MA: MIT Press.

Roth, Harold D. 1990. "The Early Taoist Concept of *Shen*: A Ghost in the Machinery?" In *Sagehood and Systematizing Thought in the Late Warring States and Early Han*, edited by Kidder Smith, 11–32. Brunswick, ME: Bowdoin College.

———. 1999. *Original Tao: Inward Training and the Foundations of Taoist Mysticism*. New York: Columbia University Press.

Rump, Ariane, and Wing-tsit Chan. 1979. *Commentary on the Lao-tzu by Wang Pi*. Honolulu: University of Hawai'i Press.

Saso, Michael. 1997. "The Taoist Body and Cosmic Prayer." In *Religion and the Body*, edited by Sarah Coakley, 231–247. Cambridge: Cambridge University Press.

Schafer, Edward H. 1981. "Wu Yün's 'Cantos on Pacing the Void,' " *Harvard Journal of Asiatic Studies* 41: 377–415.

Schwartz, Benjamin. 1985. *The World of Thought in Ancient China*. Cambridge, MA: Harvard University Press.

————. 1998. "The Worldview of the *Tao-te-ching*." In *Lao-tzu and the Tao-te-ching*, edited by Livia Kohn and Michael LaFargue, 189–210. Albany: State University of New York Press.

Seidel, Anna. 1969. *La divinisation de Lao-tseu dans le taoïsme des Han*. Paris: Ecole Française d'Extrême-Orient.

Taylor, Rodney L. 1978. *The Cultivation of Selfhood as a Religious Goal in Neo-Confucianism*. Missoula, MT: Scholars Press.

————. 1988. *The Confucian Way of Contemplation: Okada Takehiko and the Tradition of Quiet-Sitting*. Columbia: University of South Carolina Press.

————. 1990. *The Religious Dimensions of Confucianism*. Albany: State University of New York Press.

Tsukamoto, Zenryū, and Leon Hurvitz. 1985. *A History of Early Chinese Buddhism*. 2 vols. Tokyo: Kodansha.

Tu, Wei-ming. 1979. *Humanity and Self-Cultivation: Essays in Confucian Thought*. Berkeley, CA: Asian Humanities Press.

————. 1998. *Confucianism and Human Rights*. New York: Columbia University Press.

Waley, Arthur. 1989 [1938]. *The Analects of Confucius*. New York: Vintage Books.

Watson, Burton. 1968. *The Complete Works of Chuang-tzu*. New York: Columbia University Press.

Yü, Ying-shih. 1987. "O Soul, Come Back: A Study of the Changing Conceptions of the Soul and Afterlife in Pre-Buddhist China," *Harvard Journal of Asiatic Studies* 47: 363–395.

Zürcher, Erik. 1959. *The Buddhist Conquest of China: The Spread and Adaptation of Buddhism in Early Medieval China*. 2 vols. Leiden: E. Brill.

————. 1980. "Buddhist Influence on Early Taoism." *T'oung Pao* 66: 84–147.

4

The Mystical Dimensions of Buddhism
David B. Gray

The fields of Buddhist Studies and Mystical Studies are deeply entwined and arguably complementary. Buddhism has challenged and enriched the study of mysticism, and many students of Buddhism are drawn to the religion out of interest in its meditative practices that are arguably mystical. A course that brings the two fields together, on "Buddhism and Mysticism," has great potential for engaging student interest. Yet this course will also need to present a coherent rational for this integration. This is because the claim that Buddhism is "mystical" has been contested from multiple angles. On the one hand, early and influential definitions of mysticism tended to accord closely with Western religious models, which thus appear to exclude Asian religions such as Buddhism that do not share their theological presuppositions. On the other hand, during the Colonial period, Buddhist modernists began to claim that Buddhism was not a "religion" at all, but was a "science," and that it was "rational" rather than "mystical." This argument was developed in reaction to Christian criticisms during the nineteenth and twentieth centuries, and it remains a very influential discourse in Buddhist circles.

To argue successfully that Buddhism does in fact have mystical dimensions, it will be necessary to first argue for a definition of *mysticism* that is inclusive enough to accommodate religions such as Buddhism that lack a strong focus on a singular God or ultimate reality. I will then discuss the distorted view of Buddhism that has resulted from the success of the Buddhism qua science argument, and that Buddhism, contra the Buddhist modernists, does contain numerous elements that cannot be labeled "rational" and must be labeled mystical, insofar as Buddhism makes claims regarding the nature of the self and reality that are not scientifically and empirically verifiable. Rather, Buddhism, like many other mystical traditions, makes claims to special forms of nonempirical knowledge that are the results of contemplative practices. I will conclude with a discussion of resources that are helpful for the study of Buddhist

mysticism in undergraduate classes. In particular, I will focus on autobiographical works by Buddhist meditators, which, in my experience, are a rich
resource that undergraduate students tend to find far more accessible than
traditional Buddhist scriptures or commentaries, or works of secondary
scholarship.

Mysticism and the Asian Religions

The Western study of religion has had a strong tendency to presuppose Western cultural and religious superiority. Tomoko Masuzawa has shown, in her
2005 work, *The Invention of World Religions,* that Western scholarship in religion during the nineteenth and much of the twentieth century produced hierarchical taxonomies of religion that tended to privilege Christianity and
reduced to lesser positions other religions, such as Islam, Hinduism, and Buddhism. This attitude is also found in early and influential studies of mysticism.
Evelyn Underhill, in her influential work *Mysticism,* largely presupposes the
Western theological perspective, arguing that mysticism involves union with a
singular divine ultimate reality (1911, 71–73). Underhill was not explicitly engaging in comparison. Her view of mysticism derived from the Western mystical traditions, and it certainly remains a useful exposition from the perspective
of these traditions. However, definition of *mysticism* in terms of union with a
singular divine absolute reality is problematic from the perspective of Buddhism, because Buddhist philosophers tended to reject such singular absolute
realities.

From the perspective of nineteenth- and early-twentieth-century European
scholarship on religion, Buddhism certainly seemed anomalous. Religion was
commonly defined in terms of belief in spiritual entities, a god, gods, or spirits,
and Buddhism, on the surface at least, did not fit neatly into influential taxonomies of religion such as Tylor's, which classified religions as "animistic,"
"polytheistic," or "monotheistic." Because Buddhists both denied the existence
of a monotheistic creator god and downplayed (while not denying outright)
the deities of ancient Indian mythology, it was an open question whether Buddhism was even a religion, at least when *religion* is defined in terms of belief in
supernatural entities.[1] Definitions of *mysticism* that defined mysticism in terms
of union with a divine entity are likewise problematic, as far as Buddhism is
concerned.

Some later scholars of mysticism were aware of this problem. Zaehner, for
example, still defined *mysticism* as an experience of union. However, he took
into consideration a larger number of religious traditions, paying particular
attention to Islamic and Hindu mystical traditions. He thus added "monism" to
theism as a possible religious theological perspective. He thus defined *mysticism*
as follows: "In Christian terminology mysticism means union with God; in

non-theistical contexts it also means union with some principle or other. It is, therefore, a unitive experience with someone or something other than oneself" (1957, 32).

However, Buddhism even presents a challenge to this more inclusive definition. While later Mahāyāna Buddhist traditions deploy the language of "union" (*yoga, samyoga, samāyoga*) in their descriptions of the goals of meditative practices, the more conservative Theravāda tradition appears to lack any sort of unitive descriptions of the goal of practice. Zaehner made a weak attempt to argue that it does, by arguing, contra Buddhist doctrine, that the Buddha taught a doctrine of an absolute eternal self (*ātman*).[2] Other scholars of mysticism, such as Geoffrey Parrinder, have likewise followed Zaehner in arguing that Buddhists likewise seek some sort of "unitive experience" (1976, 60).

The Mahāyāna Buddhist tradition focuses on the realization of emptiness, classically defined as ultimate reality, and also equated with Buddha nature and the nature of mind. This suggests that the classical formulation of mysticism qua union with ultimate reality is at least partially relevant to Buddhism.[3] Although there are major differences between Christian and Buddhist and mystical traditions, centering around the former's focus on a singular absolute God, and the latter's rejection of this, there are nonetheless fascinating similarities between Buddhist and theistic descriptions of mystical practices and the aim or objectives of these practices. Whereas the Buddhists reject a singular creator deity or divine principle, they often use very similar language as theistic mystical traditions in describing the object of their own meditative practices, the realization of the nature of mind or Buddha nature. This similarity certainly supports the claim that Buddhism has a strong mystical dimension, as I will argue in the next section.

Moreover, it is not the case that Buddhism necessarily problematicizes the study of mysticism; it simply does not fit well with definitions that privilege theistic preconceptions. Ninian Smart, for example, has argued that the term *mystical* should not be applied to religions such as Christianity, Judaism, and Islam, which focus on an encounter with a sacred "other"; he applies the term *numinous* to these traditions. The term *mystical,* in his view, is more appropriately applied to religious traditions, such as Buddhism and Daoism, that do not posit an external "other" and that focus on the realization of nonduality, the disappearance of the subject-object distinction, in meditative practice.[4] Even though *mysticism* remains a contested category, there certainly appears to be good reason to conduct an exploration of Buddhist contemplative traditions within this rubric, as would be the case in a course on "Buddhism and Mysticism."

Given the fact that the category of *experience* has been highly contested, it is essential that this term be at least briefly addressed in a course on mysticism. The notion that "mystical experience" entails a special category of experience involving direct and unmediated access to the absolute has received considerable criticism, notably by Steven Katz (1978), Wayne Proudfoot (1985), and Robert Sharf (2000). This claim has been defended by others, such as Robert Forman (1990, 1999). Interestingly, Mahāyāna Buddhists seemingly straddle this debate. With the constructivists, Mahāyāna Buddhists of the Yogācāra-Madhyamika synthesis that came to dominate in Northern India during the time when the Buddhist tantras were composed argued for the conditioned, and hence constructed, nature of ordinary experience (Forman 1999, 81–89). However, a number of Buddhist theorists argued convincingly that awakening involves a "special" and nonempirical form of knowledge, a direct perception of ultimate reality achieved via meditative techniques. Buddhists thus join other mystical traditions in claiming a special mode of knowledge attained via mystical means.

I do not wish to make any special claims about the nature of experience as actually perceived by Buddhist meditators, past or present. Being based solely upon textual sources, this essay can only address the rhetoric of experience or self-experience contained within these texts. The exact content of any experiences that the meditative practices might engender is beyond the scope of this chapter. However, insofar as the meditative practices do yield, on a regular basis, distinctive forms of "religious experience," I agree with Matthew Kapstein, who argued that experiences, religious or otherwise, are not private and are thus reproducible by qualified agents. Rather, "religious experiences, like aesthetic experiences, are thus second order experiences, constituted by our interpretations and judgments of primary phenomenal experiences of sound, sight, and so on, and of mental and abstract phenomena as well" (2004b, 287).

Is Buddhism Rational or Mystical?

Anyone interested in arguing for the mystical dimension of Buddhism must still contend with the Buddhist modernist claim that Buddhism is not a religion at all, but is rather a "science," a "philosophy," or a "way of life." This claim, which is still quite prevalent, is rooted in interreligious debates that took place during the Colonial period. Prominent nineteenth-century Protestant missionaries, such as Robert Spence Hardy, attempted to convert Buddhists to Christianity by arguing that Buddhism really was not a religion. Hardy, in his work *Eastern Monachism,* argued that the Buddha was not really a religious figure at all, but was an "uninspired" social reformer, rather than a divinely inspired genuine religious figure (Snodgrass 2009, 27). Hardy's argument was almost certainly based on the widespread European assumption that belief in spiritual entities was the defining characteristic of "religion," as noted earlier. Because Buddhism appeared to reject such beliefs, it was, arguably, not a religion, and certainly not an "inspired" one.

Some Buddhists and advocates of Buddhism reacted to such critiques, as well as Victorian era debates concerning science and religion, by accepting Hardy's claim that Buddhism was not a "religion" (as defined by European Protestants such as Hardy) and was in fact "science." The region of the Buddhist world in which the Buddhist modernist position first developed appears to have been Sri Lanka, during the mid- to late-nineteenth century. This was almost certainly because Sri Lanka was one of the first predominantly Buddhist countries to fall under European colonial rule. It was thus a region in which Buddhists encountered Christian missionaries in the culturally unsettling colonial context.[5]

Buddhists reacted to the criticisms of missionaries such as Hardy, and they ultimately developed the strategy often employed by subaltern groups, which involves "appropriating the myths and discourse of the dominant class, which they may also refashion and employ to telling advantage" (Lincoln 1989, 49–50). That is, they reacted to the hegemonic discourse of the agents of colonial power and developed their own counterhegemonic discourse, which appropriated and cleverly redeployed elements of the colonizer's own discourse. Buddhist Modernists appear to have made use of the works of European social scientific thinkers, such as Frazer and Tylor, who argued for a taxonomy of human knowledge, with "science" in the privileged position, above religion.[6] That is, they accepted the claim that Buddhism is not a "religion," as defined in colonial era European discourse. But they then claimed that Buddhism was "science," placing it above religion in the taxonomies advanced by an influential group of European theorists. In other words, they replied to their critics, Western missionaries, by appropriating a mode of discourse advanced by the secular critiques of their critics' own position.

As Donald Lopez has argued in a recent work on the persistent claim that Buddhism is "science," this claim is ideological, and was made by Asian Buddhists and Western converts to validate Buddhism (2008, xi). The claim that Buddhism is "rational" is often made *via negativa*, by claiming that it is not a "religion." Such arguments typically assume the late-nineteenth-century European definitions of religion in terms of belief in gods or spiritual entities. Many Buddhists, past and present, claim that Buddhism is an atheistic religion; some actively resent the implication that Buddhism involves belief in gods at all.[7]

Buddhist traditions are better categorized as *nontheistic*, provided that we understand this term in a somewhat narrow sense. Buddhist philosophical traditions rejected the notion that there is a supreme deity who created the world, and upon whom living beings are dependent for their existence or salvation.[8] Buddhists, however, generally accepted the complex South Asian cosmology that included a large number of divine beings, including the "gods" (*deva*) of the Vedic Hindu tradition, and when they were transmitted to other regions in Asia, they frequently added local deities to their pantheons (Faure 1987, 341). They simply denied that any of these deities had a privileged status as creator deities and argued instead that they, like humans and animals, were "creatures." Buddhists held that all beings, from the loftiest god to the lowliest worm, are conditioned entities, created not by a creator deity, but existing in forms commensurate with their past actions or *karma*. Gods, on account of their excellent *karma*, exist in superior forms and enjoy very long lives, but they too were subject to decay and death, and hence did not enjoy any sort of ultimate status.

Ultimately, the debate about whether or not Buddhism is religion or science is, as it is ideological, irresolvable. Buddhism, like virtually all religions, contains multiple forms of discourse. Buddhism has produced convincingly rational philosophical discourses.[9] And the claim that Buddhism is a "science" or a "science of the mind" is bolstered by Buddhism's rich legacy of meditative practices and psychological analysis.[10]

However, Buddhist traditions have made a number of claims that are not empirically verifiable and, hence, cannot be reasonably labeled "scientific." These include the claim that the Buddha achieved a state of omniscience.[11] Moreover, the Buddha is supposed to have achieved this state via the cultivation of meditative practices that are believed to yield, for anyone who practices them properly, direct apprehension of ultimate reality, that is, reality as it truly is, rather than as it seems to be to ordinary individuals.

Many Buddhists traditions, like other traditions with strong mystical inclinations, claimed that it is possible to give rise to direct knowledge of the absolute. Since at least the time of Dharmakīrti (circa the seventh century CE), many Buddhists have also presumed a special mode of "yogic cognition" (*yogipratyakṣa*), resulting from successful meditation practice, which permits direct and unmediated experience of ultimate reality.[12] Thus, Buddhist traditions see awakening as proceeding through the attainment of a special gnosis, the nonconceptual gnosis of a Buddha (*nirvikalpajñāna*).[13] Meditation techniques are also believed to result in extrasensory modes of perception, which likewise go beyond the scope of empirically verifiable knowledge (Eltschinger 2001). It is precisely with respect to these beliefs and practices that Buddhism extends into realms beyond what can reasonably be termed "scientific" or "rational" (in the context of the Western academic discourse, at least) and clearly establishes itself as a religion with a very strong mystical dimension.

The Mystical Dimensions of Buddhism

While the Theravāda tradition of Buddhism presented challenges to scholars such as Zaehner who defined mysticism in a theocentric fashion, it can be easily classified as "mystical," given its focus on meditative practice, if we adopt the more inclusive definition advanced by scholars such as Ninian Smart and Robert Gimello. The Theravāda Buddhist tradition, like virtually all Buddhist traditions, conceptualizes the path to awakening as primarily a journey involving the meditative realization of the nature of the self, the nature of body-mind complex. And the Theravāda Buddhist tradition likewise privileges the mind as the generator of our sense of reality. Like other Buddhist traditions, it privileges mind to such an extent that no clear distinction is made between mental and cosmic states, which is consonant with mysticism and certainly presents a serious challenge to those who claim that Buddhism is a science.

In addition to holding the universal or nearly universal Buddhist beliefs concerning the omniscience of the Buddha and the possibility that meditation practice can result in extrasensory perceptual powers, the Theravāda tradition holds the Buddhist belief in the centrality of the mind in the shaping of our sense of reality. This idea is expressed quite clearly in a famous passage from the well-known Buddhist scripture, the *Dhammapada*, which opens with the following five verses:

> All phenomena have mind as their precursor, mind as their leader, and are mind-made. If one speaks or acts with an impure mind, suffering follows one just as the wheel follows the foot [of that which pulls the cart].
>
> All phenomena have mind as their precursor, mind as their leader, and are mind-made. If one speaks or acts with a pure mind, happiness follows one like the shadow that never departs.
>
> The hatred of those who harbor [thoughts such as] "He reviled me," "He assaulted me," "He defeated me," or "He robbed me" is never appeased.
>
> The hatred of those who do not harbor [thoughts such as] "He reviled me," "He assaulted me," "He defeated me," or "He robbed me" is easily pacified.
>
> Hatred is never appeased through hatred; through non-hatred hatred is always appeased. This is an enduring truth.[14]

This passage suggests that our experience of the world is shaped by our minds. Buddhists thus see insight into the nature of mind, and the reconditioning of mental habits, as essential steps in the path to salvation. Indeed, the Buddhist path, as presented by the Buddha in his famous "Turning the Wheel of the Dharma" sermon, is typically divided into the so-called three trainings: moral discipline (*śīla*), wisdom (*prajñā*), and concentration (*samādhi*). Concentration and wisdom are developed through meditative practice, and moral discipline is seen as a prerequisite for this practice.[15]

The centrality of mind is affirmed in the venerable Buddhist notion that the Buddha passed through a series of states of mental concentration known as *dhyāna/jhāna* prior to becoming awakened.[16] The *dhyāna* states were correlated with the different levels of the cosmos (*dhātu*) in traditional Buddhist cosmology. Buddhists explicitly blurred the boundary between the mind and cosmos in their meditative traditions. Traditionally, Buddhists viewed the cosmos as consisting of three distinct realms of experience (*dhātu*), known as the "desire" (*kāma*), "form" (*rūpa*), and "formless" (*arūpa*) realms. The very term *dhātu* here indicates an unwillingness to distinguish ontology and epistemology, for Buddhists distinguish these realms of existence on the basis of the psychological states that dominate the beings of these realms. As Paul Griffiths notes, for Buddhists the term *dhātu*

> refers both to psychological realms—altered states of consciousness—and to cosmological realms, places in which the practitioner can exist or be reborn. To attain to a particular altered state is to (temporarily) exist in the corresponding *cosmological* realm and (if other things are equal) to be reborn in that realm. There is thus an intimate link between the psychological and cosmological. (1986, 183 n. 50)

The link between the psychological and cosmological could be made manifest via meditation. Early Buddhist theorists divided the "form realm" into multiple heavens, which corresponded to the four states of meditative concentration (*dhyāna*). This implies that through entry into states of deep meditation, it is possible to access different levels of the cosmos, a claim that is in fact made in scriptures such as the *Sāmaññaphala Sutta* and the *Kevaddha Sutta*.[17] Traditional accounts of the Buddha's death (*parinirvāṇa*), and later, his awakening, relate that he traversed the levels of the cosmos via the *dhyāna* meditative states, and attained awakening and ultimate release in the highest heaven of the form realm (*rūpadhātu*) known as Akaniṣtha.[18] He also reportedly possessed the ability to ascend to heavenly realms such as the Trayastriṃśa heaven, to which he ascended to preach to his mother (Reynolds and Reynolds 1982, 15).

Buddhists claim that not only the Buddha, but also any advanced meditator, can develop the power to visit other levels of the cosmos, such as the heaven or hell realms, simply by cultivating the corresponding state of mental concentration. Popular Buddhist literature is also filled with accounts of monks such as Mahāmoggallāna (Sanskrit: Mahāmaudgalyāyana), who likewise possessed the ability to travel to different cosmic realms. Regarding this, Frank and Mani Reynolds wrote:

> In the early stages of Buddhist history cosmological motifs were established in the very center of the tradition through the visionary and meditative experiences of the Founder and his early disciples. The visionary experience that was part of the Buddha's own Enlightenment process, and a special forte of the Buddha's great disciple Mahāmoggallāna, produced a series of vivid images of the heavenly realms in which the meritorious deeds of men were rewarded and of the hells in which men received retribution for their sins. The meditative experience, which was

also a vital part of the Buddha's own Enlightenment process and the early Buddhist path, led to the development of conceptions of cosmic worlds corresponding to the various levels of meditative consciousness (*jhāna*) that especially holy men could achieve through mental discipline and concentration. (1982, 15)

The notion that advanced meditators could cultivate such powers through meditative practice was not limited to the early period, but lived on, most notably in the esoteric Buddhist traditions, which are replete with accounts of advanced meditators possessing supernatural powers.[19]

Far from advocating a rational-empirical "scientific" vision of reality, Buddhists propounded a profoundly mystical vision of reality as a mental creation, as filtered through the distorting lens of mental and physical conditioning. Indeed, one could compare these teachings with the ideas advanced by Aldous Huxley in his influential (1954) work *The Doors of Perception,* which influenced scholars of mysticism such as Zaehner.[20] This idea is expressed even more clearly by advocates of the Mahāyāna Buddhist traditions. The *Laṅkāvatāra Sūtra,* a well-known Mahāyāna scripture, makes the following bold claim about the nature of mind and reality:

> There is no subject nor object, nor is there bondage or that which is bound; [all things] are like an illusion, a mirage, a dream, a blind eye. If one who understands reality sees non-discursively (*nirvikalpa*), free of taint, then perfected in yoga he sees me without a doubt. There is nothing to cognize, like a mirage in the sky; one who cognizes things acknowledges nothing. In the relativity of being and non-being things do not arise; it is from the wandering of mind through the triple world that variety is known. The world has the same nature as a dream, and so too the various forms within it.... This mind is the source of the triple world, and wandering the mind appears hither and thither.[21]

One of the most famous examples of this idea occurs in a verse in Vasubandu's *Viṃśikakārikā,* which occurs as follows, "the mind is indefinite, as in a dream, just as all *preta* see a stream as pus and so forth, or like an injury received in a dream."[22]

In his autocommentary on this verse, the *Viṃśikavṛtti,* Vasubandu explains that a single locus of perception, the stream in the preceding example, might be viewed in radically different ways by different beings. A deity might see it as nectar luminous and pure; a human as a stream of water for bathing, drinking, and such; a hungry spirit (*preta*) as a stream of filth; and a fish as the world itself.[23] The world then is very much a matter of perceptual representation, and there is no basis for confidence that any one view of the world is complete, or even accurate. For Buddhists, realization of the nature of mind via direct meditative experience is key to the understanding of reality.

Mahāyāna Buddhist traditions were deeply concerned with the meditative realization of ultimate reality. This reality was famously defined in a thoroughly apophatic fashion by the great Buddhist philosopher Nāgārjuna as "emptiness" (śūnyatā), understood as the negation of any essential or intrinsic reality of any being or entity. Scholastic Buddhist traditions tended toward the apophatic approach, identifying emptiness qua ultimate reality with the nature of mind. This, in turn, is Buddha nature, one's fundamental capacity to attain awakening, made possible precisely because one lacks any sort of unchanging self-nature. Meditation on emptiness proceeded via largely analytical process of negation; one discovers the nature of one's self by systematically identifying what the self is not.[24]

Even though ultimate reality is characterized by Buddhists as *acintya*, inconceivable and thus indescribable, this experience has often been described in Buddhist literature in a more cataphatic fashion as "clear light" or "luminous gnosis," a direct apprehension of ultimate reality, the nature of mind itself as clear light (Kapstein 2004a, 126–130). Buddhist meditators seek to realize ultimately inconceivable nature of mind, the direct realization of which is tantamount to awakening. Thus, the Tibetan nun Orgyan Chokyi (1675–1729 CE) was instructed by her meditation master as follows: "If you understand the mind, you are a Buddha. Do not look elsewhere for Buddha. You must meditate correctly on consciousness" (Schaeffer 2004, 148).

Tantric Buddhist techniques likewise presumed the centrality of mind in the construction of our experience and sense of reality. Tantric visualization exercises typically involve the deconstruction of our ordinary sense of self and reality, via its "dissolution into emptiness," followed by a reconstruction of a divine sense of self and reality.[25] In the Tantric Buddhist traditions, the mind is seen as intrinsically pure and awakened from time beginningless, and the purpose of tantric visualization exercises is reconditioning the mind to realize its awakened nature and experience the world in a purified fashion.

This idea was expressed lucidly by Rong-zom Chos-kyi-bzang-po, an important rNying-ma scholar who lived in Tibet during the eleventh century. He explains that:

> In the mantric method, the two truths are inseparable.... Furthermore, there is no production of non-delusion by means of removing delusion, and awakening occurs through purification by means of the very actuality of delusion. Therefore, all things are completely awakened from the beginning, and things which appear in diverse states are the maṇḍala of the adamantine body, speech and mind itself; they are similar to the Buddhas of the three times who have not passed beyond the actuality of purity. The characteristics of sentient beings and Buddhas are not different from the very actuality of things. The mind attributes to them distinct appearances through the power of imagination, in the same way that things appear distinct and caused in a dream.[26]

Tantric Buddhist traditions seek to awaken, through creative visualization techniques, the innately creative powers of mind. Rather than allowing the mind to persist in its conditioned patterns, which are often conducive to suffering, the goal is to gain mastery over these powers and use them to accelerate one's evolution into a fully awakened Buddha.

Interestingly, Buddhist descriptions of ultimate reality qua the nature of mind sometimes employ language that evoke theistic traditions' discourse about God, which should not seem surprising, given the Buddhist belief in the centrality of mind in the generation of one's experience of reality. We see an early intimation of this in the *Dhammapada*'s claim that "all phenomena have mind as their precursor, mind as their leader, and are mind-made." A striking example is a scripture of the "Great Perfection" (*rdzogs chen*) of the Nying-ma (*rnying ma*) school of Tibetan Buddhism, which is titled *The All-Creating Sovereign, The Mind of Perfect Purity*. This text portrays the nature of mind as ineffable, "beyond thinking and inexplicable" (Neumeier-Dargyay 1992, 111). It describes the centrality of mind in creative terms, stating:

> A simile for all things being the mind of perfect purity is that all [things] created are in their own being like the sky; this is the main point of the mind of perfect purity. Sky, wind, water, earth, and fire, these five elements come miraculously forth from the mind of perfect purity as Buddhas, the three-fold world, the five paths, and the six [categories of] sentient beings (63).

This text, personifying the nature of mind, has it declare: "Oh, all you sentient beings of this threefold world! Because I, the All-Creating Sovereign, have created you, you are My children and equal to Me. Because you are not second to Me, I am present in you" (111). Like the *Dhammapada* and *Laṅkāvatāra Sūtra*, the mind is identified as the source of our experience of the phenomenal world, but here the vision is extended much further, with mind personified and attributed with divine powers and attributes. The somewhat unorthodox nature of this text, in fact, led to its condemnation by the eleventh-century Tibetan prince Pho-brang Zhi-wa-'od (Karmay 1980, 4).

However, this is not the only Buddhist text to metaphorically attribute lordly and creative qualities to mind. Another interesting example is the poem "The Place of Mind," composed by the Korean nun and Son master Son'gyong Sunim (1903–1994). It reads as follows:

> Mind nature is the host
> Which cannot be taught through words,
>
> ....
> Lord of the ten thousand [things].[27]

This remarkable poem describes the nature of mind in an apophatic fashion, completely inexpressible and inconceivable, yet also employs cataphatic terminology as well, evoking the classical Buddhist equation of the nature of mind and luminosity. It presents a vision of the nature of mind as sovereign amid the phenomenal world that is its creation.

Although it is only possible here to cover a limited range of examples, these should suffice to demonstrate that Buddhist traditions possess profound mystical dimensions, insofar as these traditions posit, and seek to realize via meditative exercises, a hidden dimension or root of human consciousness that underlies ordinary conscious experiences. Even though Buddhist traditions differ in many ways from other religious traditions with mystical dimensions, they share certain similarities, particularly with respect to the forms of discourse used to describe experiences of ineffable yet luminous spiritual realities.

Teaching Buddhist Mysticism

A course on Buddhist mysticism would ideally be taught as an upper level seminar, for advanced undergraduate students who have already received an introduction to religious studies methodologies. I would make an "Introduction to Buddhism" course as a prerequisite for this class, although I would admit ambitious students who have not taken the prerequisite. I thus include background readings on the basic history and teachings of Buddhist traditions as recommended readings for this course.

I conduct this seminar as a guided introduction to graduate level work in religious studies. The course is structured around a series of assignments that culminates in the completion of a research paper. Each student is also responsible for initiating the class discussion with a formal class presentation on the topic of the week's discussion. The recommended reading list for each week includes additional readings on the subject to aid the student presenter(s).

The course is designed for a fourteen-week semester and is broken down into seven two-week units. The course will open in the initial two weeks with consideration of the definitions of mysticism and their applicability to Buddhism, and the problem of religious experience in the context of the study of Buddhist meditation traditions. The course will conclude with two weeks dedicated to student presentations on the topics of their research papers. The bulk of the course, thus, will consist of five two-week units on various Buddhist meditation traditions. Each unit will open with readings of classical or contemporary works on meditation, followed by a reading of an autobiography of a practitioner of that style of meditation. In my experience, the reading of the autobiographical works deeply enriches the students' understanding of the practices that are typically described in far more abstract or mechanical ways in the works on meditation practice.

The first unit will focus on the Theravāda Buddhist tradition of *Vipassanā* meditation. This will be followed by two units on Tibetan Buddhism, focusing respectively on Tantric Yoga and Mahāmudrā practice traditions. Two units focusing on East Asian meditation traditions, the Korean Son and Japanese Zen, respectively, will conclude the survey of Buddhist meditation traditions.

Needless to say, this structure is easily adaptable for faculty teaching courses of different lengths. Those who teach in the ten-week quarter system, as I do, could delete one of the Tibetan and one of the East Asian units, resulting in a six-week "core" that would address three different traditions in three different areas of the Buddhist world. Faculty teaching a twelve-week semester course could simply delete one of the units.

Seminar: Buddhist Mysticism

This course will involve a detailed study of Buddhist traditions of meditation through the lens of the study of mysticism. We will seek to understand not only the mechanics of actual meditation practices, but also the experiences that they are purported to produce, as reported in the literature on meditation and the accounts of meditators. We will also explore their soteriological significance in the Buddhist traditions that advocate their practice. As an upper level seminar, this course will require regular advance preparation of the readings and active participation in the discussions of them in class. Students will be expected to read, reread, and take detailed notes on a short reading for the week. Each student will also be expected to lead the class discussion for one of the classes; this will require additional preparation of recommended background readings. Discussion notes will be submitted at the end of each class. Each student will also be responsible to lead the discussion for one class. The course will culminate in the submission of a research paper (3000–6000 words, 40% of grade). In preparation for this assignment, each student will submit a 150–200 word abstract and bibliography (10%) and a 6–8 page seminar paper "draft" (20%) and will give a twenty-minute class presentation on their research (20%). Class participation will account for the remaining 10% of the grade; this will be evaluated on the basis of class participation and preparation as indicated by the weekly submission of notes on the readings, as well as the quality of the class discussion leadership.

REQUIRED BOOKS (AVAILABLE FOR PURCHASE IN THE BOOKSTORE)

Batchelor, Martine, and Sun'gyong Sunim, *Women in Korean Zen: Lives and Practices*

Buswell, Robert E., *Tracing Back the Radiance: Chinul's Korean Way of Zen*

Dakpo Tashi Namgyal, *Clarifying the Natural State: A Principal Guidance Manual for Mahamudra*

Gunaratana, Henepola, *Mindfulness in Plain English*

Gunaratana, Henepola, *Journey to Mindfulness: The Autobiography of Bhante G.*

Lhalungpa, Lobsang P. *The Life of Milarepa*

Mullin, Glenn H., *Tsongkhapa's Six Yogas of Naropa*

Schaeffer, Kurtis, *Himalayan Hermitess: The Life of a Tibetan Buddhist Nun*

Sogen, Omori, *An Introduction to Zen Training: A Translation of the Sanzen Nyumon*

Waddell, Norman, *Wild Ivy: The Spiritual Biography of Zen Master Hakuin*

ON RESERVE IN THE LIBRARY

Bucknell, Rod, and Chris Kang, *The Meditative Way* (MW)

Kapstein, Matthew T., ed., *The Presence of Light: Divine Radiance and Religious Experience*

Katz, Steven T., ed., *Mysticism and Philosophical Analysis* (MPA)

Mitchell, Donald W., *Buddhism: Introducing the Buddhist Experience* (IBE)

Proudfoot, Wayne, *Religious Experience*

Sarbacker, Stuart, *Samādhi: The Numinous and Cessative in Indo-Tibetan Yoga*

Sharf, Robert H., "The Rhetoric of Experience and the Study of Religion"

Smart, Ninian, *Dimensions of the Sacred: An Anatomy of the World's Beliefs*

STANDARD REFERENCE WORKS IN LIBRARY

Encyclopedia of Religion (Lindsay Jones, ed., 2005) (ER)

Encyclopedia of Buddhism (Robert E. Buswell, Jr., ed., 2004) (EB)

SYLLABUS

Unit 1: Introductions

Week 1—Buddhism as Mysticism?

Read: MPA: "Mysticism and Meditation" (170–199)

Recommended: ER: "Mysticism," Smart: 166–195

Week 2—Meditation and Religious Experience

Read: Kapstein, "Rethinking Religious Experience: Seeing the Light in the History of Religions" (265–299), MW: "Experiences in Meditation" (197–207), Sarbacker: 27–51

Recommended: MPA: "Language, Epistemology, and Mysticism" (22–74), Sharf: "The Rhetoric of Experience and the Study of Religion," Proudfoot (entire)

Unit 2: The Vipassanā Tradition

Week 3—Insight Meditation: The Practice

Read: Gunaratana, *Mindfulness in Plain English*

Recommended: IBE: 65–102, EB: "Vipassanā," MW: 19–28

Week 4—Insight Meditation: A Practitioner's Perspective

Read: Gunaratana, *Journey to Mindfulness: The Autobiography of Bhante G.*

Recommended: MW: 208–218, 228–263

Unit 3: Tibetan Tantric Yoga

Week 5—Tantric Yoga: The Practice

Read: Mullin: 111–226

Recommended: Mullin: 19–105, IBE: 160–178, MW: 175–191

•Abstract and bibliography due

Week 6—Tantric Yoga: A Classical Hagiography

Read: Lhalungpa: 1–203

Recommended: ER: "Milarepa," Lhalungpa: vii–xxxii

Unit 4: Tibetan Mahāmudrā

Week 7—Mahāmudrā: The Practice

Read: Dakpo Tashi Namgyal: 13–104

Recommended: EB, ER: "Mahāmudrā"

Week 8—Mahāmudrā: A Practitioner's Perspective

Read: Schaeffer: 133–184

Recommended: Schaeffer: 3–132

Unit 5: Korean Son

Week 9—Son/Zen Meditation: The Practice

Read: Buswell: 98–187

Recommended: Buswell: 1–72, ER: "Buddhism: Buddhism in Korea," ER: "Chinul," ER: "Kōan," IBE: 219–226, 245–262

Week 10—Son/Zen Meditation: Practitioners' Perspectives

Read: Batchelor and Sun'gyong: 3–113

Recommended: IBE: 272–273

Unit 6: Japanese Rinzai Zen

Week 11—Rinzai Zen Meditation: The Practice

Read: Sogen: 2–220

Recommended: IBE: 275–309, ER: "Zen"

Week 12—Rinzai Zen Meditation: A Practitioner's Perspective

Read: Waddell: 1–122

Recommended: Waddell: vii–xliv, EB: "Hakuin Enkaku"

Unit 7: Student Presentations

Weeks 13 and 14—Student Presentations

•Seminar papers due on day of presentation

Notes

1. Regarding Tylor's schema see vol. 2 of his influential (1871) work, *Primitive Culture*.

2. See Zaehner (1958, 99). Note that Zaehner follows Coomaraswamy's and Horner's discredited claim that the Buddha advocated the existence of an eternal self (Coomaraswamy and Horner 1948, 147–163). For a critique of Zaehner's argument, see Smart (1986, 105–108).

3. Parrinder, for example, wholeheartedly argues that Mahāyāna Buddhism, at least, fits the expected unitive pattern. See Parrinder (1976, 60–65).

4. See Smart (1996, 167), as well as Gimello's discussion (1978, 171–172) of Smart's earlier (1958) version of this argument.

5. For a discussion of this period, see Snodgrass (2009), Hallisey (1995), and Gombrich and Obeyesekere (1988, 202–255).

6. Frazer argued for the progression from magic to religion to science, see Frazer (1890, 824–827). Tylor, on the other hand, proposed the development of human culture through religious stages, from animism to polytheism, monotheism, and, eventually, science. See Tylor (1871, vol. 2).

7. Regarding this issue, see Cohen (2006, 149–180).

8. For an excellent discussion of Buddhist nontheism, see Tilakaratna (2003), as well as Jackson and Makransky (2000).

9. See, for example, Parimal Patil's (2009) study of Ratnakīrti's critique of Hindu arguments for the existence of God.

10. For a cogent presentation of this position, see Wallace (2009).

11. Regarding this claim, see Jaini (1974) and Bühnemann (1980).

12. See Steinkellner (1999), Dunne (2006), and Woo (2009).

13. See Makransky (1997, 68–72).

14. My translation from the text edited in von Hinüber and Norman (1995, 1–2).

15. The *Dhammacakkappavattana-sutta* occurs at *Saṃyutta-nikāya* 56.11; for a translation see Rahula (1974, 92–94). The three trainings are commonly discussed in Buddhist works on meditation. See, for example, U Pandita (2006, 5–16). See also Lusthaus (2002, 110–118). Note that Bronkhorst (1986, 102–103) has argued that *prajñā*, which we might translate as "discerning wisdom" or "insight," referred in the context of Buddhist meditation to an essential insight into the altered states of consciousness that arise in meditation, and which a successful meditator must have in order to negotiate these altered states. This *prajñā* or insight was considered particularly essential in the mediations on the four *dhyāna*, which, as I suggest, have cosmic as well as psychological significance.

16. Regarding the *jhāna* meditations in the Theravāda tradition, see Cousins (1973) and Griffiths (1983). They are treated extensively in Buddhaghosa's *Visuddhimagga*; see Ñāṇamoli (1999, 85–172).

17. For a translation of these scriptures, see Walshe (1995, 91–109, 175–180).

18. Akaniṣṭha gradually gained significance as a site for awakening *par excellence*. Originally considered to be the point of exit for the Buddha from the cosmos following his physical death, in the Mahāyāna, it was understood to be the place where the tenth-level bodhisattva attained awakening. This idea occurs in the *Laṅkāvatāra Sūtra*, which states, "The Buddha awakens not in the desire nor in the formless realms; he awakens in the form

realm amidst the Akaniṣṭha [deities] who are free of passion [*kāmadhātau tathārūpye na vai buddho vibudhyate / rūpadhātvakaniṣṭheṣu vītarageṣu budhyate*]" (*Laṅkāvatāra Sūtra* 10.774, edited in Vaidya [1963, 158]; cf. Gethin [1997, 207] and Suzuki [1932, 284]). Likewise, Śāntarakṣita in his *Tattvasaṃgraha* holds that Akaniṣṭha is the actual site for a Buddha's awakening, and that the life of the historical Buddha is simply a cosmic drama enacted by one of his emanations. "In the lovely city of Akaniṣṭha, free from all impure abodes—there Buddhas awaken; but here [in this world] creations awaken" (translated in Gethin [1997, 206]).

19. This is confirmed by a brief perusal of famous accounts of the "accomplished ones" or *siddhas*, such as the hagiographies translated in Robinson (1979). For an excellent study of the *siddhas* and the artistic and literary traditions connected with them, see Linrothe (2006). Regarding the persistence of these ideas in East Asia, see Teiser (1988, 147–164).

20. One might add that this book, and also the growing use of psychedelic drugs that it inspired, also indirectly contributed to the growth of the academic study of Buddhism in the West. Regarding this phenomenon, see Badiner (2002).

21. My translation of *Laṅkāvatāra Sūtra sagāthaka*, vv. 31–36, from the text edited in Vaidya (1963, 109); cf. Suzuki (1932, 228–229).

22. My translation from Vasubandhu's *Viṃśikakārikā*, fol. 3a.

23. See Vasubandhu's *Viṃśikavṛtti*, Tōhoku catalogue of Derge canon #4,057, *sde dge* Tanjur *sems tsam* vol. shi, 4b–5a.

24. For a classical example of this approach, see Hopkins (1996).

25. For a discussion of these practices from a theoretical perspective, see Gray (2006). For a more detailed presentation of Tantric meditative practices, see Cozort (1986).

26. My translation from Rong-zom Chos-kyi-bzang-po, 127–128.

27. Translated in Batchelor and Son'gyong Sunim (2006, 113). Note that I have replaced the term *dharma* in the poem with the bracketed text *things*. The term *dharma* has multiple meanings, but here it clearly refers to a phenomenal entity. Here "ten thousand things" means simply all existing things.

References

Badiner, Allan Hunt, ed. 2002. *Zig Zag Zen: Buddhism and Psychedelics*. San Francisco: Chronicle Books.

Batchelor, Martine, and Sun'gyong Sunim. 2006. *Women in Korean Zen: Lives and Practices*. Syracuse, NY: Syracuse University Press.

Bronkhorst, Johannes. 1986. *The Two Traditions of Meditation in Ancient India*. Stuttgart: Franz Steiner Verlag Wiesbaden GmbH.

Bühnemann, Gudrun. 1980. *Der Allwissende Buddha: Ein Beweis und Seine Probleme. Ratnakīrtis Sarvajñasiddhi*. Wein: Arbeitskreis für Tibetische und Buddhistische Studien Universität Wien.

Bucknell, Rod, and Chris Kang. 1997. *The Meditative Way: Readings in the Theory and Practice of Buddhist Meditation*. London: Routledge.

Buswell, Robert E. 1991. *Tracing Back the Radiance: Chinul's Korean Way of Zen*. Honolulu: Univeristy of Hawai'i Press.

Cohen, Richard S. 2006. *Beyond Enlightenment: Buddhism, Religion, Modernity.* London: Routledge.

Coomaraswamy, Ananda K., and I. B. Horner. 1948. *The Living Thoughts of Gotama the Buddha.* London: Cassell and Company.

Cousins, L. S. 1973. "Buddhist *Jhāna*: Its Nature and Attainment According to Pali Sources," *Religion* 3 (1): 115–131.

Cozort, Daniel. 1986. *Highest Yoga Tantra: An Introduction to the Esoteric Buddhism of Tibet.* Ithaca, NY: Snow Lion Publications.

Dakpo, Tashi Namgyal. 2001. *Clarifying the Natural State: A Principal Guidance Manual for Mahamudra,* translated by Khenchen Thrangu Rinpoche. Hong Kong: Rangjung Yeshe Publications.

Dunne, John D. 2006. "Realizing the Unreal: Dharmakīrti's Theory of Yogic Perception," *Journal of Indian Philosophy* 34 (6): 497–519.

Eltschinger, Vincent. 2001. *Dharmakīrti sur les Mantra et la Perception du Supra-sensible.* Wein: Arbeitskreis für Tibetische und Buddhistische Studien Universität Wien.

Faure, Bernard. 1987. "Space and Place in Chinese Religious Traditions," *History of Religions* 26 (4): 337–356.

Forman, Robert K. C., ed. 1990. *The Problem of Pure Consciousness: Mysticism and Philosophy.* New York: Oxford University Press.

———. 1999. *Mysticism, Mind, Consciousness.* Albany: State University of New York Press.

Frazer, Sir James George. 1890. *The Golden Bough: A Study in Magic and Religion.* Abridged ed. New York: The Macmillan Company, 1958.

Gethin, Rupert. 1997. "Cosmology and Meditation: From the Aggañña-Sutta to the Mahāyāna," *History of Religions* 36 (3): 183–217.

Gimello, Robert M. 1978. "Mysticism and Meditation." In *Mysticism and Philosophical Analysis,* edited by Steven T. Katz, 170–199. New York: Oxford University Press.

Gombrich, Richard, and Gananath Obeyesekere. 1988. *Buddhism Transformed: Religious Change in Sri Lanka.* Princeton, NJ: Princeton University Press.

Gray, David B. 2006. "Mandala of the Self: Embodiment, Practice and Identity Construction in the Cakrasamvara Tradition," *Journal of Religious History* 30 (3): 294–310.

Griffiths, Paul. 1983. "Buddhist Jhāna: A Form-Critical Study," *Religion* 13 (January): 55–68.

———. 1986. *On Being Mindless.* LaSalle, IL: Open Court.

Gunaratana, Henepola. 2001. *Mindfulness in Plain English.* Somerville, MA: Wisdom Publications.

———. 2003. *Journey to Mindfulness: The Autobiography of Bhante G.* Somerville, MA: Wisdom Publications.

Hakuju, U.I., Munetada Suzuki, Yensho Kanakura, and Tokan Tada. 1934. *A Complete Catalogue of Tibetan Buddhist Canons (Bkaḥ-ḥgyur and Bstan-ḥgyur).* Sendai: Tōhoku Imperial University.

Hallisey, Charles. 1995. "Roads Taken and Not Taken in the Study of Theravāda Buddhism." In *Curators of the Buddha: The Study of Buddhism Under Colonialism,* edited by Donald S. Lopez Jr., 31–61. Chicago: University of Chicago Press.

Hopkins, Jeffrey. 1996. *Meditation on Emptiness.* Rev. ed. Boston: Wisdom Publications.

Huxley, Aldous. 1954. *The Doors of Perception.* New York: Harper.

Jackson, Roger R., and John J. Makransky, eds. 2000. *Buddhist Theology: Critical Reflections by Contemporary Buddhist Scholars.* London: RutledgeCurzon.

Jaini, Padmanabh S. 1974. "On the Sarvajñatva (Omniscience) of Mahāvīra and the Buddha." In *Buddhist Studies in Honour of I. B. Horner*, edited by L. Cousins, 71–90. Dordrecht: Reidel.

Kapstein, Matthew T. 2004a. "Rethinking Religious Experience: Seeing the Light in the History of Religions." In *The Presence of Light: Divine Radiance and Religious Experience*, edited by Matthew T. Kapstein, 265–299. Chicago: University of Chicago Press.

———. 2004b. "The Strange Death of Pema the Demon Tamer." In *The Presence of Light: Divine Radiance and Religious Experience*, edited by Matthew T. Kapstein, 119–156. Chicago: University of Chicago Press.

Karmay, Samten. 1980. "An Open Letter by the Pho-brang Zhi-ba-'od." *The Tibet Journal* 5: 2–28.

Katz, Steven T. 1978. "Language, Epistemology, and Mysticism." In *Mysticism and Philosophical Analysis*, edited by Steven T. Katz, 22–74. New York: Oxford University Press.

Lhalungpa, Lobsang P. 1985. *The Life of Milarepa*. Boston: Shambhala Publications.

Lincoln, Bruce. 1989. *Discourse and the Construction of Society: Comparative Studies of Myth, Ritual, and Classification*. New York and Oxford: Oxford University Press.

Linrothe, Robert, ed. 2006. *Holy Madness: Portraits of Tantric Siddhas*. New York: Rubin Museum of Art; Chicago: Serindia Publications.

Lopez, Donald S., Jr. 2008. *Buddhism and Science: A Guide for the Perplexed*. Chicago: University of Chicago Press.

Lusthaus, Dan. 2002. *Buddhist Phenomenology: A Philosophical Investigation of Yogācāra Buddhism and the Ch'eng Wei-shih lun*. London: RoutledgeCurzon.

Makransky, John. 1997. *Buddhahood Embodied: Sources of Controversy in India and Tibet*. Albany: State University of New York Press.

Masuzawa, Tomoko. 2005. *The Invention of World Religions*. Chicago: University of Chicago Press.

Mitchell, Donald W. 2002. *Buddhism: Introducing the Buddhist Experience*. New York: Oxford University Press.

Mullin, Glenn H. 1996. *Tsongkhapa's Six Yogas of Naropa*. Ithaca, NY: Snow Lion Publications.

Ñāṇamoli, Bhikkhu. 1999. *Visuddhimagga, The Path of Purification*. Seattle: BPS Pariyatti Editions.

Neumaier-Dargyay, E. K. 1992. *The Sovereign All-Creating Mind, The Motherly Buddha, A Translation of the Kun byed rgyal poi mdo*. Albany: State University of New York Press.

Parrinder, Geoffrey. 1976. *Mysticism in the World's Religions*. London: Sheldon Press.

Patil, Parimal G. 2009. *Against a Hindu God: Buddhist Philosophy of Religion in India*. New York: Columbia University Press.

Proudfoot, Wayne. 1985. *Religious Experience*. Berkeley: University of California Press.

Rahula, Walpola. 1974. *What the Buddha Taught*. 2nd rev. ed. New York: Grove Press.

Reynolds, Frank E., and Mani B. Reynolds. 1982. *Three Worlds According to King Ruang: A Thai Buddhist Cosmology*. Berkeley, CA: Asian Humanities Press.

Robinson, James B. 1979. *Buddha's Lions: The Lives of the Eighty-Four Siddhas, Abhayadatta*. Berkeley, CA: Dharma Publishing.

Rong-zom Chos-kyi-bzang-po. 1974. "*gsang sngags rdo rje theg pa'i tshul las snang ba lhar sgrub pa*." In *Selected Writings (gsuṅ thor bu) of Roṅ-zom Chos-kyi-bzaṅ-po*, edited by

'Khor-gdoṅ Gter-sprul 'Chi-med-rig-'dzin, 125–151. Smanrtsis Shesrig Spendzod 73. Leh: S. W. Tashigangpa.

Sarbacker, Stuart. 2005. *Samādhi: The Numinous and Cessative in Indo-Tibetan Yoga*. Albany: State University of New York Press.

Schaeffer, Kurtis. 2004. *Himalayan Hermitess: The Life of a Tibetan Buddhist Nun*. Oxford: Oxford University Press.

Sharf, Robert H. 2000. "The Rhetoric of Experience and the Study of Religion," *Journal of Consciousness Studies* 7 (11/12): 267–286.

Smart, Ninian. 1958. *Reasons and Faiths: An Investigation of Religious Discourse, Christian and Non-Christian*. London: Routledge and Kegan Paul.

———. 1986. *Concept and Empathy: Essays in the Study of Religion*. New York: New York University Press.

———. 1996. *Dimensions of the Sacred: An Anatomy of the World's Beliefs*. Berkeley: University of California Press.

Snodgrass, Judith. 2009. "Discourse, Authority, Demand: The Politics of Early English Publications on Buddhism." In *Transbuddhism: Transmission, Translation, Transformation*, edited by Nalini Bhushan, Jay L. Garfield, and Abraham Zablocki, 21–41. Amherst: University of Massachusetts Press.

Sogen, Omori. 1996. *An Introduction to Zen Training: A Translation of the* Sanzen Nyumon, translated by Dogen Hosokawa and Roy Yoshimoto. Tokyo: Tuttle Pubishing.

Steinkellner, Ernst. 1999. "Yogic Cognition, Tantric Goal, and other Methodological Applications of Dharmakīrti's *Kāryānumāna* Theorem." In *Dharmakīrti's Thought and its Impact on Indian and Tibetan Philosophy*, edited by Katsura Shoryu, 349–362. Wien: Verlag der Österreichischen Akademie der Wissenschaften.

Suzuki, D. T. 1932. *The Lankavatara Sutra*. London: George Routledge and Sons.

Teiser, Stephen F. 1988. *The Ghost Festival in Medieval China*. Princeton, NJ: Princeton University Press.

Tilakaratna, Asanga. 2003. "Buddhist Non-theism: Theory and Application." In *Approaching the Dharma: Buddhist Texts and Practices in South and Southeast Asia*, edited by Anne M. Blackburn and Jeffrey Samuels, 125–149. Seattle: BPS Pariyatti Editions.

Tylor, Edward Burnett. (1871) 1958. *Primitive Culture*. Reprinted in 2 vols. *The Origins of Culture* and *Religion in Primitive Culture*. New York: Harper Torchbooks.

Underhill, Evelyn. 1911. *Mysticism: A Study in the Nature and Development of Man's Spiritual Consciousness*. London: Methuen and Company.

U Pandita, Sayadaw. 2006. *The State of Mind Called Beautiful*. Somerville, MA: Wisdom Publications.

Vaidya, P. L. 1963. *Saddharmalaṅkāvatārasūtram*. Darbhanga: The Mithila Institute.

Vasubandhu. *Viṃśakakārikā*. To. 405. *sde dge* Tanjur *sems tsam* vol. shi, 3a–4a.

———. *Viṃśikavṛtti*. To. 4,057. *sde dge* Tanjur *sems tsam* vol. shi, 4b–19a.

von Hinüber, O., and K. R. Norman. 1995. *Dhammapada*. Oxford: Pali Text Society.

Waddell, Norman. 2001. *Wild Ivy: The Spiritual Biography of Zen Master Hakuin*. Boston: Shambhala Publications.

Wallace, B. Alan. 2009. *Mind in the Balance: Meditation in Science, Buddhism, and Christianity*. New York: Columbia University Press.

Walshe, Maurice. 1995. *The Long Discourses of the Buddha: A Translation of the Dīgha Nikāya*. Boston: Wisdom Publications.

Woo, Jeson. 2009. "Gradual and Sudden Enlightenment: The Attainment of Yogipratyakṣa in the Later Indian Yogācāra School," *Journal of Indian Philosophy* 37 (2): 179–188.

Zaehner, R. C. (1957) 1961. *Mysticism: Sacred and Profane: An Inquiry into Some Varieties of Praeternatural Experience.* Reprint, Oxford: Oxford University Press.

———. (1958) 1977. *At Sundry Times: An Essay in the Comparative Study of Religions.* Reprint, Westport, CT: Greenwood Press.

5

Teaching Islam, Teaching Islamic Mysticism
David Cook

Teaching mysticism from an Islamic perspective means teaching Sufism. Although it is clear from a historical perspective that there were and are other forms of mysticism in Islam (stronger in early Islam, weaker during the present time), for the balance of Muslim history, Sufism has been the primary means by which the Muslims sought union with God. To best convey the nuances of Islamic mysticism to students, this essay will detail the history of Islamic mysticism, focusing on its transformation into Sufism during the eighth and ninth centuries, indicating some crucial contemporary developments and offering pedagogical strategies and a sample syllabus along the way.

Early Manifestations: Zhud and Dhikr

From a very early period, there has been an ascetic strain within Islam. Although it is difficult to say whether the Prophet Muhammad (d. 632) was personally ascetic—as his character has been shaped in the stories about him both to the advantage of asceticism and against it—one finds a minority of his companions (*sahaba*) lived an ascetic lifestyle. This tendency was in sharp contrast to the luxurious and wealthy lifestyles affected by many Muslims during the early period especially in the wake of the great Islamic conquests (634–732), during the course of which, the area of the eastern Mediterranean basin and the Iranian plateau came to be controlled by Muslims. Although these conquests brought huge wealth to an elite, there were always those who abstained completely from partaking in this wealth.

In abstaining, these Muslim ascetics, the best known of whom are Abu al-Darda' (d. 651) and Abu Dharr al-Ghifari (d. 652), followed closely in the ascetic practices of the Christian monastics around them (and later when in Central Asia, the example of Buddhism monks). For centuries, Christian monks in the regions of Syria and Egypt had practiced very severe forms of bodily mortification and deprivation, and for these pains, they had acquired a high level of local social and religious prestige. In the words of Peter Brown (1971, 80–101), they had become the local holy men, looked to by the population for arbitration and miracles and feared by the secular and ecclesiastical hierarchies, respectively. This social and religious prestige is reflected in the Qur'an, where it is said, "and you will find that the closest in affection to the believers those who say 'we are Christians.' For among them are priests and monks and they are not arrogant" (5:82).[1]

However, Muslim asceticism, while maintaining deprivation, did not embrace all of the elements of Christian monasticism. From a very early stage, the chastity characteristic of monks and nuns was rejected (although there are some early examples of Muslims castrating themselves), and the complete withdrawal from society of the anchorite lifestyle was also not accepted. Otherwise, what came to be called *zuhd* (asceticism) during the seventh, eighth, and ninth centuries was a popular lifestyle of a certain segment of Muslims.

The *zuhd* literature that has come down to us consists of a large number of sayings (many of them very obviously Christian in origin, some citations even from the Bible) and accounts of early Muslim ascetics.[2] The asceticism that they practiced focused on forms of spiritual excess (staying the night in prayer, doing supererogatory actions, meditation), bodily deprivation (fasting, extensive denial of sleep), and embracing holy poverty. There is little mention in the sources of the extensive beatings and other bodily mortifications that are part of Christian asceticism. In general, the Muslim ascetic was one who embraced the contempt of other Muslims, dressing in rags, associating with the poor, performing base occupations (such as herding animals, blood-letting, or professional mendicancy), but he still tended to live in cities or at least in populated areas rather than seek out complete isolation. If one could point to an obvious difference between Christian and Muslim ascetics, it would be that the latter were urban and practiced their asceticism within civilization rather than outside of it.

Probably the most obvious characteristic of these early ascetics was the remembrance of God, called *dhikr* (remembrance or recollection). In Qur'an 2:152, it states "Remember Me and I will remember you. Give thanks to Me and do not be ungrateful." This constant *dhikr* of God became emblematic of both early ascetics and later Sufis. It involved the attempt to clear the mind completely of all thoughts that did not center around God through constant repetition of the ninety-nine names of God (*al-asma' al-husna*) or other mantric formulae.

Sufi Transformations

By the beginning of the ninth century, Muslim ascetic ideas coalesced around the term *Sufism*, with its singular *Sufi*, meaning "wool-wearer." It is uncertain where this term came from or why precisely it came to be emblematic of Islamic mysticism. Many theories have been advanced, the most obvious of which is that possibly the early Sufis did wear this type of wool, although there is no evidence that they did. Suffice it to say that the Sufi movement took over the *zuhd* heritage in its entirety and many of its spiritual examples such as al-Hasan al-Basri, Rabi`a al-`Adawiyya, `Abdallah b. al-Mubarak, and Ibrahim b. Adham were actually ascetics and belonged to the period before Sufism arose. Stories about them became mainstays in the Sufi literature from then until the present time.

Sufism has always suffered from a certain ambiguous relationship toward Islam, however. To start off with, Sufis embraced a lifestyle that stood in opposition to that of many Muslims who embraced the Qur'anic notion of "it is no offense to seek a bounty from your Lord" (2:198), which meant to accept worldly success. There was also the major issue of the mystical nature of the union with God sought by Sufis and the practical implications of their relationship toward Muslim law (the *shari`a*). For many Sufis, the absolute love that they felt for God and the union they enjoyed with Him liberated them from the strictures of the law, which they felt was merely for those people who were in need of some form of coercion to cause them to behave. What need had Sufis for the five daily prayers, basic to Islam in all of its forms, when they were constantly in prayer to God day and night?

Moreover, some Sufis took their union with God in a direction that implied complete identification with God, and perhaps even a complete dissolution of self (the *fana'* or cessation of being that was the goal of most Sufi systems). Probably the best known of these Sufis was the mystic al-Hallaj (d. 922), who is said to have stated in an ecstatic state (*hal*) "I am the Truth" (*ana al-haqq*), a statement that implied that he was God (or at least unified with Him). Al-Hallaj was crucified for these words, a process that he made no attempt to hinder, as he desired the mystical annihilation of *fana'*. But Sufism, in general, suffered as its opponents were able to demonize it as negation of the unity of God (a basis of Islam) (Massignon 1994).

The other side of Sufism was the more establishment one that embraced a duality between the open observance of the *shari`a* and the private observance of the Sufi rituals of *dhikr* and self-deprivation. An interesting off-shoot of this tendency was that of the Malamatiyya, a movement current in eastern Iran, which sought to keep its orthodoxy entirely out of the public eye, while performing good deeds in private and deliberately courting the contempt and rejection of the public. This formula was designed to avoid the spiritual pride that the Malamatis felt was characteristic of the impoverished and abstemious lifestyle of mainstream Sufis—these latter could revel in their relative poverty just as much as more successful Muslims could in their wealth (Al-Sulami n.d., 402–436).

Probably the best-known establishment figure in classical Sufism was al-Ghazali (d. 1111), who was a Sunni theologian at a prestigious Baghdad college, who, after going through a spiritual crisis that caused him to up and leave it all for fourteen years, converted to Sufism and became an ardent exponent of it in later life. As al-Ghazali was uniquely qualified to marry the mainstream *shari`a*-abiding element of Sufism with its radical antinomian wing, his influence on Sufism is immense. From his time until the present, the vast bulk of Muslims have been Sufis, and it is hard to point to a major intellectual or religious figure in Islam that was not a Sufi or at least influenced by Sufism until the middle of the nineteenth century. Al-Ghazali in many ways made Sufism intellectually and socially respectable (Algar 2001).

It was during this period (eleventh and twelfth centuries) that the process of Sufis converting people to Islam began to be a major factor. Although the ascetic literature gives examples of conversion to Islam from the early period, following al-Ghazali there were larger numbers of Sufis who began to organize themselves into brotherhoods (*tariqa*). These organizations have continued to be critical in the spread of Islam to the present time and are most usefully compared with orders (in the Catholic church) or denominations (in the Protestant world). Groups of mendicant Sufis (called *faqirs*, meaning "poor" or *dervishes*) began to gather at the borders of the Muslim world, in Central Asia, in West and East Africa, in India, and eventually in Southeast Asia. In each one of these regions, the process of conversion was remarkably similar. Sufi holy men (following in the footsteps of Christian monks of the early period) gained the reputation of a spiritual elite. They had healing and intercessory powers and could—and did—confront Islamic rulers and their religious intellectuals (the `*ulama*). This confrontation was often to the benefit of the Sufis, as they could position themselves as local heroes and gain converts.

It was not at all unusual during this period, and to the present day, for these Sufi holy men to cultivate an entire range of sanctity around their persons. This sanctity was usually conveyed by the term *baraka* or "blessing." Sometimes this *baraka* was accrued to a given person, who would then pass it down to his descendents, or to a place, usually his tomb or a place closely associated with his teachings or miracles during his lifetime and thereafter. *Baraka* was something that continued to be in effect and constituted a strong draw to the people of the region, and sometimes far beyond (as pilgrims). People would come for miracles, healing, and, most especially, to gain the intercession of the holy man for their sins against the moment during the Day of Judgment when they would be judged. It was commonly hoped that the holy man's general *baraka* would protect his followers or those who had revered his holy site. On a popular level, all sorts of amulets, prayers, and paraphernalia would be sold and cultivated at such sites (Cornell 1998).

At the same time as these popular trends were growing, there was development in Sufi cosmology and metaphysics. The Spanish Muslim figure of Ibn al-'Arabi (d. 1240) was probably the most intricate intellect that Islam has ever produced. In his voluminous works, he solidified abstract notions of

God's being, His relation to the cosmos, and the cosmos's interrelation with humanity. Bringing together many strands of Sufism and writing in the most careful yet often obscure manner (because his many opponents believed him to be destructive to Islam), Ibn al-ʿArabi formulated a theory that later became known as *wahdat al-wujud* (although he did not use that term). *Wahdat al-wujud,* as Ibn al-ʿArabi formulated it, emphasized the absolute existence of God as opposed to the finite and fleeting existence of all created creatures and God's absolute oneness. This later emphasis has opened the doctrine of *wahdat al-wujud* to charges that it is pantheistic. Ibn al-ʿArabi's emphasis and enthrallment with the nature of God's existence can possibly lead one in that direction. But it is unlikely that the man himself was a pantheist (Ansari 1999, 149–192).

Wahdat al-wujud was only part of a larger intellectual framework that Ibn al-ʿArabi developed. As William Chittick, Ibn al-ʿArabi's most comprehensive interpreter in English has stated: "Ibn al-ʿArabi's teachings come together on the issue of human perfection, which is none other than for human beings to be fully human…the degree to which they achieve this goal establishes their worth as God's servants and vice-regents and determines their situation in this world and the next" (1998, xxiii). In this manner, Ibn al-ʿArabi developed the doctrine of *al-insan al-kamil,* the Perfect Man, which became the goal to which Sufis aspired. Moving away from mystical annihilation of the earlier periods, he proposed that the Gnostic Sufi through his cognizance of God could (hypothetically) attain a level of perfection that would be similar to that of the Prophet Muhammad (the archetypal Perfect Man). This doctrine continued to have ramifications throughout Sufism for the following centuries.

Almost at the same time as Ibn al-ʿArabi was formulating his theories, the major Sufi poet and thinker Jalal al-Din Rumi (d. 1273) was composing his epic ecstatic verses on the theme of universal love. Rumi, who was a refugee from the onslaught of the Mongol invasions, based himself in Anatolia (today Turkey) where he dictated to his disciples *Mathnawi* (in Persian, *Masnavi*), in which the formulation of ecstatic Sufism took final form. Rumi avoids any Hallaj-like proclamations of complete union with God, but he emphasizes a type of universalism that has served as a spiritual attractant for many even to the present day. His followers, the Mevlevis, developed the emblematic pattern of dance (the "Whirling Dervishes") in his honor and helped bring music and dance into the repertoire of mainstream Sufism. However, it should be noted that these elements, so attractive to outsiders, have been problematic within the context of Islam (Hamarlund, Olson, and Ozdalga 2001).

A typical story of Rumi is told that he saw a group of priests dressed in black, and a number of his followers made negative comments about their appearance. Rumi, on the other hand, stated: "There are no people in the world who are more generous" even though they would eventually be sentenced to hellfire, "nonetheless, when the sun of divine favor suddenly shines on them, they will immediately become illuminated and have white (bright) faces. [poem] 'If a hundred year old infidel beholds you, he prostrates himself and quickly becomes a Muslim.'" Indeed, the group of priests did convert to Islam, and Rumi's reaction was "God Most High conceals blackness in whiteness and Hew gives whiteness a place within blackness" (O'Kane 2002, 98).

Rumi's importance within Sufism also represents the growth of Sufi poetry and epics, which, although they had their roots in early Arabic ascetic poetry, were closely linked to the revival of the Persian language in the eleventh through fourteenth centuries. Poets such as Sa'di (d. 1283 or 1291), Nizami Ganjavi (d. 1209), and Hafez (d. 1390) developed this tradition and contributed mightily to the literary tradition of Sufism. Many writers used Sufi themes or heroes inside their stories or allegories, and in this manner, Sufism and Sufi ideas came to dominate the discourse of Islam, especially in lands influenced by Persia (Iran, Central Asia, India, Turkey). Sufism thus moved away from its early roots as a low-class phenomenon and became the language of the courtly elite, and the Sufi lifestyle became the ideal to which they aspired.

Following the period of Rumi, the process of the brotherhoods' development continued apace. Starting with the Qadiriyya (associated with 'Abd al-Qadir al-Jilani, d. 1166), which today is both the oldest of the brotherhoods as well as the one that has the broadest reach throughout the Muslim world, brotherhoods became prominent in the Islamization of many regions. Each brotherhood has some specific characteristic that sets it apart from the others, but with one major exception, all of them claim a spiritual link (known as a *silsila*, a "chain") that leads from the founder of the brotherhood back to one of the prominent companions of the Prophet Muhammad (usually to 'Ali b. Abi Talib, his cousin, son-in-law, and fourth successor). Thus, the followers of a brotherhood claim spiritual continuity with early Islam as they claim to be the heirs of spiritual and esoteric knowledge that will have passed down this chain to the founder of the group, and from him to the rest.

Characteristics that set different brotherhoods apart are difficult to classify. Sufis run the range between militancy (e.g., the Sanusiyya) and pacifism (e.g., the Shadhiliyya or the Chishtiyya), from being extremely close to mainstream Sunnism (e.g., the Naqshbandiyya) to groups that almost diverge entirely from Muslim practice (the Muridiyya). In general, the Naqshbandiyya has been closely associated with Central Asia and South Asia and has been a comparatively mainstream organization that is very attractive to elites. The Chishtiyya, on the other hand, has been very much a vehicle of popular Islam and, in its practice in India, is strikingly similar to popular Hindu practices. In Africa, many of the Sufi brotherhoods have been of a militant character, and some such as the Qadiriyya under the leadership of Shehu Usuman Dan Fodio (d. 1817) spearheaded jihads against Muslims and non-Muslims alike. All major Sufi brotherhoods at one time or another fought against European encroachments during the nineteenth and early twentieth centuries.

Some specifically African organizations include the Tijaniyya, whose founder Ahmad al-Tijani (d. 1815) claimed to have seen the Prophet Muhammad in the flesh. The Tijaniyya is the only major brotherhood to eschew the *silsila*. The Tijaniyya claiming what amounted to a new revelation has proved to be very popular throughout West Africa. Similarly, the appearance of Ahmadu Bamba in Senegal at the beginning of the twentieth century heralded a complete reinterpretation of the Sufi heritage. Ahmadu Bamba tied the idea of salvation closely to practical work (especially in the groundnut culture of Senegal) and removed or allegorized many of the mainstays of Islam such as prayer and pilgrimage. The Muridiyya cultivated a social order that was conducive to the development of song, dance, and art. Even today, pictures of Ahmadou Bamba form a major component in the street art of Senegal (Roberts and Roberts 2003).

Contemporary Developments

There can be no reasonable doubt that the majority of Muslims at the beginning of the twentieth century were either Sufis or heavily influenced by Sufism. Additionally, most converts to Islam, including those of European extraction, have tended to convert to Islam through Sufism. However, consistently throughout Muslim history, there has been hostility and antagonism toward Sufis and Sufism. In general, this opposition has focused upon the Sufi beliefs in the intercessory role for holy men (the *baraka*), the veneration of the relics associated with these holy figures (which smacks of idolatry for many mainstream Muslims), and the indifferent attitude that Sufis can display toward strict observance of the *shari'a*. There has, on the part of anti-Sufis, been a striking lack of gratitude toward the role that Sufism has played in the conversion of non-Muslims, and on a number of occasions, Sufis or Sufi movements have been the targets of jihad on the ground that they were not "true Muslims."

These trends have their present roots first in the thought of Ibn Taymiyya (d. 1328), a polemicist and iconoclast, who was largely rejected during his own time, but today is seen as a prominent Muslim thinker by radical Muslims (Wahhabis or Salafis). Ironically, the best evidence is that even though Ibn Taymiyya was critical of Sufi practices, especially the veneration of holy men, he was himself a Sufi of the Qadiriyya (Makdisi 1973, 118–129). These charges were revived and amplified by Muhammad b. 'Abd al-Wahhab (d. 1797), who founded the theological-political tendency known as radical Islam (or Wahhabiyya). Again, he cited the position of intercessors within Sufism to classify it as *shirk* or "polytheism," a grave sin. Many other Sufi practices were also placed within the categories of major sins. Ibn 'Abd al-Wahhab, though viewed as an iconoclast by many Muslims, through his classifications of major sins nullifying one's belief in Islam has had a normifying effect upon the faith as well. Even if many do not agree with his harsh categories, all of them are backed up by Qur'anic verses and are not easily refuted.

Sufism faced another attack with the beginning of the twentieth century coming from Muslim liberals and reformers such as Muhammad 'Abduh (d. 1905) of Egypt. Liberals and reformers identified Sufism as the primary factor contributing to the backward social and structural status of the Muslim world (vis-à-vis European domination). They usually accused Sufis of being otherworldly, antitechnological, and passive (from a military point of view). Although this critique is not necessarily fair, especially given the fact that many of the anti-European jihad movements of the nineteenth and early twentieth centuries were led by Sufis, these were characterizations that have tended to stick to Sufism until the present day, especially in the opinions of Muslim elites. For these elites, the Sufis were the primary collaborators with European colonialists—their passivity and otherworldliness encouraged foreigners to take advantage of Muslims in general. Toward the end of the twentieth century, both liberal and radical critiques of Sufism have tended to join together in a doctrinal opposition to Sufism, in many cases saying that Sufis are either non-Muslims or even anti-Muslim.

In the face of these attacks, Sufism has demonstrated remarkable resilience. Even though the social prestige of Sufism remains low within the Arabic-speaking Middle East (the core lands of Islam), many Arabs remain associated with Sufi brotherhoods. Throughout other Muslim regions, such as South Asia, Southeast Asia, and Africa, the strength of Sufism remains phenomenal; in many cases, it can be compared in its dynamism to the concurrent growth of Pentecostal Christianity. It has usually been Sufis who have reached out to non-Muslims in dialogue, and a great many Islamic ideas have passed into common religious discourse in Europe and the United States (through the medium of New Age religion) from Sufism.

This tendency toward a somewhat ecumenical outlook was common in Sufism already in the Middle Ages, as one finds both Jewish and Christian Sufis in Egypt and elsewhere (Goitein 1967–1985, 5:471–480). Europeans such as Louis Massignon (d. 1962), his student Henri Corbin (d. 1978), and Frithjof Schuon (d. 1998) have engaged in Sufi practices or converted to Islam and have led Sufi movements. This tendency is especially strong in Europe, but it is also present in Sufi groups in the United States. Starting from the teachings of Hazrat Inayat Khan (d. 1927), who founded an International Sufi Movement in Switzerland, and continuing on through the intellectual followers of Ibn al-'Arabi (both in the United Kingdom at the Muhyi al-Din Ibn 'Arabi Society at Cambridge University and in France through the followers of Michel Chod-kiewicz and others), and to the devotees of the Haqqani Foundation (associated with the Naqshbandiyya brotherhood), Sufism has consistently been a spiritual attractant for Westerners.

Pedagogical Strategies

Teaching Sufism in an American classroom is a difficult task, most probably because the teaching of such a vast and complicated subject requires a thorough knowledge of and appreciation of Islamic culture. This fact is indicated by the difficulties of choosing a proper introduction to Sufism. Although many competent scholars such as Annemarie Schimmel (1975), William Chittick (2000), Hamid Algar (2001), Carl Ernst (1997), and Alexander Kynsh (2000) have written introductions to Sufism, there is always a certain emphasis inside any introduction. For example, Schimmel's introduction is probably the easiest to read (and in my experience the most popular with students), although it is a bit dated now, but it focuses heavily upon the South Asian and Turkish heritage of Sufism. Other introductions have also tended to focus on issues of interest to the authors rather than a broad focus on Sufism as the primary component of Islamic culture throughout the last thousand years. As globalization proceeds apace, we become more and more cognizant of the fact that Sufism cannot be merely an Arab or a Persian phenomenon, because it is equally an Indonesian and an African one as well.

For primary sources, the teacher is well served with regard to Islamic mysticism. Looking at the bookshelves of major bookstores, there are usually many English volumes of Rumi, some of Ibn al-'Arabi (who might be too complicated for a popular audience), and other prominent classical writers such as al-Ghazali and especially Persian-language literary figures such as Hafez will be represented. On the Internet, and through specialized ordering, much of the canon of Sufism can be read in English (as well as French, German, Spanish, or Italian) in competent scholarly translations, as a result of 150 years of sustained foreign interest in Sufism. The same could not be said for any other subject with regard to Islam, whether historical or literary in nature. Indeed, the major problem for the teacher in this regard is the embarrassment of riches that presents itself in reading the mystical heritage of Islam.

The appearance and prominence of Sufism on the Internet has also become a major issue for the teacher. Here the problem also lies in too much information, the inability to sift the accurate from the inaccurate, and the apologetic slant of many Sufi websites. Because many of these websites are not run by Sufis, but by associated sympathizers from a New Age bent, it is difficult to tell (for the uninitiated) what is actually classical Sufism and what is contemporary New Age religion. Without knowing the classical sources, it is difficult to know what has been suppressed from these websites and why. Even with a broad-minded writer such as Rumi, there are occasional racist or sexist comments or allegories. Should these be suppressed as offensive in contemporary society or taught because they are historically accurate and represent what Rumi (or others) truly thought?

Even more often on the Internet one comes across opposition to Sufism. Indeed, students are just as likely to discover that Sufis are not Muslims as they are to find websites conveying authentic Sufi materials. It is possible that some of that ambiguity is created not only by Salafis who reject Sufism on doctrinal grounds, but also by contemporary Western adherents of Sufism who love the cultural and literary heritage of mysticism but reject its connections with the extremist Islam about which they read in the newspapers. Sufism as a system has always been, as noted, slightly bigger than Islam itself and has contained within it a range of people who have never converted to Islam.

As more and more American Muslims are present in the classroom, there will be an additional confrontation that awaits the teacher teaching Sufism. Many second- and third-generation Muslims will either come from a Sufi background or be hostile to Sufism. Those from the former group may very well appreciate more of its local cultural aspects rather than the broad intellectual and religious heritage highlighted in this chapter. Some of the latter might be hostile to the inclusion of Sufism within the rubric of Islam at all. Certain of my Muslim students have challenged me when I have offered courses on Sufism, saying that it is not Islam. Although it is clear that such challenges are deliberately provocative, they could very well proliferate as the trend in American Islam continues away from what are considered to be "cultural accretions" (i.e., locally based Sufi practices not rooted in the *sunna*) toward radical Islam, especially among students.

Just as definitions of mysticism overall are problematic, one of the chief difficulties of dealing with Sufism is not merely the vastness of the subject or the fact that Sufism has intertangled itself with many of the constituent cultures of Islam, but that it is so difficult to define. In this regard, radical Muslims, depending upon Ibn 'Abd al-Wahhab's "Ten Nullifiers of Islam" (discussed in "Contemporary Developments") to define what they consider to be non-Muslim Sufism out of Islam, have the edge. It is far easier from this dogmatic perspective to state what is "not" Islam than to state what "is" Sufism. From the earliest stages of the movement in the ninth and tenth centuries, Sufism embraced a number of logical oppositions: those who followed the *shari'a* carefully together with the most extreme types of antinomians, Arab and non-Arab Muslims, rich and poor, free-born and slaves, as well as many other oppositions. Uniquely for Islam, there is well-documented evidence of the participation of women in Sufi circles; al-Sulami's eleventh-century treatise on the subject proves as much.[3]

All of these differences mean that both classical and contemporary definitions of Sufism (and mysticism in general) suffer from incoherence and a tendency to mean all things to all people and have only a few commonalities. These include the desire to achieve union with God, a belief in the efficacy of spiritual guides for the Sufi "path," a willingness to read the Qur'an (and the tradition literature) in an allegorical fashion, and a preference for experience-based religious knowledge or Gnostic knowledge (*ma'rifa*) as opposed to the revelation-based knowledge of the *shari'a* (the *'ilm*). These commonalities continue to hold and influence the mystic of today.

Syllabus

Sufism: Islam's Mystical and Esoteric Tradition
    Week 1. Early holy men/women in Islam

    Brown (1971), 80–101
    Ogen (1982), 33–48
    'Attar (1990), 39–51 (Rabi'a al-'Adawiyya), 63–79 (Ibrahim b. Adhham), 87–99 (Dhu al-Nun al-Misri), 199–213 (al-Junayd)
    Al-Sulami (1999), introduction, 54–70

    Week 2. Beginnings of Sufism

    Schimmel (1975), chaps. 1, 2
    Massignon (1994), 10–23, 117–156, 208–290
    al-Suhrawardi (1975), 27–83
    Al-Qushayri (1992), 1–11, 25–31, 47–54, 215–22

    Week 3. al-Ghazali

    Schimmel (1975), chap. 3
    al-Tirmidhi (2003), 11–56
    al-Ghazali (1980)
    Sharma (1972), 65–85

    Week 4. al-Ghazali

    al-Ghazali (1998)
    al-Ghazali (1997), 105–192
    al-Ghazali (1986), 23–29

    Week 5. Ibn al-'Arabi

    Chittick (1998), ix–xxxix, sec. 1
    Husaini (1979)
    Ansari (1999), 149–192
    Rosenthal (1988), 1–35

    Week 6. Ibn al-'Arabi

    Schimmel (1975), chap. 4
    Chittick (1989), chaps. 1, 2
    Chittick (1989), 1–11; (1994), 31–38

Week 7. Ibn al-'Arabi

Chittick (1989), chap. 3
Chittick (1988), 51–82; (1994), 97–112
Arrach (1997), 97–113

Midterm: in class

Week: 8. Persian Sufism

al-Hujwiri (2000), chap. 14
Hafiz (1953), 1–34 (introduction)
Hafiz: http://www.HafizOnLove.com
Bashiri (1979), 34–67

Week 9. Persian Sufism

Nasr (1999), 1–11
al-Sulami (1991), pt. 4
al-Razi (2003), 268–278, 310–334

Week 10. Jalal al-Din al-Rumi and Turkish Sufism

Chittick (2001), pts. 1, 2
Iqbal (1991), 353–384
Ernst (1997), chap. 7

Week 11. Jalal al-Din al-Rumi

Chittick (2001), pt. 3
Schimmel (1975), chaps. 6, 7
Thackston (1999), 1–54 (discourses 1–11)

Week 12. Indian and Chinese Sufism

Rizvi (2002), 1:chap. 6, 2: chaps. 4, 5
Rajgiri (2001), 184–211
Murata (2000), 376–388

Week 13. Sufi orders in India, Indonesia, and North Africa

Schimmel (1975), chap. 5
Martin (1976), chaps. 3, 6
van Bruinessen (1990), 150–179
Lawrence (1981), 119–152

Paper due

Week 14. Contemporary Sufism

Hermansen (1998), 155–178

Wilson (1998), 179–210
www.naqshbandi.org
Roundtable discussion

Final exam: take home

Notes

1. All Qur'anic translations are from Fakhry (1997).
2. For many of them, see Khalidi (2001).
3. Al-Sulami (1999).

References

Algar, Hamid. 2001. *Imam Abu Hamid Ghazali: An Exponent of Islam in its Totality*. One-onta, NY: Islamic Publications.

Ansari, Abdul Haq. 1999. "Ibn 'Arabi: The Doctrine of *Wahdat al-wujud*," *Islamic Studies* 38: 149–192.

Arrach, Samer. 1997. "The World of the Imagination in Ibn 'Arabi's Ontology," *British Journal of Middle Eastern Studies* 24: 97–113.

Attar, Farid al-Din. 1990. *Muslim Saints and Mystics: Episodes from the Tadhkirat al-Auliya' (Memorial of the Saints)*, translated by Arthur Arberry. New York: Penguin.

Bashiri, Iraj. 1979. "Hafiz and the Sufic *Ghazal*," *Studies in Islam* 16: 34–67.

Brown, Peter. 1971. "The Rise and Function of the Holy Man in Late Antiquity," *Journal of Roman Studies* 61: 80–101.

Bruinessen, Martin van. 1990. "The Origins and Development of the Naqshbandi Order in Indonesia," *Der Islam* 67: 150–179.

Chittick, William. 1988. "Death and the World of the Imagination," *Muslim World* 78: 51–82.

———. 1994. *Imaginal Worlds: Ibn al-'Arabi and the Problem of Religious Diversity*. Albany: State University of New York Press.

———. 1989. "Microcosm, Macrocosm and Perfect Man in the View of Ibn al-'Arabi," *Islamic Culture* 63: 1–11.

———. 1998. *The Self-Disclosure of God: Principles of Ibn al-'Arabi's Cosmology*. Albany: State University of New York Press.

———. 1989. *The Sufi Path of Knowledge: Ibn al-'Arabi's Metaphysics of Imagination*. Albany: State University of New York Press.

———. 2001. *The Sufi Path of Love: The Spiritual Teachings of Rumi*. Albany: State University of New York Press, 1983.

———. 2000. *Sufism: A Short Introduction*. Oxford: Oneworld Publications.

Chodkiewicz, Michel. 1993a. *An Ocean without a Shore: Ibn 'Arabi, the Book and the Law*, translated by David Streight. Albany: State University of New York Press.

———. 1993b. *Seal of the Saints: Prophethood and Sainthood in the Doctrine of Ibn 'Arabi*, translated by Liadain Sherrard. Cambridge: Islamic Texts Society.

———. 1995. *The Spiritual Writings of Amir 'Abd al-Kader*, translated by James Chrestensen and Tom Manning. Albany: State University of New York Press.

Cornell, Vincent. 1998. *The Realm of the Saint: Power and Authority in Moroccan Sufism.* Austin: University of Texas Press.

Ernst, Carl. 1997. *The Shambhala Guide to Sufism.* Boston: Shambhala.

Fakhry, Majid, trans. 1997. *The Qur'an: A Modern English Version.* London: Garnet Press.

Ghazali, Abu Hamid Muhammad al-. 1980. *Deliverance from Error: Five Key Texts Including His Spiritual Autobiography al-Munqidh min al-Dalal,* translated by R. J. McCarthy. Reprint, London: Fons Vitae.

———. 1998. *The Niche of Lights,* translated by David Buchman, Brigham Young University— Islamic Translation Series. Provo, UT: Brigham Young University Press.

———. 1997. "On Breaking the Two Desires." In *Disciplining the Soul,* translated by T. J. Winter, 105–192. Cambridge: Islamic Texts Society.

———. 1986. *Sawanih: Inspirations from the World of Pure Spirits,* translated by Nasrollah Pourjavady. London: Routledge.

Goitein, S. D. 1967–1985. *A Mediterranean Society.* Berkeley: University of California Press.

Hafiz, 1953. *Fifty Poems of Hafiz,* translated by A. J. Arberry. Cambridge: Cambridge University Press.

Hamarlund, Andreas, Tord Olson, and Elizabeth Ozdalga, eds. 2001. *Sufism, Music and Society in Turkey and the Middle East.* Istanbul: Swedish Research Institute.

Hermansen, Marcia. 1998. "In the Garden of American Sufi Movements." In *New Trends and Developments in the World of Islam,* edited by Peter B. Clarke, 155–178. London: Luzac.

Hujwiri, al-. 2000. *Kashf al-mahjub,* translated by Reynald Nicholson. Cambridge: Gibb Memorial Trust.

Husaini, Abdul Qadir. 1979. *The Pantheistic Monism of Ibn al-'Arabi.* 2nd ed. Santa Clara, CA: Sh. Muhammad Ashraf.

Iqbal, Afzal. 1991. "Mevlana Rumi on the Perfect Man," *Islamic Studies* 30: 353–384.

Khalidi, Tarif. 2001. *The Muslim Jesus.* Harvard: Harvard University Press.

Kynsh, Alexander. 2000. *Islamic Mysticism: A Short History.* Leiden: E. J. Brill.

Lawrence, Bruce. 1981. "Sufism and the History of Religions," *Studies in Islam* 18: 119–152.

Makdisi, George. 1973. "Ibn Taimiya: A Sufi of the Qadiriya," *American Journal of Arabic Studies* 1: 118–129.

Martin, B. J. (1976) 2003. *Muslim Brotherhoods in 19th Century Africa.* Reprint, Cambridge: Cambridge University Press.

Massignon, Louis. 1994. *The Passion of al-Hallaj, Mystic and Martyr,* translated by Herbert Mason. Abridged ed. Princeton, NJ: Princeton University Press.

Murata, Sachiko. 2000. "Sufi Texts in Chinese." in *The Heritage of Sufism,* Vol. 3, edited by Leonard Lewisohn and David Morgan, 376–388. Oxford: Oneworld.

Nasr, Seyyed Hossein. 1978. *An Introduction to Islamic Cosmological Doctrines.* Boulder, CO: Shambhala.

———. 1999. *Sufi Essays.* Chicago: KAZI Publications.

———. 2008. *The Garden of Truth: The Vision and Promise of Sufism, Islam's Mystical Tradition.* New York: HarperCollins.

———. 1999. "Persian Sufi Literature: Its Spiritual and Cultural Significance." In *The Heritage of Sufism.* Vol. 2, edited by Leonard Lewisohn and David Morgan, 1–11. Oxford: Oneworld.

Ogen, Göran. 1982. "Did the Term 'Sufi' Exist before the Sufis?" *Acta Orientalia* 43: 33–48.

O'Kane, John, trans. 2002. *Shams al-Din Ahmad-e Aflaki: The Feats of the Knowers of God* (Manaqeb al-arefin). Leiden: E. J. Brill.

Qushayri, al-. 1992. *Principles of Sufism*, translated by B. von Schlegell. Berkeley: Mizan Press.

Rajgiri, Mir Sayyid Manjhan Shattari. 2001. *Madhumalati: An Indian Sufi Romance*, translated by Aditya Behl and Simon Weightman. Oxford: Oxford University Press.

Razi, Najm al-Din al-. 2003. *The Path of God's Bondsman: From Origin to Return*, translated by Hamid Algar. North Haledon, NJ: Islamic Publications International.

Rizvi, Saiyid Athar Abbas. 2002. *A History of Sufism in India*. Reprint, New Delhi: Munshiram Manoharlal.

Roberts, Allen F., and Mary Nooter. 2003. *Saint in the City: Sufi Arts of Urban Senegal.* Los Angeles: Fowler Museum at University of California, Los Angeles.

Rosenthal, Franz. 1988. "Ibn `Arabi between 'Philosophy' and 'Mysticism,'" *Oriens* 31: 1–35.

Schimmel, Annemarie. 1975. *Mystical Dimensions of Islam*. Chapel Hill: University of North Carolina Press.

Sharma, Arvind. 1972. "The Spiritual Biography of al-Ghazali," *Studies in Islam* 9: 65–85.

Suhrawardi, Abu al-Najib al-. 1975. *A Sufi Rule for Novices: A Translation of the Kitab Adab Al-Muridin*, translated by Menachem Milson, Harvard Middle Eastern Studies 17. Cambridge, MA: Harvard University Press.

Sulami, al-. 1991. *The Book of Sufi Chivalry*, translated by Tosun Bayrak. Rochester, NY: Inner Traditions.

Sulami, Abu `Abd ar-Rahman as-. 1999. *Early Sufi Women: Dhikr an-Niswa al-Muta `Abbidat as-Sufiyyat*, translated by Rkia Cornell. Louisville, KY: Fons Vitae.

Sulami, Muhammad b. al-Husayn al-. n.d. 1980-1993. *Majmu`at-i athar-i Abu `Abd al-Rahman Sulami*. 2 vols. Tehran: Markaz-i Nashr-i Danishgahi.

Thackston, Wheeler, trans. 1999. *Signs of the Unseen: The Discourses of Jalaluddin Rumi.* Boston: Shambhala.

Tirmidhi, al-Hakim al-. 2003. *Three Early Sufi Texts: A Treatise on the Heart, Stations of the Righteous, The Stumblings of Those Aspiring*, translated by Nicolas Heer. Louisville, KY: Fons Vitae.

Wilson, Peter. "The Strange Fate of Sufism in the New Age." In *New Trends and Developments in the World of Islam*, edited by Peter B. Clarke, 179–210. London: Luzac.

6

Teaching Jewish Mysticism

CONCEALING THE CONCEALMENT
AND DISCLOSURE OF SECRETS

Elliot R. Wolfson

Mysticism as Radical Thinking

In an age that is hypersensitive to diversity and loathes to accept generalizations, teaching courses on religion within the academy has become increasingly more difficult, even as accessibility to sources, both primary and
secondary, has greatly increased.[1] Mysticism presents an additional challenge
insofar as the experiences studied under this rubric push at the limits of what
we can know and of what we can speak. Although I, too, am inclined to shun
positing a rigid understanding of mysticism that would be applied universally
and unconditionally, I assent to the possibility that, above all else, mysticism
relates to the capacity of the human mind to imagine what cannot be imagined
and to think what cannot be thought. Such an understanding, in my judgment,
is flexible enough to satisfy both the essentialist claim that there is something
we can identify as the unchanging essence of the mystical and the constructivist claim that mystical elements need to be studied and evaluated within specific cultural contexts. The formlessness of the experience that is implied by
this conception may account for both the commonality and distinctiveness of
the mystical elements expressed in the different traditions.[2] The point is formulated lucidly by Jess Hollenback (1996, 75–76):

> When I say that the mystical experience is amorphous, I am observing
> that its content (and its effects) differ from one religious tradition to the
> next. . . . It should now be clear that when one says that mystical experi-
> ence is amorphous this is simply another way of stating that, in the vast
> majority of cases, one can never isolate either its content or its effects
> from the mystic's historical context. Indeed, the content of almost every
> mystical experience seems to be structured in such a manner as to
> empirically validate or otherwise legitimize many elements of that

description of reality that are either expressly or implicitly present in the mythologies, dogmas, or rituals that form the core of that religious tradition to which the mystic adheres. Not only do mystics empirically confirm the existence of a domain of experience that remains inaccessible to the five senses but also the structure of what they perceive to be ultimate reality is consistent with the descriptions given or implied of it by the revelation(s) or rituals that found their particular religious traditions.[3]

To delineate the mystical as the trail that leads human consciousness to its limit—a testing of the center at the margins—presumes that subversion is characteristic of its demarcation: that is, innate to its very structure is the possibility of its undermining. In communicating to students the value of a comparative approach to the study of mysticism that is respectful of the contextualist perspective, I frequently emphasize that by digging deep into the ground of one particular tradition, one finds the way to its ungrounding, as that tradition invariably opens the door to other traditions. The specificity of a path, in other words, leads to the discovery of alternate paths that are the same in virtue of being different—what they share with each other is their difference from one another.[4] It is in this sense that mysticism may be called a *radical thinking*, a taking hold of the root that is at the same time an eradication.

Open System and Generalizing from the Particular

In assessing the task of teaching Jewish mysticism, it must first be noted that there is no single definition of this phenomenon or even a consensus regarding the best way to identify its salient characteristics. The basic framework to approach the topic remains the one established by Gershom Scholem. Although Scholem's own work built on the foundation laid by scholars who preceded him, an obvious point that is sometimes obfuscated in the historiography of the field, he did go further than anyone before in establishing the historical contours of what he called the "major trends" of Jewish mysticism. For Scholem, Jewish mysticism is a postbiblical phenomenon, and it includes the throne or chariot mysticism from Late Antiquity, the Rhineland Jewish pietism of the twelfth and thirteenth centuries, the prophetic Kabbalah first enunciated by Abraham Abulafia in the thirteenth century, the theosophic Kabbalah whose major expression is found the compilation *Sefer ha-Zohar* from the thirteenth and fourteenth centuries, the Kabbalah of Isaac Luria in the sixteenth century, the Sabbatian and Frankist messianic movements of the seventeenth and eighteenth centuries, and the east-European Hasidism of the eighteenth and nineteenth centuries (Scholem 1956). In spite of the serious lacunae in Scholem's delineation—for instance, his leaving out of the picture the intellectual mysticism promulgated by Moses Maimonides (1138–1204),[5] as well as the Jewish Ṣūfism cultivated by his descendants in Egypt for two centuries, Abraham (1186–1237), Obadyah (1228–1265), and David ben Joshua (c. 1335–1415)[6]— and in spite of the impressive growth of the field in the last few decades, incorporating an assortment of alternative approaches, including but not limited to philosophy, psychology, sociology, anthropology, literary criticism, and gender studies, the historical-philological remains the most effective pedagogical method. Particularly influential is the typological distinction advanced by Scholem to classify two major schools of mystical speculation that evolved in the thirteenth century, theosophic and prophetic Kabbalah; as I noted, the former is represented by the zoharic anthology and the latter by the works of Abulafia and his students. Theosophic Kabbalah is a form of contemplative mysticism that sets its focus on the visualization of the ten divine gradations or luminous emanations (*sefirot*) in the form of an anthropos confabulated in the imagination; prophetic Kabbalah is focused on the cultivation of meditative practices centered around the divine names and the letters of the Hebrew alphabet that lead to unitive states of consciousness, the separation of the intellect from the body and its conjunction with the divine intellect.[7]

Scholem resisted the notion that there is a grand narrative to explain coherently the various manifestations of Jewish mysticism. The apprehension of Scholem has only intensified in the current environment where appeal is made to theoretical models that accentuate *différance* in the Derridean sense, the emphasis on differing and deferring, a privileging of indeterminacy and multivocality. As one who is sympathetic to the hermeneutical sensibilities of both deconstruction and postmodernism, I do not eschew the call for pluralism or appeal to multivocality as an effective explanatory tool; nevertheless, I do not think this precludes the possibility of presuming a unifying scheme in studying and teaching this corpus. The positing of recurrent patterns does not come at the expense of being attentive to heterogeneity; on the contrary, it is precisely difference that allows us to recognize sameness just as it is sameness that allows us to recognize difference. The assumption that there are enduring structures does not ignore specific details and historical changes. The generic claims are rooted in and must be tested against particularities. I do think, however, that it is plausible to speak of concepts and symbols that persist through the phases of temporal evolution. Lest there be any misunderstanding, let me state unequivocally that this surmise does not presuppose that the variegated history of Jewish mystical doctrines and practices should be subsumed monolithically under the stamp of immutable essences. Jewish mysticism as a religious phenomenon illustrates that the immutability of system occasions novel interpretation. In the indigenous wisdom of the tradition, the teaching is new if it is old but it is old because it is new.[8]

Jewish mysticism, and especially the different trends of medieval Kabbalah, exemplifies the dialectical confluence of innovation and conservation. The simultaneity of truth as unprecedented and erstwhile is linked to an underlying conception of time as the instant of genuine iteration, that is, the repetition of the same as different in the renewal of the different as same. For Kabbalists, this fundamental axiom is legitimated not by reason but by prophetic experience, the first link in the unbroken chain of the tradition believed to have been transmitted orally from master to disciple (*qabbalah mi-peh el peh*).[9] In the mindset of Kabbalists, system is what accounts for interruption of order by chaos, the intervention of the moment that renders time continuously discontinuous and discontinuously continuous. Much like the technical term for the Ṣūfī, *ibn waqtihī*, literally, the "son of the moment,"[10] the Kabbalist—and, by extension, one who desires to understand kabbalistic doctrines—experiences the eventfulness of time as the constant resumption of what is always yet to be, the return of what has never been, the vertical diremption that opens the horizontal timeline to the spherical fullness of eternity, which is not a static timelessness set in opposition to the motion of time but rather the deeper modulation of the temporal flow (Wolfson 2006a, 176–177). That I assume structures of thought may be recovered philologically, structures influenced but not causally determined by historical factors, does not subject kabbalistic texts to a standard of rigid uniformity; on the contrary, structure accounts for heterogeneity, system for unpredictability. In the interpretive praxis of scholar and practitioner alike, innovation and repetition are not mutually exclusive; they well forth from the spot where the novel is recurringly ancient and the ancient interminably novel.

Aniconism and the Quest to See God: Biblical Roots of Jewish Mysticism

The theme in the history of Jewish mysticism that I would identify as persistent is the desire to envision the presence, the divine glory, in forms forbidden for priests and other Israelites to worship iconically, though seemingly permissible for poets and prophets to depict imaginatively.[11] That is, Israelite cult was distinguished from other ancient Near Eastern societies by the explicit injunction against worshipping an idol of God, but this did not stop visionary souls from depicting God in very graphic form. It is sometimes assumed that the ban on graven images is related to the further presumption that God has no visible form and, by extension, no tangible body. A growing consensus in biblical scholarship, however, maintains that for the ancient Israelites, the burning issue seemed not to be God's corporeality, but rather the problem of depicting that body in material images. Indeed, already in the early monarchic period, the official cult in Jerusalem was aniconic, but this aniconism did not imply the incorporeality of God, an inference made repeatedly by rationalist interpreters of Judaism from Philo of Alexandria in the first century to Maimonides in the twelfth century and to Hermann Cohen in the twentieth century. One theological premise shared by the various denominations of Jewish practice today is the belief that God is not a body and hence anthropomorphic depictions of God must be interpreted figuratively. Notwithstanding the tenacity by which this conviction is held, the evidence from the Bible and later sources suggests that many Jews presumed that God was capable of assuming tangible forms even as the use of icons in liturgical service has been steadfastly prohibited in the long and variegated development of Judaism as a religious phenomenon. The will to envision God in images without succumbing to idolatry, on the one hand, or rejecting iconoclasm, on the other, is the ultimate ordeal of the prophetic imagination as it has expressed itself in a plethora of Jewish texts through the ages.

The tension between aniconism and visualizing the deity played an especially distinctive role in the development of the mystical currents within Jewish history. By turning the lens in this way, the roots for Jewish mysticism, phenomenologically speaking, can be unearthed in the biblical canon. Didactically, to locate the beginnings of the story of Jewish mysticism in scripture represents a major shift from the Scholemian model. Indeed, I would go so far as to say that the various streams that have been studied under the taxon of Jewish mysticism consistently exhibit a yearning to envisage the divine in a manner that is congruent with the visionary experiences preserved in the literary accounts of prophetic epiphanies. Hence, there is no reason not to read the latter as testimonies of a mystical inclination. Ironically, the iconoclastic orientation has fostered a fecund theological imagination, which has been particularly prolific in the writings of mystic visionaries in their quest to see the invisible God. Although the experiences of the divine related by Jewish mystics engaged other senses, including hearing, scent, and touch, the sense of sight assumed an epistemic priority, reflecting and building upon the biblical verses that privilege the ocularcentric nature of revelatory experience. To name but a few of the most prominent examples: Jacob's vision of God face-to-face (Gen. 32:30); the appearance of the glory of the Lord to the Israelites in the cloud (Exod. 16:10) or as a consuming fire (Exod. 24:17). The vision of the back of the fleeting glory accorded Moses (Exod. 33:21–23); Isaiah's seeing the Lord sitting on a high and lofty throne (Isa. 6:1); Ezekiel's beholding the image of the glory in the likeness of the image of a man enthroned on the sapphire stone (Ezek. 1:26); and Daniel's gazing at the Ancient of Days (Dan. 7:9–10). In a scriptural religion like Judaism, one cannot speak of mystical experience (of which vision is one specific type) divorced from an interpretative framework that is shaped by the cultural matrix of that tradition. This is not to deny that the experience of immediacy, which is often singled out as a distinguishing characteristic of mystical experience, is impossible, but only that even such experiences are mediated by specific contexts. Instead of setting immediacy and mediation in binary opposition, as one finds frequently in scholarly analyses of mysticism, we would do better to speak paradoxically of a mediated immediacy. The Jewish mystic may experience the God of Israel without any intermediary, but it is still an experience that takes shape within the parameters of Judaism, however that is to be construed, and hence what the Jewish mystic experiences is not the same as what the Christian, Muslim, Hindu, or Buddhist mystic would experience in the immediacy of his or her experience.

In medieval Jewish mysticism, the locus of the vision is typically situated in the heart/imagination of the visionary, the site where the normal division between inside and outside is dissolved in the play of double mirroring, that is, the heart mirrors the image of the imageless as the image of the imageless mirrors the divine. Mystics in various traditions have considered the imagination to be the divine element of the soul, the element that enables them to gain access to the realm of incorporeality by transferring or transmuting sensory data and/or rational concepts into symbols. Through images within the heart, the divine, whose pure essence is incompatible with any form, is nonetheless manifest in *imaginal* forms—a term that I borrow from Henry Corbin, the historian of Islamic esotericism—expressed philologically in Jewish mystical texts by the expressions *demuyot*, *dimmuyot*, and *dimyonot*. To ascribe these forms to God does not imply that the divine assumes a corruptible body in the historical plane. It entails, rather, that the spiritual reality can be apprehended only through an image configured in the imagination of the visionary, an image that is most often anthropomorphic in nature. Locating these forms in the imagination is not to divest them of objective reality or to reduce them to the subjective stance of the individual, however, because the theophanic image of that which transcends images is accorded the status of reality only inasmuch as it is imagined as real. This perspective implies the identity of symbol and what is symbolized, albeit an identity that preserves the difference of that which is identified as the same—the world, accordingly, may be considered the imaginal body in which the divine light is instantiated, the garment through God is manifest by being hidden.

The idea of the imaginal body, moreover, intimates another understanding of enfleshment, which, in my view, may be applied to the esoteric teaching cultivated by Jews from the throne mysticism of Late Antiquity through the kabbalistic speculation of the Middle Ages. It is this notion that justifies thinking of incarnational tendencies that are distinct from—albeit in dialogue with—the prevailing Christian dogma. From the vantage point of Jewish mysticism, we must adopt a docetic interpretation of the incarnation along the lines articulated by Corbin: the incarnated body is not "found on the plane of materially realized existences, of events accomplished and known once and for all, but always in the transcendent dimension announced by theophanies—because 'true reality' is the internal event produced in each soul by the Apparition that impresses it. In this domain we require a faculty of perception and mediation very different from the demonstrative or historical reasoning which judges the sensible and finite data relating to rationally defined dogmas or to the irreversible events of material history" (Corbin 1969, 153).[12] For the Jewish mystic, the site of the incarnational insight is the ontographic inscripting of flesh into word—as opposed to the transubstantiation of the word into flesh— and the consequent transfiguration of the carnal body into the ethereal, luminous body, finally transposed into the literal body, the body that is the letter, hyperliterally, the name YHWH, which is the Torah in its esoteric valence (Scholem 1965, 32–86; 1972, 79:78–80, 80:178–180, 193–194; Tishby 1989, 1079–1082; Idel 2002, 69–74). The use of anthropomorphic imagery to delimit God is meant to convey the ontological claim that the Hebrew letters assigned to each of the relevant limbs constitute the reality of the body on both the human and divine planes of being. Indeed, as any number of scholars have discerned, a basic tenet of Jewish esotericism consists of this principle of the "semiotics of creation," that is, the conviction that the letters of the Hebrew alphabet are not only the instruments of divine creation, but that they comprise the hyletic stuff of being. In the medieval kabbalistic context, this cosmological view is coupled with an apophatic dimension, insofar as the ciphers of the holy language were thought to be contained in the tetragrammaton, the ineffable name, the garment in and through which the Infinite is clothed. Essential to my understanding of the kabbalistic notion of poetic incarnation, consequently, is appreciating the extent to which the kataphatic description of the Torah as the name that is the textual body is juxtaposed with the apophatic notion that the body that is seen is the image of the imageless. Hence every manifestation is perforce an occlusion, every affirmation a negation (Wolfson 2005, 190–260).

The vision of God in the history of Jewish mystical speculation is engendered, therefore, by the concomitant presence of absence and absence of presence. The God who is envisioned is the invisible God, and that which is revealed is revealed in its concealment. Despite the significant historical differences that separate the anonymous mystics of the Hekhalot literature, the Rhineland Jewish Pietists, the enlightened Castilian Kabbalists responsible for the zoharic compilation in its earliest redactional layers, and the prophetic Kabbalists who followed the teachings of Abraham Abulafia, they all shared a common biblical heritage that affirmed the possibility of God assuming visible form and the denial that the God of Israel could be iconically represented. This point is related succinctly in one passage from *Sefer ha-Zohar*, wherein the divine emanations (*sefirot*) are depicted as the "glorious garments" (*levushin diqar*), "veritable garments" (*levushin qeshot*), "true arrayments" (*tiqqunei qeshot*), and "true sparks" (*boṣinei qeshot*), which reveal the hidden light of the infinite, the "supernal spark" (*boṣina ila'ah*) that is beyond the polarity of light and darkness, the luminous dark that is the dark luminosity, neither light nor dark.[13] The sefirotic gradations, therefore, embody the central paradox that informed the logic central to the Jewish mystical *imaginaire*—they reveal the concealed by concealing the concealment, for if it were otherwise, how could the concealed be revealed?

Secrets of Torah: Esotericism and the Contours of Jewish Mysticism

The conflict between vision and invisibility provided the ideational framework within which Kabbalists articulated the esoteric dialectic of concealment and disclosure. Every act of disclosure is a form of concealment when what is disclosed is what has been concealed, but the disclosed can be concealed as the disclosed only to the extent that the concealed is disclosed as the concealed. The image of circumcision in particular was employed by Kabbalists to communicate this dialectic: an integral part of the rite according to the rabbinic ruling is the unveiling of the phallus after the foreskin has been cut away. In Lacanian fashion, what is unveiled is that which must remain veiled even in—precisely on account of—its unveiling (Wolfson 2005, 128–141). The teaching of truth, like truth itself, is characterized by this hide-and-seek drama. Hence, the hermeneutic of esotericism, the dissimilitude of the secret, is predicated on letting that which is hidden appear as what is hidden and that which appears remain hidden as what appears, an orientation that revolves about the paradox that what is most visible is the invisible. Alternatively expressed, the form that is seen preserves the invisibility of the unseen, just as the liturgical tradition to vocalize YHWH as Adonai secures the ineffability of the name. To attend this paradox is to ascertain that every act of uncovering is a recovery, every act of undressing a redressing. This paradox was enunciated explicitly by sixteenth-century Kabbalists in Safed using a maxim that can be traced textually to the Muslim philosopher Avicenna (c. 980–1037), "disclosure is the cause of concealment and concealment the cause of disclosure" (Wolfson 2002, 110–111).

Is it possible to apply this method in the academic setting, and if it is not, then can the exposure of secrets be executed effectively in the classroom? The reticence to divulge secrets constitutes one of the greatest obstacles to the teaching of mysticism within secular institutions—how does one translate this reticence into an acceptable form within the university? And if one is compelled to divulge all of the secrets, in what sense has one communicated these secrets? Have we come to the spot where the scholar and the adept are separated by an irreconcilable distance? Can there be a meaningful way in which the scholar can perform the disclosure of secrets by concealing them? Or is the ethos of the academy such that the unqualified imparting of knowledge requires a full and categorical disclosure? But how can this be accommodated if the content of what is to be revealed can only be revealed to the degree that it is hidden? Scholem famously wrote that an "authentic tradition" must remain secreted and that a tradition that becomes overt is a "fallen" one (Biale 1987, 103–104).[14] The truly esoteric knowledge cannot be propagated and thus a secret that is transmitted is by definition inauthentic; in the most exact sense, there can be a secret tradition but no tradition of secrecy. To be unveiled, the secret must be veiled; in the veiling lies the power of unveiling.

This may very well expose the insufficiency of the prevailing academic method to provide an adequate mechanism to teach about one of the most archaic features of mysticism. As a number of scholars have noted, the alleged origin of the term *mysticism* in the ancient mystery cults is linked to the emphasis on the esoteric character of the knowledge attained by the adept who receives the mysteries (*mysteria*) through specific rites (*orgia*) or initiations (*teletai*).[15] It has been suggested that the root for the word mystery is *muein*, to close the eyes or the lips and probably had the connotation of the oath of secrecy by which those initiated into the mysteries were bound (Parrinder 1976, 8; Cupitt 1988, 23–24). More recently, it has been conjectured that the notion that mystery cults involved the revelation of secret doctrines was enhanced by Plato's use of the term *mysterion* to denote secret knowledge (Bowden 2010, 24). This knowledge was thought to be mysterious in at least two senses. First, as I have already intimated, it is not to be readily and indiscriminately disclosed to everyone, and even with respect to other initiates, the modality of acceptable speech to converse about secrets was through passwords (Bowden 2010, 129–130). Second, it is not acquired through normal perception or ratiocination but through an extraordinary revelation, a closing of the eye to the sensible world. Mystical secrets are, to borrow a Ṣūfī expression, known in an immediate and direct fashion that may be considered as a form of tasting (*dhawq*) (Schimmel 1975, 193, 253; Meier 1999, 254, 674) or, as some Kabbalists were wont to say, contemplation by way of sucking (*yeniqah*) (Scholem 1987, 275; Wolfson 2005, 212, 523n145). The goal of the mystical path, therefore, is portrayed as illumination or enlightenment that ensues from the direct encounter with the ultimate source of all being, a gnosis that is not cognitive but intuitive.

The historical manifestations of Jewish mysticism betray both connotations of the term *secret* outlined herein. Indeed, a more appropriate term to characterize this body of lore is *esotericism* (*ḥokhmat ha-nistar*). I do not think it an exaggeration to say that nothing is more important for understanding the mentality of the Jewish mystic than the emphasis on secrecy. In the formative period of classical Judaism, the rabbis viewed select issues as arcane and, therefore, improper for public discussion or exposition. There is the well-known Mishnah in Ḥagigah 2:1 in which three subjects, illicit sexual relations, the account of creation, and the account of the chariot, are signaled out as sections of scripture that cannot be studied openly. Additionally, in several places in rabbinic literature, mention is made of the "mysteries of the Law" (*sitrei torah*), which are transmitted orally from a master to the disciple that has mastered all forms of study and lives an exemplary life of piety. The possession of secret gnosis, which relates to both dogma and ritual, empowers the individual, as he or she alone has the keys to unlock the arcane mysteries of God, the human, and nature. On occasion, these secrets are portrayed as being recorded in books of limited circulation (sometimes the secrets are said to be inscribed on the heavenly tablets) that can be revealed again to the visionary. The topos of celestial or hidden books, whose primary aim is to establish a credible chain of tradition as a source of esoteric knowledge, continued to influence Jewish mysticism through the generations. The receiving of esoteric knowledge from a text was combined with the emphasis on oral reception from a master, the primary connotation of the term *qabbalah*.

Secreting Secrets: Dispelling Mysteries of Torah

The distinctive view of secrecy that emerges from medieval kabbalistic teaching is that the inability to communicate the secret is not due to the unworthiness of a particular recipient, but it is associated with the ineffability of the truth that must be kept secret. This is not to suggest that Kabbalists did not also embrace the idea that secrets must be withheld from those unworthy to receive them. The hermeneutic of esotericism displayed in many kabbalistic sources does indeed attest to this elitist posture, but it certainly goes beyond it as well, inasmuch as the concealment of the secret is dialectically related to its disclosure. Simply put, the utterance of the mystery is possible because of the intrinsic impossibility of its being uttered. Even for the expert who demonstrates unequivocally that he deserves to be a recipient of the esoteric tradition, there is something of the secret that lingers in the very act of transmission.

The secret has an ontological referent that is presumably separate from the phenomenal realm and thus transcends the limits of human understanding and modes of conventional discourse. A classical example of the point is the mystery of the Trinity in Christianity. To apprehend the mystery is not to resolve the fundamental paradox of one God being three. The sacramental experience of the Trinity is predicated on holding the paradox in place. If I logically solve the paradox, my faith in the Trinity is questionable. The mystery as such involves the belief in and practice based on the fundamentally incomprehensible notion of one God being manifest in three hypostases. As a further illustration of the point, let me mention a secret that many scholars have signaled as one of the characteristic doctrines of medieval Kabbalah, the mystery of the androgyne in the Godhead (*sod du-parṣufin*). To receive the secret about the androgynous nature of the divine is not to resolve the problem of the mystery; on the contrary, this gnosis is what opens the mystery to its deeper depths as a mystery, for what is it to say that the oneness of the God of Judaism is predicated on the comprehension of and experiential participation in the sacred union between the King and the Matrona, the bridegroom and the bride? From the one example, we may generalize: In kabbalistic texts, apprehension of the secret does not settle the apparent conflict between the external and the internal meaning, which correspond, respectively, to the poles of revelation and reason, but it forges the paradoxical awareness that the external veil and the internal face are identical because they are different. The secret as such must be exposed if it is to be a secret, but being a secret precludes its being exposed except as a secret that cannot be exposed.

The secret, consequently, presupposes the concurrent projection and withholding on the part of the one in possession of the secret. If I possess a secret and transmit it to no one, the secret has no relevance. By the same token, if I readily divulge the secret without discretion, the secrecy of that secret is rendered ineffectual. What sanctions me as the keeper of a secret is not only that I transmit it to some and not to others, but that in the very transmission I maintain the secret by withdrawing in the act of dissemination. The secret is a secret to the extent that it is concealed in its disclosure, but it may be concealed in its disclosure only if it is disclosed in its concealment.

The investiture of power necessitates that diffusion of the secret invariably demands preserving the secret.[16] The words ascribed to Jesus in response to the query of his disciples regarding the use of parables capture the posture of duplicity implicit in the hermeneutical structure of secrecy: "To you has been given the secret of the kingdom of heaven of God, but for those outside everything is in parables so that they may indeed see but not perceive, and may indeed hear but not understand; lest they should turn again, and be forgiven" (Mark 4:11–12). The disciples represent the elect circle that have no need for parables, because they directly know the mystery of the kingdom, and thus they perceive and understand; by contrast, the masses addressed by Jesus can only see and hear and thus they must receive the truth in the form of parables, which conceal even as they reveal. "With many such parables he spoke the word to them, as they were able to hear it; he did not speak to them without a parable, but privately to his own disciples he explained everything" (Mark 4:33–34). In this passage is a crucial dimension of the Jewish mystical sensibility (Kermode 1979, 2–3). The use of the parabolic idiom is essential to the proliferation of mystical wisdom, because this is a rhetorical form that allows one to stay faithful to the secret nature of the secret by holding back even as one comes forward. Without the parabolic framing, the more one attempts to express the secret, the further one is from it. If the secret were to be fully revealed, there would be no secret to reveal, insofar as there would be no secret to conceal. The logic of esotericism is predicated on the dialectical relation that pertains between the secret that is disclosed and the secret that is withheld. For a secret to be genuinely secretive, it cannot be divulged, but if it is not divulged in any manner, it is hardly a secret.

When this paradox is fully comprehended, the binary distinction between speech and silence is transcended. That is, the esoteric nature of the secret is predicated on the ultimate ineffability to which the secret refers, but the ineffability itself is the measure of what is spoken. That mystics in certain traditions (Judaism, Islam, and Hinduism come to mind) bestow a positive valence on language as the medium by which the enlightened can participate in the creative process (especially through scriptural exegesis) does not mean that they oppose in principle the restraint on speech that is often associated with mystical experience and the strict code of esotericism. On the contrary, the avowal of language as inherently symbolic facilitates the acceptance of that which inevitably exceeds the boundary of language. The phenomenon to which I refer has been expressed by Michel de Certeau in his telling reference to the "split structure" of mystical language by which he intends that the "only way to establish a 'symbolic' expression is to separate two terms that are necessary, but contrary to each other." From that perspective, mystical speech is always a "manifestation of a cut," and consequently the ineffable is "not so much an object of discourse as a marker of the status of language" (de Certeau 1995, 443). In teaching about mysticism, however, the mission is to transform that marker of the ineffable into an object of discourse. On this score, the one who is instructing others about mysticism is obliged to deploy jargon that mimics the mystic. Here an affinity between the poet and mystic can be noted: the attempt to portray what cannot be portrayed, the absence that is more real than presence, surpasses language through language. The symbolic understanding of language promoted by the Kabbalists, the saying of the unsayable, is encapsulated in the rabbinic custom that I mentioned briefly, the vocalization of the tetragrammaton by the epithet Adonai—one word yields both the name that is not pronounced and the name that is pronounced. The audibility of the latter safeguards the inaudibility of the former. The Torah, which esoterically is the name YHWH, is similarly marked by a twofold nature, the overt and the latent, and just as the epithet gives voice to the name by keeping it mute, so the external meaning, the letter of the text, reveals the internal meaning by concealing it (Wolfson 2005, 9–10, 17–21, 25–27; 2007b, 258–294). It is incumbent upon the professor of Jewish mysticism to perform the play of disclosure and concealment and thereby assist the student in envisioning the invisible and uttering the unutterable. To be sure, this is by no means an easy undertaking, but mysticism, as we well know, has never been a commodity that is exchanged straightforwardly.

Notes

1. For a good review of the problem, see Jensen (2001, 238–266).
2. See Scholem (1965, 8–9).
3. Hollenback (1996, 75n1) explicitly credits Scholem for discussing the "essential amorphousness" of mystical experience.

4. Compare my formulation in *Venturing Beyond: Law and Morality in Kabbalistic Mysticism* (Wolfson 2006, 262–263): "The particular path of the Jewish mystical experience leads out of the specificity of this one tradition, but it does so in a manner that compels walking the path repeatedly to find the way out. If one contemplates the possibility of following the path to get beyond the path definitively, then one is off the path and thus will never get beyond the path. To traverse the path of law one must travel the path lawfully. In my estimation, this is a distinctive feature of the mystical phenomenon in the history of religions."

5. See the essays collected in Blumenthal (2006, 51–151) and (2009, v–xxv [English section]). In the same volume, see Freudenthal (2009, 77–97 [Hebrew section]).

6. A number of scholars has worked on this material and here I will mention three essays that serve as good introductions. See Fenton (1998, 127–154), (2003, 201–217, esp. 206–212), and (2004, 95–112).

7. The typological classification has been developed in many of the studies of Moshe Idel of which I will here only mention his first major monograph, *Kabbalah: New Perspectives* (1988).

8. The summary account here is based on Wolfson (2007c, 143–167, esp. 156–158).

9. A more detailed analysis of the interface between the oral and written can be found in Wolfson (2000, pp. 166–224).

10. For references, see Wolfson (2006a, 214n93).

11. This is the thesis of Wolfson (1994).

12. See Wolfson (2007a, 121–122).

13. *Zohar* 3:291b (Idra Zuṭa). See Wolfson (2005, 9).

14. See Biale (1979, 101–102).

15. See Burkert (1995, 79–100) and the recent study by Bowden (2010, 14–15, 23–24).

16. The emphasis on power accords with the approach of Jantzen (1995).

References

Biale, David. 1979. *Gershom Scholem: Kabbalah and Counter-History*. Cambridge, MA: Harvard University Press.

———. 1987. "Gershom Scholem's Ten Unhistorical Aphorisms on Kabbalah." In *Gershom Scholem*, edited by Harold Bloom, 99–123. New York: Chelsea House.

Blumenthal, David R. 2006. *Philosophic Mysticism: Studies in Rational Religion*. Ramat-Gan, Israel: Bar Ilan University Press.

———. 2009. "Maimonides' Philosophic Mysticism." In *Maimonides and Mysticism Presented to Moshe Hallamish on the Occasion of His Retirement*, edited by Avraham Elqayam and Dov Schwartz [*Da'at* 64–66], v–xxv (English section). Ramat-Gan, Israel: Bar Ilan University Press.

Bowden, Hugh. 2010. *Mystery Cults of the Ancient World*. Princeton, NJ: Princeton University Press.

Burkert, Walter. 1995. "Der Geheime Reiz des Verborgenen: Antike Mysterienkulte." In *Secrecy and Concealment: Studies in the History of Mediterranean and Near Eastern Religions*, edited by Hans G. Kippenberg and Guy G. Stroumsa, 79–100. Leiden: E. J. Brill.

Corbin, Henry. 1969. *Creative Imagination in the Ṣūfism of Ibn 'Arabī*, translated by Ralph Manheim. Princeton, NJ: Princeton University Press.

Cupitt, Don. 1988. *Mysticism after Modernity*. Oxford: Blackwell.

de Certeau, Michel. 1995. "History and Mysticism," translated by A. Goldhammer. In *Histories: French Constructions of the Past*, edited by Jacques Revel and Lynn Avery Hunt, 437–487. New York: New Press.

Fenton, Paul B. 1998. "Abraham Maimonides (1187–1237): Founding a Mystical Dynasty." In *Jewish Mystical Leaders and Leadership in the 13th Century*, edited by Moshe Idel and Mortimer Ostow, 127–154. Northvale, NJ: Jason Aronson.

———. 2003. "Judaism and Sufism." In *The Cambridge Companion to Medieval Jewish Philosophy*, edited by Daniel H. Frank and Oliver Leaman, 201–217. Cambridge: Cambridge University Press.

———. 2004. "The Literary Legacy of Maimonides' Descendants." In *Moses Maimonides (1138–1204): His Religious, Scientific, and Philosophical Wirkungsgeschichte in Different Cultural Contexts*, edited by Görge K. Hasselhoff and Otfried Fraisse, 95–112. Würzburg: Ergon Verlag.

Freudenthal, Gideon. 2009. "The Philosophical Mysticism in Maimonides." In *Maimonides and Mysticism Presented to Moshe Hallamish on the Occasion of His Retirement*, edited by Avraham Elqayam and Dov Schwartz, 77–97 (Hebrew section). Ramat-Gan, Israel: Bar Ilan University Press.

Hollenback, Jess Byron. 1996. *Mysticism: Experience, Response, and Empowerment*. University Park: The Pennsylvania State University Press.

Idel, Moshe. 1988. *Kabbalah: New Perspectives*. New Haven: Yale University Press.

———. 2002. *Absorbing Perfections: Kabbalah and Interpretation*, foreword by Harold Bloom. New Haven, CT: Yale University Press.

Jantzen, Grace M. 1995. *Power, Gender and Christian Mysticism*. Cambridge: Cambridge University Press.

Jensen, Jeppe Sinding. 2001. "Universals, General Terms and the Comparative Study of Religion," *Numen* 48: 238–266.

Kermode, Frank. 1979. *The Genesis of Secrecy: On the Interpretation of Narrative*. Cambridge, MA: Harvard University Press.

Meier, Fritz. 1999. *Essays on Islamic Piety and Mysticism*, translated by John O'Kane with editorial assistance of Bernd Radtke. Leiden: Brill.

Parrinder, Geoffrey. 1976. *Mysticism in the World Religions*. New York: Oxford University Press.

Schimmel, Annemarie. 1975. *Mystical Dimensions of Islam*. Chapel Hill: University of North Carolina Press.

Scholem, Gershom. 1956. *Major Trends in Jewish Mysticism*. New York: Schocken.

———. 1965. *On the Kabbalah and Its Symbolism*, translated by Ralph Manheim. New York: Schocken Books.

———. 1972. "The Name of God and the Linguistic Theory of the Kabbala," Pts. 1 and 2, *Diogenes* 79: 59–80; 80: 164–194.

———. 1987. *Origins of the Kabbalah*, edited by R. J. Zwi Werblowsky, translated by Allan Arkush. Princeton, NJ: Princeton University Press.

Tishby, Isaiah. 1989. *The Wisdom of the Zohar*, translated by David Goldstein. Oxford: Oxford University Press.

Wolfson, Elliot R. 1994. *Through a Speculum That Shines: Vision and Imagination in Medieval Jewish Mysticism*. Princeton, NJ: Princeton University Press.

————. 2000. "Beyond the Spoken Word: Oral Tradition and Written Transmission in Medieval Jewish Mysticism." In *Transmitting Jewish Traditions: Orality, Textuality and Cultural Diffusion*, edited by Yaakov Elman and Isaiah Gershoni, 166–224. New Haven, CT: Yale University Press.

————. 2002. "Divine Suffering and the Hermeneutics of Reading: Philosophical Reflections on Lurianic Mythology." In *Suffering Religion*, edited by Robert Gibbs and Elliot R. Wolfson, 101–162. London: Routledge.

————. 2005. *Language, Eros, Being: Kabbalistic Hermeneutics and Poetic Imagination*. New York: Fordham.

———— 2006a. *Alef, Mem, Tau: Kabbalistic Musings on Time, Truth, and Death*. Berkeley: University of California Press.

————. 2006b. *Venturing Beyond: Law and Morality in Kabbalistic Mysticism*. Oxford: Oxford University Press.

————. 2007a. "Imago Templi and the Meeting of the Two Seas: Liturgical Time-Space and the Feminine Imaginary in Zoharic Kabbalah," *RES* 51: 121–122.

————. 2007b. *Luminal Darkness: Imaginal Gleanings from Zoharic Literature*. Oxford: Oneworld.

————. 2007c. "Structure, Innovation, and Diremptive Temporality: The Use of Models to Study Continuity and Discontinuity in Kabbalistic Tradition," *Journal for the Study of Religions and Ideologies* 6: 143–167.

PART II

Negotiating Mysticism

EXPANDING THE MAP

7

Chosen by the Spirits

VISIONARY ECOLOGY AND INDIGENOUS WISDOM

Lee Irwin

Teaching Native American religion and spirituality is a difficult and demanding task; one that requires constant attention to formative issues within Religious Studies and within the interdisciplinary context of Native Studies. These difficulties stem from shallow or artificial representations that mask a long history of brutal political and religious oppression, false characterizations, the denial or underevaluation of native epistemologies and spiritual values, and the constant tendency to rewrite, reinscribe, and reassimilate native beliefs into alien, nonnative constructs of meaning. The need to avoid essentializing attitudes and falsifying "trickster hermeneutics" (Vizenor 1999, 15–18) in native interpretations of religious practices creates a context of tension, uneasy resistance, and often anger and suspicion on the part of native persons toward any (false) claims to represent native religious thinking. As a scholar of native religious history, I am keenly aware of the ambiguity that informs a field of study whose history is overshadowed by 400 years of oppression, denial, and marginalization through aggressive colonialism and government control, followed by an unexpected late-twentieth-century turn toward romanticization, commodification, and a naive fixation on native spirituality unmoored from its usual grounding in place, language, tradition, and required social relationships. An authentic context for teaching native religions requires conscious commitment to bring fully into view, for discussion and debate, the long and painful history of religious denial and constant mis/reinterpretation that has dominated most discussions of native religions (Irwin 2000).

Another challenge in teaching native spirituality is its base in complex oral traditions, visual arts, ritual symbols or actions, and expressive cultural media that are not easily interpreted and which are not accompanied by explanatory texts. Traditional native religious expression is strongly embodied and enacted rather than inscribed or reflexive through written texts. Further, many of the written texts that do exist, often transcribed by nonnatives, are mythopoetic narratives whose dense symbolism and embeddedness in a wide variety of languages are not supported by any history of interpretation of those texts. The semiotics of religious expression are primarily coded in bodily signs, visual images, carved and constructed objects, and communicated in dance, gesture, song, storytelling, and initiatory instructions often not accessible to uninitiated natives (Irwin 1994, 185–236). Advanced and developed teachings within these oral traditions are not commonly shared, printed, or disseminated to others outside of a relatively small circle of those most expert and informed through requisite instruction and successful ritual practices. Thus the participatory nature of native religious knowledge, its enacted practice in ritual, and its oral articulation in small initiative societies, further shrouded by a history of religious oppression, make it difficult to articulate core teachings, particularly in the area of revelatory, visionary experience (Ferrer 2009, 136–138).

In developing a context for discussion of native spiritual and visionary teachings, a larger issue further obscures the pointedness of explicit discussion—how primary is a given tradition, among a particular people, in representing a native spiritual teaching? My own view on this is that the complexity of five hundred highly diverse native nations makes judicious selection a necessity, one based in humility, honest self-appraisal of skills, and familiarity that teaches by example, not by creating an artificial pose of expertise. Pedagogically, this is the initial move, to identify those traditions and communities that best fit the context of the course goals and with which the instructor has a sufficient degree of familiarity that allows for a genuinely comparative approach. This does not mean, however, that the selected communities can be fully represented; there are always and inevitably gaps, lacunas, and insufficiencies in the materials available for study that make it difficult, if not impossible, to give a comprehensive review of a particular tradition. Even though we have over one hundred years of ethnography, the lack of primary language texts, the theoretical bias of ethnographers, and a selectivity that often misses or ignores areas of importance, particularly in religious beliefs and native epistemology, makes it challenging to assemble a coherent and accurate view of any particular community. Although another strategy commonly used is to focus on more thematic materials, themes that may cut across diverse traditions, the rudimentary knowledge required for such thematic views, to avoid false essentializing, still requires some degree of expertise in each tradition solicited for comparison. My own pedagogical strategy has been to develop a specific knowledge of each native community, its beliefs, practices, religious lexicon, historical development and transformations through colonial oppression, before attempting any comparison between native groups. Thematic approaches are often fraught with falsifications based on a lack of distinctive knowledge concerning a particular community's beliefs and practices.

In constructing a practice for teaching Native American visionary traditions, and contextualizing those traditions in terms of nonnative discourses on mysticism, it is important to realize that in the native context, there is no repository of texts or any written, reflexive tradition that addresses the topic of mysticism. At the very least, it is necessary to recontextualize the subject as one related to native epistemologies based in visionary practices, dream knowledge, and revelatory events whose contents are inseparable from distinctive tribal traditions in an overarching history of religious encounter, struggle, and oppression through Christian missionization and government (Bureau of Indian Affairs) repression of religious practices. Following the preceding methodology in locating native religious traditions in explicit communities, I will give three examples to explicate the visionary epistemologies engaged by native practitioners to establish a comparative sense of how mystical thinking and encounter has resulted in paradigmatic views that embrace translingual, culturally specific, and symbolically rich interpretations that might be characterized as mystical. These examples are: the Ojibwa-Saulteaux shaking tent rite, the Lakota vision quest, and in a more pan-Indian sense, the visionary revelations of native prophets. However, I also want to review the problematic application of the concept of *mysticism* to native spirituality and illustrate how that concept can impose limitations, constrictions, and misdirections that lead to a false hierarchical evaluation of native spirituality. Conversely, I also want to show how native traditions can give added value to mystical theory and offer perspectives that are congruent with embodied, lived spirituality fully immanent and actual in creative processes of human innovation (Brown 2007). And I will articulate a pedagogical theory for the presentation of this material in ways I have found highly engaging and emotionally powerful in teaching native religions.

Mysticism and Pedagogical Theory in Native Religions

How relevant is discourse in Religious Studies on mysticism to the actual practice and orientation, to the thought worlds, of Native American practitioners? To what degree can the implicit and overly determined meanings of the term *mysticism* be applied to the rich panoply of native religious traditions? In teaching native spirituality, it is quite possible to do so without a single reference to the term *mysticism* and, in fact, the introduction of the term requires that it be problematized. A sound pedagogy of Native American religion and spirituality requires a historical context; the tendency to present native traditions as though they were ahistorical artifacts, or exotic examples of "long ago and far away" traditions, needs to be countered by a genuine commitment to articulate the oppression and denial of native religions (which made practice and participation in native ceremonies a crime punishable by imprisonment, coupled with denial of necessary annuities goods). In doing this, the instructor needs to have a thorough and coherent view of that history; the goal is to sensitize students to issues of religious freedom, the oppression of native values, the marginalization of those values as "pagan superstition," and the constant imposition of categories and terms that are completely alien to native religious thinking. From the outset, I discuss with students the general denial of the value and significance of native epistemologies in the face of dominant theologies, scientism, and inflated academic theories that claim to reveal the underlying significations of native thinking. When this is accomplished in a thorough manner, students become very sensitive to the use of analytic terms that are clearly nonnative in origin. Thus the introduction of a conceptual frame from nonnative intellectual traditions can and will cause students to question the category and the relevance of its application.

I engage the problematizing of mysticism on three fronts: the historical development of the category, a review of mainstream theoretical debates from which indigenous epistemologies are generally excluded, and the alignment of the category with written texts, as compared to embodied, enacted manifestations. It is perhaps ironic that mystical encounters are usually translingual, yet the scholarly emphasis has privileged the written account often over other types of expression, reflecting the pervasive "linguistic turn" in Anglo-American theory (Ferrer and Sherman 2009, 4–6). This is a turn that does not sit well with native traditions of enacted spirituality. In addressing the historical development of the term *mysticism,* I use an article by Leigh Schmidt (2003) whose careful historical analysis parallels a simultaneous historical criminalization of native religions. In brief, Schmidt identifies the English formative period of the concept with the "mid-18th c. critique of enthusiasm … and the 'deluded votaries' of mysticism" that had no place in the world of Enlightenment rationality (2003, 276–277). Here a keynote is sounded, the identification of the mystical with sectarian delusion and antirational behavior contra rationalized theology and emotional control. This certainly challenges the intense, emotional character of native vision-seeking. Increasingly, the category of mysticism became identified, in Protestant writings, with "inner purity" distinct from all ritual practices. In American writings, by mid-1850s, the concept sheds its partisan, sectarian aspects and became universalized as "higher spirituality" liberated from historical contingency, "rarefied and stripped of rituals, material symbols, sacramental hosts, and bleeding bodies" (Schmidt 2003, 287). All of which challenges native spiritual practices as enacted, embodied interpretations of the visionary encounter. William James (1902) furthered this process of decontextualizing *mysticism,* making it a psychological phenomena of individual subjects removed from any particular practices and linked to written accounts that take precedence over the more subtle, translingual affects of the encounter. Finally, this ahistorical, universalized, and essential concept of mysticism became a liberal construct meant to counter the increasing dogmatism of scientific reductionism that would deny any real significance to the idea of mysticism (Schmidt 2003, 290–291).

At the very time that mysticism was being progressively disidentified from social context and universalized as a transcendent core within world traditions or psychologized as the private experiential domain for rare and exceptional individuals, Native American religions were under attack as pagan (lacking transcendence), barbarous (rituals with bleeding bodies), irrational (lacking written sacred texts), and demonic (worshipping lower, dangerous spirits). The juxtaposition here signifies a widespread, nonnative view that whatever was mystical was not inherent to native religious traditions and that the particularity of native traditions demonstrated a lack of the supposed universal, transcendent core. And, in the name of "civilization," native traditions should be repressed, and their practitioners punished for their supposed religious ignorance and instructed by appropriate missionaries of the Christian tradition in order to reveal to them authentic sources of transcendence and salvation. The conceptual distancing of the mystical from the culturally specific and the increasing focus on highly select written texts within the "great traditions" in no way served to enhance appreciation for native religions in all their specificity, ritual expression, and embodied symbolism.

A second, and more current, stage of development within theories of mysticism, post-mid-twentieth century, has also problematized mysticism in the study of native religions. I highlight three dominant perspectives of mysticism: "pure consciousness" (Forman 1990), strictly "contextual" (Katz 1978), and the intermediary position of "convergence" (Idel and McGinn 1989) at least among Western Semitic mystical traditions, as all deconstructive for native religions (Short 1995; Brainard 1996). The contextual position might seem to favor native traditions but at the expense of undermining the epistemological priorities of native visionaries and truncating the deep ontological claims made by them. As I demonstrated some years ago, native visionaries and mystic dreamers are primary agents for innovation and creative change within their respective traditions, particularly among traditions institutionalizing forms of vision seeking, as well as among native communities that recognize wholly new, revelatory teachings stemming from visionary or "prophetic" knowledge (Irwin 1994, 164). Contextual theories of mysticism offer no adequate account for the creative, revelatory, innovative aspects of mystical visions; further, by reducing the account to immediate, local context, as a function of sociocultural conditioning, the theory undermines native ontological claims that are translingual and reflect a visionary epistemology in which a transcultural spiritual agent interacts with the visionary to empower him or her as a mediator of cultural development and change. Because contextual theory denies any "universal referent" and subsumes all such accounts as linguist artifacts, nominal expressions encoding sociocultural values and forms, the theory builds a dualistic divide between cultural context and the ontological depths affirmed by native visionaries (Short 1995, 659; Brainard 1996, 361–362).

The problematic issue of the "pure consciousness" theory, that is, a capacity to forget, surpass, and outreach any cultural or social contextual conditions in the mystical event, an ability to reach an "unmediated" ground that is then assumed to be common and universal across religious traditions disempowers any tradition that does not characterize its visionary epistemology in the limited transcendentalism of the "pure event." This form of hierarchical phenomenology stems from a lexical concern to describe, delimit, and hypostasize through verbal description a "core experience," thereby establishing an authoritative validity by which religious experience can be valued as mystical or not. Such a strategy, though particularly applicable to written reflexive, meditative, and philosophical traditions and to texts that encode a transcendental core, does not support an epistemic process by which the encoding of visionary experience is signified through aesthetic, symbolic, gestural, and visual forms. A lack of transcendental text does not mean a lack of transcendental perception; however, it may mean that what is sought in the mystic event is in fact not a transcendent context or "pure consciousness" but rather a reification of mystical knowledge in the form of visual, communal, enacted expressions. Finally, the limitations of the convergence theory is its obvious commitment to the core Semitic religions of Judaism, Christianity, and Islam, none of whose proponents recognize any particular value in native religions as contributing to the theory, and most of which support a clear dependence on comparative textual-theological analysis, thus highlighting linguistic parallels, a methodology which is not applicable to native religions.

A recent nominal attempt to mediate these diverse theoretical tensions by offering such defining characteristics of mystical experience as "nonordinariness" and "profundity" is intriguing but problematic insofar as *nonordinary* means unexplainable and more particularly not naturalistic (Brainard 1996, 372–377). Native visionaries do not seek explanations but enactments, and those enactments are utterly integral to a naturalistic, native account of the world in which mystical agencies are described in terms of kinship and familial relations. If *profound* is taken to reference "ultimate meaning," then this too is problematic when the goals of visionary encounter are directed toward the affirmation and appointment of recognized social and religious roles. Finding one's place through visionary guidance seems something less than ultimate and something more than merely conventional. In this sense, native visionary practices might be described as creatively mediating socioreligious life through dramatic visionary encounters that result in holistic expressive forms that are aesthetic, somatic, symbolic, and communally interactive but not necessarily written or phenomenologically descriptive.

Pedagogical Constructions and Practices

Having cleared the ground methodologically, I then proceed to develop a native-centered description of select examples of visionary encounter, each contextualized in a specific native community and historically related to ongoing tactics of enculturation by Anglo-American agencies of church and state. *lecture*
The first example is certainly one of the oldest, known as the "Shaking-Tent" rite and more modernly among the Lakota as the Yuwipi, "tie them up" ceremony. An excellent, though dated, historical ethnography of the rite in the northern plains by Father John Cooper introduces the ritual, offers a comparative analysis, and gives significant detail of the rite among the Gros Ventre (A'aninin, White Clay people). Problematically, this article reflects a widespread view of native peoples as "primitive" and "mythic"—issues that must be addressed in reviewing the material (Cooper 1944). Dating from roughly the same period is another classic article that locates the rite in a particular native community, the Canadian-American Saulteaux (Ojibwe/Anishinaabe). This article is based on careful firsthand observation and gives a remarkably unbiased account of the rite as witnessed by the author (Hallowell 1942). Using selections from this article, it is possible to reconstruct a mid-twentieth century example of the rite, demonstrably much older, that has clear mythopoetic and mystical contents. This is a possession rite in which an individual chosen by the spirits (*pawaganak*) through dreams and visions becomes a medium for spiritual communication with "more than human persons" (Hallowell's famous description) or with autonomous spiritual agencies that are called forth through the rite by the visionary as mediator to answer communal needs, to heal, and confirm the reality of those agencies. The epistemology is constructed in mythopoetic narratives in which the visionary speaks in the voices of the various spirits and the small but sturdy tent holding the visionary shakes, even though he is tied up with ropes, demonstrating the presence of various spiritual agents.

This material engages the question of mysticism from the ground up in a native context in which the performative, storied, enacted ritual demonstrates an opening to ontological depths, into a spirit-laden world, through the communicative efficacy of the visionary (*tcisaki*), who is believed to fully embody the invisible agencies of that world. Here the "core experience" is constructed as an interactive relation between the two communities, the native peoples and the spirits, mediated through specific verbal arts that indicate authentic communication. The visionary speaks in the unique voice of each spirit, some to comical effect, as an illustration of an expansive kinship that harmonizes the visible and invisible domains. This is not mysticism in the service of individual transformation, even though the visionary is indeed transformed, but in service to the community, to validating the intentional structures of dreaming by which individuals in the community acquire personal connections with piritual agencies. The shaking tent visionary is a vivid, dynamic rit-in-action, of spirit breaking out of the confines of a narrow in order to demonstrate the vitality of an interactive, com- ...work of shared intelligences that, in native thinking, are not reducible to purely subjective states. The mystical content is thoroughly socialized at the same time that it functions to demonstrate an expansive cosmology of transphysical relations, in service to human communal health, well-being, and proper order (*pimadaziwin*). This is mysticism as the ritualization of "right relations" linked to both communal well-being and to an individual process of empowerment by agencies that make those relations exceptional and creatively dynamic. As a complement to this material, I have students look at the art and writing of Noval Morriseau, a brilliant Ojibwa painter and artist, whose work captures the spiritual quality of the mystical in vivid imagery and x-ray visions of the interior life.

Moving to a more contemporary account, specifically among the Lakota, I use materials by Gary Holy Bull (Ampohoksila), a contemporary Lakota practitioner of the Yuwipi rite from the Cheyenne River reservation (Keeney 1999). This material also includes a CD with songs that link to his personal experiences and gives an excellent illustration of the role of music, song, and prayer in the expression of native spiritual teachings. Three of the tracks on the CD are personal narratives that tell the story of his transformation into a Yuwipi healer and *pejuta wicasa*, or "medicine man" who has also led the "Sun Dance" (*wi wanyang wacipi*) and other ceremonies for over twenty years (Keeney 1999, 60). By listening to selections from the CD, students gain a better sense of oral culture and are exposed to the rhythm and pace of native speaking, so very different from ordinary American English. The narrative, mirrored in the text but delivered Lakota style, demonstrates the struggle and fear that Holy Bull faced in trying to accommodate the intrusion of voices, spirit talk, and visions into his life from a young age.

Holy Bull talks about his training under a highly respected Lakota healer, Two Sticks (and Frank Fools Crow), and how he was tied up in a blanket and placed on a high butte for four days and nights to bring him into visionary relations with the grandfather spirits of the Yuwipi lodge. He also narrates his experiences in the purification lodge (*ini kagapi*), his obligations in being a keeper of a sacred bundle, and his experiences in "crying for a vision" (*hanble-lachia*) that resulted in his vision of a coyote spirit, in animal and human form, who taught him the proper songs for the Sun Dance (Keeney 1999, 56–59; on sacred language, Brown 2001). Holy Bull makes an important distinction in separating the *luwapi* "spirit calling" rite by song and prayer from the more intense Yuwipi rite in which he is tied up, interacts in trance, and ends the ceremony untied, illustrating the presence of active spiritual agencies. He also narrates miraculous healing power of the Yuwipi, including his wife's cure from cancer. He notes how "spirit often presents itself as a light, be it bluish or white sparks or a mellow glow of warm light" (Keeney 1999, 68–73). These narratives capture very brief glimpses of powerful transformative events and spiritual encounters embedded in an enactive paradigm whose purpose is not personal revelation, but service to the community, attaining multiagent healing capacities, and gaining a wisdom based in spirit communion that emphasizes kindness, honesty, sharing, and courage (Keeney 1999, 95; Powers 1982; Lewis 1992, 77–85).

This text also makes the transition from the Yuwipi rite to the vision seeking rite and links the old shaking tent practice with other forms of enacted spirituality, epitomized by the vision quest *(hanblelachia)*. The classic text for this rite is the visionary experience of the famous Oglala holy man Black Elk *(Hehaka Sapa)* at the age of twelve, while very sick, as recorded by John Neihardt in the 1930s at Pine Ridge reservation; the stenographic account made by Neihardt's daughter was later published by Ray DeMallie and offers the most accurate text for the vision (DeMallie 1984, 114–142; also Neihardt 1932, 20–47). In this extensive narrative, one of the most complete Lakota vision narratives recorded, students are introduced to the full scope of visionary, mythopoetic language as a vivid account of an "out of body" flight into the sky, and meetings with the spirits in the form of Lakota elders gathered in the celestial rainbow tipi. The four grandfathers, each representing a power of the four directions, plus Skan, the great power above, integrate him into the full cosmology of Lakota thought as the Sixth Grandfather, the power of earth. He is given the authority to hold the Horse Dance as each grandfather gifts him with religious symbols, in the presence of four distinctive sets of colored horses, one set from each direction. He then walks the black road of sorrow and suffering and the "good red road" of healing and reconciliation, seeing along each the struggles he must face and the actions he must take for the spiritual preservation of the Lakota nation. After witnessing much suffering, the vision culminates is a world renewal where the four-rayed herb "shines its light everywhere" and he experiences his breath as lightning. On waking, Black Elk was healed of his sickness and imbued with the heavy responsibilities of saving his nation from the forthcoming loss of culture, land, and religion (for unpacking this vision, see Holler 2000; also DeMallie 1987).

This vision offers a context for exploring the mythopoetic aspects of native mystical language; the encoding of mystical visions in vivid imagery of action; the use of sacred objects, the importance of song, prayer, and gesture; and the whole as a template for ritual action directed toward the good of the community. Further, the vision reflects the individual and unique aspects of Black Elk as a creative vision-dreamer whose visionary knowledge integrated traditional Lakota symbols and actions with innovative elements, including some elements taken from Christianity. Black Elk does not seek this vision, it comes to him in a time of crisis, both for himself and for his people; he is "chosen by the spirits" in a way similar to the call that came to Gary Holy Bull, reflecting an epistemology in which the gifted individual is identified by archetypal encounters through voices, visions, and signs (Wise 2000). The mystical elements of this encounter are not simply a reflection of cultural context (innovation, Christian influences, historical crisis are present) or pure consciousness (pervasive light and the lightning-breath reflect deep penetration and expanse), but a mediated, participatory event in which the ontological depths of native perception are shaped into actions, objects, and goals meant to serve the needs of the community. The participatory aspect is the way in which visionary encounters introduce the visionary into the dense revelatory world of a vaster web of spiritual agencies regarded as imbued with unique powers and abilities beyond the ordinary human capacity and given to the visionary as gifts and responsibilities. The knowledge is revelatory for the individual and healing for the community; the mysticism is cocreative, socially diffuse, and supports a visionary epistemology that marks the individual as an agent of transformation and healing change.

The vision reflects a creative tension, an unambiguous call for spiritual action and connection with spiritual agency transmitted as a vision of what might be or become for a boy of twelve. The atemporal aspect, the call for action and role-taking beyond the present, acts to instigate an intentional development, to invoke a call for successful action as a spiritually empowered individual whose efficacy will require actual manifestation of that potential. Black Elk's first healing, a successful healing of a young boy, occurred years later only after he had first enacted his great vision with the whole village participating (in a Horse Dance) and then undertaken a successful vision quest rite that confirmed and supplemented the great vision. The embodiment of the vision requires multiple stages of instruction, ritual, and disciplined commitment to fully bring forth the intentions of the original vision encounter. The enactive paradigm is not simply based in a sudden and complete mystical knowledge, but requires years of preparation, instruction, and purification to fully realize the potential gifts revealed. Visionary knowledge must be brought into alignment with communal needs and adapted according to the individual capacities, current circumstances, existing performative genres, and the directions given by the sacred powers. This maturation process is crucial to the mystical paradigm and is vividly evident in native visionary practices; the pragmatic test of the vision is a demonstration by the visionary that validates the vision for the community.

At this point, I then introduce a third example of a mystical type, the "prophet" as a founder of a native religious movement, one that usually combines traditional and nonnative elements. The history of native prophecy is fully embedded in visionary epistemology such that every founding figure (most are men) will reference his visions as an authenticating source for the new teachings. The history of these movements span a time period from the pre-Columbian to the present, and the narratives are dense with visionary en-

form and image. In terms of mysticism, the goals of the course involve expos-
ing students to cultural alterity where a mystical encounter is confirmed in
relationship to indigenous traditions worldwide, among peoples of other cultures, whose embodied mystical encounters and enactive practices resonate
with Native American traditions. For example, a colleague and I brought an
Inuit Kalaallit Elder and spiritual teacher, Angaangaq Angakkorsuaq, from
Greenland to classes to give a talk, drum, tell stories, and narrate an account of
his mystical development. Students quickly picked up the similarities with
Native American traditions and also recognized how his teachings reflected
influences from other indigenous cultures, as well as from more contemporary
nonnative thinking comparable and syncretic with his own visionary knowledge. This interaction allowed students to gain a comparative perspective that
affirmed the diversity of indigenous traditions, their creative development,
and helped them to identify the intersecting mystical elements of an enactive,
participatory spirituality.

I never teach course material apart from also teaching some historical account of native loss of religion, land, language, and culture as many native
people still live under the shadow of oppression, poverty, alcoholism, and loss
of identity. Native religious traditions have tended to be primary sources of
reaffirmation and spiritual strength for the reconstruction of native identities
through ritual participation, renewed interest in explicit communal religious
practices, and a reverence for native wisdom and spirit-guided knowledge.
Such knowledge has a mystical base as many rituals are constructed to foster
deep participatory encounters in those who meet the strict requirements of
the rite. The transmission of teachings and practices do not involve adoration
for the teacher (or a text) but a deep commitment to fully attend to the web of
relations that extend into the invisible world and there constitute spiritual
agencies meant to empower the participants. Confirming the spiritual and
mystical validity of the rite requires an appreciation of its potential to induce
transformation, inducted from deep ontological sources, as those most congruent with visionary knowledge. Students learn that this knowledge requires
discipline, commitment, training, and reverent actions that meet the highest
standards of spirituality as in any other religious tradition.

Reflections on native religious experience often raise another linguistic
problem, the relationship between the semantic domains of mysticism and
shamanism. In teaching native religions, I rarely use the terms *shaman* or *shamanism* (or *mystic*) as they, like *mysticism*, carry a history of imprudent connotations that mask or erase the many careful distinctions made by native
peoples linguistically in naming experts and various practitioners of native
religions. Every native religious tradition I have studied has, in the native language of that people, multiple descriptive terms based on the training, experience, and level of skill of a practitioner that indicate the unique knowledge or
area of expertise of the individual. Subsequently, within actual communities,

there is rarely a generic term that functions to categorize all practitioners under a single designation and when such a term ("medicine person") is used, it tends to be directed to nonmembers of the community or "outsiders" who do not know or comprehend a native language. Expertise in religious function, in terms of deeply respected knowledge, does not depend on a particular species of mysticism as much as it does on pragmatic, demonstrated results that illustrate a successful relationship to the spirit world. Members of native communities make careful linguistic distinctions about an individual's ability and skill without invoking specific metaphysical criteria to validate that ability. Generally, *shamanism* is an alien term imported into the native context by nonnatives who use the term as a substitute for a lack of a more precise knowledge of actual native languages (Irwin 2003). Like *mysticism,* the term tends to decontextualize the more nuanced and distinctive linguistic typologies that designate explicit areas of expertise in an embodied, enacted context of communal spiritual practices.

As for metagoals, I am reminded of Thomas Moore's statement that real education is education of the soul, not just the mind, and that "soul-oriented teachers need wisdom rather than information and a strong imagination" (Moore 2005, 15). This is because the language of soul development requires *eros,* a passionate connection to needs and desires that animate a life of curiosity, inquiry, and possible transformation. In teaching about religions, I want students to feel and sense as well as to think, I want them to develop empathy and intensity, to be moved soulfully by the worlds, thoughts, passions, aspirations, and suffering of others (Sloan 2005, 28). I do not teach intellectual detachment, but passionate interest and critical evaluation, feeling sensitivity and clarity of thought, multisensory engagement, and an accurate, explicit understanding for personal relevance and wisdom (Hart 2001). I bring in physical objects used in religious ceremony and show images of crafts, art, and the contemporary lived world of native peoples for heightened aesthetic and visual appreciation. I play music to sensitize students to diverse emotional perceptions and show video clips of real people speaking, singing, or praying to heighten the sense of person-to-person contact. I draw visual representations of cosmology and socioreligious symbolism on the board, using a wide range of natural and symbolic images that I can deconstruct and reconstruct as the discussion flows along. I engage students in continual discussion, encouraging them to bring forward their concerns, and I treat them as equals, not as subordinates. I willingly admit to not knowing or lack of certainty and to complete ignorance when questions arise that challenge or supersede my own understanding. I see teaching as partnership, relational and interactive, not dictatorial. I stand *with* my students, not over them, in cocreative relation (Chow et al. 2003).

Transformative, holistic education must engage the heart as well as the mind, touch feelings and evoke outrage at injustice and abuse, not simply make a

pretense of neutrality or embrace an artful methodology of detac
as though human beings were merely rational, merely reflective. W
passionate beings. We need to engage the issues of education pass
authentically, and we need to teach our students that emotional er~~~~~~ ~~
the very source of intentional development. What we love, what moves us, and
what influences and motivates us can come through education that then results
in action, in carrying the learning experience into the world of daily life with
invigorating commitment. Students have contacted me years later, noting how
the Native American course, its contents and learning outcomes, have stayed
with them, motivated them, influenced them. The key here is engagement, a
judicious mix of sobriety, humor, caring, and a constant process of refining and
developing what one knows and how to share and communicate that learning
with inspiration. These goals go beyond the course content, and yet, are crucial
to the delivery of any course; they reflect the very heart of the educational process: to motivate students to apply what they learn because it touches them
deeply and contributes to their development. The course contents are stepping
stones, the stable points where knowledge and learning provide genuine insight
and value. On the farther postgraduate shore, one hopes that such learning will
be applied because we, as teachers, modeled genuine caring in the context of
sharing our knowledge. In this sense, mysticism becomes simply one strand in
the greater project of full human development. The weaving of that strand into
the lives of real persons requires that we treat the subject with respect and humility, not imposing a particular ideology or overdetermined interpretation of
what constitutes the "mystical" but instead, cultivate a willingness to engage in
dialogue with cultural perspectives that often challenge our own views. Mysticism, in this sense, is a context for human exploration and discovery, an opening into participatory knowing that is partnered, communal, and creatively rich
with individual and shared discovery.

References

Brainard, Samuel F. 1996. "Defining 'Mystical Experience,'" *Journal of the American Academy of Religion* 64: 359–393.

Brown, Joseph Epps. 2001. "Silence, the Word, and the Sacred: Evoking the Sacred through
Language and Song." In *Teaching Spirits: Understanding Native American Religious
Traditions*, ed. Emily Cousins, 41–59. New York: Oxford University Press.

———. 2007. "The Question of Mysticism." In *The Spiritual Legacy of the American Indian,
With Letters While Living with Black Elk,* 81–86. Indiana: World Wisdom.

Cave, Alfred. 2006. *Prophets of the Great Spirit: Native American Revitalization Movements
in Eastern North America.* Lincoln: University of Nebraska Press.

Chow, Esther Ngan-Ling, Chadwick Fleck, Guang-Hua Fan, Joshua Joseph, and Deanna
M. Lyter. 2003. "Exploring Critical Feminist Pedagogy: Infusing Dialogue, Participation,
and Experience in Teaching and Learning." *Teaching Sociology* 31: 259–275.

Cooper, John M. 1944. "The Shaking Tent Rite among the Plains and Forest Algonquians," *Primitive Man* 17: 60–84.

DeMallie, Raymond J. 1984. *The Sixth Grandfather: Black Elk's Teachings Given to John G. Nihardt*. Lincoln: University of Nebraska Press.

———. 1987. "Lakota Belief and Ritual in the Nineteenth Century." In *Sioux Indian Religion*, edited by Raymond J. DeMallie and Douglas R. Parks, 25–44. Norman: University of Oklahoma.

Dowds, Gregory Evans. 1993. *A Spirited Resistance: The North American Indian Struggle for Unity, 1745–1815*. Baltimore, MD: The Johns Hopkins University Press.

Fenton, William N., ed. 1975. *Parker on the Iroquois*. Syracuse, NY: Syracuse University Press.

Ferrer, Jorge, and Jake Sherman, eds. 2009. *The Participatory Turn: Spirituality, Mysticism, and Religious Studies*. Albany: State University of New York Press.

Ferrer, Jorge. 2009. "Spiritual Knowing as Participatory Enaction: An Answer to the Question of Religious Pluralism." In *The Participatory Turn: Spirituality, Mysticism, and Religious Studies*, edited by Jorge N. Ferrer and Jacob H. Sherman, 135–169. Albany: State University of New York Press.

Forman, Robert K., ed. 1990. *The Problem of Pure Consciousness*. New York: Oxford University Press.

Hart, Tobin. 2001. "Teaching for Wisdom," *Encounter: Education for Meaning and Social Justice* 14: 3–16.

Hallowell, A. Irving. 1942. *The Role of Conjuring in Saulteaux Society*. Publications of the Philadelphia Anthropological Society 2. Philadelphia: Philadelphia Anthropological Society.

Holler, Clyde, ed. 2000. *The Black Elk Reader*. Syracuse, NY: Syracuse University Press.

Idel, Moshe, and Bernard McGinn, eds. 1989. *Mystical Union and Monotheistic Faiths: An Ecumenical Dialogue*. New York: Macmillan Press.

Irwin, Lee. 1994. *The Dream Seekers: Native American Visionary Traditions of the Great Plains*. Norman: University of Oklahoma.

———. 2000. "Freedom, Law, and Prophecy: A Brief History of Native American Religious Resistance." In *Native American Spirituality: A Critical Reader*, edited by Lee Irwin, 295–310. Lincoln: University of Nebraska Press.

———. 2003. "Shamanism." *Encyclopedia of Religion and American Cultures,* edited by Gary Laderman and Luis León, 3: 223–226. Santa Barbara: ABC-CLIO Publishers.

———. 2008. *Coming Down from Above: Prophecy, Renewal and Resistance in Native American Religions*. Norman: University of Oklahoma Press.

James, William. 1902. *The Varieties of Religious Experience: A Study in Human Nature*. New York: Longmans, Green, and Company.

Katz, Steven T., ed. 1978. *Mysticism and Philosophical Analysis*. New York: Oxford University Press.

Keeney, Bradford, ed. 1999. *Lakota Yuwipi Man: Gary Holy Bull*. Philadelphia: Ringing Rocks Foundation .

Lewis, Thomas H. 1992. *The Medicine Men: Oglala Sioux Ceremony and Healing*. Lincoln: University of Nebraska.

Mooney, James. (1896) 1990. *The Ghost-Dance Religion and the Sioux Outbreak of 1890*. Reprint, Lincoln: University of Nebraska Press.

Moore, Thomas. 2005. "Educating the Soul." In *Holistic Learning and Spirituality in Education*, edited by John P. Miller, Selia Karsten, Diana Denton, Deborah Orr, and Isabella Colalillo Kates 9–16. Albany: State University of New York Press.

Neihardt, John G. 1932. *Black Elk Speaks*. Lincoln: University of Nebraska Press.

Powers, William. 1982. *Yuwipi: Vision and Experience in Oglala Ritual*. Lincoln: University of Nebraska Press.

Schmidt, Leigh Eric. 2003. "The Making of Modern 'Mysticism.'" *Journal of the American Academy of Religion* 71: 273–302.

Short, Larry. 1995. "Mysticism, Mediation, and the Non-Linguistic." *Journal of the American Academy of Religion* 63: 659–675.

Sloan, Douglas. 2005. "Education and the Modern Assault on Being Human: Nurturing Body, Soul, and Spirit." In *Holistic Learning and Spirituality in Education*, edited by John P. Miller, Selia Karsten, Diana Denton, Deborah Orr, and Isabella Colalillo Kates, 27–35. Albany: State University of New York Press.

Vizenor, Gerald. 1999. *Manifest Manners: Postindian Warriors of Survivance*. Lebanon, NH: University Press of New England.

Wise, R. Todd. 2000. "The Great Vision of Black Elk as Literary Ritual." In *The Black Elk Reader*, edited by Clyde Holler, 241–261. Albany: Syracuse University Press.

{ 8 }

Teaching African American Mysticism
Joy R. Bostic

> It is the insistence of mysticism...that there is within reach of every
> [person] not only a defense against the Grand Invasion but also the
> energy for transforming it into community.
>
> —THURMAN (1961, 4)

This quote speaks directly to the tension that lies at the core of African American mysticism—the tension between interior and exterior life. This tension exists within the boundaries of two types of negotiations. The first type involves the negotiation that individuals and communities plagued by the violence and violation of hegemonic power must make to self-define in the face of externally imposed circumscriptions. The second relates to the ways in which the struggle to *be* in light of this self-definition effectively and authentically translates into concrete, embodied action in community. Both of these negotiations turn on access to legitimated forms of knowledge.

In this essay, I discuss the significance of epistemology and its relationship to embodied action in African American mysticism and how to structure a course inclusive of both elements. I start with the importance of theories and definitions as well as identify religious world views that inform African American mysticism. Next, I discuss the historical problem of demonization that affects student views of African American religious traditions and practices. Throughout the chapter, I propose pedagogical strategies and tools that include student exercises and the use of narrative, film, art, music, and dance to help students enter into and more deeply engage African American mystical traditions.

Theories and Definitions

Epistemological theories that speak to how we know what we know are critical theories to interrogate when teaching about mysticism from the perspectives of marginalized groups. It is our epistemological bearings that help us ˎ mine what we deem to be "legitimate" mystical experience. Thus, in a co African American mysticism, I would begin with an exploration of how cism has been historically defined, both specifically in African America.. culture and, more generally, in Western Christian traditions. With respect to the latter, it is important to discuss the ways in which the issues of power, race, and gender have factored into these definitions. Against this backdrop, the course I describe gives special attention to African American mystical and religious worldviews, as well as the epistemological frameworks they inform. These frameworks provide a lens through which we can better understand the complexity of African American mystical traditions.

Knowledge and how we know what we know are central concerns in the study of mysticism. Whenever I teach a course in religious studies, I spend the first one or two weeks establishing the methodological framework for the course and defining primary terms. Though I teach mostly undergraduate students, I find that at any level it is important to begin by generating student definitions. Therefore, in a course on mysticism I might ask, "When I say the words *mystical* or *mysticism* what comes to mind?" or "How would you define the terms *mystical* or *mysticism*?" I write student answers on the board and ask a student to volunteer to take notes, type up our list, and send it to me electronically. Later I disseminate copies to everyone in the class. In this way, the class has a record of our collective starting point. After we compile the list of definitions, I follow up by asking students to identify what sources have informed their opinions. Therefore, students become self-reflective and are more aware of the basis for their own definitions. As a teacher, these exercises give me an idea of where my students are and what assumptions they hold.

In the past, student responses have ranged from "union with God" to "weird voodoo stuff." These answers usually indicate definitions that are influenced by particular Western constructions of religious experience. Oftentimes these constructions are also shaped by specific notions of race and gender. Whatever their responses, this process provides me with an understanding of how I should map out the rest of the course in a way that takes seriously the knowledge that students bring to the course, as well as assumptions that need to be unpacked. This kind of informed mapping enables me as a teacher to structure the course so that students gain a deeper knowledge of the subject matter and expand narrow assumptions into broader perspectives about African American mysticism. At certain points during the semester, we review our lists of definitions to see how our perspectives have changed.[1]

After these initial exercises, I present material on the contextual factors that have influenced the development of African American mysticism. I emphasize how African American mysticism has developed and flourished within culturally pluralistic milieus. As a result of European colonialism and the modern slave trade, Africans arrived on the shores of the Americas as early as the sixteenth century from diverse geographical areas on the African continent. Consequently, both enslaved and free blacks came from diverse ethnic groups with diverse languages and religious expression. Therefore, cross-fertilization has necessarily occurred between European and African continental cultures, as well as among racial and diverse ethnic groups in North America, in ways that have resulted in regional and cross-continental transmissions. European Western religious thought and practices have necessarily influenced and been influenced by African American religious worldviews and practices in individual and collective ways. Thus, the language and constructs of how African Americans describe and interpret mysticism have both informed and been informed by the various cultural strains that have converged in North America over the course of the last five centuries.

With the starting point anchored in the contextual landscape of African American culture, I then present a survey of the works of such scholars and theologians as Howard Thurman, Alton Pollard, and Barbara Holmes and discuss how each of them defines mysticism with these cultural milieus in mind. These religionists fundamentally view mysticism and mystical experience as an intimate encounter with the sacred. How the sacred is identified may vary. For Thurman, intimate encounter with a transcendent God grows out of practices of "pause and rest" (1999, 29). He situates the object of mystical experience within a monotheistic notion of a transcendent deity. Nevertheless Thurman does not merely relegate mysticism and mystical experience to the realm of the Other or the transcendent. Thurman views mysticism as a part of a continuum. Even though the object of mystical encounter may be a transcendent Other, an authentic mystical encounter is manifested in the concrete world. Human beings encounter a God who relates to them personally and intimately. An individual who encounters God in mystical experience is so inwardly transformed that she or he is compelled to respond to this encounter by way of embodied action based upon a vision of "the good" revealed in said experience (Thurman 1939, 27–29). Embodied action is then translated into social change and transformation by way of the subject's work in the world to make the vision a reality. Thus, Thurman takes seriously and values highly the human dimensions of life and how individual mystical experience affects living communities.

Pollard, who is trained as a sociologist of religion and a Thurman scholar, also grounds his definition of mysticism within this human dimension. For Pollard, mystical experience involves "intimate discourse and practices that speak to what it means to be human in relationship to the transcendent and the mundane" (2009, 4). Pollard views mysticism not as a way of escaping the world but as a way of holding the tension between transcendent and mundane realities. For him, mystical experience marks the human as well as the transcendent dimension as sacred space.

In her book *Joy Unspeakable*, Holmes (2004) discusses the role of contemplation in mystical life on both an individual and communal level. She also sees African American approaches as taking seriously both the transcendent and the mundane. Holmes identifies African American contemplative practices as negotiations of intimate space in which the "Spirit and flesh can wrestle and embrace" (2004, 25). This quote presents the quintessential struggle between what Thurman identifies as the needs of the "familiar altar" of the individual and the physical, social, economic, and political concerns of human community (Pollard 1992, 56). In this way, the mystical impulse within African American religious traditions speaks to the need for the individual spirit to "pause and rest" in intimate embrace with the divine and, thereby, shield itself from the "Grand Invasion" of external impositions. At the same time, African American mysticism is understood as a source of knowledge, authority, and empowerment for prophetic and healing social engagement.

Multivocality and Meaning-Making

Authority, legitimacy, and knowledge are all bound up in claims of intimacy with what we might think of in traditional Western terms as an ultimate source. For African American scholars, theologians, and practitioners, intimate communication with the divine is certainly at the core of African American mystical experience. In fact, Thurman contends that one can only truly know God and be known by God by way of personal encounter. Whereas Thurman acknowledges that there is a universal aspect to God as Ultimate Being, God relates to human beings in personal and intimate ways. It is within the interpenetrating dance of the human and the divine that true knowledge is realized. Again, it is important to note here that Thurman presents his views within a Western monotheistic framework.

One should not assume, however, that the object of African American mystical encounter is limited to a traditional Western monotheism. Rather, one should also understand any notion of the divine within the multivocal context of the African diaspora. In his work on African mysticism, Kofi Opuku (1995) acknowledges that there is a "vital unity" in mystical experience. He also assumes, however, that the divine is expressed in multiple forms, for example, ultimate reality, ancestors, spirit or spirits, deities, nature spirits (Opuku 1995, 326). This sense of multiplicity is also central to an African American theological worldview. It is within this theological worldview that African Americans claim intimacy with diverse objects of mystical experience. Here I use David L. Weaver-Zercher's (2004, 6) notion of theology as the way persons understand and relate to sacred power. This definition allows for a more inclusive discourse on how diverse individuals and groups think and talk about religious experience.[2] It also overcomes the limitations of a traditional Western Christian equation of sacred power with a sole, often masculine, God. Within the pluralistic context of lived religion, African American mysticism can assume a sacred-social world replete with multiple inhabitants and multiple forces of power that make up a coherent, whole reality. This sacred-social world is created and recreated by shifting concepts of time in which the past, present, and future converge and the adaptation of materials, symbols, and texts in service of whole community—the living, the dead, and the yet-to-be born.

To help students grasp this concept of multivocality with respect to sacred power, I include the use of visual arts in the classroom to help students understand general religious theory and methodology. The use of such visual arts as collages and quilts are particularly helpful in gaining a better understanding of African American religious traditions. Both use diverse extant materials to create meaning and reinterpret forms within a contemporary context. For example, Romare Bearden's mixed-media collages, Faith Ringgold's painted story quilts, and Harriet Powers's appliqué quilts, provide rich images, patterns, and textures that communicate complex, multilayered meanings within a coherent whole. These patterns of African American meaning-making employ particular approaches to concepts of time, use of materials, and the construction of sacred-social worlds.

Student Exercise

To expose students to these patterns of meaning-making, I have students view examples of artists' collages and quilts in class or take students on a field trip to an art museum to view relevant works. Afterward, I invite students to develop their own collages as an experiential exercise.[3] For this exercise, each student selects images and creates a collage that expresses her or his own worldview. Students then present their collages to the class. Each person then gives an oral presentation addressing the following questions about her or his creative process: Why did you select these particular images? What images did you keep and why? What images did you throw out and why? What was the overall message or meaning you intended to convey? Classmates respond with their own interpretations of the presenter's work. Consequently, student responses yield diverse interpretations that open up the group's understanding of experience, meaning, and multiplicity. In this way, students gain a better sense of the relationship between the experience of a multivocal sacred-social world and knowledge creation.

Art, Music, and Dance as Pedagogical Tools

Collage and quilting as art forms communicate knowledge and meaning-making. These are effective media for exploring African American sacred-social

worldviews. Other art forms are useful as well. For example, the sculptures of
Betty Saar and her daughter Alison Saar are an example of two African American artists who embody aspects of a communal sacred-social worldview.[4] Betty
Saar's sculptures express the mystical symbols resident within African American traditions. Alison Saar continues creating art in the same vein as that of
her mother. The use of the Saars' work can serve as visual representations of
mystical attention,[5] practice and worldview that can effectively enable students
to more deeply understand African American mysticism. Also, the life and
works of musicians such as John Coltrane and Cassandra Wilson are instruc-
tive for showing how artists rely on mystical experience as a source of knowledge and creativity. Coltrane's *A Love Supreme* is a prime example of how
contemplative practices inform creative processes.[6] The music of Cassandra
Wilson, born in Jackson, Mississippi, is a good example of the relationship
between creativity and folk as well as African-derived traditions. Her music
also expresses a multivocal sacred-social worldview.[7]

Finally, dance is also an important medium for the understanding of African American mystical traditions. For my course "Black Women and Religion
in the United States," I brought in a consultant who is a college dance instructor and a Yoruba priestess to teach students about the relationship between
dance and the sacred in African-derived religions. She taught students about
the Yoruba tradition's deities, religious communal structure, history, and
sacred songs. She also made connections between some of the movements
with which my mostly Christian, African American students would be familiar, especially those from Pentecostal traditions and classical dances and movements associated with particular rites, deities, and occasions within other
African-derived religions. This session proved to be very effective in getting
the students to relate to the significance of the body in religious experience
and practice.

Mind-Body/Spiritual-Material

Because of the centrality of dance and the body, it is important to stress that
both the material and the spiritual are fundamental constituents of the sacred-
social world in African American mysticism. The focus on movement, the body,
and the material in African and African American religious worldviews is what
gives rise to mischaracterizations and demonization of African and African
American religious and cultural practices. Historically, Western philosophical
and Anglo-Christian theology have been rooted in a sharp dichotomy between
the mind or spirit and the body or the material world with the former categories
representing a higher order.[8] The body and sensual expressions have been depicted and theologized as a "lower nature" by Anglo-Christians who colonized
North America. As a result, it is assumed that that which is of a lower nature will

inevitably lead to chaos and evil. The body and sensuality, therefore, are a threat to the human soul and, thus, should be contained, suppressed, and controlled. Women and blacks historically have been associated with this lower nature, the body, and sensuality.[9] Consequently, they, too, must be contained, suppressed, and controlled. In contrast, African and African American mystical practices and epistemological findings are often rooted in sensual imagery, vision, and ecstatic dreams. Moreover, the body serves as a site for human-divine communication and knowledge-making within these mystical traditions in complex ways. For example, in African-derived religions practiced in the Americas such as Vodou and Ifa, the reception and communication of divine knowledge is located in the "mindful body" (Brown 1991, 254).

Though at various points in history, classical Western philosophical and Anglo-Christian traditions have accepted the ecstatic as an avenue of divine union, it has also been characterized as a lower form of mystical experience.[10] Grace M. Jantzen (1995) argues that Western Christian mysticism as a category of religious experience has been historically defined in ways that reflect relationships among gender, power, and knowledge. These relationships are important because throughout the history of interpretation of mystical experiences there has remained an "overt link" between knowledge and authority based on mystical claims (Jantzen 1995, xv). For example, Jantzen argues that when women increasingly laid claim to religious authority based on mystical encounter, particularly ecstatic experiences, the institutional authority that usually accompanied these claims when made by men was rendered suspect or relegated to the domestic sphere.

Demonization of the Marginalized and the Ecstatic Encounter

This argument also applies to the mystical experiences of African and African American practitioners, both female and male. The knowledge claims of those marginalized within dominant Anglo-Christian history and culture have often been dismissed as outside the religious norm. Moreover, the epistemological assertions and visionary descriptions of the marginalized have often been considered to be those of the emotionally unbalanced or disturbed.[11] Persons of African descent have been characterized as "superstitious," heathens, and devil worshippers.[12] Student depictions of mysticism as "weird voodoo stuff" reveal a bias that has been influenced by these historical mischaracterizations. Moreover, these mischaracterizations have been perpetuated by cinematic and media images of black religion based on the historical and cultural demonization of African-derived religion and culture.[13] These demonizing images of African and African American mystical practices have been consistent fare in Hollywood versions of black religion in films as recent as Disney's *The Princess and the Frog.*

Film

In *The Princess and the Frog*, the character Dr. Facilier was portrayed as a power-hungry magician who is indebted to "the spirits." He seeks to repay the debt by seizing power from the white plantation owner, "Big Daddy" La Bouff. The treatment of Dr. Facilier's character in *The Princess and the Frog* merely hints at an aspect of mystical religion vital to those who are marginalized—the ways in which spiritual power enables persons to overcome and transcend the death-dealing actions of the powerful. Dr. Facilier, however, is portrayed as one who wants something he has not earned and who works his magic and relies on the aid of the spirits to manipulate, exploit, and even destroy the film's protagonist. In addition, La Bouff is depicted as a jovial, benevolent community leader and well-respected business man. The film does not reveal the true origins of his wealth nor does it reveal the kind of exploitation of African American labor, bodies, and lives that resulted in the riches La Bouff and his family enjoy. Even with the presence of Mama Odie, who is a type of fairy godmother and is intended as a benevolent counterpart to Dr. Facilier, the film does not overcome its negative portrayal of the religion. In fact, Mama Odie's character operates as a feminine stereotype parallel to Dr. Facilier's character. Vodou remains mired in the stereotypical mischaracterizations associated with voodoo dolls, toothless "old hags," and demonic manipulations of power. These images and characterizations have made a strong imprint on the cultural imagination of America and the world.[14]

In order to counter the demonizing and stereotypical depictions of African American religion, I use films such as *Daughters of the Dust, Legacy of Spirits,* and *The Book of Eli* as pedagogical tools. *Daughters of the Dust* is a movie replete with sensual imagery that powerfully represents an African-derived rendering of time and a sacred-social world that contains a profoundly mystical element. Set at the turn of the twentieth century, this film tells the story of a family living on one of the Sea Islands off the Georgia coast. Nana Peazant, the family matriarch, serves as the clan's link to enslaved African ancestors who worked on the islands' indigo plantations. She still bears the mark of her own labor—hands stained by the midnight blue dye. She also continues to practice the rituals of the clan's ancestors and even communes with their spirits. Nana Peazant serves as a transmitter of knowledge between worlds and among generations that include those not yet born. The past and future collide in the present as family members struggle with their collective and individual identities, uncertain prospects on the mainland, and questions regarding the continuity of their familial connections across the waters. This family's attempts to find new meaning in such precarious circumstances culminates in the multivocal combination of African, folk, and Christian elements as Nana Peazant attaches an *nkisi* to a Bible and family members express their commitment to the whole of their traditions.

Legacy of the Spirits is a documentary film that explores the religious and communal life of Vodou devotees in Brooklyn, New York. This documentary portrays the complex structures of Vodou communities, initiation practices, religious leadership, and the multilayered traditions of Vodou that are inclusive of African-derived, Caribbean American–indigenous, and French Catholic elements. Students whose only knowledge of Vodou or "voodoo" is from cinematic caricatures are often surprised by the complexity of the community's traditions. It is precisely this communal context that is often missing from the depictions of lone "voodoo witch doctors" in films such as *The Princess and the Frog*. A particularly pointed response in the documentary film is a practitioner's answer to the interviewer's question about the stereotypical association of Vodou with "voodoo dolls."[15] This long-time practitioner explains that he does not know where the stereotype comes from. "I've never seen any voodoo dolls." He chuckles to himself and then adds, "Sometimes I wish there were such a thing as voodoo dolls though." This line usually strikes students as a significant point, even if it is in a humorous way. They too are able to identify with the practitioner's sentiments as well as both recognize and laugh at their own participation in this typical mischaracterization.

One aspect of the film stimulated animated discussion and presented a teachable moment: a scene that suggests the sacrifice of an animal, in this case a chicken. After showing this film in one of my courses, one student immediately objected to the animal sacrifice. I was surprised that, of all the images and information communicated in the film, this was the one that stuck with him. I asked the entire class, "How many of you eat chicken?" Every student raised his or her hand. I then asked them whether or not those of us who eat chicken have somehow distanced ourselves from the killing of the very chickens that we eat. The student who offered the initial objection responded by saying, "Yes, but that's different." For him "our" eating of chickens was more "civilized." I countered by asking students whether or not they were aware of how poultry was processed in this country. This opened up a lively discussion of the poultry farm industry in the United States. Several of the students were knowledgeable about the questionable treatment of animals and processing of meat and poultry on corporate farms. One student described her own experience of seeing chickens sacrificed in a village in Ghana, recently. She argued how quick and humane it was.

As a class, we discussed the ways in which animal sacrifice is considered sacred and the animal is thanked for its life. This discussion did not necessarily settle the debate, nor was I attempting to discourage them from raising questions about these issues. It became an opportunity, however, to get students to recognize the ways in which we often assume privileged positions by claiming normativity with respect to our own cultural practices and demonize practices of those whom we consider "the Other." I try to stress how important it is for students not to distance themselves from those who are different—to see themselves as subjects and others as objects—for, as we have seen in the example of the sacrifice/killing of animals, many of us participate in actions that have similar results. The question becomes how and why do we make moral distinctions when members of another group act as agents.

Narrative

One way to traverse the gulf between one as subject and the other as object is through narrative. African American spiritual narratives and autobiographies present black people as religious subjects. Historically marginalized cultures have had their collective political and social power, knowledge and cultural productions subordinated to dominant cultures. This means that dominant cultures have assumed the power to define and exploit the marginalized as objects. Religious narratives provide mystical accounts of the ways in which African American women and men have claimed authority as subjects and engaged in emancipatory practices of self-definition and self-construction. The mystical encounters described take multiple forms from subtle disclosure to dramatic dreams and visions. Narrative materials are good sources for investigating and analyzing these forms. For example, Clifton H. Johnson's *God Struck Me Dead: Voices of Ex-Slaves* provides a particularly telling glimpse into the complexity of African American sacred-social worlds. These accounts combine Christian and non-Christian notions of the personality, sin, and redemption.

Within the pages of these narratives, the reader is exposed to the significance of nature in mystical encounter, the use of biblical imagery, and prophetic themes that inform profound instances of self-examination, conversion experiences, and other epistemological shifts. Ex-slaves speak as subjects in a divine-human exchange. This exchange is the intimate embrace, or, more appropriately, an intimate wrestling, between the human soul and spiritual forces of sacred-social worlds that include deities, nature, living souls, dead ancestors, angels, and spirit guides. Within this intimate exchange, knowledge is revealed to spiritual travelers that provide avenues of self-discovery and disclosure of worldly and otherworldly vistas that are experienced as liberatory and salvific.

For the marginalized, who have been exploited and demonized as objects, communing with the divine yields knowledge of self, the world, and social and political systems that in many ways subvert the definitions, patterns, and rationalizations of oppressive interlopers. In other words, divine authority trumps dominant ideology. Having crossed the thresholds of these "familiar altars," enslaved Africans seem to be empowered with a more expansive worldview that enables them to transcend the limited and narrow constructions of the slave master or members of their own communities. They know what they know based on an authority that is more powerful than their detractors. While these slave narratives show evidence of a theological worldview that may not be wholly defined by Christian concepts and principles, nineteenth-century autobiographies written by African American women fit more distinctly within a traditional Christian framework.

Nineteenth-century spiritual autobiographies express more specifically a Christian evangelical, theistic understanding of sacred power. The spiritual autobiographies of Jarena Lee and Julia A. Foote are good examples of this type (Andrews 1986). However, even these autobiographies rely on a connection to a sacred-social world that informs how they understand religious experience and the resulting epistemological fruits. For these women, community is a crucial theme to their own sense of self-understanding and vocation as they perceived it in light of their mystical encounters. Moreover, it is the immanent presence of "holy energy" (Andrews 1986, 36) within community that also provided mystical authority and power for their lives. These women have not only claimed authority to preach and teach within communities that exhibit racial and gender bias, but they also developed the theological and biblical arguments they used to confront the hypocrisies and misuse of power within African American and Anglo-Christian communities. For women such as Rebecca Cox Jackson, however, traditional Christian evangelical perspectives were combined with nontraditional views of sacred power.[16] For example, Jackson, by way of mystical vision, embraced the divine feminine as well as the ability through prayer to affect change in the material world.

Other nineteenth-century figures such as Nat Turner and Sojourner Truth are examples of the ways in which prophetic calling and mystical experience combine to provide knowledge and authority to confront unjust systems. These prophetic mystics began their lives fettered by the institution of slavery. It was their respective mystical experiences that informed their own constructions of a liberated self and compelled them to engage in heroic acts intended to bring about justice in the world. Nat Turner's apocalyptic visions informed the slave revolt he led in Virginia. Sojourner Truth's mystical experiences led her to reject the system of slavery, to change her name, and to become an itinerant preacher who confronted the sins of racism and sexism. Though all of these narratives should be read critically with respect to audiences as well as the cultural and historical values of their times, the latter narratives of Turner and Truth deserve extra scrutiny because they are not firsthand accounts (Sernett 1985, 88–99; Washington 1993). In any event, narratives serve as pedagogical resources that enable students and teachers to explicate and compare diverse African American mystical experiences, practices, and epistemological findings. It is critical, however, to contextualize these texts in ways that expose their limitations.

Once again, film can serve as a tool for analyzing problematic interpretations of African American mysticism. *The Book of Eli* provides a good example of apocalyptic mysticism and might serve as a useful tool with which to explore and discuss the structure of prophetic calling, apocalypticism, and the role of violence. The film is set in a postapocalyptic United States. As a result of devastating religious wars, human beings have "burned a hole in the sky" and the sun has "burned up everything." The image of the sun-scorched Earth is reminiscent of such apocalyptic figures as Nat Turner. Because of the evil actions of humans, Eli, played by Denzel Washington, delivers such lines as "cursed is the ground because of us." Eli's prophetic words call out that the Earth will only yield "thorn and thistle" and that human beings made of mere dust can only hope to return to dust. Eli tells the leader of a group of bandits, "I know who you are....Murderers of innocent travelers. You will be held accountable." Eli's journey to deliver a special book which turns out to be a King James version of the Bible to the West Coast of the United States speaks of pilgrimage, mystical power, and knowledge. One day he hears an internal voice. This voice leads him to the book. The voice then tells him to take the book to the West, reveals his path and assures him that he will be protected along the way. Eli stresses to fellow traveler Solara that he is "not crazy." "I know what I heard. I know what I hear. And I know I would have never made it without help." Eli is protected from death and follows signs along the path. What we find out later in the movie is that Eli is physically blind, yet he has the power to strike down his foes. He even escapes from a locked room with a guard stationed in front without being seen. *The Book of Eli* also links together mystical vision, power, and action. Late in the movie, Eli realizes, when he has been forced to turn over the book to Carnegie to protect Solara's life, that he was so focused on the object that he "forgot to do what the book says and live by it." Therefore, part of the protagonist's character arc in *The Book of Eli* was to translate the Bible's ethical mandates into action.

In the twentieth-century, religious activists such as Howard Thurman, Malik El Shabazz, Malcolm X, and Martin Luther King Jr. translated the ethical mandates of their religious experiences into social activism. It was their respective mystical encounters that proved critical in these translations. These encounters may be introduced to students through different media. In his autobiographical text, Thurman describes how his spirituality was deeply informed by the religious sensibilities and ethical formations of his grandmother Nancy Ambrose. He also discusses how his brand of mysticism was nurtured by his early practice of solitude and his communion with nature. For Thurman, the night sky was his companion and the ocean a source of knowledge. A large oak tree served as a counselor and dialogue partner as he shared his "bruises and [his] joys" (1981, 9).

Malcolm X engaged in strict spiritual practices as a Muslim, first as a minister in the Nation of Islam and then as a seeker in a more orthodox tradition. However, it was his mystical vision and prison-cell conversion that first set his feet on the path to spiritual discipline and social engagement. Spike Lee's film

Malcolm X includes a visually stunning depiction of this event and of Malcolm's initial meeting with Elijah Muhammad, as well as the pilgrimage to Mecca that inspired his conversion to Sunni Islam.

In his sermon "God is Able" (King 1981, 113–114; 1964, 114–115), Martin Luther King Jr. recounts his kitchen table experience of divine presence that gives him the courage and the vision to overcome fear of death and recommit to a life of social justice work rooted in his Christian commitment. Holmes also identifies twentieth-century activists such as Fannie Lou Hamer and Rosa Parks as "public mystics" (2004, 152). Hamer's "spiritual focus and resolve" is evidence of what Holmes describes as contemplative practices (2004, 154). Narrative examples of her resolve are included in the biography *This Little Light of Mine* (Mills 1993). In addition, film footage, transcripts, and audio recordings of Hamer's speeches on the Mississippi Freedom Democratic Party and problems of representation at the 1964 Democratic National Convention provide good resources for her public work.[17] Still photography, websites, and biographies reveal the contemplative practices and sacred worldview of Rosa Parks.[18] Thus, as we can see, there are myriad forms through which to capture how the sacred-social world of African American religious experience gives rise to authoritative epistemological claims.

Conclusion

In teaching African American mysticism, I see as primary goals establishing and enabling students to understand the operating sacred-social worlds of religious practitioners. These sacred-social worlds are multivocal, take seriously the marriage between the spiritual and the material, and involve particular concepts of time. It is within certain sacred-social worlds that religious subjects commune and communicate with the divine and experience intimacy with spiritual beings. As a result, the individual and/or the gathered community lay hold to knowledge claims that assist them in negotiations of interior leadings and external circumscriptions. Such knowledge claims aid in the process of self-definition that seals the practitioner against the "Grand Invasion" of hegemonic power and enables her or him to reclaim and embrace embodied ways of being and knowing that counter demonizing stereotypes. Consequently, mystical communion gives rise to concrete action in the world whereby practitioners participate in social change and transformation.

I have proposed several pedagogical tools and strategies that help to convey the complex constructions of African American sacred-social worlds that inform mystical experiences and interpretations. These tools and strategies include uses of film, art, music, and dance. By contextualizing African American mysticism and using these tools, teachers can expose the demonizing aspects of Western culture and history as these relate to black religion and mysticism, privilege African Americans as meaning-making subjects in American mysticism, and lead students to a deeper engagement with these traditions.

Notes

1. I include myself in this process as well.

2. Although the relationship between sources of sacred power may be hierarchical, practitioners include and give appropriate attention to each through ritual.

3. I am grateful to my colleague Velma Love at Florida A & M University, who suggested that I use my work with collages in the classroom and invite my students to create their own as pedagogical tools for teaching African American religion.

4. See Collins (2006).

5. Rachel Harding referred to the "mystic attention of black women" during a session at the 2009 Annual Meeting of the American Academy of Religion in Montreal, Quebec.

6. In the acknowledgments of the liner notes for *A Love Supreme*, Coltrane states that he experienced a spiritual awakening in 1957. He also describes the album as an "offering" to God. See Coltrane (1986).

7. See, for example, Wilson (1993, 1999).

8. See Carr (2003, 5).

9. See, for example, Uzukwu (1997), Paris (1995) and Asante (1996).

10. See, for example, Underhill (1980, 27).

11. At a panel on mysticism that took place as a part of the annual meeting of the American Academy of Religion several years ago, I was asked to offer a psychological explanation for the knowledge claims of nineteenth-century African American women. The questioner assumed that the experiences these women described could be reduced to some sort of pathology.

12. We see evidence of this historical demonization of black religion by Western cultures even in the contemporary context with the characterizations of Haiti by Pat Robertson and French Prime Minister Nicolas Sarkozy following an earthquake that devastated the country in January 2010. Both described the country as being "cursed."

13. In the past when I have asked students what has informed their perceptions of Vodou, for example, they consistently identify film as their sources.

14. See, for example, the representation of "voodoo" in the 1973 James Bond movie *Live and Let Die*.

15. Many references have been made to voodoo dolls in film and television where a doll that supposedly resembles a person is used to inflict pain or to otherwise manipulate a person.

16. See Humez (1981).

17. For archival footage of Fannie Lou Hamer see, for example, Parmer (1991).

18. See, for example, www.rosaparks.org, and Parks (1992).

References

Andrews, William L. 1986. *Sisters of the Spirit: Three Black Women's Autobiographies of the Nineteenth Century*. Bloomington: Indiana University Press.

Asante, Kariamu Welsh. 1996. *African Dance: An Artistic, Historical and Philosophical Inquiry* Trenton, NJ: Africa World Press, Inc.

Brown, Karen McCarthy. 1991. *Mama Lola: A Vodou Priest in Brooklyn* Berkeley: University of California.

Carr, David. 2003. *The Erotic Word: Sexuality, Spirituality, and the Bible.* New York: Oxford University Press.

Clements, Ron, and John Musker, dirs. 2010. *The Princess and the Frog.* DVD. Burbank, CA: Walt Disney Studio.

Collins, Lisa G. 2006. "The Arts of Loving." In *Women and Religion in the African Diaspora,* edited by R. Marie Griffith and Barbara Dianne Savage. Baltimore: The Johns Hopkins University Press.

Coltrane, John. 1986. *A Love Supreme.* MCA Records, compact disc.

Dash, Julie, dir. 2000. *Daughters of the Dust.* DVD. New York: Kino International.

Hamilton, Guy, dir. 1999. *Live and Let Die.* DVD. Los Angeles: Metro Goldwyn Mayer.

Holmes, Barbara. 2004. *Joy Unspeakable: Contemplative Practices of the Black Church* Minneapolis: Augsburg Press.

Hughes, Albert, and Allen Hughs. 2010. *The Book of Eli.* DVD. Burbank, CA: Warner Brothers.

Humez, Jean, ed. 1981. *Gifts of Power.* Ann Arbor: University of Michigan Press.

Jantzen, Grace. 1995. *Power, Gender and Christian Mysticism.* London: Cambridge University Press.

Johnson, Clifton H., ed. 1993. *God Struck Me Dead: Voices of Ex-Slaves.* Cleveland: Pilgrim Press.

King, Martin Luther, Jr. 1964. *Stride Toward Freedom.* New York: Harper and Row.

——— . 1981. *Strength to Love.* Philadelphia: Fortress Press.

Kramer, Karen, dir. 1985. *Legacy of the Spirits.* DVD. Watertown, MA: Documentary Educational Resources.

Lee, Spike, dir. 2000. *Malcolm X.* DVD. Burbank, CA: Warner Brothers.

Mills, Kay. 1993. *This Little Light of Mine: The Life of Fannie Lou Hamer.* New York: Dutton.

Opuku, Kofi. 1995. "African Mysticism." In *Mysticism and the Mystical Experience,* edited by Donald H. Bishop. Cranbury, NJ: Associated University Press.

Paris, Peter J. 1995. *The Spirituality of African Peoples: The Search for a Common Moral Discourse.* Minneapolis: Fortress.

Parks, Rosa, with James Haskin. 1992. *My Story Rosa Parks.* New York: Puffin Books.

Parmer, Pratibha, dir. 1991. *A Place of Rage.* VHS. New York: Women Make Movies.

Pollard, A. B. 1992. *Mysticism and Social Change.* New York: Peter Lang.

——— . 2009. "African American Mysticism." In *African American Religious Cultures.* Vol. 1, edited by Anthony B. Pinn. Santa Barbara: ABC-CLIO.

Sernett, Milton C., ed. 1985. *Afro-American Religious History: A Documentary Witness.* Durham, NC: Duke University Press.

Thurman, Howard. 1939. "Mysticism and Social Change," *Eden Seminary Bulletin* 4 (Spring): 27–29.

——— . 1961. *Mysticism and the Experience of Love.* Lebanon, PA: Pendle Hill.

——— . 1981. *With Head and Heart: The Autobiography of Howard Thurman.* New York: Harcourt, Brace, Jovanovich.

——— . 1999. *Meditations of the Heart.* Boston: Beacon Press.

Underhill, Evelyn. 1980. "The Essentials of Mysticism." In *Understanding Mysticism*, edited by Richard Woods. Garden City, NY: Image Books.

Uzukwu, Elochukwu E. 1997. *Worship as Body Language: Introduction to Christian Worship an African Orientation*. Collegeville, MI: Liturgical.

Washington, Margaret, ed. 1993. *Narrative of Sojourner Truth*. New York: Vintage Books.

Weaver-Zercher, David L. 2004. "Theologies." In *Themes in Religion and American Culture*, edited by Philip Goff and Paul Harvey. Chapel Hill: University of North Carolina Press.

Wilson, Cassandra. 1993. "Sankofa," *Blue Light 'Til Dawn*. Capital Records, compact disc.

———. 1999. "Run the VooDoo Down," *Traveling Miles*. Capital Records, compact disc.

9

Teaching Experiential Dimensions of Western Esotericism
Wouter J. Hanegraaff

In an article on the history of the word *mysticism* published in 1980, the influential Roman Catholic theologian Louis Bouyer (1980, 42) made some remarks that go to the heart of Western esotericism as a field of academic research:

> According to whether we admire Christian, or Christianized, Hellenism or, instead, distrust it, so must we regard mysticism, and particularly Christian mysticism, with favor or disfavor. Some see in it the very heart of religion.... Others, on the contrary, see it as a pagan leprosy.

Bouyer was calling attention to the religious Platonism of late Hellenistic culture as central to what mysticism was all about. And he was emphasizing the sharp opposition that existed, already among the early church fathers, between those who saw Christianity as the supreme form of an inclusive "perennial philosophy" that shared its essential tenets with the ancient pagan nations, and exclusivists who rejected any concordance with pagan "wisdom" as an open invitation to pagan idolatry. The dialectics of these two positions, pagan versus antipagan (and inclusive versus exclusive), constitutes one of the most fundamental "deep structures" in the history not only of Christianity, but of Western culture up to the present day (Hanegraaff 2012a). For instance, when conservative Christians attack James Cameron's blockbuster *Avatar* (2009) as a pagan narrative reflecting left-wing liberal values, the director and his critics still move within the same apologetic and polemical discourse.

The field of research nowadays referred to as *Western esotericism* (a term invented in the eighteenth century) is grounded in the Renaissance revival of Platonic Orientalism: the widespread Hellenistic belief, shared by many of the church fathers, that Plato had been preaching a supreme spiritual wisdom whose origins were not in Greece but in the ancient pagan cultures of the Orient, and their legendary religious founders—the Egyptian Hermes Trismegistus, the Persian Zoroaster, or the Hebrew Moses. Renaissance humanists such as Marsilio Ficino and Giovanni Pico della Mirandola not only revived that patristic tradition, but were able to expand it greatly, because they had access to a wealth of newly discovered textual sources that could be attributed (although mistakenly, as we know today) to these "ancient sages": Hermes was believed to have written the *Pimander*, Zoroaster the *Chaldaean Oracles*, and Moses had received the secret teachings of Kabbalah at Mount Sinai. In this manner, pagan philosophies of late antiquity were fused with medieval scriptural Jewish hermeneutics and Roman Catholic theology, resulting in a powerful vision of religious unity—ultimately on Christian foundations, to be sure—that was profoundly inspiring for progressive intellectuals before the Council of Trent, and remained a highly significant, although gradually discredited, current until far into the seventeenth century. Moreover, the humanistic rediscovery and integration of Hellenistic learning did not stop with strictly philosophical and religious sources. It also included the many ancient materials concerned with study of the natural world, which had been preserved, commented on, and expanded by Islamic scholars during the Middle Ages, and translated from Arabic into Latin since the eleventh century: astrology, natural magic, and alchemy. From the sixteenth century on, all these elements were frequently mixed together as parts of a synthetic worldview on Platonic foundations, known under labels such as "Hermeticism" and "occult philosophy." Everything nowadays studied as *Western esotericism*—from eighteenth-century illuminism and nineteenth-century occultism or theosophy to the New Age spiritualities since the 1960s—has its foundations, historically and conceptually, in these contexts.

However, as formulated by Bouyer, there were always those who saw anything adopted from Hellenistic culture as "pagan leprosy" by definition. The antipagan reaction against the "perennial philosophy" can be traced, again, from church fathers such as Tertullian (*De praescriptione haereticorum* 7.7–9: "What has Athens to do with Jerusalem, the Academy with the Church, heretics with Christians?"), through Renaissance humanists such as George of Trebizond or Pico della Mirandola's younger cousin Gianfrancesco, and from witchcraft theorists such as Johannes Wier to Counter-Reformation intellectuals such as Giovanni Battista Crispo, who described in dramatic terms how the church had been infiltrated by paganism through the machinations of Satan's chief instrument, Plato. Predictably, the antipagan polemic was taken up with even greater fervor by Protestant authors, who described Roman Catholic theology as the pernicious product of the "Hellenization (that is: paganization) of Christianity." On these foundations, the seventeenth-century theologian Ehregott Daniel Colberg was the first to conceptualize all the heresies as belonging to one large countertradition, "Platonic-Hermetic Christianity"; and, in a very similar way, the extremely influential Protestant and Enlightenment historian of philosophy Jacob Brucker outlined a "family tree" of pagan pseudophilosophies, from Zoroaster to the Christian theosophers of his own time. During the same period, and in close relation with these developments, the ancient disciplines of astrology, alchemy, and natural magic, which had become part and parcel of the occult philosophy since the sixteenth century, lost most of their earlier credit: relying frequently on hidden spiritual influences and invisible correspondences in nature, and strongly associated with the same pagan currents that were being discredited in the domain of philosophy, they lost the battle with the mechanical paradigm in science. As such, by the eighteenth century, they had acquired their present status as occult sciences, and together with the Platonic/Hermetic philosophies of ancient pagan wisdom they became the "other" of mainstream Western religion, science, and philosophy. Mainstream intellectuals abandoned the critical and historical study of these topics almost completely, routinely referring to them as mere superstitions that could not be taken seriously by academics. As a result, throughout the nineteenth and much of the twentieth centuries, the book market concerned with these domains was dominated by amateur scholars, some inspired by antiquarian curiosity about the strange beliefs of the past, others by nostalgia for the magical worldviews that seemed to have fallen prey to the "disenchantment of the world," and by hopes of seeing them revived.

The dominance of amateur scholarship made the entire field look even more doubtful and unattractive for academics, and the revival of critical research in these domains during the twentieth century has been slow and hesitant. A decisive breakthrough occurred in the 1960s because of the writings of Frances A. Yates on the "Hermetic Tradition" and the "Occult Philosophy" of the early modern period (Yates 1964; 1979), followed by a growing flood of studies about the role of Hermeticism in the scientific revolution, including famous examples such as the alchemy of Isaac Newton and Robert Boyle. The general effect of this development has been one of demonstrating how the dominant grand narratives of modernity have resulted in highly selective, anachronistic, and, hence, misleading historiographies. From present-day perspectives, it is evident that scholars of earlier generations systematically highlighted what they saw as "true" or "serious" philosophy, religion, and science, while systematically ignoring and distorting the abundant evidence that showed how many of the most important philosophers, theologians, or scientists had been involved, deeply and persistently, in the "false" or "superstitious" beliefs of Hermeticism, astrology, alchemy, or magic.

As regards the history of how these currents and concerns have developed *after* the seventeenth century, academic research has been even slower in catching up. Here, a breakthrough similar to that of Yates is associated with the French scholar Antoine Faivre. Holder of the first university chair in the history of Western esotericism (École Pratique des Hautes Études, Sorbonne), and originally a specialist of the theosophical and "illuminist" currents of the eighteenth century, his prolific oeuvre eventually covered the entire scope from the Renaissance to the twentieth century and began to make an international impact when his works started to be translated into English by the end of the 1980s. Since the early 1990s, coinciding with the emergence of a new generation of scholars, this has led to a rapid development of academic research, as reflected in a flood of international conferences, scholarly journals such as *Aries: Journal for the Study of Western Esotericism* and associated book series (both published by Brill Academic Publishers), international organizations such as the European Society for the Study of Western Esotericism and the Association for the Study of Esotericism in the United States, a proliferation of monographs in these fields, and last but not least, the development of academic teaching programs. Having had the honor of being appointed, in 1999, at the world's second chair for Western esotericism at the University of Amsterdam, I was given the opportunity of building up the first full-time academic program in this field (Hanegraaff and Pijnenburg 2009). Since the introduction, in 2002, of a master's degree taught in English, it has attracted considerable numbers of Dutch and international students at the undergraduate, graduate, and postgraduate levels.

Have I been teaching any "mysticism" in this context? To answer that question, I have to return once more to the opening quotation by Louis Bouyer. As it turns out, he believed that common understandings of Christian mysticism as "an invasion of Christianity by Hellenistic religiosity" were ultimately incorrect, because the term μυστικός did not originally refer to an "ineffable religious knowledge" but to "the secret of a rite in its purely material aspect." The term acquired its later meaning in the specific context of early Christian speculation focused specifically on "Christ and his mystery," and only here did it begin to acquire the experiential connotations that still adhere to it today (Bouyer 1980, 43–45). Underlying this argument, it is not hard to perceive a dogmatic agenda of claiming the orthodoxy of *mysticism* as something that inherently belongs to the Roman Catholic tradition and protecting it from any dependence on (read: contamination by) Hellenistic paganism. Most important for our concern is the logical implication: It may be true that other religious traditions have "experiential" dimensions of their own, but these should not be described as *mysticism,* for that term is reserved for the mysteries of Christ as understood by Roman Catholic theology. In short, the only true mysticism is the one of the church, and paganism can have nothing to do with it.

The influence of this subtle argumentative logic has been pervasive, and its hidden theological agenda has determined much that has been written about mysticism in the twentieth century. The important implication for our present concerns is that, by definition, it condemns non-Catholic manifestations of experiential religion—and particularly the pagan and heretical competitors of what eventually emerged victorious as orthodox, "centrist" Christianity—to the status of *pseudomysticism.* In a rather confused manner, this implication has been widely adopted even by secular scholars who do not share the theological criterion by which pseudomysticism could be distinguished from the genuine article. Vague assumptions about "respectable" versus "nonrespectable" forms of religion associated with the occult have usually taken its place. As a result, routine denigrating remarks about the "Underworld of Platonism" and its manifestations, such as Gnosticism, Hermeticism, or theurgy (Dillon 1977, 384), have been common in scholarly literature until quite recently. And if their experiential dimensions were recognized at all, they were typically dismissed as obscure, embarrassing forms of "occult" irrationality far removed from the dignity of the great Christian mystics.

None of this will do, if we are really serious about critical and unbiased approaches to historical research and teaching. It is not the business of scholars of religion to make pronouncements about the truth or falsity of religious traditions, let alone to choose sides in theological debate by adopting the claims of religious or secular orthodoxies about the falsity or foolishness of their competitors. Have I, then, been teaching mysticism in our program at the University of Amsterdam? No, for if the term depends on its contrast with pseudomysticism, it is precisely the *latter* category that captures the experiential phenomena central to my field of research! Particularly while studying the very types of religion against which the church fathers were so concerned to construct their own identity, it just does not make sense to apply to them precisely the terminology that they were reserving exclusively for themselves.

An alternative could be the term *gnosis*. It was prominent in the very currents of late antiquity under discussion here, and it emphasizes the conviction that true and fully convincing "knowledge" of divine things can be attained not by means of reasoning, the senses, or revealed scriptures, but only by gaining direct, experiential access to the higher spiritual realities themselves (Hanegraaff 2012b). Although such a noetic dimension has been part of classic forms of Christian mysticism, it has always been problematic there because of theological strictures against *curiositas* and moral objections against the idea of human beings actively searching out the divine mysteries instead of receiving them by divine grace. The exaggerated notion that pagans and heretics are obsessed by the arrogant idea of breaking through to the divine realities by their own human powers is part of the anti-Gnostic polemic and has been used to bolster the normative opposition of "magic versus mysticism" (e.g., Underhill 1977, 149–164). In fact, the definitive breakthrough toward gnosis was typically experienced as a gift of divine grace in Gnostic and Hermetic contexts as well, and "mystics" can take a quite active attitude in their search for union with the divine. Nevertheless, it is true that the deliberate search for "superior knowledge," often linked to specific spiritual training programs or ritual techniques, is particularly characteristic for experiential traditions in Western culture that are derived directly and explicitly from Hellenistic paganism. This makes *gnosis* a convenient term for the central experiential dimension of Western esotericism.

In one of the standard master's degree courses in our program at the University of Amsterdam, my students and I have been exploring the search for gnosis in Western esotericism under the general heading of "altered states of consciousness" (ASCs). Of course I was well aware that the choice for this particular focus and terminology is not without its risks, to say the least, because of its association with the countercultural agendas of the 1960s and their well-known fascination with psychoactive substances such as LSD. However, if one has the courage to consider the ASCs concept in and for itself (that is to say, without implications of a "politics of consciousness" geared toward the transformation of society or a glorification of psychedelics), one finds that it has considerable benefits as well. There are signs that serious discussion of ASCs is returning to the agenda of cognitive psychology (Baruš 2003; Shanon 2002), and the more I have studied it, the more have I become convinced of its potential in text-based historical research. In the study of Western esotericism specifically, the ASCs concept provides us with an interpretative framework that often makes better sense of the sources than its more traditional alternatives, whether one is dealing with Hermetic gnosis in late antiquity, Ficino's use of the Platonic *furores* in the Renaissance, somnambulic trance in German Romantic *Naturphilosophie*, or New Age neoshamanism (Hanegraaff 2001; 2008; 2010a; 2010b). I will illustrate this below.

Using the ASCs concept as a conceptual framework in studying historical sources has a number of implications. First of all, it means accepting the possibility that, in many cases, their authors are not just using "mystery language" as a conventional literary genre or rhetorical trope, but are doing exactly what they claim to do: trying to describe impressive and life-changing experiences that have either (in first-person narratives) happened to themselves, or (in third-person narratives) are believed to have happened to others, or (in idealized fictional narratives) are believed to be possible for those who are blessed with success in the quest for gnosis. Furthermore, in studying sources from this perspective, one must accept that the authors were faced with the delicate paradox of using discursive language for describing experiences that are typically said to resist verbalization; in short, they are trying to say what they say they cannot say.

Both points imply a methodology that is willing to begin by taking the authors seriously on their own terms, rather than reducing them to instruments of discourse. In other words, it is concerned first and foremost with trying to find out what the authors were trying to tell their readers, and only secondarily with what the discourse may be telling *us*. Therefore, it is not surprising that, in teaching the course in question, I was confronted on an almost daily basis with a sharp contrast between the background assumptions that most of my American students appeared to have adopted from the post-Foucauldian discursive approaches widespread in academic teaching in the United States, and those of most students from the Netherlands and other European countries, where such

approaches are far less dominant. It is not my intention here to polemicize against
the academic culture associated with terms such as *theory* or *Cultural Studies,*
but I could not help noticing at least one transparent reason for its attraction to
an academic context where knowledge of foreign languages can no longer be
expected. Because lack of linguistic competence makes close, critical, and philologically informed reading of primary sources impossible, it is logical that one
tries to make a virtue out of necessity by replacing it by a type of abstract theorizing that focuses largely on theory and requires no more than occasional references to a convenient-chosen quotation here or there (in English translation).

A first task for me, therefore, consisted in a certain degree of deprogram-
ming. Although I had to rely on English translations in my classes as well,
I tried at least to explain and demonstrate why it is so crucially important to go
ad fontes to the best of one's ability, and I did my best to stimulate students to
get a competitive edge by learning at least one foreign or ancient language,
preferably more. By the time of the most recent edition of my course, I had
adopted a mantra that I explained during the first class and kept repeating
later: "Sources—Writing—Criticism." As regards the first element, though I am
happy to say that the general intellectual level of my American and Canadian
students was high, sometimes very high, it nevertheless proved necessary to
press home the elementary insight that, for historically oriented scholarship, at
least, there simply is no such thing as studying religion (esoteric or otherwise)
unless it is grounded in the study of primary sources, and the further point
that no translation can ever be trusted at face value. As I hope to show in the
present chapter, the entire meaning of a passage or even a complete text can
sometimes change completely according to how a few crucial words are translated. As for the second element, I insisted on the Wittgensteinian principle
that "whatever can be said at all, can be said clearly" (muddled writing equals
muddled thinking) and was forced to reject several papers full of badly di-
gested quasi-Deleuzian jargon but empty of any clear content. Esoteric writing
was not rewarded! Finally, I had to insist very explicitly on the virtues of criticism, starting with self-criticism. Sad but true, each year's group of students
from across the Atlantic has told me that where they came from, it was not at
all appreciated for students to voice criticism of what their teachers told them
and failure to respect this was likely to result in lower grades. To the puzzle-
ment of some, I told them exactly the opposite. As far as I am concerned, a
scholar who cannot accept criticism (expressed in a respectful manner, of
course) has no business in the academy and should better look for another line
of work. As paradigmatically expressed by Immanuel Kant, what is at stake
here is one of the very foundations of the Enlightenment enterprise: *sapere
aude,* "dare to think" for yourself instead of just buying what you are told.
Instead of teaching our students to accept blindly what authorities are telling
them, we are supposed to help them cultivate their faculties of critical judgment. Arguments count, not the fragile egos of professors.

On these foundations, my students and I have been reading and discussing a wide range of textual materials concerned with experiential dimensions of Western esotericism, with a particular focus on ASCs. They included the passages in Plato's *Phaedrus* about the four forms of μανία or "divine madness" and their later fortunes in Western culture, linked to notions such ecstasy or rapture in authors like Ficino or Giordano Bruno; various attempts at interpreting the initiatic experience of the Eleusinian mysteries, including the notorious psychedelic interpretation by the classicist Carl Ruck in the 1970s and its criticism by Walter Burkert; the step-by-step initiation into gnosis that can be traced through *Corpus Hermeticum* I and XIII to the *Discourse on the Eight and the Ninth*; visions of the witches' sabbath in relation to Carlo Ginzburg's *Benandanti* and the witches' ointment as described by Della Porta in his *Magia Naturalis*; the ecstatic techniques of Abraham Abulafia as analyzed by Moshe Idel; the visions of Emanuel Swedenborg and modern attempts at neuropsychiatric diagnosis; the spectacular visions and trance states of the "Seeress of Prevorst" (Friederike Hauffe) described by Justinus Kerner in the early nineteenth century; mesmeric descriptions of "astral travel" in occultist novels such as *Ghost Land* and modern theosophy; Aleister Crowley's and Victor Neuberg's trance experiences in the Egyptian desert described in *The Vision and the Voice*; Carl Gustav Jung's creative imagination and numinous visions from the unconscious during the time of his psychotic breakdown (made fully accessible recently by the long-awaited publication of *The Red Book*); and the psychedelic trance states described, with copious Hermetic and alchemical references, by contemporary neoshamanic esotericists such as Terence McKenna or Daniel Pinchbeck.

What, exactly, does the combination of close text-critical reading with a focus on ASCs contribute to the understanding of such materials in the context of Western esotericism? This question cannot be answered in the abstract, but must be demonstrated by some specific examples. The importance of linguistic precision is immediately evident in the case of Plato, for nobody has ever been able to find a satisfactory translation for his central term μανία. Literally, it means "madness," but this will not do. Plato makes a point of emphasizing that he means a state of divine inspiration that is granted to the true philosopher, but confused with insanity by the common crowd: "Standing aside from the busy doings of mankind, and drawing nigh to the divine, [the true philosopher] is rebuked by the multitude as being deranged, for they do not realize that he is full of God" (*Phaedrus* 249d). The term that is used here, ἐνθουσιάζων, might suggest that the philosopher is in a state of "enthusiasm," but this will not do either, because that word has long lost its original connotations. The most common modern solution has been "frenzy," but that term is confusing in that it has retained none of the intended connotations of a state of divine ecstasy and merely suggests that a person is excited and "out of his mind." Indeed, ἔκστασις may be closest after all, as it does suggest something like being "beyond oneself" and is used for unusual states of the kind that must have been intended here (e.g., Lewis [1971] 1989). The truth is that Plato's μανία is part of a very complex discursive field (Pfister 1959), consisting of multiple terms to refer to unusual, "altered" states of consciousness that occurred in religious contexts. The *Phaedrus* focuses on four types of μανία: under the influence of the first, one is able to prophesy (as, for example, the Delphic oracle or the Sibyls); a second "telestic" one seems to have to do with healing rites and purifications (Linforth 1946); a third one is induced by poetry (and by extension, music); and the fourth and highest one is induced by love (eros): the central topic of the dialogue. Moreover, such altered states are not just objects of discussion in the *Phaedrus*, but they turn out to function as a means of finding the answer to philosophical questions. Socrates himself does not at all behave like a rational philosopher engaging his interlocutor in Socratic dialogue. On the contrary, his decisive speech (which includes the famous image of the chariot of the soul) is delivered *ex cathedra*, under the spell of divine inspiration. Socrates is merely the instrument through which the true nature of love is revealed to Phaedrus. As it turns out, this fact was a cause of profound worry for some of my students with a background in philosophy. They found it hard to accept that in this famous dialogue, Plato himself was presenting rational thinking as useful but limited, because the attainment of certain knowledge about the highest realities required a more-than-rational altered state inspired by the gods. To this, my only response could be that whether we like it or not, this is what we find in the *Phaedrus*. That we may find it hard to accept says more about our own biases than about Plato.

As my course progressed, it quickly became evident to my students that studying ancient texts with special attention to ASCs led to a profound and sometimes embarrassing "deconstruction" of common academic discourse. Modern scholars in general, but classicists and philosophers in particular, are simply not used to paying much attention to these dimensions and are quite capable of ignoring their very presence even when they are looking right at them; even if they are forced to take them into account, they typically do not know what to do with them. Beautiful illustrations of this phenomenon can be found in the study of the "philosophical" Hermetica. For example, the first treatise of the *Corpus Hermeticum*, the Poimandres, has been studied in depth by generations of scholars, who have generally adopted its subdivision as suggested in 1946 by the great scholars of Hermetism Nock and Festugière. They saw the text as consisting of a short Introduction (1–3); a Revelation consisting of a Cosmogony (4–11); an Anthropology (12–23); an Eschatology (24–26); the apostolic mission of the prophet (27–29); and a final prayer (30–31) (Nock and Festugière 1992, 2–6). The effect is that the Poimandres is reduced to a conventional philosophical treatise, and its central emphasis on gnosis is suppressed. Nock and Festugière did not pay any special attention to the fact that almost the entire text is explicitly presented as the description of a vision that occurs during an altered state: it all happens while the visionary's thinking is soaring high while his bodily senses are suspended (CH I:1). In this state, he sees an enormous being, who introduces himself as Poimandres, the "mind of sovereignty," and offers to answer his questions. Crucial for the text as a whole but, amazingly, overlooked by all commentators, is the fact that the visionary responds by posing two questions (he wants to know the true nature of things, and he wants to know God), and these are answered in rapid succession by means of two visions-within-the-vision (4–7). In other words, the answers do not come in the form of rational explanations: the visionary *sees* the truth directly. Only afterward does Poimandres explain to him what he has just seen and answer his questions (8–26), and that is where we find Nock and Festugière's cosmogonical, anthropological, and eschatological discussions. Obviously this commentary is much longer than the visionary episodes, for verbal explanation takes time, whereas one can see a vision in a flash; but structurally, the center of the Poimandres is in those short visionary episodes, *not* in the commentary. Interpreting the structure of the text in this manner is not arbitrary, but follows from a basic principle that is emphasized repeatedly in the Hermetic corpus. Those who aspire to gnosis have to engage in practices to "steel themselves against the deceit of the cosmos," and they have to study what is referred to as the "General" and "Further discourses." In all likelihood, these terms refer to discussions of the basic Hermetic philosophy concerned with the nature of the world, man, and God, as found in many of the surviving Hermetic treatises. However, although this philosophical training is considered necessary as a preparation, it is ultimately insufficient, for the simple reason that discursive language "does not get as far as the truth" (CH IX:10; see Hanegraaff 2008, 133–137). In CH X:5–6, we read the following:

> In the moment when you have nothing to say about it, you will see it, for the knowledge [gnosis] of it is divine silence and suppression of all the senses. One who has understood it can understand nothing else, nor can one who has looked on it look on anything else or hear of anything else, nor can he move his body in any way. He stays still, all bodily senses and motions forgotten.

This is the description of an altered state: the body is immobilized and the senses are suppressed; the truth is seen directly; and what is seen cannot be expressed by words. If such passages are merely noted but their implications not taken seriously, the very structure of a dialogue such as the Poimandres gets misunderstood; its contents are incorrectly evaluated as philosophy (according to modern understandings of that term); because they are measured by the wrong yardstick, that of reason, they inevitably fall short and are seen as obscure and inconsistent; and the end of the story is that the most important part of the message is overlooked. No need for the anonymous author to hide his true meaning under a veil so as to shield it from the profane. One can rely on the rationalist bias of its commentators to make the message "occult" (hidden) or keep it "esoteric" (secret)!

Perhaps the most fascinating text in the *Corpus Hermeticum* is treatise XIII, on spiritual rebirth. The pupil Tat has completed the standard preparations: he has "steeled himself against the deceit of the cosmos" and has thoroughly studied the "General Discourses." However, he has found that they speak in riddles about divinity, claiming that one must first be born again. Fortunately for him, his master Hermes Trismegistus has just returned from the mountain where he has gone through that very experience of rebirth. Understandably, Tat wants to know from him what he should do. But to his frustration, Hermes begins speaking in riddles too. When pressed by Tat, he says that he really does not know what else to say, for up there on that mountain, something has happened to him that he cannot express in words: first he saw an "immaterial vision" within himself, and then he went "out of himself into an immortal body." His old, material body is no longer of any importance, but his new body is invisible, untouchable, and without size.

Then we encounter a particularly perfect example of why no understanding is possible without close textual analysis with reference to the original language. According to the standard translation by Brian Copenhaver, Tat responds with the words "you have driven me quite mad, father, and you have deranged my heart" (Copenhaver 1992, 50); a more recent translation has "O father, you have cut me to the quick, and destroyed my faculties" (Salaman, van Oyen, and Wharton 1999, 66); and Nock and Festugière write, "Tu m'as jeté dans une folie furieuse et dans un égarement d'esprit, ô père" (you have thrown me into a furious madness and mental confusion, o father) (Nock and Festugière 1992, 202). But although these texts have been footnoted in extreme detail in modern editions, no translator or commentator has seen anything worthy of note in the fact that Tat uses the term μανία—and yet, this is the indispensable key to understanding what is going on. Tat's sentence is not just an exclamation, but an observation about what is happening with himself as a result of Hermes' words: They have thrown him into an altered state. And what is more, in this state, he suddenly no longer sees his own body ("Now I do not see myself"). That the term μανία is meant to have exactly this meaning is confirmed by the continuation of the dialogue, for Hermes takes Tat's words as a hopeful sign that he might indeed be experiencing an altered state similar to the one he has just been describing. His formulation could not have been more explicit: "My child, could it be that you, too, would have passed out of yourself, as happens to those who are dreaming in sleep, but then in full consciousness?" (CH XIII:4).

But although Tat's mind is now in a state of transformation, he still sees Hermes' physical body the way he used to see it, and this surprises him. If he had been truly reborn like his master, he should now be able to see his regenerated body. Hermes confirms this, pointing out that true reality is entirely different: It is "the unsullied,...the unlimited, the colorless, the figureless, the indifferent, the naked-seeming, the self-apprehended, the immutable good, the incorporeal" (CH XIII:6). To perceive it, Tat must ardently wish for the power that is given through rebirth, suspend (again!) the activity of his bodily senses, and most of all, his body must be cleansed of its "tormentors." What follows looks very similar to a shamanic ritual of exorcism. Hermes tells Tat to be silent and proceeds to summon ten divine powers that drive out those twelve tormentors. They are clearly conceived of as a kind of demonic entities, for having been vanquished by the divine powers, they leave Tat's body "with a flapping of wings" (CH XIII:9). And then, as a result of this purification, Tat does indeed enter an exalted state of consciousness, described exactly in the terms that had been used elsewhere (CH XI:20) to capture how God himself perceives the world by means of participation: "I am in heaven, in earth, in water, in air; I am in animals and in plants; in the womb, before the womb, after the womb, everywhere" (CH XIII:11).

The process continues even further (see Hanegraaff 2008), but this must suffice for explaining how ancient Hermetic texts can be interpreted in a novel manner by combining a method of close reading attentive to linguistic detail with a focus on ASCs. In studying other and later materials, my students and I kept encountering examples of the strange resistance of many scholars against even looking in this direction. For example, it is very rare to find specialists of witchcraft who are willing to even consider the famous witches' salve as a factor that might be relevant to understanding visions of the sabbath. We have contemporary recipes of this salve (notably in Giovanni Della Porta's *Magia Naturalis*), so we know that they contained ingredients with strong hallucinogenic properties (usually from the Solanaceae family, such as datura or belladonna), experiments with the salve have confirmed that they cause very strong dreamlike sensations that may include flying through the air and participating in erotically charged feasts (e.g., Will-Erich Peuckert: see Hanegraaff 2010c, 280), and contemporary documents leave no doubt that some women accused of witchcraft had been smearing such a salve in their armpits and on their genitalia and were found in a deep stupor during which they claimed they had visited the sabbath (Harner 1973). How much more evidence does one need to at least consider an altered states hypothesis for at least some dimensions of the witchcraft phenomenon? Nevertheless, it plays no role even in Stuart Clark's monumental 827-page *summa* of modern witchcraft scholarship (Clark 1997). The general attitude is well captured by Robin Briggs's statements that "we do not need any pseudo-empirical observations" such as the drug cults that have been "imagined" by some, because the ingredients of the witches' salve turn out to be "harmless substances" that "only acquired their virtue by being placed in a symbolic system, through preparation at particular times and so forth" (1996, 56). Anybody who takes the trouble to get informed about the dramatic effects of plants such as belladonna or datura knows better.

A final aspect of teaching these subjects concerns the delicate relation between textual study and the scholar's personal experience. It will come as no surprise that some of the students who decide to pursue a master's degree in the study of Western esotericism originally got interested in this field because of some kind of personal involvement in contemporary esoteric practice. Some of them turned out to be members, or former members, of occultist organizations or esoteric traditions such as Wicca, the Theosophical Society, Freemasonry, or the Ordo Templi Orientis. Almost all of them understood that they needed to leave their personal commitments outside the classroom, although a few of them went through a difficult process of "disenchantment" and "losing faith" as the implications of textual and historical criticism with respect to their own tradition began to dawn on them. A particularly interesting discovery in working with these students concerned their attitude toward the (sometimes sensational) descriptions of visionary experience that we were studying in class. For example, what to make of Carl Gustav Jung's descriptions in the famous chapter in his *Memories, Dreams, Reflections* about his psychotic period, where he describes how at a certain moment he made the conscious decision "to let himself fall" and literally plunged into an underworld that apparently was as real to him as the room from which he had made the plunge (Jung 1965)? Or what to do with the extreme visions and demonic encounters described in meticulous detail by Aleister Crowley in *The Vision and the Voice* (Crowley, Neuburg, and Desti 1998)? Again, how to think about the many years that a respected intellectual and scientist like John Dee spent in conversation, by means of a medium, with angelic entities in a black mirror, who even taught him a complete "Enochian" language (e.g., Harkness 1999)? For me as an academic without any strong talent for visualization, such descriptions were (and remain) staggering testimonies and a genuine puzzle. They are so far beyond the range of ordinary experience that one cannot just shrug one's shoulders and describe them matter-of-factly as if there is nothing remarkable about them. They cry out for an explanation of some kind. However, to my considerable surprise, I discovered that many of my students simply did not see the problem. "Of course one can have such visions," some would tell me outside the classroom: "I have them all the time!" And "of course one can see entities in a black mirror and speak with them," a student with an occultist background told me: "just follow the instructions, and you will see for yourself."

I did not follow his advice (yet); but in fact, I realized that these responses make perfect sense against the background of the researches by the anthropologist Tanya Luhrmann in her seminal study of contemporary occultist culture, *Persuasions of the Witch's Craft*. Luhrmann had done participatory research among modern magicians in London, initially inspired by the classic anthropological question "why do they practice magic when, according to observers, the magic doesn't work?" (Luhrmann 1989, 4) What she discovered was that it *did* work, but very differently from how she had expected. The key was a learning process described by Luhrmann as "interpretive drift" (1989, 307–323): magicians went through an elaborate curriculum, which typically took years, through which they learned elaborate symbolic systems and systematically trained themselves in developing specific mental faculties such as visualization. Luhrmann discovered that by diligently doing the exercises, learning the techniques, and practicing the ritual prescriptions, her own ability to visualize (among other things) developed to an extent that she had not considered possible before. The basic process did not seem much different from what happens to a professional athlete, who trains his body to perform feats that are completely unthinkable for the average person. Most academics, who have come to excel in their line of work by learning very different sets of mental skills (verbal rather than imaginal, analytic rather than meditative, rational rather than poetic), seem to underestimate how vivid and subjectively convincing can be the experiences of a talented visualizer who has spent years on training his or her mental abilities.

My experience of teaching about experience can be summarized in terms of one central and deceptively simple requirement: that of taking the texts seriously and putting oneself in second place. Their authors might mean exactly what they write, and therefore, our first task consists in listening as well as we can, while trying to understand what they were attempting to tell their readers. Fashionable references to the "death of the author" are premature to say the least, and perverse in principle, for even though the authors of our texts may no longer be alive, they appear to have found a way to keep speaking to us. If we refuse to listen because we do not expect to hear anything but the reflection of our own voices, then we should not be surprised if we cease learning anything new. My central motivation as a teacher is exactly opposite. The careful and critical reading of texts can play a crucial emancipatory role in intellectual development, for students as well as teachers, by undermining our ingrained assumptions about the way things are. The reason is that, for once, this type of study is *not* about what we as twenty-first-century readers think we know and understand, but about what somebody from a very different time and place is trying to communicate across the abyss of cultural and historical estrangement. Paradoxically, texts about states of consciousness that defy verbalization are particularly effective means of such communication, because they do not allow us to smooth over the gap by means of translation into our own habitual concepts and vocabulary, thereby maintaining the illusion of unproblematic understanding. Instead, they force us to focus on what we share fundamentally with other human beings: the biological mechanisms, physical and mental, that allow us to experience a reality we do not understand, and then try to understand it.

References

Barušs, Imants. 2003. *Alterations of Consciousness: An Empirical Analysis for Social Scientists.* Washington, DC: American Psychological Association.

Bouyer, Louis. 1980. "Mysticism: An Essay on the History of the Word." In *Understanding Mysticism*, edited by R. Woods, 42–55. Garden City, NY: Image Books.

Briggs, Robin. 1996. *Witches and Neighbours: The Social and Cultural Context of European Witchcraft.* London: Fontana.

Clark, Stuart. 1997. *Thinking with Demons: The Idea of Witchcraft in Early Modern Europe.* Oxford: Oxford University Press.

Copenhaver, Brian B. 1992. *Hermetica.* Cambridge: Cambridge University Press.

Crowley, Aleister, with Victor B. Neuburg and Mary Desti. 1998. *The Vision and the Voice, with Commentary and other Papers.* Boston: Weiser Books.

Dillon, John. 1977. *The Middle Platonists: A Study of Platonism 80 B.C. to A.D. 220.* London: Duckworth.

Hanegraaff, Wouter J. 2001. "A Woman Alone: The Beatification of Friederike Hauffe née Wanner (1801–1829)." In *Women and Miracle Stories: A Multidisciplinary Exploration*, edited by Anne-Marie Korte, 211–247. Leiden: Brill.

———. 2008. "Altered States of Knowledge: The Attainment of Gnōsis in the Hermetica," *The International Journal of the Platonic Tradition* 2: 128–163.

———. 2010a. "'And End History. And Go to the Stars': Terence McKenna and 2010." In *Religion and Retributive Logic*, edited by Carole M. Cusack and Christopher Hartney, 291–312. Leiden: Brill.

———. 2010b. "The Platonic Frenzies in Ficino." In *Myths, Martyrs and Modernity*, edited by Jitse Dijkstra, Justin Kroesen, and Yme Kuiper, 553–567. Leiden: Brill.

———. 2010c. "Will-Erich Peuckert and the Light of Nature." In *Esotericism, Religion, and Nature*, edited by Arthur Versluis, Claire Fanger, Lee Irwin, and Melinda Phillips, 281–305 . Michigan: North American Academic Press.

———. 2012a. *Esotericism and the Academy: Rejected Knowledge in Western Culture.* Cambridge: Cambridge University Press.

———. 2012b. "Gnosis." In *The Cambridge Handbook of Western Mysticism and Esotericism*, edited by Glenn A. Magee. Cambridge: Cambridge University Press.

Hanegraaff, Wouter J., and Joyce Pijnenburg, eds. 2009. *Hermes in the Academy: Ten Years' Study of Western Esotericism at the University of Amsterdam.* Amsterdam: Amsterdam University Press.

Harkness, Deborah E. 1999. *John Dee's Conversations with Angels: Cabala, Alchemy, and the End of Nature.* Cambridge: Cambridge University Press.

Harner, Michael J. 1973. "The Role of Hallucinogenic Plants in European Witchcraft." In *Hallucinogens and Shamanism*, edited by Michael J. Harner, 125–150. London: Oxford University Press.

Jung, Carl Gustav. 1965. "Confrontation with the Unconscious." In *Jung, Memories, Dreams, Reflections*, 170–199. New York: Vintage Books.

Lewis, I. M. (1971) 1989. *Ecstatic Religion: A Study of Shamanism and Spirit Possession.* Reprint, London: Routledge.

Linforth, I. M. 1946. "Telestic Madness in Plato, Phaedrus 244de," *University of California Publications in Classical Philology* 13: 163–172.

Luhrmann, Tanya M. 1989. *Persuasions of the Witch's Craft: Ritual Magic in Contemporary England*. Cambridge, MA: Harvard University Press.

Nock, A. D., and A.-J. Festugière. 1992. *Corpus Hermeticum,* vol. II. Paris : Les Belles Lettres.

Pfister, F. 1959. "Ekstase," *Reallexikon für Antike und Christentum*, vol. IV, 944–987. Stuttgart: A. Hiersemann.

Salaman, Clement, Dorine van Oyen, and William D. Wharton. 1999. *The Way of Hermes*. London: Duckworth.

Shanon, Benny. 2002. *The Antipodes of the Mind: Charting the Phenomenology of the Ayahuasca Experience*. Oxford: Oxford University Press.

Underhill, Evelyn. 1977. *Mysticism: A Study in the Nature and Development of Man's Spiritual Consciousness.* New York: New American Library.

Yates, Frances A. 1964. *Giordano Bruno and the Hermetic Tradition*. London: Routledge and Kegan Paul/Chicago: The University of Chicago Press.

———. 1979. *The Occult Philosophy in the Elizabethan Age*. London: Ark Paperbacks.

PART III

Investigating Mysticism

PERSPECTIVES, THEORIES
AND INSTITUTIONAL SPACES

10

Teaching the Graduate Seminar in Comparative Mysticism

A PARTICIPATORY INTEGRAL APPROACH

Jorge N. Ferrer

How should we teach the graduate seminar in comparative mysticism? Is it enough to offer a survey of the field, training in comparative methodological skills, and/or a focus on a selected number of mystics, texts, or traditions? Or should we stress the primacy of inquiry in graduate education, supporting students' research on their own mystical interests while providing them with methodologically fruitful and personally significant inquiry tools? And should these inquiry tools be restricted to the mind's reflexive skills, or are we willing to create a more participatory learning environment in which students can incorporate other ways of knowing—such as somatic, emotional, and contemplative—in their investigations?

My main aim in this chapter is to describe a participatory pedagogy that engages multiple epistemic faculties in the teaching of an advanced doctoral seminar in comparative mysticism. First, I offer a brief account of the academic and curricular context, structure, and content of the seminar. Second, I introduce the seminar's participatory pedagogy, contrasting it with two other approaches to integral education: mind-centered and bricolage. Third, I discuss several pedagogical strategies employed in the course. Fourth, I argue that this type of pedagogy paves a methodological middle way between engaged participation and critical distance in the teaching and study of mysticism. In conclusion, I stress the integrative thrust of participatory knowing and reflect on the future of participatory approaches in the teaching of religion.

The Graduate Seminar in Comparative Mysticism

ACADEMIC CONTEXT

For ten years, I have taught "Comparative Mysticism" as a doctoral seminar offered by the department of East-West Psychology at the California Institute of Integral Studies (CIIS), San Francisco. The alternative educational mission

stitute makes it crucial to preface my discussion with some words
,e seminar's larger academic context. CIIS was founded in 1968 by
,s Chaudhuri, a leading exponent of the integral philosophy of the
In. ,i mystic Sri Aurobindo (1872–1950). The Institute is not committed to
any single philosophical or spiritual perspective, but some principles of integral philosophy have shaped its educational mission. This mission includes the
following principles: integration of mind/body/spirit, multiple ways of knowing, spirituality in higher education, cross-cultural understanding and multi-
culturalism, a multidisciplinary curriculum, transdisciplinary inquiry, and
experiential and transformative learning.[1]

Founded in 1976, the multidisciplinary department of East-West Psychology is concerned with the meeting of Eastern, Western, and indigenous psychological and spiritual traditions. The department seeks to ground academic
excellence and the acquisition of professional skills in both students' personal
transformation and a spiritually informed scholarship. As an academic field,
we think of East-West Psychology as a larger context for disciplines that explore the interface between psychology and spirituality: for example, transpersonal and integral psychology, Consciousness Studies, depth psychology
(Jungian, archetypal, and psychoanalytic), contemplative psychology, Shamanic and Indigenous Studies, and ecopsychology. Pedagogically speaking,
we strive to provide an *integral transformative education* that encourages students to engage in the integration of knowledge and of multiple ways of
knowing.

CURRICULAR CONTEXT

Approaching the encounter among Eastern, Western, and indigenous worldviews in the spirit of transformative dialogue and open inquiry, the department offers master's and doctoral East-West Psychology programs as well as a
certificate in East-West Spiritual Counseling.[2] In this context, "Comparative
Mysticism" is a one-semester advanced doctoral seminar, usually taken in the
students' last years. Participants are thus prepared by prior course work in
East-West psychological disciplines, world religions, and research methods in
the human sciences. Advanced seminars have a cap of twelve students and are
restricted to a doctoral level of instruction.

STRUCTURE AND CONTENT OF THE SEMINAR

The seminar has three main goals. The first is to provide a foundation through
an examination of classic and contemporary approaches to the comparative
study of mysticism. The second goal is to foster individualized inquiry by guiding students in the selection or development of a comparative approach appropriate to their research interests. To learn how to approach the study of

mysticism in an empathic, participatory, and contemplative manner that integrates critical perspectives is the third, pedagogical goal of the seminar.

"Comparative Mysticism" is usually structured as fifteen three-hour weekly sessions. After an introductory meeting, the seminar proceeds through three sections: "Methodological Foundations," "Interpretive Models in Comparative Mysticism," and "Contemporary Issues in the Study of Mysticism."[3]

"Methodological Foundations" consists of three sessions. The first explores the various meanings of the term *mysticism* existing in both the literature and the classroom. The second discusses problems of definition, offers a historical overview of the field, and continues the exploration of students' preunderstandings of mysticism. The third presents methodological foundations and challenges of the field, critiques of the comparative method in religious studies, and the study of mysticism as a mystical-hermeneutical path.

"Interpretive Models in Comparative Mysticism" comprises five sessions surveying the main families of hermeneutic approaches in the field: traditionalist, perennialist, constructivist, feminist, neo-perennialist, postmodern, contextualist, pluralist, and participatory.

"Contemporary Issues in the Study of Mysticism" includes five topical sessions on areas of critical inquiry in the modern study of mysticism, including subjects such as intermonastic dialogue and the ethics of mysticism. During this section, students offer oral presentations of their research projects.

At the final session, students complete their presentations, reflect on how their understanding of mysticism may have changed throughout the seminar, and assess collaboratively the collective inquiry process and research outcomes.

Many sessions employ case studies linked to specific readings. Case studies illustrate particular methodological issues, interpretive models (e.g., the construction of Buddhist mystical experience), and contemporary topics in the study of mysticism. In addition, students critically analyze sample comparative papers in class using the integral hermeneutical method described herein.

For their final assignment, students select two or more mystical traditions, texts, authors, notions, or phenomena and compare them, applying one of the interpretive models studied or developing their own approach. Students are encouraged to incorporate accounts of their personal experience in support of their thesis. As mentioned, the assignment includes oral presentations of comparative projects in which students receive feedback from both instructor and peers.

The seminar differs from traditional courses on mysticism not only in its pedagogy but also in its contents. Most mysticism courses either offer a survey of mysticism in world religions or focus on the comparison of two or more mystics, texts, or traditions selected by the instructor. In contrast, "Comparative Mysticism" presents a rich array of hermeneutical models, methodological tools, and thematic explorations as the context in which students focus their comparativist efforts on mystical subjects of their choice—an approach that may not be suitable for undergraduate or graduate introductory courses. Such an increased political participation enhances students' personal involvement and empowers the extended epistemic participation sought by a participatory integral pedagogy.[4]

A Participatory Approach to Integral Education

Briefly, a participatory pedagogy seeks to incorporate as many human faculties as appropriate into learning and inquiry. A participatory pedagogy should be sharply distinguished from both mainstream education and a *mind-centered approach* to integral education that is based on the intellectual study and/or elaboration of holistic frameworks or understandings. Even though intellectual discernment is important, mystical phenomena partake of many nonmental dimensions; thus, an eminently mental approach can arguably lead to partial understandings and even significant distortions. To fully understand their knowledge claims, mystics insist on the necessity of transcending purely intellectual knowledge and engaging a fuller range of epistemic competences (Ferrer 2000, 2002). In addition, most mystical traditions posit the existence of an isomorphism or deep resonance among the human being, the cosmos, and the mystery out of which everything arises (e.g., see Chittick 1994; Faivre 1994; Jónsson 1988; Lincoln 1986; Saso 1997; Shokek 2001). If we entertain the plausibility of these emic claims, it can be argued that the more human dimensions participate in the study of mysticism, the greater will be the dynamic congruence between the inquiry approach and studied phenomena and the more coherent with the nature of mysticism will be the resulting knowledge (Ferrer 2002, 2008).

A participatory pedagogy should also be distinguished from a *bricolage approach* (the most widespread in alternative education), which either incorporates experiential practices such as meditation or ritual into an essentially mind-centered education or offers an eclectic curriculum engaging many human attributes (e.g., hatha yoga for the body, contemplation for spiritual awareness). Although these practices engage nonmental dimensions, these dimensions rarely, if ever, become part of the substance of the educational process, which is entirely planned, conducted, and assessed from the perspective of the mind.[5]

In contrast, by fostering access to multiple ways of knowing, a *participatory approach* invites the engagement of the whole person, ideally at all stages of the educational process.[6] The novelty of the participatory proposal is essentially methodological. It stresses the exploration of practical approaches that combine the power of the mind and the cultivation of consciousness with the epistemic potential of human somatic, vital, and emotional worlds.

"Comparative Mysticism" uses a partial (versus complete) participato
On the one hand, a fully participatory approach requires more poten.
ential practices than those described herein to access and activate th
deeply buried, undeveloped, and/or repressed) epistemic powers of tl_ ion-
mental worlds.[7] On the other hand, though the inquiry process is facilitated by
a wide array of human attributes, the seminar places a strong emphasis on the
intellectual elaboration, discussion, and critical appraisal of knowledge. This
emphasis is perfectly legitimate in courses focused on methodological training, critical discussion of textual sources, or hermeneutic study. Whereas edu-
cators should strive toward the inclusion of as many ways of knowing as
possible in the classroom, the extent and range of this epistemic participation
needs to be determined case by case.

Though standard lectures have their place in participatory education, a
graduate seminar should stress the *primacy of inquiry* and provide students
with practical methods and tools to carry out individual and collective investigation. As learners move from undergraduate to graduate education and
from master's to doctoral level, there needs to be a gradual but increasing shift
of emphasis from an educational praxis based mostly on offering content (arguably more appropriate for young adults requiring epistemic foundations) to
one that predominantly facilitates inquiry (arguably more appropriate for
adults aspiring to make an original contribution to their discipline and the
world).

Participatory Pedagogical Strategies

Objective

"Comparative Mysticism" is the fruit of a ten-year pedagogical experimentation exploring the incorporation of participatory knowing in a graduate seminar. A chief pedagogical assumption of the seminar is that a deeper and yet
critical understanding of mysticism and its study can be gained by moving
beyond eminently mind-centered approaches and accessing participatory
ways of knowing. What follows is a description of nine pedagogical strategies
used to this end in the seminar: (1) invitation to participatory knowing;
(2) guided contemplative inquiry; (3) unconditional acceptance and somatic
grounding; (4) analogical inquiry and mandala drawing; (5) dialogical inquiry;
(6) meditative reading; (7) empathic attunement through role play; (8) integral
hermeneutics; and (9) spiritually informed scholarship.

INVITATION TO PARTICIPATORY KNOWING

At the first meeting, I introduce the notion that a fuller understanding of
mysticism and a more integral approach to its study may be optimized
by accessing participatory ways of knowing—ways that can involve the

intellectual discernment of the mind, somatic transfiguration, erotic communion, the awakening of the heart, visionary cocreation, and contemplative intuition. After some discussion, I stress the importance of cultivating an attitude of "critical subjectivity" during participatory knowing in order to discern the possible biases of one's situated experiential perspective and seek a balance between engaged participation and critical distance in the study of mysticism (see "Methodological Discussion").[8] Later in the seminar, students read scholarly essays that elaborate these points, such as Frits Staal's (1975) plea to avoid an "armchair" approach to the study of mysticism by combining rational analysis and spiritual practice, Jeffrey Kripal's (2001) account of the hermeneutical-mystical experiences of scholars of religion and articulation of the mystical dimension of hermeneutics, and contemporary proposals for a "participatory turn" in religious studies (Ferrer and Sherman 2008a, 2008b).

The invitation to participatory knowing continues throughout the seminar. In this regard, it is especially helpful to begin many sessions with an *opening walk,* in which students are invited, for example, to explore mindfully the classroom space through different sensory modalities; stretch the body to make it more present and porous; move or dance at the tempo of background music; and/or become aware of the state of their bodies, vital energy, hearts, minds, and consciousness. I consider these opening walks to be healing rituals of remembrance; students are consciously and/or unconsciously reminded that they do not need to leave their nonmental attributes and associated ways of knowing outside the classroom, as they have implicitly learned to do during most of their adult education. The opening walks notify students that they do not need to begin the session as "disembodied heads" and invite them to remain as present as possible during class activities—mentally, somatically, vitally, emotionally, and so forth.

GUIDED CONTEMPLATIVE INQUIRY

Some weeks, the opening walks are followed by a guided contemplative inquiry into questions connected to the session's readings or topics. To this end, students find a place in the room to lie down or sit in a posture that invites a state of relaxed alertness and optionally cover their eyes with a bandana offered as an aid for inner recollection. (Here I remind students about the etymological meaning of the Greek term *mūstikos*: "to cover the eyes or the lips"). Meditative music plays in the background. After some simple relaxation instructions, I announce that I will read a set of open questions and/or guide an experiential inquiry connected to the week's topic: examples include the ontological status of mystical knowledge, and an experiential exploration of Robert Forman's (1988) "pure consciousness events" using Roberto Assagioli's (1972) disidentification exercise.

Before I read the questions, I ask students to be receptive to my words and the personal resonances (e.g., physical sensations, emotional states, memories) that my words may awaken in them. As the object of the contemplative inquiry, students can either focus on the question(s) that most influenced them (concentrative approach) or simply remain present, open, and receptive to the fullness of their multidimensional experience without trying to search for anything in particular (mindfulness approach). I encourage students to explore which approach may be most fertile for them and to optionally place their hands over specific parts of their bodies—such as their forehead, heart, and/or lower belly—in an attitude of deep listening to what these centers may have to say about the question(s). After spending some time in silence to develop the inquiry, students form dyads or small groups to share their experiences and insights in a fresh, unrehearsed way. To close the session, everybody stands up or sits in a circle and each student optionally shares a selected aspect of his or her experience using words, gestures, and/or movement.

UNCONDITIONAL ACCEPTANCE AND SOMATIC GROUNDING: WORKING WITH HERMENEUTICAL PREUNDERSTANDINGS, I

In the first week, I announce that the next session will start with a ritual sharing of our hermeneutical preunderstandings of mysticism. The ritual has three aims: first, to raise awareness of students' presuppositions about mysticism; second, to become familiar with the diversity of understandings of the mystical coexisting in the classroom prior to the seminar's inquiry; and third, to foster the grounding of students' inquiry in their embodied reality. To help students get ready for the ritual, I request the following homework:

> Mindfully prepare a space at home to carry out the following three-step inquiry: (1) Articulate, as clearly and succinctly as you can, your current conceptual understanding of mysticism. (2) Identify any possible biographical roots of this understanding (e.g., personal experience, intuition, readings, teachers, a mix of the above). (3) If your conceptual understanding stems to some extent from personal experience, examine how such an experience may have been shaped, consciously or unconsciously, by adopted views about mysticism, presuppositions about reality, or religious beliefs. All these questions will eventually enter our discussion, but in the ritual space you will be asked to share *only* your current conceptual-experiential understanding of mysticism. Please limit your sharing to three minutes.

The ritual is a circle of sharing shaped by the practices of unconditional acceptance and somatic grounding. This is its basic structure: (1) Participants sit in a circle and for a few minutes reconnect in silence with their conceptual-experiential understanding of mysticism. (2) A bell marks the time for the first sharing, during which the group is encouraged to practice active listening. (3) After sharing, the student lies down in the middle of the circle and the other participants respectfully place an open hand over various body parts, cultivating an attitude of unconditional acceptance. (4) The physical contact ends and everybody sits back in the circle. A moment of silence is observed before another bell indicates that it is time for the second student to go through the cycle. The ritual ends once all participants, including the instructor, have shared their understandings of the mystical.

Two features of this practice require commentary. First, the social codes regarding what constitutes safe and appropriate physical contact in contemporary American culture make it fundamental to stress the optional nature of the somatic grounding. In addition, given that the body can unconsciously store traumatic memories, students should be advised to stop the practice if they experience any discomfort, anxiety, or bodily contraction unrelated to the inquiry process. Students who decide that somatic grounding is not for them—and I make sure that everybody feels that both options are equally valid—simply return to the circle after sharing and the group practices the unconditional acceptance of the sharing without physical contact. Second, as background for the practice, I explain that unconditional acceptance can be transmitted simply through an open presence and, crucially, that it is not equivalent to uncritical agreement. To accept the place from which others begin the inquiry does not mean one agrees with their views. "In subsequent sessions," I tell students, "there will be plenty of time to agree or disagree among ourselves; now it is the time to simply accept where everybody is coming from." This practice makes students more sensitive to the horizons of understanding shaping the starting point of the group's inquiry, minimizing the emergence of disagreements based on semantics versus actual discrepancies.

ANALOGICAL INQUIRY AND MANDALA DRAWING: WORKING WITH HERMENEUTICAL PREUNDERSTANDINGS, II

The next session extends the work with hermeneutic preunderstandings from the linguistic, the logical, the conceptual, and the propositional to the imaginal, the analogical, the symbolic, and the presentational. Important for any inquiry, to engage analogical ways of knowing seems particularly relevant in the teaching and study of mysticism; mystics often stress the limitations of discursive language and resort to a rich variety of symbolic means—such as poetry, painting, or radical action—to convey their insights.[9]

The analogical inquiry proceeds as follows: I first ask students to bring to class an object that evokes or captures symbolically their felt-sense of the mystical. Typical objects include depictions of holy men and women; religious symbols, statuettes, and relics; paintings and drawings; and nature's elements, such as feathers or stones. After an opening walk, students sit or lie down, optionally cover their eyes with a bandana, and are invited to let go of intellectual considerations. Then I ask them to invoke and hold in their awareness whatever felt-sense of the mystical they may have, inviting them to (re)enact an experiential state they associate with the mystical. Here I have found it helpful to remind students that mysticism is as much about knowing as it is about not-knowing, as much about unfolding vision as it is about what remains hidden. In this spirit, I suggest to the students that they let go of any goal to achieve or see anything extraordinary and simply remain unconditionally receptive to whatever vision, symbolic expression, or embodied enactment may come to them. If they find it useful, students can place their hands over different parts of their bodies in an attitude of humble but deep listening to what these human dimensions may have to say about mysticism.

Once the inquiry ends, I provide drawing materials (colored papers, crayons, and markers) and invite students to craft an image or symbol. Though emphasis is placed on spontaneous expressions emerging from their experiential felt-sense, students can also depict something they may have seen or felt during the inquiry,[10] write poetry, or prepare a brief embodied dramatization through movement and gesture. After completing their creations, students collaboratively craft a collective mandala. To do this, they one-by-one place their paintings, poetry, and/or symbolic objects in the center of the room. Then all the students sit in a circle and contemplate the mandala in order to become familiar with the group's analogical culture about the mystical and to honor analogical ways of knowing; participants may remain in silence or verbalize, Quaker style, and/or somatically enact anything they might feel while contemplating.

This practice admits many variations, such as the creation of another circle for poetry readings or storytelling about the objects brought to class. As optional homework, students can explore the connection between their conceptual and imaginal takes on the mystical.

DIALOGICAL INQUIRY

During the discussion of readings and thematic issues, students are encouraged to practice dialogical inquiry, which seeks to integrate the strengths of Bohmian dialogue and standard academic discussion so that argumentation and polemics may become penetrating tools to inquire into the possibilities and limitations of all views. Moreover, dialogical inquiry reframes class discussion as an opportunity to practice contemplative skills in the intersubjective world. Examples of these skills are mindfulness (i.e., a nonjudgmental awareness of one's thoughts, emotions, and sensations), active listening as an act of generosity, mindful speech (e.g., offering criticism without sarcasm, mockery, or condescension), service (e.g., to truth, truthfulness, or the generation of shared meaning), nonattachment to views, and openness to transformation (see Ferrer 2003a).

To reinforce the dialogical competence of the group, I may begin some sessions by asking students to blindly pick up a card with the name of a particular skill (e.g., active listening) that becomes the focus of their practice. These sessions can end with a brief round of sharing in which students disclose the practiced skill, reflect on their performance, and receive feedback from the group. Pedagogically, I have found it more effective to break up the practice of dialogue into a number of concrete microskills than to simply ask students to try to "be dialogical" in an abstract way. The number of sessions in which I use the cards varies from group to group.

MEDITATIVE READING: INTERRELIGIOUS *LECTIO DIVINA*

After a short lecture on the contemplative status that reading sacred texts has in many traditions, I introduce an interreligious version of the Christian practice of *lectio divina* (meditative reading).[11] Throughout the semester I ask two to four volunteers to bring to the next session a brief mystical passage. At the opening of these sessions, students read the mystical passages, seeking to evoke the emotional tone they perceive in them (e.g., burning passion, unshakeable equanimity, or exhilarating joy). While the students listen to the passages, I invite them to empathically enter their meaning and use the power of their visionary imagination to experientially reconstruct the mystical event conveyed in the texts. Each reading is followed by one or two minutes of receptive contemplation in silence until a bell indicates the beginning of the next reading. The practice ends with a longer period of receptive contemplation.

Three remarks: First, I see this practice as an attempt to cultivate a hermeneutical-mystical union with the texts (Kripal 2001, 15–19) via the reenactment of both the semantic meaning (Sells 1994, 9–10) and the experiential qualities of the mystical event. Second, though potentially interreligious, the practice retains essential elements of the *lectio divina* tradition, such as the dialectic between an active movement of reading/listening to understand/apprehend (*lectio* and *meditatio*) and a more receptive movement of turning inward (*oratio*) and being open to the gifts of spirit (*contemplatio*). Third, the practice also admits many variations and can catalyze follow-up discussion. For example, students can read a single passage many times or form small groups to discuss the universality versus plurality of mystical states in light of their experiences during an interreligious *lectio divina*.

EMPATHIC ATTUNEMENT THROUGH ROLE PLAY

In the practice of role play, two or more students take the identities of scholars holding conflicting views on particular issues as a platform for subsequent

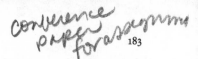

group dialogue. For example, students might be requested to recreate in class the exchange between Seyyed Hassein Nasr (1993, 2001) and Sally King (2001) on the validity of traditionalist metaphysics to account for Mahayana Buddhism. The task here is to sum up the content of these essays and engage in a dialogue that gives voice to their authors' perspectives. I may even add a theatrical touch: I introduce the presenters as Dr. Nasr and Dr. King, speaking in a panel at an American Academy of Religion meeting, for example. As the dialogue opens to the group, presenters are free to "let go of their role" and express their own viewpoints (which at times may have changed through the role play).

I have found that the practice of role play not only enhances students' empathic attunement with the different interpretive models of mysticism surveyed in the seminar but also deepens the understanding of the views under discussion. In some cases, students might benefit from taking the role of authors whose perspectives they find questionable or even disturbing. Besides bolstering emotional intelligence, this practice fosters cognitive developmental competences, such as the ability to take the role of the other, and trains students in scholarly activities such as public speaking and debate. Finally, students love these engaging dramatizations, and I believe it would be an oversight to undervalue the role of fun in effective learning.

INTEGRAL HERMENEUTICS

As the seminar proceeds, students analyze sample papers that have been carefully selected to illustrate particular virtues or pitfalls of the comparative enterprise (see note 3). Unknown to students, one sample may have been selected, for example, because of the biased nature of its comparative categories; another, for its elegant and comprehensive comparative framework. Students are encouraged to analyze the samples using an "integral hermeneutic approach"— or extended spiral of understanding—that comprises four hermeneutical moments:

1. *Hermeneutics of recovery:* Students first seek to discern, retrieve, and articulate the intended meaning of the text. The focus here is on what the author is saying, the text's main thesis or objectives, the main arguments offered, and the conclusion. At this stage, the task is to achieve the clearest comprehension possible of the text's meaning.

2. *Hermeneutics of the heart:* Here students pay attention to somatic, vital, and emotional reactions emerging while reading the paper (e.g., anger, joy, boredom) and take these reactions as a starting point for inquiry. By looking deeply into the roots of these embodied experiences, students often recognize previously unseen layers of meaning of the text and are able to articulate more clearly their appreciative and critical

perspectives. Though the hermeneutics of the heart can lead to positive considerations, the emergence of "negative" responses leads to critical hermeneutics.

3. *Critical hermeneutics:* Students identify argumentative flaws, content inaccuracies, and possible biases in the comparative analysis, raising questions such as: Who benefits from the conclusions this article reached? Are the compared mystics or traditions fairly represented? Or is one tradition grossly or subtly distorted to show the superiority of another? Has the author avoided the pitfalls of comparative hermeneutics surveyed in the course (e.g., "going native" or naïve universalism)? Students also look at the design of the comparative framework, evaluate the neutrality and productive fit of its comparative categories, and situate the author's methodological standpoint (e.g., along the engagement/detachment continuum).

4. *Mystical hermeneutics:* Adapting and combining Kripal's and Sells's proposals, students explore the degree of hermeneutical-mystical union achieved with the text and the possible emergence of a "meaning event" of semantic (as Sells proposes) and experiential dimensions. Here students may inquire into the spiritually transformative or challenging impact of their hermeneutical engagement with the text, and the influence such personal responses may have on their understanding.

Seeking to exhaust the meaning units of a text, students may go through several cycles of this extended spiral of understanding. As they gradually identify or develop their own hermeneutic style, they can change the sequence of these hermeneutical moments or work through all four simultaneously. I often insist on the value of starting with the hermeneutics of recovery at the initial stages of students' work, because I have noted that students who start with, or move too quickly to, the critical stance usually have difficulties in describing the text's meaning in its own terms or unfiltered by their critical lens.

SPIRITUALLY INFORMED SCHOLARSHIP

A general feature of my participatory pedagogy is the integration of spirituality into academic work. As we have seen, one way to pursue this goal is by engaging a multiplicity of ways of knowing in the inquiry process; another is by encouraging students to take all aspects of research and writing as opportunities to practice spiritual values. In this regard, I point out the likeness of many contemplative qualities and the traits of the paradigmatic critical thinker, such as intellectual humility, courage, or integrity.[12]

In this context, I identify five meeting points between spirituality and scholarship: (1) The *nature of scholarship* is the understanding of the hermeneutic production of meaning as potentially emerging from human participation in the creative power of life or the spirit. (2) *Content,* for example, considers the fairness in the selection of sources or the explicit discussion of spiritual questions. (3) *Form,* for example, encompasses considerations of elegance, grace, and beauty in writing; questions of tone such as avoiding condescension in criticism; or work with spiritually evocative scholarly styles such as storytelling, dialogue, visual materials, or poetry. (4) *Process,* for example, considers the commitment to truthfulness and truth in inquiry and writing. And (5), *impact* is the extent to which one's scholarship fosters the spiritual edification of both author and readers.

A full account of this approach to scholarship would require an entire paper, but, to offer a few examples, I might recommend to students that they change the root metaphor of scholarly work from "production" to a "pregnancy and birthing process" whose creative seed needs to be nourished; consider Deena Metzger's (1992) advice to prepare their desk as an altar—or as the bridal chamber for the beloved (i.e., the creative wellspring within); or keep a dream journal and pay attention to synchronicities.[13]

Methodological Discussion: The Way of Critical Participation

The general point of this section is that a participatory pedagogy like the one just outlined paves a middle way between the extremes of engaged participation and critical distance in the teaching and study of mysticism. Articulations of this (less-traveled) middle road have a long pedigree in religious studies. Almost thirty years ago, Robert C. Neville (1982) offered a vigorous defense of the value of combining the virtues of the dao (i.e., participatory engagement and existential access to religious phenomena) and the daimon (i.e., critical distance and vulnerability to correction) in the study of religion. Such a combination, argues Neville (2002), can prevent both the "blindness of uncritical participation" and "the projection of one's methodological, theoretical, and more broadly cultural assumptions onto the religious path being studied" (109). Today, the fact that an increasing number of scholars of religion display both religious commitments *and* critical perspectives on traditional religious beliefs (Barnard 1994; Cabezón 2006) further problematizes this and other related modernist dichotomies such as insider/outsider, emic/etic, or confessional/academic.

In her discussion of insider/outsider perspectives, for example, Kim Knott (2005) situates various degrees of detached observation and engaged participation along a continuum of possibilities, ranging from the "complete observer" to the "observer-as-participant" to the "participant-as-observer" to the "complete participant." Commenting on the work of scholars of religion who value participation and critical distance, Knott writes:

> Such an insider-researcher acts as both insider and outsider, and the movement back and forth opens him or her up to a range of types of information: that which is available to outsiders, that which is only available to those within the researched community (insiders), and that which becomes available to the researcher through his or her reflexive participation in the research process (254).[14]

My position on this question is germane not only to Knott's observation but also to Kripal's (2001) "methodological nondualism," which intends to

> challenge the dichotomy between insider and outsider and not assume *either* that the historian, psychologist, or anthropologist who seems to be outside...does not also know and appreciate something of the shimmering truths of which the insider so passionately speaks *or* that the insider, however devoted to an ideal, cannot also see clearly and bravely something of the actual of which the scholar tries to speak (323).[15]

But how may walking this middle path influence the teaching of mysticism? To begin, given that these standpoints can be combined in scholarly sound and fruitful ways, to present them as dichotomous not only is fallacious but also may constrain students' methodological choices. I have repeatedly witnessed how a participatory pedagogy naturally fosters the adoption of a perspective of "critical participation"—one that can also potentially dance between insider and outsider positions.

It cannot be stressed enough that to embrace a participatory approach does not mean to eschew critical perspectives of mystical phenomena. On the contrary, going into the depths of one's emotions (and their fierce moral discrimination) via a hermeneutics of the heart, cultivating empathic attunement through role play, paying attention to one's bodily reactions while engaged in dialogical inquiry, and being receptive to visions or insights in contemplative exercises—all these strategies can offer potent resources for critical discernment in the teaching and study of mysticism.

Here are some examples: Looking deeply into her anger, one of my students discerned a subtle patriarchal bias in a paper's comparative categories; becoming aware of a constriction in the flow of his vital energy, another raised questions about a sexually dissociative account of spiritual realization presented in class; and a third student, paying attention to her body's experience of lifeless stagnation while reading, developed a critical account of certain types of mysticism as disembodied and even ecologically pernicious. Thus, a critical-participatory approach opens a vast methodological sea between the extremes of engaged participation and critical distance that, if skillfully navigated, can integrate the virtues of both standpoints while avoiding their shortcomings.[16]

As should be obvious, however, there is not a generic formula to integrate engaged and detached perspectives in the teaching and study of mysticism.

Both teachers and students need to locate themselves at a point of the continuum described by Knott, justify their methodological choice, and clearly state the specific manner in which they develop (or plan to develop) their scholarship. That said, students can legitimately reject the value of participatory engagement and choose to develop their scholarship from an entirely detached or critical perspective—an approach prevalent in the socioscientific study of religion and theoretically developed by authors such as Robert Segal (1992), Donald Wiebe (1999), Ivan Strenski (2006), J. Samuel Preus (1987), and Bernard McCutcheon (2001). Likewise, students can reject the value of detached observation and choose to work from a strictly engaged or participatory perspective, as in certain forms of theological and confessional scholarship. In both cases, however, students (and teachers) should not be allowed to remain nonresponsive to the many criticisms raised about these extreme standpoints. Strictly "detached" students will need to address the challenges to the value and very possibility of pure objectivity or metaphysical agnosticism issued by the postempiricist philosophies of science, feminism, social constructivism, poststructuralism, and religious emic epistemologies, among other disciplines. And strictly "engaged" students will need to respond to the charges of dogmatism, circularity, and epistemological blindness raised by modern critical thinkers. The bottom line is that in both cases students need to justify their positions in the wake of these critiques and display a high degree of self-reflexivity about their chosen methodological standpoint—both basic features of any robust scholarship.

Conclusion

In this chapter, I have described a participatory integral approach to the teaching of a doctoral seminar in comparative mysticism. I believe it is fair to say that this participatory pedagogy engages a fuller range of epistemic competences than those usually accessed in mainstream graduate education. Besides intellectual reason, the seminar's pedagogical strategies foster the development and participation of students' somatic, emotional, intuitive, imaginal, and spiritual intelligences. I have also argued that this pedagogical approach forges a methodological stance capable of integrating the strengths of engaged participation and critical distance.

My pedagogical experimentation is motivated by the conviction that the teaching and study of mysticism must be neither exclusively guided by a "participatory heart," which feels deeply but lacks critical rigor, nor by a "cognicentric mind," rightfully critical of religious dogma and ideology but usually out of touch with the person's intuitive powers and the world's mysteries. As Daniel Gold (2003) persuasively argues, what defines the work of the most successful interpretive writers of religion—from Mircea Eliade to Clifford

Geertz to George Dumézil to Wendy Doniger—is *precisely* a synthesis of a "soft heart," characterized by empathic imagination and intuition, and a "hard mind" capable of penetrating analysis through the use of the critical intellect. From a participatory perspective, however, an integrated cognition is not exhausted by a fusion of head and heart; it also needs to incorporate the epistemic powers of the body, the erotic, and the mystical (Ferrer and Sherman 2008a, 39–41).[17]

As a final thought, I am mindful that the application of some of the participatory strategies described herein may be more fitting in alternative institutions such as CIIS than in standard universities. After all, most students come to the Institute seeking a more integral education that offers intellectual rigor, engages multiple ways of knowing, values personal experience, and takes seriously the potential cognitive value of spirituality. In addition, most students at the Institute are spiritual practitioners of various sorts, whose intellectual and spiritual paths are often intimately intertwined and who combine rational inquiry with experiential practice. In this context, the "cash value" of dancing between the engaged stance of the insider and the critical stance of the outsider is a "no brainer" for most CIIS students. That said, I feel confident that an increasing number of teachers and students of mysticism (and religion) in academia may recognize the value of exploring participatory approaches, and that in future years, mainstream education will embrace pedagogies that systematically engage multiple ways of knowing. The explicit inclusion of all human attributes in learning and inquiry goes a long way in reconnecting education with its root meaning (*edu-care*: "bringing out the wholeness within") and, therefore, with transformative healing and spiritual growth, both of which involve a movement toward human wholeness.

Notes

1. On the history and educational mission of CIIS, see the essays by McDermott (2005), Subbiondo (2005), and Wexler (2005) in Bronson (2005). Subbiondo (CIIS current president) outlines ten principles of integral education drawn from a course of my design (see Subbiondo 2006). For the current mission statement of the Institute, see www.ciis.edu.

2. For a description of the programs' curricula and courses, see http://ciis.edu/Academics/Graduate_Programs/East_West_Psychology_.html.

3. For references of the sources used in these sections, as well as of the case studies and sample comparative papers mentioned, see the seminar syllabus at http://ciis.edu/Academics/Graduate_Programs/East_West_Psychology_/Jorge_Ferrer.html.

4. Space does not allow me to discuss here the relationship between epistemic and political participation in higher education not only in course design but also regarding assessment. For a provocative essay on participatory assessment, see Heron (1988).

5. For an extended discussion of the differences between mind-centered, bricolage, and participatory approaches, see Ferrer, Romero, and Albareda (2005).

6. For discussions of validity and assessment in multidimensional inquiry, see Braud (1998) and Heron (1996).

7. For a report of a fuller participatory inquiry developed in another of my courses, see Osterhold, Husserl, and Nicol (2007), and for some narrative accounts of students' transformative learning experiences in a version of this course recently taught at Ritsumekian University (Kyoto, Japan), see Nakagawa and Matsuda (2010). For a discussion of the body of practical work from which the course's main inquiry tools are drawn, see Ferrer (2003b).

8. For valuable discussions of critical subjectivity in the human sciences and spiritual inquiry, see Heron (1996, 1998).

9. I cannot elaborate on this point here, but I also indicate the striking parallels between Johnson's (1987) cognitive theory of the imagination—as an epistemic bridge between the embodied and the mental—and esoteric and mystical takes on the epistemic role of the active Imagination (to be distinguished from "imagination" or merely mental fantasizing) in raising sensual/perceptual experience to a visionary status in that isthmus between physical and spiritual realms that Corbin (1995, 1998) calls *mundus imaginalis*.

10. For a thorough account of the incorporation of art into scholarly inquiry, see Sullivan (2010).

11. To increase their understanding of the practice, students read Arico (1999).

12. For example, as identified by Paul and Elder (2002, 17–36). A notable exception is the critical thinker's (over)reliance on discursive reason as the final arbiter of truth claims.

13. For an extended discussion, see Ferrer, Romero, and Albareda (2005). Also see Romanyshyn's (2007) important account of research with soul in mind and articulation of an alchemical hermeneutics.

14. Cf. Taves's sustained argument for "the value of cultivating both the engaged and detached roles relative to the study of spirituality and for the value of learning to move back and forth between these roles" (2003, 187).

15. In a later work, though affirming the import of insider perspectives, Kripal privileges the outsider standpoint in the study of religion (Kripal 2006, 139–140). My own view is that each case needs to be assessed independently, and that no *a priori* or generic hierarchical relationship between these standpoints can be legitimately established to ascertain what the privileged interpretation of a religious phenomenon (say a Kalua tantric ritual or a Shipibo *ayahuasca* ceremony) may be. Paraphrasing Kripal, I would argue that it is as important to let go of the pride of the insider and embrace the "gnosis of the outsider," as it is to let go of the pride of the outsider and embrace the "gnosis of the insider."

16. Space has not allowed me to discuss the challenges involved in implementing participatory pedagogies, such as overcoming of cognicentrism, avoiding anti-intellectualism, or integrating in the classroom difficult personal materials that may be activated as students engage nonmental worlds. For discussions of some of these challenges, see Ferrer, Romero, and Albareda (2005) and Barnard (1999).

17. The "gnostic epistemology" outlined by Kripal (2006) is another example of a contemporary approach to the study of religion that relies not only on reason and the critical intellect, but also on the symbolic and contemplative, the mystical body and its erotic energies.

References

Arico, Carl. 1999. "The *Lectio Divina* Tradition: Lost and Found." In *A Taste of Silence: A Guide to the Fundamentals of Centering Prayer*, 103–122. New York: Continuum.

Assagioli, Roberto. 1972. *Psychosynthesis: A Manual of Principles and Techniques*. New York: Viking Press.

Barnard, William G. 1994. "Transformations and Transformers: Spirituality and the Academic Study of Mysticism," *Journal of Consciousness Studies* 1: 256–260.

——. 1999. "Meditation and Masks, Drums and Dramas: Experiential and Participatory Exercises in the Comparative Religion Classroom," *Teaching Theology and Religion* 3: 169–172.

Braud, William. 1998. "An Extended View of Validity." In *Transpersonal Research Methods for the Social Sciences: Honoring Human Experience*, edited by William Braud and Rosemarie Anderson, 213–237. Thousand Oaks, CA: Sage Publications.

Bronson, Matthew, ed. 2005. "Revisioning Higher Education." Special issue of *ReVision: A Journal of Consciousness and Transformation* 28.

Cabezón, José Ignacio. 2006. "The Discipline and Its Other: The Dialectic of Alterity in the Study of Religion," *Journal of the American Academy of Religion* 74: 32–34.

Chittick, William C. 1994. "Microcosm, Macrocosm, and Perfect Man." In *Imaginal Worlds: Ibn al-'Arabi and the Problem of Religious Diversity*, 31–38. Albany: State University of New York Press.

Corbin, Henry. 1995. "*Mundus Imaginalis* or the Imaginary and the Imaginal." In *Swedenborg and Esoteric Islam*, translated by Leonard Fox, 1–33. West Chester, PA: Swedenborg Foundation.

——. 1998. "A Theory of Visionary Knowledge." In *The Voyage and the Messenger: Iran and Philosophy*, translated by Joseph Rowe, 117–134. Berkeley, CA: North Atlantic Books.

Faivre, Antoine. 1994. *Access to Western Esotericism*. Albany: State University of New York Press.

Ferrer, Jorge. 2000. "Transpersonal Knowledge: A Participatory Approach to Transpersonal Phenomena." In *Transpersonal Knowing: Exploring the Horizons of Consciousness*, edited by Tobin Hart, Peter Nelson, and Kaisa Puhakka, 213–252. Albany: State University of New York Press.

——. 2002. *Revisioning Transpersonal Theory: A Participatory Vision of Human Spirituality*. Albany: State University of New York Press.

——. 2003a. "Dialogical Inquiry as Spiritual Practice," *Tikkun: A Bimonthly Jewish Critique of Politics, Culture, & Society* 18: 29–32.

——. 2003b. "Integral Transformative Practice: A Participatory Perspective," *The Journal of Transpersonal Psychology* 35: 21–42.

——. 2008. "Spiritual Knowing as Participatory Enaction: An Answer to the Question of Religious Pluralism." In *The Participatory Turn: Spirituality, Mysticism, Religious Studies*, edited by Jorge Ferrer and Jacob H. Sherman, 135–169. Albany: State University of New York Press.

Ferrer, Jorge, Marina T. Romero, and Ramon V. Albareda. 2005. "Integral Transformative Education: A Participatory Proposal," *Journal of Transformative Education* 3: 306–330.

Ferrer, Jorge, and Jacob H. Sherman. 2008a. "Introduction: The Participatory Turn in Spirituality, Mysticism, and Religious Studies." In *The Participatory Turn: Spirituality, Mysticism, Religious Studies,* edited by Jorge Ferrer and Jacob H. Sherman, 1–78. Albany: State University of New York Press.

———, eds. 2008b. *The Participatory Turn: Spirituality, Mysticism, Religious Studies.* Albany: State University of New York Press.

Forman, Robert K. C. 1998. "Introduction: Mystical Consciousness, the Innate Capacity, and the Perennial Psychology." In *The Innate Capacity: Mysticism, Psychology, and Philosophy,* edited by Robert K. C. Forman, 3–41. New York: Oxford University Press.

Gold, Daniel. 2003. *Aesthetics and Analysis in Writing on Religion: Modern Fascinations.* Berkeley: University of California Press.

Heron, John. 1988. "Assessment Revisited." In *Developing Student Autonomy in Learning,* edited by David Boud, 77–90. London: Kogan Page.

———. 1996. *Co-operative Inquiry: Research into the Human Condition.* Thousand Oaks, CA: Sage Publications.

———. 1998. *Sacred Science: Person-Centred Inquiry into the Spiritual and the Subtle.* Ross-on-Wye, UK: PCCS Books.

Johnson, Mark. 1987. *The Body in the Mind: The Bodily Basis of Meaning, Imagination, and Reason.* Chicago: University of Chicago Press.

Jónsson, Gunnlaugur A. 1988. *The Image of God: Genesis 1:26–28 in a Century of Old Testament Research,* translated by Lorraine Svendsen. Lund: Almqvist and Wiskell.

King, Sally. 2001. "The *Philosophia Perennis* and the Religions of the World." In *The Philosophy of Seyyed Hassein Nasr. The Library of Living Philosophers,* vol. 28, edited by L. E. Hahn, R. E. Auxier, and W. Stone, 203–220. Chicago: Open Court.

Knott, Kim. 2005. "Insider/Outsider Perspectives." In *The Routledge Companion to the Study of Religion,* edited by John Hinnells, 243–258. New York: Routledge.

Kripal, Jeffrey, J. 2001. *Roads of Excess, Palaces of Wisdom: Eroticism and Reflexibility in the Study of Mysticism.* Chicago: University of Chicago Press.

———. 2006. *The Serpent's Gift: Gnostic Reflections on the Study of Religion.* Chicago: University of Chicago Press.

Lincoln, Bruce. 1986. *Myth, Cosmos, and Society: Indo-European Themes of Creation and Destruction.* Cambridge, MA: Harvard University Press.

McCutcheon, Bernard. 2001. *Critics Not Caretakers: Redescribing the Public Study of Religion.* Albany: State University of New York Press.

McDermott, Robert. 2005. "An Emersonian Approach to Integral Education." *ReVision: A Journal of Consciousness and Transformation* 28: 6–17.

Metzger, Deena. 1992. "Writing as a Spiritual Practice." In *Writing for Your Life,* 183–244. San Francisco: Harper.

Nakagawa, Yoshi, and Yoshiko Matsuda, eds. 2010. *Integral Approach: Integral Transformative Inquiry.* Kyoto, Japan: Institute of Human Sciences, Ritsumekian University.

Nasr, Seyyed Hassein. 1993. "The *Philosophia Perennis* and the Study of Religion." In *The Need for a Sacred Science,* 53–68. Albany: State University of New York Press.

———. 2001. "Reply to Sally B. King." In *The Philosophy of Seyyed Hassein Nasr. The Library of Living Philosophers:* vol. 28, edited by L. E. Hahn, R. E. Auxier, and W. Stone, 221–231. Chicago: Open Court.

Neville, Robert C. 1982. *The Tao and the Daimon: Segments of a Religious Inquiry*. Albany, NY: State University of New York Press.

———. 2002. *Religion in Late Modernity*. Albany: State University of New York Press.

Osterhold, Helge M., Elisabeth R. Husserl, and David Nicol. 2007. "Rekindling the Fire of Transformative Education: A Participatory Case Study," *Journal of Transformative Education* 5: 221–245.

Paul, Richard W., and Linda Elder. 2002. *Critical Thinking: Tools for Taking Charge of Your Professional and Personal Life*. Upper Saddle River, NJ: FT Press.

Preus, J. Samuel. 1987. *Explaining Religion: Criticism and Theory from Bodin to Freud*. New Haven, CT: Yale University Press.

Romanyshyn, Robert D. 2007. *The Wounded Researcher: Research with Soul in Mind*. New Orleans: Spring Journal Books.

Saso, Michael. 1997. "The Taoist Body and Cosmic Prayer." In *Religion and the Body*, edited by Sarah Coakley, 230–247. New York: Cambridge University Press.

Segal, Robert. 1992. *Explaining and Interpreting Religion*. New York: Peter Lang.

Sells, Michael. 1994. *Mystical Languages of Unsaying*. Chicago: University of Chicago Press.

Shokek, Shimon. 2001. *Kabbalah and the Art of Being*. London: Routledge.

Staal, Frits. 1975. *Exploring Mysticism*. Berkeley: University of California Press.

Strenski, Ivan. 2006. *Thinking about Religion: An Historical Introduction to Theories of Religion*. Malden, MA: Blackwell.

Subbiondo, Joseph L. 2005. "An Approach to Integral Education: A Case for Spirituality in Higher Education." *ReVision: A Journal of Consciousness and Transformation* 28: 18–23.

———. 2006. "Integrating Religion and Spirituality in Higher Education: Meeting the Global Challenges of the 21st Century," *Religion & Education* 33: 1–19.

Sullivan, Graeme. 2010. *Art Practice as Research: Inquiry in Visual Arts*. 2nd ed. Thousand Oaks, CA: Sage Publications.

Taves, Anne. 2003. "Detachment and Engagement in the Study of 'Lived Experience,'" *Spiritus* 3: 186–208.

Wexler, Judie. 2005. "Toward a Model of Integral Education." *ReVision: A Journal of Consciousness and Transformation* 28: 29–34.

Wiebe, Donald. 1999. *The Politics of Religious Studies: The Continuing Conflict with Theology in the Academy*. New York: St. Martin's Press.

11

Teaching Mysticism in Dialogue with Gender and Embodiment at a Quaker Seminary

A FEMINIST APPROACH

Stephanie Ford

Intro

Teaching mystical texts in a seminary classroom is a challenging task, particularly given the constraints of a semester-long time frame, the plethora of texts and materials that might be considered, and the needs of contemporary seminary students. Also, liberation theologies and global consciousness bring constructive tensions to the selection of texts and the approach taken to the course content. Furthermore, in a way specific to seminary teaching, students' developing ministerial competency is critical to course design. Here, too, the denominational ethos and theological vision of the school—named and understood—are factors in developing the course emphases.

This chapter describes a pedagogy that employs self-reflection, historical inquiry, and liberation hermeneutics—with particular focus on gender and embodiment issues—used in the "History of Christian Spirituality," a course that I taught for nine years at Earlham School of Religion (ESR) that is focused around Christian mystical texts. First, I consider the particular academic context of ESR, a Quaker seminary, and the feminist standpoint and vision that I bring to the course, followed by an overview of the structure and content of the course itself, with a reflection on the particular concerns on teaching mysticism to seminarians. Then, I seek to identify the dynamics among readers and texts—the "*invisible hermeneutical community*" (Kripal 2001, 9). In particular, I consider the pedagogical approaches I employ to foster a liberation hermeneutics attentive to issues of gender and embodiment in teaching a unit on Mechthild of Magdeburg. Finally, to ascertain how the course supports students' ministerial formation, I offer some examples of students' independent research and creativity, considering their critical, mystical, and embodied engagement with primary and secondary sources.

Teaching History of Christian Spirituality: Academic Context

As one of two seminaries in the United States in the Quaker tradition, ESR's primary mission is to offer an inclusive Christian theological education at the intersection of several streams of Quakerism, a tradition rooted in the Separatist movement of seventeenth-century England and founded by an enigmatic mystic himself, George Fox (1624–1691). The seminary, established in 1960, promotes a centrist Quaker vision of universal ministry. Pastoral ministry, along with peace and justice activities, pastoral care, spiritual formation and direction, and writing represent some of areas of study students pursue in their professional studies as ministers.[1]

From their origin, members of the Religious Society of Friends have waited upon the Inner Light for spiritual sustenance for the work of social justice in the world. Friends became convinced that their "experimental" discovery of the Inner Light, which might manifest bodily as trembling or quaking during moments of prophetic speech, would eventually lead to the purification of all Christendom.[2] Therefore, it is not surprising that spiritual formation would have a vital role in a Quaker curriculum, one connected to the work for gender, racial, and class justice. ESR was one of the first Protestant seminaries to give spirituality a distinctive place in a divinity school curriculum. The school identifies a vision of transformative education along the lines of what could be called an "ethical mysticism."[3] A range of spirituality courses enable students to consciously reflect on religious experience, to learn and practice forms of prayer and other spiritual disciplines, to consider a theology and practice of Christian discipleship, and to develop skills in offering spiritual direction and spiritual formation leadership—all with a concern to further peace and justice. In the "History of Christian Spirituality," students are introduced to several core mystical texts as well as some nontraditional sources. The course emphasizes an experiential-reflective encounter with these primary sources. In preparation, students must take a required introductory course in spiritual formation and a course of their own choosing in church history. These prerequisites enable students to (1) gain skill reflecting on religious experience, (2) learn nonjudgmental listening skills vital to the safe sharing of personal spiritual experiences in the class setting, and (3) develop some competence in redacting texts within their historical context.

Although the seminary is Quaker, over half of the student body is ecumenical, ranging from mainstream Protestants to members of the Swedenborg Church. Residentially centered until 2001, the school now has a flourishing distance-learning program. *Access* students take online classes and residential intensive courses to complete master of divinity and master of arts degrees. Every faculty member contributes to the development of intensives and online courses to flesh out the core curriculum for the *Access* program. In 2008–2009,

her life and visionary experience. Cultural rules of the courtesan, medieval classism, and ecclesiastical hierarchy also reverberate through her multivalent text. Her writing must be read with a consciousness of her otherness. Thus the study of historical context and biography (recognizing that interpretative lenses are layered there as well) is also essential to my pedagogical approach using a liberation hermeneutics in the study of mystics of times past.[12]

[handwritten: course objective]

Course Structure and Content

The "History of Christian Spirituality" is a thirteen-week, upper level spirituality course at ESR. The structure of the course is a seminar in which class members participate in culling questions and facilitating discussion around concerns that they bring to the authors and texts, both primary and secondary sources. My role as instructor is to (1) provide the groundwork on the subjects of mysticism and Christian history; (2) bear witness to my own experiential engagement with mysticism and the mystical texts we study, sharing with appropriate vulnerability in order to facilitate student sharing; and (3) bring critical questions to the topics, themes, and persons of our study, thus fostering the application of a liberation hermeneutics to our sources. The students, in addition to engaging in class discussions, also prepare essays and create a final project emerging from questions at the intersection of their experiential dialogue with and critical reflection on primary texts. As the instructor, I provide a selection of topics and questions for three synthesis essays, but the students themselves discern the topic for their final project (with instructor approval).

Ideally, if time and money were not at issue, students would be assigned several volumes of full-length mystical texts so that they would have primary texts for their ongoing study; however, in one semester, these texts could not receive adequate attention, at least in the course as currently conceived. Almost every time I have taught "History of Christian Spirituality," I have debated narrowing to one or two texts and delving into them deeply versus conducting a broader survey. I keep returning to the latter. A critical aspect for me in discerning the number of texts is the feminist hermeneutics I apply around gender and the body, which requires a significant cross-section of material. It is likely that if we used in-depth literary analysis of a few texts, the same questions and range of thought might emerge; nevertheless, seminary students also want to become familiar with broad selection of resources in order to be equipped for ministry in a variety of contexts (such as being able to quote a mystical writer thoughtfully in a sermon). *[handwritten: syllabus]* Furthermore, it is not only the texts but the authors' lives that class members want to engage. Thus, the variety of female and male mystical personalities, from Clare of Assisi to Julian of Norwich to Teresa of Avila and Therese of Lisieux and from Origen of Alexandria to Francis of Assisi to Meister Eckhart and Thomas Merton, also provides important experiential data regarding the mystical journey.

The face-to-face class is a weekly seminar of three hours, and the online class revolves around weekly discussion through continuous, asynchronous interaction (three posts required per week). In both versions, the course is designed around weekly units focused on one or more mystics from a similar time period. During the first week of the course, definitions of mysticism and spirituality are considered—and students write an essay proposing their own tentative definitions; in the weeks that follow, biographies and secondary sources become vital tools for students to make experiential, yet critical encounters with primary mystical texts and their authors. At the end of the course, students are asked to revisit those initial essays to see how their views have changed or not on questions of definition.

Although the overall vision for course content has not changed substantially since I began teaching the class in 2001, what has changed have been secondary sources that I and students read (taking advantage of new scholarship) and the course emphases.[13] In early offerings of the class, I was zealous to introduce students to the Beguine movement of the thirteenth century, given its rich gender alterity on the medieval landscape. Therefore, I took two to three weeks with primary and secondary sources on Beguine mysticism, focusing on Mechthild of Magdeburg, Hadewijch of Brabant, and Beatriz of Nazareth.[14] However, this emphasis left little room for engaging other women mystics, while also keeping overall gender balance. Therefore, I shifted the content on Beguine mystics to a single unit in a complementary study of Mechthild of Magdeburg and Meister Eckhart, with material provided on the Beguine movement as background. This shift turned out to be fruitful because of the dramatic difference between the embodied, kataphatic Mechthild and the apophatic Eckhart (even as there are striking similarities in theology);[15] the juxtaposition became an important pedagogical tool, enabling rich discussion. Following that, I decided to pair Carmelites John of the Cross and Teresa of Avila in a later unit (more typical in studies of mysticism), which again enabled students to witness contrasting approaches alongside rich theological similarities on prayer and the Dark Night experience. Already the course included a unit on Francis and Clare of Assisi, in which their biographies and writings were compared. Altogether, the three pairings provide significant fodder for conversations on gender and mystical experience just by virtue of their concurrence.

As a major text for the course, *Light from Light: An Anthology of Christian Mysticism,* offers selections from a number of the primary texts that we cover.[16] Of course, as an anthology, the selections are contextually spare, and the gender inclusiveness of the text, though stronger in the second edition, does not include the Beguine mystics—though it does their counterpart, Meister Eckhart. The advantage is that the book covers a number of mystical works, with contextual introductions to each, so that it proves a valuable resource for students' personal archives. (For the unit on Mechthild, I provide selections from her treatise, *The Flowing Light of the Godhead*). I supplement *Light from Light* with a volume, *Celtic Spirituality*, as well as the text on African American spirituals and a collection of Thomas Merton's writings from the *Modern Spiritual Masters Series*.[17] As a secondary text, Janet Ruffing's edited collection, *Mysticism and Social Transformation*, brings worthwhile discussion on the mystical foundations of Franciscan praxis, Meister Eckhart's preaching, Teresa of Avila's work of justice, and African American female spiritual leaders of the nineteenth century.

Our overview of Christian mysticism in the Western tradition begins with Origen of Alexandria, Gregory of Nyssa, and the Desert tradition in the third and fourth centuries in North Africa. Next, we examine the life and writings of Augustine, particularly his *Confessions*, alongside the work of the Pseudo-Dionysius (although not influential in the West until the ninth century). From there, we skip several centuries to a study of the life and texts of the Italians Francis and Clare of Assisi in the twelfth century. At this point, the course deviates from the standard corpus and turns to a unit on Celtic Christian spirituality.[18] We then consider the German mystics Mechthild of Magdeburg and Meister Eckhart of the thirteenth century. The next unit covers the life and writings of Julian of Norwich (fourteenth century), followed by a unit on the sixteenth-century Carmelites John of the Cross and Teresa of Avila, along with some all-too-brief attention to the later Carmelite mystic Therese of Lisieux (1873–1897). For a second time, the course leaves classical texts for a study of African American spirituals and to discuss Joy Bostic's essay on mystical experience and activism among African American women in the nineteenthcentury.[19] We then turn to Evelyn Underhill (1875–1941), exploring in addition to primary texts in *Light from Light*, selections from my own dissertation on the British spiritual writer.[20] Finally, we explore the life and writings of Thomas Merton (twentieth century) before the last week when class members share their independent projects. As one option for the third synthesis essay and then for their final projects, students can choose to study a mystic that we have not encountered. Catherine of Siena and Marguerite Porete have been two women mystics whose lives and writings have often inspired further independent student research.

As mentioned, before we delve into the texts themselves, I facilitate a class discussion on defining mysticism with the hope that the students may begin naming their own mystical encounters and so that they might become critically cognizant of the cultural stereotypes and universalizing glosses that arise around the term *mysticism* and related notions of *spirituality*. Generalizations that I hear frequently are that mystics are otherworldly, introverted, and unwilling to engage the work of justice (because they are focused on ethereal endeavors). In the introduction to her text, Ruffing addresses that concern skillfully, pointing out that in the Christian tradition, the testimony of social justice goes hand-in-hand with the mystics' love for God. The essays that follow *objective*

support her thesis, and the evidence bears true in our overall study. Mystical experiences seem to enhance and even enable these faithful ones to do the work of peacemaking in the world.[21] A second and more challenging problem arises in the debate between essentialist and constructivist views on the nature of mysticism. Perhaps because divinity students are typically believers, they project a theistic premise onto mystical experiences; furthermore, the mystics we study are theistic. Students who have taken a course on interreligious dialogue have a better grasp of the issues, but it is not a required prerequisite. For our course, students read a number of definitions of mysticism as well as quotes from mystics,[22] and then write a definition essay. This process begins to tease out their assumptions.

As a scholar and teacher of mysticism, I am persuaded by Michael Stoeber's argument for an experiential constructivist perspective, which "overcomes the problems associated with the extreme constructivist thesis" by maintaining "the positive impact of the Real upon the mystic" (1994, 16). Yet, enabling students to even acknowledge the constructivist's position is challenging. Several weeks into the course, whether offered on campus or online, some students seem to revert to an essentialist gloss in their view of mysticism, particularly after reading Underhill's writings in the modernist period (which arguably present an essentialist view). I attribute this "slippage" to two factors: first, as I have indicated, there is that inherent missionary desire in Christianity for a unified theistic core, and second, students bring a recurring hope for potential unity across traditions (or at least some shared core of experience) that will further peace.

Cultivating the "Invisible Hermeneutical Community": A Pedagogy of Experiential Reflection

There is a joke at the seminary that students have to reflect *on* their own reflections when it comes to spirituality courses! Certainly, extensive oral and written reflection of personal and corporate spiritual experience is emphasized; still, there are two important contextual caveats to what might at first appear to be a solipsistic pedagogy of experiential reflection. One of them is that the Quaker posture of listening within has always been vital to its mystical spirituality. Quaker philosopher and mystic Thomas Kelly describes this testimony of attentiveness to the Inner Light:

> For by this very Light within you, is your recognition given. In this humanistic age we suppose man is the initiator and God is the responder. But the Living Christ within us is the initiator and we are the responders. God the lover, the accuser, the revealer of light and darkness presses within us. (Kelly 1941, 4)

A second caveat also follows this fundamental tenet of Quaker practice, which is that one's inward listening is done in community, in dialogue with others (who are also listening to the Spirit) for the purpose of discernment and ultimately creative action in the world.[23] In the case of our course, I would contend, the class becomes a kind of invisible hermeneutical community consisting of the historical subject, that is, the mystic (who, of course, is part of his or her own historical hermeneutical community), the hermeneutical-mystical experiences of the scholar, and hermeneutical responses of the scholar's readers (Kripal 2001, 9).

Moreover, I simply follow Kripal's point further by noting that the class members as readers bring their own mystical experiences to this invisible community. Indeed, it is my pedagogical intention to foster a productive space for internal recovery, appropriate sharing, and deepening self-understanding of personal mystical experiences, in addition to the mystical hermeneutics of engaging mystics and their scholars. I believe that the students come with "implicit mystical concerns" and that at times in the class community, these "hermeneutical encounters [take] on powerful and sometimes genuinely transformative dimensions" (Kripal 2001, 6).

Lectio Divina and the Hermeneutical Community

The practice of *lectio divina* supports the creation of this hermeneutical community. *Lectio divina* is taught as a primary spiritual practice in the introductory formation course, and in later courses, the practice constitutes a pillar in the approach to autobiographical and devotional texts.[24] Nevertheless, particularly in "History of Christian Spirituality," *lectio divina* is not naïvely applied, but rather entails a study of context (religious, social, philosophical, and political influences), the author and her or his community, with attention to enhancing self-awareness of the critical lenses that we as contemporary readers bring. Moreover, as a hermeneutical encounter with the text, the reader-student is encouraged to be aware of affirming, clarifying, and transformative movements within her- or himself.[25] The sharing of these inner movements is optional, but having taken foundational course in spiritual formation and experienced the exploratory ethos that typifies ESR, students often share in both residential and online versions of the course. Indeed, in the seminary context, where spiritual formation is an important dynamic in the minister's development, this kind of critical-spiritual reading of texts hopefully provides a crucible for strengthening ministerial identity. In the Quaker context, it could be argued that the practical formation of the minister might be likened to that of a mystic, given that a posture of waiting upon the Spirit is central. Thus, such hermeneutical encounters with spiritual forebears, Quaker and ecumenical, are important to the formation of these students-as-ministers.[26]

for introduction
to course

The Case of Mechthild of Magdeburg

The four movements of *lectio divina*—reading, meditation, prayer, and contemplation—may be reconsidered for educational endeavors as attention, reflection, receptivity, and transformation.[27] In order to truly attend to the
otherness of a mystical writing, student-readers must study historical context
and biography. As readers of Mechthild of Magdeburg's *The Flowing Light of
the Godhead*, students must consider the medieval church, the economic and
social realities for medieval women, the Beguine movement, the courtly love
tradition, and the radical nature of a text written in the vernacular (Mechthild
wrote in German rather than Latin) among other issues. A careful reading of
Mechthild's writings also entails examining the sparse, but important biographical data to be found about her life, such as the fact that Mechthild described having regular ecstatic visitations from the age of twelve on.

Students are invited "attend" to Mechthild's writing by engaging particular
visions of hers as they might a sacred text. Such an approach allows the text to
ask questions of them in their relationship to God, soul, and the body. It also
allows students to witness Mechthild's "otherness," which indirectly promotes
safe space for their own embodied mystical experiences to be expressed. One
of those visions, a Eucharistic vision from Book II of *The Flowing Light of the
Godhead*, is wonderfully multivalent, and reading it enables the class as a whole
to consider several contextual issues before and alongside a hearing of the
text.[28] In that vision, we find evidence of Mechthild's critique of the priesthood
(since John the Baptist, a priest of unsanctified lineage, offers the Eucharist in
the vision); we infer her self-understanding as a Beguine, identify medieval
views of the heavenly hierarchy, hear a song in the *troubaritz* tradition, and
experience the powerful divine feminine role of Mary the mother of Jesus.

Staying close to Mechthild's visions prevents romanticized generalizations
about medieval woman mystics and female embodiedness, while also enabling
students to experience a sensual mysticism in which the body is a locus for
contact with God. Mechthild's conscious conflicts around the body are quickly
evident in the vision: She refers to herself as a "foul puddle" and "wretched"
and then at other moments, looks down to see her body transformed into "a
noble maiden" who wears "a garland of splendid gold" (Mechthild 1998, 74).
Not unsurprisingly in the ecstasy of a heavenly Eucharist, Mechthild wonders
aloud about death, revealing both her longing for heaven and her grief over the
potential loss of earthly existence. As she, the "poor girl," finally approaches
the altar, the host is transformed into a wounded lamb with "sweet eyes" that
can never be forgotten. Mary facilitates the communion, and the poor girl arrives at the altar "with great love and an open soul." Taking the lamb into her
mouth, Mechthild finds that it has moved downward, suckling her heart in a
sensual feeding moment that she gives herself over to.[29] The scene is intense, a
bit grisly for contemporary readers, and deeply erotic. The *troubaritz* that was

inscribed on her garland earlier comes to fruition: "His eyes into my eyes, / His heart into my heart, / His soul into my soul / Untiringly enclosed" (74).

The metaphor of fluidity is a key to Mechthild's images; Michelle Voss Roberts describes Mechthild as having a "fluid ontology" (2008, 644). Divine moisture is imaged as dew, rain, blood, honey, milk, and wine. The soul also carries this same fluid nature. The soul, in fact, is likened to God in her capacity for immanence and transcendence as she flows back to God "according to her ability" (VII.45). The driving force of this communion between God and the soul is desire. The divine feminine image of Lady Love in courtesan poetry, *Minne*, becomes for Mechthild a divine "imagistic container" for her ecstatic spirituality. As a feminine divine image, *Minne* is "a symbol of power, authority, boldness, mental and spiritual well-being and free" (Wiethaus 1991, 50). *Minne* can be problematic in her forcefulness, and a few students have worried about her abusive tendencies.

The *lectio* experience for students in reflection and receptivity emerges in various responses. Some wonder about Mechthild's mental health; others find the eroticism uncomfortable even though they might also consider bridal or love mysticism a valid expression of communion with the Divine. Many students reflect on the major differences between Mechthild's visions and Eckhart's sermons, read during the same week. As noted earlier, this moment enables both a discussion of apophatic and kataphatic mysticisms as well as an opportunity to wrestle with generalizations about men and women mystics, embodiment, and the centuries-long absence of Mechthild's voice from the received tradition.[30] Because of the unsettling paradoxes revealed in Mechthild's Eucharistic vision, students tend to refrain from proto-feminist generalizations, as well as to reconsider their own self-understandings of the body-soul relationship. Some students respond that Mechthild's visions are refreshingly evocative of divine-human mutuality, with the soul daring in her vulnerability and human desire a powerful agent in mystical union.

How students are transformed by such a hermeneutical encounter with Mechthild's visions and writings can be more difficult to assess. Students often make comparisons to other erotic mystical poetry they have read, like that of Kabir and Rumi, but the comparisons are fleeting. More profoundly, some acknowledge that they have had mystical experiences that seem unconventional, and depending on the perceived level of safety in the class, students may recall visions, dreams, and embodied experiences of the Divine that they have had. In papers or informal responses that I as the instructor read or hear, students have often shared deeply; in online discussion, students are sometimes more detached in self-reference, but nonetheless willing to name embodied spiritual experiences as something they have experienced.

Creative Expressions, Ministry, and Mysticism

For their essays and final projects, students are encouraged to think about
the ministries they are involved in currently or imagine participating in in
the future. Because ESR does not narrow ministry to congregational settings
only, students consider a variety of settings for ministry. Students may envision themselves leading retreats, teaching within a congregation or alternative setting, offering comfort as a chaplain, preaching, and leading small
groups. One student designed a richly textured pilgrimage to three distinct
cultural sites in New Mexico, one of which was El Santurario de Chimayó.
The mystical range in his text, embodied, nature-centered, kataphatic, and
apophatic, was thorough. Focusing on writing as ministry, another student
wrote a one-woman script—the protagonist having a dialog with several
mystics. Another student designed an eight-week course for a congregation,
introducing participants to a variety of mystics ranging from Gregory of
Nyssa to Julian of Norwich. Several students over the years have designed
retreats, some focused around the ever-popular Celtic Christian theme;
others have developed retreats centered around women mystics like Teresa
of Avila and Julian of Norwich. One student wrote poetry in the vein of
Mechthild; another painted a stormy terrain in which the same mystic with
open arms toward heaven cries: "I cannot dance, o Lord, unless You lead me;
if You wish me to leap joyfully, let me see You dance and sing—then I will
leap into Love" (Mechthild 1998, 59).

In a final "exam," students are asked to consider how their minds may have
changed through the encounter with these female and male mystics of the
Christian tradition. The responses are rich in self-identification and inspiration. One student expressed his transformation in the metaphor of new
"friends" in his balcony:

> I have people in my balcony that were not there before. My commu-
> nion of saints is bigger and better. Gregory of Nyssa, the anonymous
> writer of the Cloud of Unknowing, and the Pseudo-Dionysius are
> waving me out of bed in the morning, whispering about the gifts of
> silence, helping me to light my candle, inviting me down the apophatic
> way and pointing to the gifts along the way. I have Francis nudging me
> to kiss my lepers. I have Claire praying that I kiss the Christ within
> me. I have Julian blessing my senses and their ability to reveal the
> amazing delights of God's creation. I have Teresa calling me to bold
> and loving action in the face of resistance.... And while there are
> layers of complexity that each names in their own way, the song this
> balcony chorus sings to me is quite simple, "Do what you need to do
> to stay awake—don't miss the graceful glimpses of the Great Mystery
> that come your way—it is what life is about."[31]

Conclusion

Seminary students bring to their study of the Christian mystical tradition curiosity, some biases understandings of mysticism, and yet a real hunger to study mystics as they prepare for ministry. By taking this course after they have gained some experience in self-reflection and in the interpretation of historical texts, students are better prepared to do the critical-spiritual reading that is foundational to the hermeneutical encounter. Nevertheless during the course, it is important to periodically return to definitions of mysticism so that the tendency toward essentialist glossing may be acknowledged and critiqued. A liberation hermeneutics attentive to issues of gender and the body bring nontraditional voices to the fore, such as Mechthild of Magdeburg's as well as Celtic and African American voices. By staying close to the text, students may be checked before making generalizations about women mystics and embodiment, while also reckoning with sensual mystical data. Students benefit from these dialogues with a variety of persons within the Christian tradition, often finding creative expressions of their study for ministry. Moreover, they often become comfortable identifying their own embodied and gendered mystical encounters. ✓

Notes

1. For a description of ESR's mission and guidelines, see http://esr.earlham.edu/experience-esr.

2. Thus, the term *Quakers* was originally a derisive term used by outsiders, but gradually became accepted within the movement. Members generally speak of one another as "Friend."

3. See Brinton (1967).

4. My online design is simple. What is unique to online learning in my experience is that each student must "talk" in class, must bring reflections on the readings and specific questions related to the primary and secondary texts provided. I also provide feedback to each student weekly. This particular dynamic is the most effective aspect of online instruction, enabling for many students, particularly introverts, a thoughtful hermeneutical community. However, because of missing vocal cues and gestures, some discussions do not develop or deepen as they do in face-to-face instruction.

5. In using *standpoint*, I am applying Nancy Hartsock's insight that I as a woman and part of an oppressed group may potentially be able to see reality with at least two lenses: that of my own, as an Anglo-American woman; and with keen awareness, the male dominant group whose rules I must negotiate. Nevertheless, there are countless binaries that I cannot experience firsthand. See Hartsock (1998).

6. In the course itself, there is a unit on African American spirituals, a multivalent and rich resource for Christian spirituality, but I identify myself as a facilitator of this study rather than as a teacher of this tradition. The text we use is Arthur C. Jones (1993) *Wade in the Water: The Wisdom of the Spirituals* (Maryknoll, NY: Orbis Books). Likewise, more as a

guide to research and discussion, I facilitate a unit on Celtic Christian spirituality. While I have in the past used secondary sources to support class reflection, the last time I taught the course, I assigned readings from the volume *Celtic Spirituality* (1999) in *The Classics of Western Spirituality*, translated and introduced by Oliver Davies.

7. For example, I do not typically chose Marguerite Porete, fascinating though she is, because her writing tends toward the apophatic. Although I am more than amenable to elevating a woman mystic in the apophatic stream of mysticism, there is not enough time in a semester-long course to include her as I have other priorities for content and gender balance.

8. *The Cloud of Unknowing* is a good example of a synthesis of these two streams, for the "cloud of unknowing" is finally penetrated by the "longing dart of love." See Jantzen (1995).

9. In *Power, Gender and Christian Mysticism*, Jantzen (1995) gives credit to Origen for an intellect driven by desire and love. "Nevertheless," notes Jantzen, "it is reason, not the body or the emotions or the will, that is the human faculty amenable [in Origen's thought] . . . to union with God."

10. See Jantzen (1999).

11. See Ruffing (2001, 5).

12. Indeed, as I taught the course over the last ten years, I began to see that students needed more critical awareness of historical context in the study of mysticism and, thus, decided to require the additional prerequisite of at least one church history course.

13. One horizon that I have explored in teaching the course is to give a global context for the history of Christian Spirituality, using the concise and valuable *Spirituality and Mysticism: A Global View* by James A. Wiseman as a secondary text for students. However, my initial attempt at working with a primary Asian Christian text was frustrating because of the time limits in a one-semester course, as well as linguistic and cultural obstacles. I continue to review materials with the hope of creating a more global course.

14. For a helpful secondary source that I have used, see Murk-Jansen (1998).

15. This pairing was not original with me. Bernard McGinn (1994) edited a scholarly work examining Meister Eckhart in dialog with the Beguine mystics, including a fine essay by Frank Tobin, "Mechthild of Magdeburg and Meister Eckhart: Points of Coincidence."

16. See Dupré and Wiseman, eds. (2001).

17. See Bochen, ed. (2000).

18. There are several reasons for the focus on Celtic Christian spirituality. One is that until recently, the tradition had been marginalized in the study of Western Christianity. It also offers an interesting array of both literary hagiography, which includes stories of the strong female mystical prophet, St. Brigit, and lay prayers, songs, and poetry that are nature-centered and embodied. The overview has also been happily received by students, several of whom have followed up with creative projects related to Celtic Christianity.

19. See Bostic (2001).

20. See Ford (2002). My dissertation examines the life and work of Underhill in light of the feminist critique of Grace Jantzen. My assessment is that although Underhill's legacy is not a contemporary feminist one, her work did resist the dominant male hegemony in significant ways. Moreover, through a broad reading of her texts, Underhill's own ecstatic mysticism and bold feminist energy emerge. In particular, her political activism against the war near the end of the war reveals the social transformation her own mysticism furthered. See also Ford (2006).

21. See Ruffing (2001).

22. In the face-to-face lecture as well as an audio file online (and written notes), I make reference to definitions of mysticism by Evelyn Underhill, William James, W. T. Stace, Steven Katz, Bernard McGinn, Robert Ellwood, and Michael Stoeber.

23. See Birkel (2004), particularly chapter 3 on discernment.

24. See Brown (2003) for an introduction to *lectio divina,* along with other prayer forms.

25. See Liebert (2002) and Wright (1996). Liebert refers to Wright's point that the work of the scholar "can be both self-implicating and transformative precisely in the way it brings us face to face with the radical otherness of what it is that we study" (42).

26. Students read primary mystical and spiritual texts in the Quaker tradition in the course "Quaker Spirituality"; therefore, we do not directly study Quaker mystical texts. However, students regularly draw comparisons or make allusions to Quaker writings.

27. See Lichtmann (2005).

28. See Tobin's translation of Mechthild of Magdeburg, *The Flowing Light of the Godhead* (1998). The vision is found in book II, number 4. The title speaks to its diverse characteristics: "The Poor Girl, the Mass of John the Baptist, the Transformation of the Host into the Lamb, the Beauty of the Angels, Four Kinds of Sanctified People, and the Golden Penny."

29. See Mechthild (1998, 75).

30. See Poor (2004).

31. Mark Siler (2009), Response to final exam, "History of Christian Spirituality," Earlham School of Religion.

References

Birkel, Michael. 2004. *Silence and Witness: The Quaker Tradition.* Traditions of Christian Spirituality Series. Maryknoll, NY: Orbis Books.

Bochen, Christine, ed. 2000. *Thomas Merton: Essential Writings.* Maryknoll, NY: Orbis Books.

Bostic, Joy R. 2001. "Mystical Experience, Radical Subjectification, and Activism in the Religious Traditions of African American Women." In *Mysticism and Social Transformation,* edited by Janet K Ruffing. Syracuse: Syracuse University Press.

Brown, Patricia D. 2003. *Paths to Prayer: Finding Your Own Way to the Presence of God.* San Francisco: Jossey-Bass.

Brinton, Howard. 1967. *Ethical Mysticism in the Society of Friends.* Pendle Hill Pamphlet 156. Wallingford, PA: Pendle Hill Publications.

Dupré, Louis, and Wiseman, James, eds. 2001. *Light from Light: An Anthology of Christian Mysticism.* New York: Paulist Press.

Ford, Stephanie. 2002. "Evelyn Underhill's Mystical Theology in Light of the Feminist Critique of Grace Jantzen." PhD diss., Catholic University of America.

———. 2006. "Crossing Over to God's Side: Evelyn Underhill and the Problem of Security," Weavings 21 (5): 30–36.

Hartsock, Nancy. 1998. *The Feminist Standpoint Revisited and Other Essays.* Boulder, CO: Westview Press.

Jantzen, Grace. 1995. *Power, Gender and Christian Mysticism.* New York: Cambridge University Press.

———. 1999. *Becoming Divine: Towards a Feminist Philosophy of Religion*. Bloomington: Indiana University Press.

Kelly, Thomas. 1941. *A Testament of Devotion*. San Francisco: Harper.

Kripal, Jeffrey J. 2001. *Roads of Excess, Palaces of Wisdom: Eroticism and Reflexivity in the Study of Mysticism*. Chicago: University of Chicago Press.

Lichtmann, Maria. 2005. *The Teacher's Way: Teaching and the Contemplative Life*. Mahwah, NJ: Paulist Press.

Liebert, Elizabeth. 2002. "The Role of Practice in the Study of Christian Spirituality," *Spiritus: A Journal of Christian Spirituality* 2 (1): 30–49.

McGinn, Bernard. 1994. *The Foundations of Mysticism: Origins to the Fifth Century*. Vol. 1, *The Presence of God: A History of Western Christian Mysticism*. New York: Crossroad.

———, ed. 1994. *Meister Eckhart and the Beguine Mystics*. New York: Continuum.

Mechthild of Magdeburg. 1998. *The Flowing Light of the Godhead*, translated and introduced by Frank Tobin. Mahwah, NJ: Paulist Press.

Murk-Jansen, Saskia. 1998. *Brides in the Desert: The Spirituality of the Beguines*. Traditions of Christian Spirituality Series, edited by Philip Sheldrake. Maryknoll, NY: Orbis Books.

Poor, Sara S. 2004. *Mechthild of Magdeburg and Her Book: Gender and the Making of Textual Authority*. Philadelphia: University of Pennsylvania Press.

Roberts, Michelle Voss. 2008. "Flowing and Crossing: The Somatic Theologics of Mechthild and Lasseswari," *Journal of the American Academy of Religion* 76 (3): 638–663.

Ruffing, Janet K. 2001. "Introduction." In *Mysticism and Social Transformation*, edited by Janet K Ruffing. Syracuse: Syracuse University Press.

Stange, Mary Zeiss. 1987. "Treading the Narrative Way Between Myth and Madness: Maxine Hong Kingston and Contemporary Women's Autobiography," *Journal of Feminist Studies in Religion* 3 (1): 15–28.

Stoeber, Michael. 1994. *Theo-Monistic Mysticism: A Hindu-Christian Comparison*. New York: St. Martin's Press.

Wiethaus, Ulrike. 1991. "Sexuality, Gender, and the Body in Late Medieval Women's Spirituality: Cases from Germany and the Netherlands," *Journal of Feminist Studies in Religion* 7 (1): 35–52.

Wright, Wendy M. 1996. "Keeping One's Distance: Presence and Absence in the History of Christian Spirituality," *Christian Spirituality Bulletin* 4: 21.

12

Mysticism, Spirituality and the Undergraduate: Reflections on the Use of Psychosocial Theory

William B. Parsons

The value of a volume such as this is that one could easily create the fabled "Introduction to Mysticism" course at the undergraduate level by simply culling relevant sections of the various individual essays on mystical traditions, as well as the methods and perspectives used to study them. Given the diversity of personal proclivities, curriculum needs, and institutional settings, I suspect that may be the preferred option for many. The pedagogical reflections and methodological perspectives offered in this particular essay, which presents one version of a mid- to upper-level "Mysticism and Spirituality" course for undergraduates, could be adapted to help in that cause or used as presented, namely, as advice on how one might use psychosocial methodology as part of a course on mysticism and spirituality.

Some preliminaries are in order. First, this essay is based on several years of teaching at a small, southern liberal arts university (Rice University). Rice is religiously and ethnically diverse, the undergraduate student body (approximately 3,500 students) comprises approximately the same number of women and men in their young adulthood years. Second, because my own area of expertise lies in religion and the social sciences (with an emphasis on psychology), my pedagogical strategies have been influenced by humanistic social scientific methodology and a tendency to favor using, when available, a case-history approach. Following Philip Rieff (1966), I think it most plausible, at least with respect to the United States, that we are living in a psychological culture in which therapeutic language and lifestyles have triumphed, its nomenclature governing the introspective lives of many students. My strategies have also been influenced by being thrust, if somewhat unwillingly, into the role of an "insider" (or, more technically, being enjoined to engage in a form of ethnography which can be loosely characterized as consisting of psychologically informed Geertzian thick descriptive activity). The latter is due in part to my status as a humanities divisional advisor to undergraduates, as well as being designated as a "faculty associate" of one of the college dormitories. These administrative responsibilities have afforded me privileged access to student culture. Through no virtue of my own, students apparently trust me enough to share with me (sometimes a bit too much) their "culture" of existential concerns involving gender identity, sexuality, career choices, religious anxieties, and the exigencies of life as young adults. It is imperative to keep in mind that most Western universities can still be characterized in terms of what Erik Erikson referred to as a *moratorium*: an institutional structure which is often *liminal* (in Victor Turner's sense), providing a laboratory for experimenting with age-appropriate existential concerns and life choices. It has been my experience that any class whose subject matter deals with mysticism and spirituality will invariably bring forth such concerns. Following the model of the *tantrika*, it is better to admit their inevitable influence in the classroom and to "ride" them, so to speak, than to proceed in blissful denial of their reality, as if such repression would annul their substantial influence vis-à-vis the task of learning. Given the latter, this essay proceeds on the assumption that ideas are most effective when conveyed (with all due apologies to the psychologist D. W. Winnicott) in a "good-enough" interpersonal context that takes into account the reigning sociocultural milieu and existential concerns of students. This is not to suggest that the pedagogical task should involve watering down the intellectual aim of conveying the substantial scholarship on mysticism, that the professor should be a therapist, or that it gives one license to model the class after that of a therapeutic session (a different and distinct institutional space). It *does* ask one to acknowledge the benefits that accrue when one submits to the more laborious task of making scholarship on mysticism engage both intellectually and existentially the lives of students who, in electing to take such a class, bring substantial personal (and often unconscious) baggage along for the ride.

My approach, then, in reflecting this orientation and set of concerns, is hardly doctrinaire or traditional (but not, I would argue, overly idiosyncratic), as if the best way to construct a course on mysticism and spirituality is one that proceeds by way of history and comparison, the aim being an encyclopedic overview of the variety of mystical themes, experiences, figures, and doctrines apparent in multiple religious traditions (although a strong case for the latter could easily be marshaled). As far as that project is concerned, it really *would* be better to exercise the option of creating a wider, more comprehensive introductory course by culling together preferred portions of the essays that constitute this volume. In this chapter, I outline a few sections or teaching modules, beginning with the necessary, if perfunctory, section on terms and definitions. Subsequent sections build intellectual sophistication, the hope being that the psychosocial approach and pedagogical strategies championed here are portable, fostering those intellectual capacities and tools that, once mastered, can be used to address any aspect of the mystical element of any religious tradition.

Beginning with Definitions

At the outset of a course such as this (in which the students typically number between twenty and thirty), I have them write a brief paragraph on what they think the word *mysticism* signifies, why they are taking the course, and where their religious commitments lie. What I have invariably found are several linked facts that, being based on a small sample size and with regard to a specific university culture, cannot be readily universalized. Nevertheless, they may well be helpful even for those teaching in different settings. First, there is little if any sophistication among my students as regards what academics understand by the terms *mysticism* or *spirituality*. The typical student response is that it involves certain kinds of stereotypical Maslowian peak experiences, most linking the latter to Yoga, meditation, and other kinds of exercises that are available at the university and surrounding community. Second, most students take the course not simply for intellectual reasons but also for existential ones (e.g., "I want to achieve enlightenment"). Third, although some are in fact committed to a specific faith tradition, most (about 75%, although this is admittedly a small sample size and will undoubtedly vary depending on the institution, the class, and, yes, even the professor) classify themselves as "spiritual but not religious." By the latter designation, I mean what Robert Fuller conveys in his book of the same name when he states that much of contemporary spirituality is run in individualistic ways where one literally creates a personal, "therapeutic" religious life that is nontraditional, noninstitutional, oriented around practices focused on mystical experiences and individuation, and ideologically dependent on bits and pieces of the pluralistic religio-cultural surround (Fuller 2001).

As a result, and in order to get the students to become conscious that what they understand to be mysticism is affected by an unconscious social reality (which is but a psychological way of conceptualizing the invariable effects of any socialization process), I begin historically with a set of essays and excerpts from books that trace the emergence of the terms *mysticism* and a modern, nontraditional form of *spirituality* (e.g., Bouyer 1980; De Certeau 1992; Schmidt 2003; MacDonald 2005; Principe 1983; Heelas and Woodhead 2005; Fuller 2001; McGinn 2005; and one could also use various essays of this volume). The essay by Bouyer documents the Greek and early Christian contributions to the meaning of the term *mysticism*, the latter in particular illustrating its dependence on a total Christian matrix (involving liturgy, scripture, theology) for its full meaning, reference, and use. The De Certeau and Schmidt essays trace historical developments, including the shift away from understanding mysticism as dependent on a religious tradition and the link between the emergence of mysticism as a noun and its being rendered in highly psychological, individualized, nontraditional (if not generic) terms. In this sense, there is a real overlap between what can be called "modern mysticism" and what Mary MacDonald calls "modern" (as opposed to "classic" and "churched") spirituality. One can use excerpts from the books by Fuller and Heelas et al. to frame the cultural shape and characteristics of this unchurched or nontraditional form of modern spirituality. Finally, I have found it helpful to bring in a sociological category, that of Weber's "inner-worldly mysticism," especially as elaborated by Roland Robertson (1978) and Parsons (2008), to further circumscribe this form of being mystical in contemporary culture.

To add comparative sophistication, one can also introduce several excerpts representing the perspective of multiple religious traditions (e.g., McGinn 1991; Gimello 1979; Ernst 2003) that serve to problematize the use of the term *mysticism* from a comparative perspective. For example, McGinn eschews the valorizing of "union" or any single term to designate *Christian mysticism,* instead defining it broadly in terms of the multiple ways the "Presence of God" (his preferred substitute for *mysticism*) is manifested in both episodic *experience* and the *process* of the life of the mystic in a churched setting; Gimello questions whether the term *mysticism,* which harbors Western cultural assumptions, can be applied at all to specifically Vipassanā forms of meditative insight; and Ernst cautions that Islamic forms of mysticism cannot omit the centrality of its sociopolitical dimension.

Along these lines, multiple essays in this volume are especially adept at unpacking several linked issues: the value-laden Orientalist, colonialist, gendered, and racial dimensions of the term; the objective ontological (as opposed to entirely psychological and subjective) nature of mystical visions; the focus on the shared life of the community (as opposed to the atomistic individual); the need to take into account an oral tradition (as opposed to valorizing the text); and the multiple forms of embodiment, expression, and participatory nature of some forms of mysticism (e.g., the essays in this volume by Bostic, Irwin, Gray, Ford, Ferrer). Certainly one could also include any number of other objections as well, and introducing these matters certainly opens up a Pandora's box of problematic issues that can be dealt with increasing sophistication as the course proceeds. But at the very least, this material has the virtue of affording the student insight into how the term *mysticism* is not only of Western origin and how the nontraditional, contemporary spirituality they have been socialized into is the product of a long history of sociocultural change, but also how the casual, cursory, and modern views of mysticism and spirituality are not easily transferable to the mystical dimensions found in religious traditions of various kinds. Most importantly, some usable nomenclature and a basic conceptual framework have been established, even if it brings with it the need for continual monitoring and qualification.

Psychology and Modern Spirituality Unpacked

Banking off the historical developments and cultural meanings ascribed to mysticism and spirituality, and with the rationale that one should begin with a cultural form of mysticism most easily understood by the student both existentially and intellectually, one can next turn to examine in detail modern forms of nontraditional or modern spirituality with an eye to the role of psychology in both its cultural emergence and in the study of mysticism and spirituality. One natural place to start is with a discussion of the first important modern psychological analysis of mysticism, lectures 16 and 17 of James's *The Varieties of Religious Experience*. The major pedagogical aim here is to gain initial access to the "marks" of mysticism, now understood in the modern sense as focusing on "experience" (a problematic term, as is well addressed by Sharf 1998) and his ladder or spectrum model of mystical experiences. An additional bonus is that James illustrates the difference between *churched,* or *traditional,* and *unchurched* or modern spiritual forms of mysticism. This is so, for James valorizes personal experience and the individual—standing in relation to whatever he or she consider to be the Divine—over against the institutional framing of the mystical element. For James, dogma, scripture, ecclesiastical authority, and church accoutrements of all kinds are understood as secondary outgrowths, routinized products of original charismatic experience (to be Weberian about it). As such, James stands in direct contrast to the early church fathers' view that "mystical experience," being inseparable from "mystical theology" and "mystical contemplation," requires participation in a total religious (here read "Christian") matrix that may bequeath, depending on the divine Other and grace, the presence of an objective religious reality distinct from one's psyche and unconscious. Modern spirituality, which sees institutional religion as the enemy and focuses on the individual, "experience" and "individuation," stands in contrast to *churched mysticism,* which is defined with respect to a wider context that includes scripture, tradition, and institutional accoutrements.

I have found that James and modern spirituality speaks, at least initially, more directly to the psyche of the contemporary undergraduate. It helps that James, in speaking of degrees of mystical experience (his ladder or spectrum model of mystical experience), also references his own personal experiences: that of a sense of heightened awareness while hiking in the Adirondacks, and another while under the influence of nitrous oxide (which led James to the central existential conclusion that normal waking consciousness is but one type of awareness, that all about lie potential other forms of consciousness, and that all these various and even contradictory forms are inevitably reconciled into a greater unity). This entheogen-generated insight and felt merging with the natural world, being capable of access outside a religious tradition, are easily communicable to students, some of whom are familiar with such states.

In furthering this avenue of exploration it is helpful to continue on with works on "nature" (or panenhenic/extrovertive mysticism) and the literature on entheogens. The former can be profitably elaborated through Paul Marshall's *Mystical Encounters with the Natural World* (2005), which has the further advantage of offering, in addition to rich descriptions of extrovertive experience, multiple theoretical models for their interpretation. For the controversy over entheogens, one can turn to many texts, but I have found the analysis and debates instigated by R. C. Zaehner (1980) to be particularly successful. Huston Smith's (2000) response to Zaehner and Robert Fuller (2000), who looks at the role of entheogens in multiple religious traditions, are also quite helpful. It should be noted that the relating of this material has proved to be immensely popular with my undergraduates through the years. At the same time, it should be noted that introducing this literature is not without risks. Many undergraduates are not sufficiently aware of the distinction between the religious and ritual use of entheogens and what can be referred to as a more casual, recreational use of "drugs." Indeed, the material on entheogens must be used with a certain measure of awareness of not only the fertile psyche of the undergraduate but existing social reality. One of my more memorable teaching experiences involved a young woman, clearly the brightest student in that particular class, who wished to write her term paper on the role and history of entheogens in mystical literature—the proposal of which, as a result of her meticulous research and outline, I was ready to give a green light to until, upon turning to the last page of her proposal, I read how she also wished to include an appendix reporting on her personal experimentation with altered states. Given that the latter is not only illegal, that Rice is in fact in Texas, *and* that her father was a well-known Texas judge, I had to politely inform her that her planned project, however enthusiastic the departed Timothy Leary might have been about it, was inappropriate for my class (I remark on this for while she was the first to propose such a paper, she has not been the last). In any event, beginning with nature mysticism and entheogen-based mysticism enables students an experiential basis on which to begin to understand what "mystical experience" may (and may not) designate. Given Zaehner's response to Huxley, it also allows them to begin to build more sophistication into the question of comparative mysticism and whether there is a "common core" to mysticism and ways of thinking about that core.

Second, because Zaehner equates Huxley's project (which is to say nature mysticism and entheogenic-driven mysticism) with one particular theoretical model (Jung and his psychology), it allows one to look into the "therapeutic" cultural strand and its contribution to nontraditional forms of spirituality. It is important to note that Zaehner distinguishes between mystical experience per se and mysticism as "process" (which for Zaehner, at least with respect to nature mysticism, means Jungian individuation). In this regard, one can now begin to see how spirituality and mysticism can be thought of as a therapeutic (or soteriological) regimen and not simply equated with an episodic event and its analysis. In other words, on the one hand, for Zaehner, Jungian theory is the preferred method for interpreting various cases of nature or panenhenic experience. The latter, now understood as instances of the emergence of the Self archetype, are to be distinguished in kind from theistic mystical experiences, the understanding of which requires a theological lens. On the other hand, nature mysticism can give rise to an introspective process that is but an instance of Jungian individuation. Jungian theory, then, is not only used as a preferred psychology of mysticism, but it also becomes an instance of a mystical path or process (i.e., "psychospirituality"). In this way, modern spirituality and the therapeutic process become linked; the mystical and spiritual path is clearly seen to be transformative, even if "from what" and "to what" (and the meaning of these terms should be framed as dependent on different sociocultural as well as religious contexts) still lies in question. Here again, as with the issue of the nature of mystical "experience," a basic intellectual platform concerning mystical "process" is established on which sophistication can be built as the course proceeds.

Third, to supplement this avenue of thought, it is helpful to introduce excerpts from other psychospiritual theorists and debates (e.g., R. M. Bucke [1993]; Abraham Maslow [1994]; Freud's debate with Romain Rolland on the famous "oceanic feeling" [Parsons 1999]; the influence of transpersonal psychology [Ferrer 2002]) in order to cement how psychology has been a determinative cultural contributor to the rise and ascendancy of modern spirituality. It is important to point out that although many of these theorists equate mysticism with an "experience" and espouse a common core to mysticism, the designation of what that core is varies (e.g., a peak experience, the emergence of a Self archetype, the oceanic feeling, cosmic consciousness), as does the nature of mystical process. These ruminations further prepare the student for the inevitable fact that "mysticisms" differ. As a segue to the next section, and in order to accentuate the latter point with regard to religious traditions proper, this section can conclude with excerpts from the constructivist/perennialist debate (Forman 1990; Katz 1979).

Psychology, Modern Spirituality, and the Mystical Element in the Traditions

The literature on mysticism certainly involves the description of altered states of a specific kind and the often lifelong development of spiritual dispositions, capacities, and virtues, as well as a vast assortment of theoretical models for their interpretation. The preceding section is designed to enable the student to have the beginnings of both an existential and intellectual grasp of the variety of ways of thinking about mysticism in psychosocial terms. It is at this point in the course that the student is prepared for the foray into mysticism "in the traditions" and the issues they invariably raise. Although one could easily run the next part of the course in a variety of ways and with respect to a variety of religious figures, texts, and traditions, I prefer, in keeping with my focus on psychosocial methodology, a case-history approach that centers around specific mystics. My preference, then, is for depth rather than breadth; for exploring in detail the representatives of only a few traditions in the expectation that intellectual tools and capacities for thinking about mysticism are portable, enabling the student to focus on other courses (which fortunately are available in our department) that center exclusively on the mystical element in a particular religious tradition.

A suitable bridge between modern spirituality with its psychological focus and a more traditional churched form of mysticism can be found in St. Augustine's *Confessions*. The latter has the advantage of being an ancient text— but one with a peculiarly modern, psychological feel. It is certainly akin to a contemporary autobiography even if such a view must be qualified with respect to Augustine's rhetorical (and Christian) embellishment of many of the supposed "events" and "episodes" that marked the course of his life (Jonte-Pace 1993). Surely there is much here that students can identify with: Augustine's struggles with his mother, Monica, during adolescence; the onset of puberty, his adoption of a concubine, and his struggle with sexuality; his religious impulse and the various figures and movements that captured his fancy; his ruminations on tragedies; his relationship with friends and mentors. At the same time, Augustine's narrative is meant to transcend a focus on a single individual (i.e., himself) in order to speak to the "everyman"—which translates to how Christianity can and should influence the life of every person. The pedagogical strategy here is to get the student to think about life and mysticism/spirituality in a *churched* context, which means understanding mysticism in the broad expanse of a life—as a *process* that is punctuated by significant encounters with the divine. Above all, there are two significant autobiographical narratives of mystical visions in books 7 and 9 (the visions at Milan and Ostia) that serve as crucial pillars of Augustine's religious journey.

By grappling with Augustine's life journey from both the theological and psychosocial perspectives, one can begin to put autobiographical flesh on some of the substantial issues and debates previously raised (e.g., the problem of the epistemological status of mystical vision and, specifically with respect to Augustine, the matter of "intellectual visions"; perennialist and constructivist views of mysticism; mystical experience and mystical process; the individualistic, "therapeutic" form of modern spirituality and the churched, communal, and "soteriological" form of mystical theology). Helpful with regard to these issues and with respect to the encounter between psychosocial methods and theological perspectives are two groups of secondary sources: (1) the psychosocial essays and theological responses as compiled by Capps and Dittes (1990) in their edited book, *The Hunger of the Heart* (and here I include also my own essays on psychology and Augustine's visions [1990; 2003; forthcoming]); and (2) J. P. Kenney's (2005) overview of Augustine's full teaching on mysticism (the Christian qualification for which I use McGinn's (1991) introductory comments), which incorporates texts outside the *Confessions*, and which articulates the totality of the spiritual architecture of Augustine's worldview (his "mystical theology"). The inclusion of the latter does not simply add sophistication to the definitions and debates surveyed thus far but also eventuates in the evaluation of the strengths and weaknesses of psychosocial methodology viewed relative to a theological response.

One can comparatively expand on the preceding by examining psychobiographical studies of another pivotal religious figure: Sri Ramakrishna. One can begin, as with the preceding section on Augustine, with qualifications as to how to use the term *mysticism* when speaking of Hinduism (see Hugh Urban's essay in this volume) followed by Neeval's (1976) comprehensive summary of the various "stages" of Ramakrishna's spiritual journey. The latter can be supplemented with selections from the Upaniṣads, the Bhagavad-Gita, Puranas, and Tantric material, giving the student a general Hindu framework within which to view Ramakrishna's practices.

Once the religious groundwork has been laid, one can proceed to compare three psychosocial perspectives on Ramakrishna. Although the studies by Sil (1991), Kakar (1991), and Kripal (1995) all champion psychosocial methodology, they arrive at very different conclusions and can be contrasted with respect to a few general rubrics (Parsons 1997). First, all value that enterprise that can be called *textology*. Sil, for example, is aware that in the earlier part of the twentieth century, Ramakrishna's disciples selectively translated extant biographical accounts to omit those salacious passages that would have impeded the acceptance of Ramakrishna by the relatively puritanical Protestant ethos that ruled America. Kripal takes this to an even more nuanced and provocative level, unearthing what he calls Ramakrishna's "secret talk": highly erotic and homoerotic accounts of mystical practices and visions found in the original Bengali texts yet absent from bowdlerized translations. The importance of attention to the text is one that was already encountered in Augustine and as such becomes a portable lesson, being of pedagogical importance not simply with respect to psychosocial method (one must get the "case" right before any attempt at interpretation) but as a general rule: Mystical texts in their original language evince nuances that determine meaning and, hence, cannot be dispensed with as an integral part of studying mysticism.

Second, the three theorists, while all relying on psychosocial method, employ very different models within that approach, resulting in very different conclusions about the nature of Ramakrishna's mystical visions. Sil, the most reductive of the three, discounts the possibility that mystical vision offers deep insight into the human condition or that attention to cultural context is a necessary part of the hermeneutic enterprise. Sil's study, then, has the virtue of being a textbook case of classic reductionism (a fact that receives additional importance insofar as it models the greater bulk of psychological assessments of mysticism during the twentieth century). He portrays Ramakrishna as infantile, antisocial, vulgar, crude, prone to defensive trances, misogyny, and gender confusion, being as he was beset by a host of developmental issues (e.g., seduced by wandering monks and neighbors; affected by the important deaths of his father and brother; prone to identification with women). So it is that Sil telescopes early on his preferred methodological stance and thesis: "it is necessary to understand the origins and nature of Ramakrishna's psychosis....in order to make any sense of his theosis" (5). Ramakrishna's mystical visions are dismissed with respect to well-established psychiatric categories (e.g., manic denial, psychasthenia, reaction formations, fragmented self, deautomatization, derealization, and depersonalization). In contrast, Kakar calls for the use of recent theoretical shifts within psychoanalytic theory, the originative theorists of which (specifically Lacan 1982 and Winnicott 1980) he refers to as the "mystics" of psychoanalysis. Learning from his tutelage under anthropologists of various stripes, he cautions that such theories need to be fitted to the cultural context. So it is that, in using Lacan's terminology, he conceives of Ramakrishna's intent to achieve vision of true reality "beyond the illusion of the Imaginary...and the Maya of the Symbolic Register" (Kakar 1991, 27). The Hindu notion of bhava becomes a culturally specific defense mechanism that is on a par with sublimation, the later being further rooted (and here he relies on Winnicott) in "the unknowable ground of creativeness as such" (29) and which, defined as a passionate form of devotion done with "all of one's heart...soul....might" (18) engenders mystical visions, now understood as transformative and "the preeminent way of uncovering the vein of creativity that runs deep in all of us" (29). Kripal, on the other hand, while agreeing that Ramakrishna suffered from certain forms of developmentally induced trauma, rejects the dogmatic pathologizing of Sil and, in going further than Kakar, and banking off the researches of Ricoeur, Lacan, and Obeyesekere, insists that Ramakrishna's visions were at times revelatory, accessing a bona fide ontological dimension. In displaying a form of psychological postmodernism, and by way of interpreting both Freud and Ramakrishna within a Tantric worldview, he claims "Freud only got to the third Cakra" (Kripal 1995, 43).

Third, while all three agree that Ramakrishna exhibited an unusual form of gender expression, all three differ in how to interpret it. Sil sees in Ramakrishna the behavior of a *puer aeternus* ("eternal boy"), who, when he engaged in ritual practices like madhurya bhava, understood as a culturally perverse form of cross-dressing, also revealed gender confusion. Kakar departs from Sil when he sees the latter's conclusion as betraying a Western gloss. Properly contextualized, what Ramakrishna engaged in through bhava was a ritual act whose aim is the cultivation of Winnicott's "pure female element" in us all, revealing a culture that offers males new ways of experiencing and integrating their femininity and advocates "being" and "receptive absorption" over "doing" and "active opposition" (Kakar 1991, 34). Finally Kripal sees in Ramakrishna a Tantric practitioner whose visions were fueled by unconscious, repressed homoerotic energies, the latter evident in his symptomatic acts (e.g., putting his foot in his disciples laps in ecstatic states) and use of a "vocabulary of desire" ("anxious longing," "enkindling," "attraction," "strange sensation," and "wrung like a wet towel"), all of which were terms directed at his boy disciples. Given the sensitive nature of mystical eroticism, and the fact that many students in the class may well be going through gender confusion and decisions regarding sexual orientation, this series of psychological perspectives, which may well speak directly to the heart and mind of the undergraduate, should be approached with sensitivity and can be harnessed as a real opportunity for speaking to issues concerning the relations among religion, gender, and sexuality.

The final section concentrates on a series of case studies that address the interaction between psychology and Buddhism. Again, though I am reluctant to universalize the small sample size of my classes, I have found that many of my students are very familiar with Buddhist meditational practices and have integrated them into their Western form of modern spirituality. As with the previous sections, then, it is initially helpful to bring in essays that, on the one hand, remind them of the problematic use of the term *mysticism* with regard to Buddhism (Gray in this volume and Gimello 1979) and, on the other hand, how Buddhism, particularly under the auspices of D. T. Suzuki, took a radical turn toward the psychological when it entered American soil in the twentieth century (as is well documented by Sharf 1995). Once that historical trajectory has been established, it is then quite easy to segue into the "dialogue" between Buddhist practices and various psychosocial approaches. Because the latter is now quite sophisticated and widespread, my own strategy is to provide an overview with respect to a few central theoretical perspectives: psychoanalytic, Jungian, and neurocognitive (see, for example, Austin 1998; Molino 1998; Meckel and Moore 1992; Cooper 1998; 1999; 2000; Engler 1986; 2003; Epstein 1995; Bulkeley 2005; Parsons 2009; Woods 1980). It is important to acknowledge that much of this literature emerged as a result of the 1960s, when the contemporary clinicians who are now exploring the intersection between psychology and Buddhism first became attracted to Eastern religions and went on retreats, integrated meditational practices and mystical experiences into their own therapeutic work; and so, they can be classified as "cultural insiders" insofar as they have firsthand knowledge of meditational practices and intimate relationships with multiple masters and gurus of various Buddhist schools. Many of these authors wear more than one therapeutic hat: practicing psychologists (who have been analysands) as well as teachers of Buddhist meditation (who have been students of an assortment of Buddhist masters/gurus). Their aim consists in how to put together the two modes of introspection.

In this body of literature, one can discern a wide spectrum of analyses ranging from those studies that see Buddhist practices inducing pathological states to those that seek to create room for a truly soteriological dimension to Buddhism. For example, some see Buddhism and its practices as exhibiting behavior that can be classified as symptomatic, pathological, and defensive—how teachings such as anatta (i.e., no-self) can be used (especially for adolescents and those entering middle age) to ward off the burden of creating an adaptive identity as well as to rationalize the lack of self-esteem and feelings of emptiness. Again, they show how the notion of enlightenment can be cathected narcissistically to cater to the needs of archaic forms of grandiosity, or how student-teacher relationships, transported to Western cultural soil, activate debilitating mirroring and idealizing forms of transference. Others have extolled the adaptive and therapeutic effects of meditation. Meditation can cultivate the capacity for self-observation and increase empathy, listening skills, and evenly hovering attention, further helping one become more sensitive to transference and countertransference issues. Finally, there are those who insist that beyond the pathological and adaptive dimensions of Buddhist practice lies yet a third area of inquiry—one that speaks to the fact that Buddhist practice is not simply therapeutic but soteriological, and that newer forms of brain science technology can be framed to support this line of argument.

Additionally, I leave room for addressing the psychosocial dimension of the various cultural disasters that have befallen the entry of Buddhism to the West, including surveying models for the developmental dynamics that can accrue between master and student (Kakar 1991) and the unfortunate sexual and political controversies that have dotted the cultural landscape over the past thirty years (here one can rely on excerpts from Fields 1992 and Rubin 1996). It may well be that some members of the class (and I have had more than a few) are personally familiar with such tragedies, and classroom discussion of such issues, structured around existing empirical data and scholarly reflection, can be charged yet illuminating.

Concluding Reflections

A final word about social space is in order. A course such as this occurs within the confines of a university, which is understood as a secular social space. The task is to gain what James refers to as knowledge "about" a subject (in this case mysticism). At the same time, the course is, in many ways, an academic appropriation of the kinds of insights and theory-building bequeathed through the auspices of modern spirituality and of a different social space: the clinic. The latter can be framed as a ritual designed to legitimate the experience of altered states. This is so, for psychological rituals operate by virtue of withdrawal into a liminal realm. The door that marks off the "sacred space" of the room of the therapeutic session represents the "repression barrier" and the cultural superego. Once safely behind that door, a different set of social rules is operative: the repression barrier is lifted, one gains analytic access to the unconscious through a variety of introspective techniques, and a new form of experiential awareness accrues. Engaging in this form of the introspective life constitutes knowing by acquaintance (e.g., it is one thing to endlessly describe what an apple tastes like and a whole different matter to simply bite into one). Here, then, the terms *understanding* and *knowing* admit of various degrees.

The tension between the two sorts of knowing animate a good deal of the course outlined herein. There are admittedly limits to such an approach. The initial point of departure banks off the assumption that most students have had a glimpse of the inner world and of altered states through participating in relevant cultural forms, psychological narratives, and extant introspective techniques. But one can safely assume that authentic experiences of anatta, bona fide locutions, or grace-driven intellectual visions, in lying outside the experiential reach of most students, will remain clothed in abstraction. In this regard, it is always helpful to remind the student of that line of anthropological thought that depicts all psychosocial theory as cultural and therapeutic regimens as ethnopsychological systems born of specific historical and cultural coordinates. From this perspective, therapists and analysands alike share a more or less range of accepted introspective states, the latter being fodder for theory building. The matter changes when one enters into other social spaces as found in the extremer forms of religious introspective communities (e.g., shamanistic, monastic). It is there, by virtue of engaging in a new set of introspective techniques, that one might find a whole new understanding of the self and its capabilities, which, while often quite bizarre to the uninitiated, are, to the initiate, valorized as constituting the ideal life. The average student is probably not familiar with such communities. In light of the absence of such total immersion, knowing "about" will simply have to do.

References

Austin, J. 1998. *Zen and the Brain*. Cambridge: MIT Press.

Bouyer, L. 1980. "Mysticism: An Essay on the History of the Word." In *Understanding Mysticism*, edited by Richard Woods, 42–56. Garden City, NY: Image Books.

Bucke, R. M. 1993. *Cosmic Consciousness*. New York: Citadel.

Bulkeley, K. 2005. *The Wondering Brain*. New York: Routledge.

Capps, D., and J. Dittes. 1990. *The Hunger of the Heart: Reflections on the Confessions of Augustine*. Society for the Scientific Study of Religion Monograph Series 8. West Lafayette, IN: Society for the Scientific Study of Religion.

Cooper, Paul. 1998. "The Disavowal of the Spirit: Integration and Wholeness in Buddhism and Psychoanalysis." In *The Couch and the Tree*, edited by Andrew Molino, 231–246. New York: North Point Press.

———. 1999. "Buddhist Meditation and Countertransference: A Case Study," *American Journal of Psychoanalysis* 59 (1): 71–86.

———. 2000. "Unconscious Processes: Zen and Psychoanalytic Versions," *Journal of Religion and Health* 39 (1): 57–69.

De Certeau, Michel. 1992. "Mysticism." *Diacritics* 22: 11–25.

Engler, Jack. 1986. "Therapeutic Aims in Psychotherapy and Buddhism." In *Transformations of Consciousness*, edited by Ken Wilber, Jack Engler, and Dan Brown, 17–52. Boston: Shambhala.

———. 2003. "Being Somebody and Being Nobody: A Reexamination of the Understanding of Self in Psychoanalysis and Buddhism." In *Psychoanalysis and Buddhism,* edited by Jeremy Safran, 35–80. Boston: Wisdom Publications.

Epstein, Mark. 1995. *Thoughts without a Thinker*. New York: Basic Books.

Ernst, C. 2003. "Between Orientalism and Fundamentalism: Problematizing the Teaching of Sufism." In *Teaching Islam*, edited by B. Wheeler, 108–193. New York: Oxford University Press.

Ferrer, J. 2002. *Revisioning Transpersonal Theory*. Albany: State University of New York Press.

Fields, R. 1992. *When the Swans Came to the Lake*. Boston: Shambhala.

Forman, R. 1990. *The Problem of Pure Consciousness*. New York: Oxford University Press.

Fuller, Robert. 2000. *Stairways to Heaven*. Boulder, CO: Westview.

———. 2001. *Spiritual but not Religious*. New York: Oxford University Press.

Gimello, R. 1979. "Mysticism and Meditation." In *Mysticism and Philosophical Analysis*, edited by S. Katz, 170–199. New York: Oxford University Press.

Heelas, P., and Woodhead, L. 2005. *The Spiritual Revolution: Why Religion is Giving Way to Spirituality*. Oxford: Blackwell.

James, W. 1929. *The Varieties of Religious Experience*. New York: The Modern Library.

Jonte-Pace, D. 1993. "Augustine on the Couch: Psychohistorical (Mis)readings of the Confessions," *Religion* 23: 71–83.

Kakar, Sudhir. 1991. *The Analyst and the Mystic*. Chicago: University of Chicago Press.

Katz, Steven, ed. 1979. *Mysticism and Philosophical Analysis*. New York: Oxford University Press.

Kenney, J. 2005. *The Mysticism of St. Augustine*. New York: Routledge.

Kripal, Jeffrey. 1995. *Kali's Child*. Chicago: University of Chicago Press.

Lacan, J. 1982. "God and the Jouissance of Women." In *Feminine Sexuality*, edited by Juliet Mitchell and Jacqueline Rose, 37–48. New York: W. W. Norton.

MacDonald, Mary. 2005. "Spirituality." In *The Encyclopedia of Religion*, 2nd ed., edited by Lindsey Jones, 8718–8721. New York: Macmillan.

Marshall, P. 2005. *Mystical Encounters with the Natural World*. New York: Oxford University Press.

Maslow, A. 1994. *Religion, Values, Peak-Experiences*. New York: Penguin.

McGinn, B. 1991. *The Foundations of Mysticism*. New York: Crossroad.

———. 2005. "The Letter and the Spirit: Spirituality as an Academic Discipline." In *Minding the Spirit: The Study of Christian Spirituality,* edited by E. Dreyer and M. Burrows, 25–41. Baltimore: John Hopkins University Press.

Meckel, Dan, and Robert Moore, eds. 1992. *Self and Liberation*. New York: Paulist.

Molino, Andrew, ed. 1998. *The Couch and the Tree*. New York: North Point Press.

Neeval, W. 1976. "The Transformation of Sri Ramakrishna." In *Hinduism: New Essays in the History of Religions,* edited by B. Smith, 53–98. Leiden: Brill.

Parsons, W. B. 1990. "Augustine; Common-Man or Intuitive Psychologist?," *Journal of Psychohistory* 18: 155–179.

———. 1997. "Psychoanalysis and Mysticism: The Case of Ramakrishna." *Religious Studies Review* 23 (4): 355–361.

———. 1999. *The Enigma of the Oceanic Feeling.* New York: Oxford University Press.

———. 2003. "Psychoanalysis and Mysticism: The Case of St. Augustine." In *Mysticism: A Variety of Psychological Perspectives,* edited by J. Belzen and A. Geels, 151–178. Amsterdam: Rodopi.

———. 2008. "Psychologia Perennis and the Academic Study of Mysticism." In *Mourning Religion,* edited by W. B. Parsons, D. Jonte-Pace, and S. Henking, 97–123. Charlottesville: University of Virginia Press.

———. 2009. "Psychoanalysis Meets Buddhism: The Development of a Dialogue." In *Changing the Scientific Study of Religion: Beyond Freud?,* edited by Jacob Belzen, 179–209. New York: Springer.

———. Forthcoming. "On Seeing the Light: Assessing Psychoanalytic Interpretations of Vision in Augustine's *Confessions.*" In *Augustine and Psychology,* edited by K. Paffenroth and S. Dixon. Lanham, MD: Lexington Books.

Principe, Walter. 1983. "Toward Defining Spirituality," *Studies in Religion* 12: 127–141.

Rieff, Philip. 1966. *The Triumph of the Therapeutic.* New York: Harper and Row.

Robertson, Rolland. 1978. *Meaning and Change.* New York: New York University Press.

Rubin, Jeff. 1996. *Psychotherapy and Buddhism.* New York: Plenum Press.

Schmidt, Leigh. 2003. "The Making of Modern Mysticism," *Journal of the American Academy of Religion* 71: 273–302.

Sharf, Robert. 1998. "Experience." In *Critical Terms for Religious Studies,* edited by Mark C. Taylor, 94–116. Chicago: University of Chicago Press.

———. 1995. "The Zen of Nationalism." In *Curators of the Buddha: The Study of Buddhism under Colonialism,* edited by Donald Lopez, 107–161. Chicago: University of Chicago Press.

Sil, N. 1991. *Ramakrishna Paramahamsa: A Psychological Profile.* Leiden: Brill.

Smith, H. 2000. *Cleansing the Doors of Perception.* New York: Jeremy Tarcher.

Winnicott, Donald. 1980. *Playing and Reality.* New York: Penguin.

Woods, R. 1980. *Understanding Mysticism.* Garden City, NJ: Image.

Zaehner, Richard C. 1980. *Mysticism Sacred and Profane.* New York: Oxford University Press.

{ 13 }

Mysticism in Ecumenical Dialogue

QUESTIONS ON THE NATURE AND EFFECTS OF MYSTICAL EXPERIENCE

Michael Stoeber

Teaching Context and Introduction

I teach in the areas of spirituality and philosophy of religion at Regis College—a Jesuit institution associated with the Toronto School of Theology and the University of Toronto. Its mission is inspired by Ignatian spirituality. This includes promoting a spirituality that seeks for the integration of all facets of the person, openness to critical dialogue with global cultures, and commitments both to social justice and ecumenical cooperation in theological education.[1] Regis College is a founding member (1970) of the Toronto School of Theology (TST)—the largest multidenominational Christian theological center in North America and the United Kingdom. The colleges of TST grant civil graduate degrees conjointly with the University of Toronto. Established in 1930 as a seminary, Regis College is also authorized to grant Roman Catholic ecclesiastical degrees in theology.[2]

Mysticism has been a research interest of mine for over twenty-five years, and currently, I focus or touch on the topic in many of my courses.[3] Graduate students from various departments and centers of the Univesity of Toronto can take courses at TST—and I am cross-appointed to the Centre for the Study of Religion—but most of our students are from the seven member and four affiliated theological schools. Students come from over twenty Christian denominations and occasionally from non-Christian religious traditions, with about one-fifth being non-Canadian students.[4] Regis College has alumni from at least twenty-eight different countries. Almost all the students at TST come with an undergraduate degree, with the average age per program between thirty and fifty-three years in 2008–2009. Most students have firmly developed faith orientations, and many are active in their churches. Although some students question some of the theological teachings of their tradition, I rarely encounter religious skeptics in my courses.

There are two general categories of students at TST: those who focus on ministry, professional development, or general interest; and students who are in research-oriented master's and doctoral programs. In terms of overall student numbers for courses in 2008–2009, the split between these categories was almost equal. In terms of gender in that year, the first category had a female/male split of 49%/51%, whereas the research category had a female/male split of 36%/64%. I teach higher level courses, most of which combine both categories of students. Also, most of my courses are cross-listed to both the Theology and Pastoral Theology Departments of TST, some of my courses are cross-listed to the Centre for the Study of Religion, and some of my students major in the History and Biblical Departments of TST. I have very diverse class make-ups, typically with a small majority of Roman Catholic students.

Course enrollment also varies, normally ranging from about eight to twenty students—occasionally up to thirty students—which allows me to use a teaching method combining both lecture and discussion/question styles for most of my courses, with some references to PowerPoint images and outlines. In many of my courses, I distribute possible discussion questions for some of the course readings and instruct students to reflect on these in preparation for class. When lecture material relates to one of these specified questions, I will at times shift the teaching style to class discussion, posing these and related questions to students, before returning to a lecture format.

Some courses are seminars that include only students who are research-focused. Occasionally I will ask students in these courses to provide their own written questions or comments related to course readings. At the beginning of the seminar, we read each of these questions/comments before I lead a discussion in reference to them. Also, student presentations are significant assignments of seminar courses. In all of my current courses, students are evaluated through shorter essay assignments or presentations related to assigned readings, brief philosophical/pastoral/theological reflections on themes and issues,[5] longer research papers on course topics either assigned by me or of the student's choice, and my observation of the contributions students make to class discussions.

In my teaching and research, I have reflected on the relation of mysticism to spirituality and on how mysticism potentially functions as a common creative thread (or threads) between various religious traditions. In this essay, I will outline my approach to teaching mysticism in a diverse and multidenominational context. I will also discuss how my view on the subject has changed, in part through the ecumenical dialogue I have had with my students. I have come to appreciate benefits in being open to a broad understanding of mystical phenomena and in enabling students to participate creatively and constructively within the field. In my courses on mysticism, I have found it helpful to encourage extended dialogue and reflection on certain questions related to four major guiding issues: (1) the nature of mystical experience, (2) the subjective dynamics of mystical experience, (3) the effects of mystical experience for the mystic and the community, and (4) the practices associated with mystical experiences. I will introduce many of these questions herein and contextualize some of them. A general goal is to enable students to respond to these questions in critical and creative ways, as they arise in specific courses. Often I raise these questions to students within the context of preliminary working definitions of spirituality and mysticism. I will outline these definitions before returning to these questions related to mysticism.

Defining Spirituality and Mysticism

Mysticism is sometimes treated synonymously with *spirituality*, especially in the context of popular culture, and many of my courses fall within the general area of spirituality, so I begin some of them by briefly exploring its meaning. Typically I will do this in reference to a number of definitions of spirituality that I have drawn together over the years from various theologians and popular cultural figures (for example, Oprah Winfrey defines spirituality as "knowing yourself and knowing there is something bigger than yourself").[6] We read these various definitions together, and I illustrate them through a probing dialectic that pushes students to think about key ideas, similarities, and differences between the views.

Toward the end of this process, I introduce the understanding of spirituality that I myself work with throughout the course. It is influenced especially by essays by Annice Callahan (1989) and Walter Principe (1983): "Spirituality is lived religious experience: It is the way in which people interpret and integrate their life, either in relation to the Divine or to spiritual realities that transcend or underlie the person, or in relation to what she or he feels to be ultimate values." I think it is likely that authentic spirituality involves a religious significance, even if some people do not interpret their spiritual experiences that way, and this working definition can include spiritually minded secular atheists. However, in introducing this view of spirituality to students I remind them that some scholars prefer different definitions. I ask students to be open in the course to refining their own view, one that best reflects the reality of the phenomena and provides the most creative and fruitful context for thinking about it.

Some of my courses also require a preliminary working definition of mysticism. Defining mysticism is just as difficult and controversial because it is sometimes associated with occult and paranormal phenomena or with various kinds of experiences across religions and more secular, aesthetic contexts. A helpful way to begin to think about mysticism is to situate it within different types of spiritual experiences that might apply across religious and secular lines. This has the advantage also of pushing students to begin to think about their own religious experiences within the context of initial, illustrative categories: depth experiences, visionary experiences, numinous experiences, and mystical experiences.

Depth experiences are quite common and significant human experiences (such as love, joy, grief, or insight) that are associated with important relationships or major life events (such as the death of a loved one, birth of a child, or profound aesthetic encounter). They also occur within the context of religious ritual, prayer, or meditation. Such experiences powerfully affect a person and they are granted a deep spiritual significance. They sometimes become an integrative force for a person, inspiring her or him creatively in different ways. For people of religious faith, depth experiences are *interpreted* within a religious framework or worldview. They are understood within the person's account of what it is to be human, the purpose of life, and the religious ideal. Key characteristics include drama (they break normal patterns of experience), affective power (they have a profound effect on various aspects of a person's life), and value thinking (they stimulate deep emotional and moral reflection).

Visionary experiences are more unusual than depth experiences and come in the form of typically internal images or voices in dreams, prayer, or meditation. They have the same key characteristics as depth experiences, but they involve the use of imagination in contemplative reflection. These might include visions of popular religious figures, narratives, or various kinds of spiritual presences. I do not presume that all visionary experiences are solely subjective phenomena, and I am open to expanding this category to include other more paranormal realities, such as different forms of extrasensory perception (Stoeber and Meynell 1996). These experiences border on the mystical, in that they can involve feelings of communion or sensorial penetration with the presences or the source of the voices or vision. They also edge toward numinous experiences.

Certain visionary experiences might be regarded as numinous experiences, but the numinous normally refers to a more powerfully affective experience. These are encounters or an awareness of the Divine as the "wholly Other," quite distinct and radically different from oneself. Rudolph Otto has called them the experience of the "Holy," where holy does not include the usual moral and rational connotations of the word, but points to a supernatural reality of tremendous strength (*numen*). In Otto's phenomenological account, it includes the characteristics of *mysterium* (extraordinary, unfamiliar), *tremendum* (awe, dread), *fascinans* (attraction, enchantment), and *majestas* (adoration, glorification) (Otto 1978; Smart 1958). C. S. Lewis describes the experience as a profound disturbance, one of "wonder and a certain shrinking—a sense of inadequacy to cope with such a visitant and of prostration before it..." (Lewis 1956, 5).

In mystical experience, the distinction between subject and object is blurred and there is not always the sense of dread that is associated with the numinous experience. These experiences, like the other types previously described, are socioculturally influenced, so come in different forms depending on the interpretive-experiential context. As Michel De Certeau observes: "Spiritual perception does indeed unfold within a mental, linguistic, and social organization that precedes and determines it" (De Certeau, 1992, 21). At the risk of oversimplification—for example, some types of Buddhism do not fit well into these categories—I highlight for students three major types of accounts of mystical experience: (1) an interconnection or unity with the "essence" of the natural world (nature mysticism); or (2) an intimate communion or union with the Divine experienced as personally good, loving, intelligent, and creative (theistic mysticism); or (3) a unity or identity with an impersonal and inactive Oneness or Unity (nondual or monistic mysticism). All of these experiences are transitory, but they have a powerful and long-lasting effect on the mystic's personality. They require an extremely passive orientation, where the mystic is said to move to an altered state of awareness beyond or underlying normal ego-consciousness, one which cannot be aptly or completely described given its altered sensory or nonsensory and nonintellectual nature.

These various categories of spiritual experience are introduced to students as working definitions that are open to adjustment or correction. Moreover, a major question is if one should not regard certain depth, visionary, and numinous experiences as located within the general family of mysticism, where they might all play a positive role in the spiritual growth or transformation of a person. This question was stimulated in part by some of my students of evangelical and charismatic backgrounds, who questioned what they considered to be narrow understandings of mysticism that are often contrasted with "lesser forms" of more embodied kinds of spirituality. It is also influenced somewhat by my interests in Ignatian spirituality, which strives in its religious vision for the creative integration of all aspects of the person. In the next section, we will explore briefly a more general definition of mysticism that is proposed by Evelyn Underhill. However, for now, I note that there are apparent differences as well as common features between experiences, which allow us to develop a framework or typology for initial study and dialogue. This provides an initial context for discussing key questions related to major issues of mysticism.

Questions Related to the Nature of Mystical Experience

What is the nature of mystical experience? Using the singular *mysticism* in reference to certain cross-religious phenomena raises the question whether all mystical experiences are basically or fundamentally the same. Is there an essential core or element of all religious mysticism? What would that be? Would it be undifferentiated unity, as some mystics claim, or infinite love as other mystics experience it, or creative power, or something else?

Recent statistics indicate that mysticism is a more prominent reality in contemporary society than some people might think (Ellwood 1992, 2). Some of my students are attracted to courses on mysticism because of their own spiritual experiences and they sometimes provide accounts of them in class discussions and assignments. Karl Rahner, a very influential twentieth-century Roman Catholic theologian, predicted that the "Christian of the future will be a mystic or he or she will not exist at all" (Rahner 1981, 149–150). He suggested that as society in the modern and postmodern West has become increasingly secularized and pluralistic, traditional institutional supports for Christianity have weakened. Postmodern Christianity will need to be grounded in and driven by individuals who have more immediate experiences of God, rather than by those whose perception of God is largely formal and conceptual and of a secondhand nature.

Many mystics and theorists have regarded mystical experience as the essential core of religion, though this view has come under criticism in recent years, especially from some of the more socially minded and actively oriented theologians. For example, Karl Rahner has been criticized by Johann Baptist Metz and David Tracy for espousing a spiritual theology that is one-sidedly personal and mystical, and not sufficiently socially prophetic (Wiseman 1993, 54–57). Indeed, in surveying the various dimensions of religion—the social, the liturgical-ritual, the ethical-legal, the doctrinal-creedal, the scriptural-mythological, the material, and the experiential (Smart 1989, 9–24)—one might ask why mysticism should be considered primary and more significant.

Though the various dimensions of religion are tremendously diverse cross-culturally, and even at times conflicting, some theorists claim that one can uncover a common thread of mystical practice and experience between different traditions that inspires and influences these other dimensions of religion. These kinds of claims about mysticism are what initially aroused my own interest in the area as a student in the 1980s. In one of my courses, "Comparative Mystical Traditions," we explore various themes of mysticism in some of the major world religions. We begin by focusing on selected readings and ideas of different theorists of mysticism,[7] before studying mystics from different traditions in light of our reflections in that context. In the current version of the course, we study aspects of Roman Catholic, Jewish Kabbalistic, and Native American spiritual traditions, along with some references to features of Christian Pietism, Kundalini Yoga, Theosophy, and the visual arts. We attempt to uncover and illustrate common features between mystical traditions, their differences, and the significant implications of this comparative context, through reflection on questions related to the major guiding issues mentioned previously.

One feature that is common across mystical traditions is the view that persons and the phenomenal world as we know it are somehow limited, inadequate, or distorted. Cross-culturally, many mystics also agree that one can come to an inner awareness of a higher spiritual Reality or truth, one that underlies or transcends normal consciousness and has a powerfully transformative effect on the person. This includes heightened feelings of integration and creative stimulation, bliss, joy, and a deep-felt sense of fulfillment. Although the positive effects of these experiences are long-lasting and perhaps even permanent, the personal struggles in the dynamic can be quite severe. The process of self-surrender involved in mysticism is difficult and can involve extended periods of disappointment and depression, which eventually culminates in positive spiritual realizations. These typically transient experiences involve an altered state of consciousness wherein the subject is thought to transcend or override his or her normal means of knowing and perceiving in the world.

Rahner defines mysticism as "an ultimate and absolutely radical experience of Transcendence in the mystery of God...." "In the mystical experience, the 'mystical' subject undergoes an 'immediate' experience, transcending mediation by categorical objects of the everyday,..." (Rahner 1983, 70, 72). De Certeau writes: "In a very real sense, [mystical experience] alienates. It pertains to the same order as ecstasy: that is, to that which transports one outside oneself. It expels one from the self instead of gathering one to it" (de Certeau 1992, 18). As such, mysticism is quite different from religious experiences in ordinary faith, where the relationship with the Divine is mediated through normal categories of experience. Rahner argues that the grace given by God in normal religious experiences is mediated through categorical objects of history and culture, whereas in radical Christian mysticism, one's normal categories of experience are transcended in a direct and immediate experience of divine love.

This is in line with a characteristic of mysticism observed by William James (1961)—"passivity." Mystics advocate a radical surrender of one's normal consciousness and will in letting go of our natural tendency to intend, control, and manipulate our surroundings. Bernard Lonergan, a modern Roman Catholic philosopher and theologian, speaks of consciousness as normally involving four categories of interiority: where we experience things via our attentive senses; or we question, grasp, and understand things intelligently; or we assess, affirm, and judge things rationally; or we decide and act responsibly. These normal modes of consciousness are all intentional in relation to the phenomenal world. Mystical consciousness, Lonergan suggests, does not intend anything. It is strictly passive and vital. In such extreme surrender of one's emotions, will, and intellect, one becomes aware of one's primary, vital unity with God, a condition that underlies and supports all intentional consciousness. For Lonergan, Christian mysticism is not an intentional response to God but simply the consciousness of God's love itself, of which we are not usually aware (Lonergan 1979; Price 1985). This contemporary interpretation is in line with traditional Roman Catholic spirituality that postulated a condition of "infused contemplation" as the mystic ideal—where the person is given an "experiential sense" of divine being and love (Johnston 1989, 40).

Nontheistic mystics who do not believe in a creative and personal God would not speak of it as the experience of "God's love," but many would agree with Lonergan that normal intentional consciousness overlays and inhibits the mystical consciousness. This helps explain another common characteristic of mysticism offered by William James. He writes, the "incommunicableness of the transport is the keynote of all mysticism," though Ninian Smart notes insightfully how mystical experiences are not strictly ineffable (James 1961, 318; Smart 1958, 137). Because they do not involve our normal categories of perceiving and knowing, it is hard to say precisely what occurs in that context. However, all mystics are clear that something extremely special is going on—that there is a certain kind of "content"—what James calls its "noetic aspect," as well as the powerful affect of mystical experience. Michel de Certeau observes that "mystics...spoke of 'something' that could really no longer be said in words. They therefore proceeded to a description that ran the gamut of 'sensations',...The 'emotions' of affectivity and the alterations of the body thus became the clearest indicators of the movement produced before or after the stability of intellectual formulations" (de Certeau 1992, 15).

Given these various, apparently common aspects of mysticism cross-religions, I find it helpful at some point in my "Comparative Mystical Traditions" course to explore with students a simple and general definition proposed by Evelyn Underhill in *Practical Mysticism*: "*Mysticism is the art of union with Reality. The mystic is a person who has attained that union in greater or less degree; or who aims at and believes in such attainment*" (Underhill 1942, 23). On first reading, this definition might appear overly facile to some students. However, as they reflect on the terms art, Reality, and union, they come to notice how mysticism clarified as an art—and not as a science, for example—suggests a kind of creative and intuitive openness, rather than a rigidly structured discipline and path. Nevertheless, art involves practices and skills, and so there are various mystical means and activities, and a sense of progressive movement and learning. Moreover, art involves teachers: and cross-culturally one finds spiritual directors, elders, gurus, masters, and exemplars of the mystical path and ideal, people who help the aspiring mystic find her or his way in the discipline of mystical practice (Feuerstein 1991).

In referring to the "object" of mystical experience as capital R Reality, Underhill leaves open the possibility that this definition might function beyond Christian and even theistic contexts. There is something much greater and radically different than one's normal self that a mystic becomes aware of in a nonsensory and nonintellectual consciousness. Underhill speaks of this awareness as a "union," which could mean a very loose relation that might include a wide variety of spiritual experiences or which might suggest an intimacy between the subject and the Reality that goes beyond the sense of relations or

fellowship that some unions or communions imply. Union can mean an intimate connection—a "coalition" or even a "junction" between two things. So
some mystics will speak of the unity of the experience; in some cases, they
claim that one loses one's sense of self within the Reality of the union.

This is where Underhill's definition of mysticism begins to break down in the
face of different accounts given among different religions. For, rather than claiming the experience of *communion* or *union* with a personal Reality, some mystical traditions speak of an *identity* or *oneness*, where the underlying or transcending
condition is described as nonpersonal, nondual, and even monistic. This kind of
issue brings into question the view that mysticism is the essential and common
feature of all religious traditions. De Certeau suggests we do not have the means
to decide. He claims, "there exists no single point of observation from which it
would be possible to contemplate mysticism independently of some sociocultural or religious tradition, thereby specifying 'objectively' the relationship that it
maintains with such traditions: there is, for any consideration of mysticism, no
viewpoint from Sirius" (de Certeau 1992, 23).

All mystical experience is socioculturally embedded and influenced. However, such a limitation applies to all disciplines that might cut across cultural
and historical traditions and is not to say that there might not, in the end, be
some *type* of mysticism that might exist, or come to exist, cross-culturally and
cross-religiously. Even De Certeau admits that mysticism "indicates the unity
of a modern lay reaction before sacred institutions" (de Certeau 1992, 23),
which makes one wonder why similar claims might not be made about other
common aspects between mystical experiences. In any case, under this first
major guiding issue we are still left with the interesting question of how different spiritual experiences might be similarly *mystical*. And how do different
types of mystical experiences differ? Can they be related or interconnected
psychologically? Can they be related or interconnected theologically? Is there
a *hierarchy* of mystical experiences? Are some mystical experiences better than
others? Are some more redemptive or liberating? Can mystical experiences be
understood within a framework of spiritual process and development? What
are the various dynamics of such a mystic process? Although these questions
that pertain to difference fall under the first guiding issue, some of them turn
up regularly under other major issues, including the subjective dynamics of
mystical experience.

Questions Related to the Subjective Dynamics
of Mystical Experience

What goes on in one's mind, emotions, and body during a mystical experience? Is there any knowledge content in mystical experience? What are its psychological and spiritual dynamics? What does one learn or come to know or

include course summary in summary *for book*

come to feel during mystical experience? What are the religious dynamics of mystical experience? Are there nonreligious mystical experiences? If there are mystical experiences that are not religious, can they be related to religion? Are mystical experiences wholly subjective or is there a Reality apart from the subject that is experienced mystically? If there is a Reality apart from the person, what is its nature?

Contemporary research in neuroscience has established evidence that mystical contemplation produces electrochemical brain states that are not associated with normal consciousness. Certain pathways and regions of the brain seem to be specifically related to mystical experience. There is evidence of a neurological substrate in the human brain that enables or corresponds to mystical consciousness (Beauregard and O'Leary 2007; Hick 2006; Newberg and D'Aquili 2001). Although the question remains whether or not mystical experience arises solely by natural causes related to neurological processes or by the human experience of actual spiritual realities that are stimulating these processes, this current neuroscience research seems to provide some support for what many theorists of mysticism have argued—that a person's senses and intellect cease to function normally in the intuitive awareness of a fundamental Reality underlying the differentiated and changing phenomenal reality. Joseph Marechal and Louis Dupré are modern Roman Catholic philosophers who characterize it as a "unique connaturality—born of identity" and contrast it from other cognitive processes: "Where knower and known are substantially united, that union no longer allows any distance for subject-object oppositions that determine ordinary epistemic processes. The mind functions here in a different mode of being-with reality, rather than of reflecting upon it" (Dupré 1989, 5). For Marechal and Dupré, this identity with one's ontological Source means that one participates and shares in its nature, as "life-giving Love" (Dupré 1989, 8).

Other theorists and mystics tend to think of this unity as the essence of the experience. Even William James, who speaks of "the mystical ladder" in citing a wide variety of accounts of mystical experience, observes a "pretty distinct theoretic drift" toward "monism" in mystical phenomena (1961, 302, 326). W. T. Stace, a modern philosopher, characterizes it as "the apprehension of *an ultimate nonsensuous unity of all things*, a oneness or a One to which neither the senses nor the reason can penetrate" (Stace 1960, 15–16). Agenanda Bharati, a modern Advaitic scholar, is even more adamant in referring to it as the "zero experience," insisting that "it is the person's *intuition of numerical oneness with the cosmic absolute, with the universal matrix, or with any essence stipulated by the various theological and speculative systems of the world*" (Bharati 1976, 25). As such, both Stace and Bharati provocatively characterise mysticism as intrinsically a nonreligious phenomena.

Some of my students are very surprised by this claim, and further, they are annoyed by Stace's observation that "some Christian mystics, such as St. Teresa of Avila...did not have a sufficiently analytical mind to distinguish between the experience [of undifferentiated unity] and its interpretation [as union with the Christian God]" (Stace 1960, 23–24). Bharati's view on the matter is more nuanced and respectful of Teresa's intelligence, but not necessarily more acceptable to these students. He suggests that she and many other famous Christian mystics knew exactly what was going on in their mystical experiences, but they needed to camouflage the truth about its nature (as amoral and inactive oneness) in order to avoid the inquisitorial fire: "Having had the zero-experience their theological culture prompts them to do and say the 'right' thing about the experience. Those who did not quite grasp this theistic code were the deviants, or in Christian and Islamic situations, the heretics.'"...Teresa of Avila, Suso, and virtually all Christian mystics talked Christian code when they talked about their experience, and whenever they deviated from the code they risked trouble for themselves, as did Meister Eckhart" (Bharati 1976, 58–59, 49).

I will return to the question of the nature of Teresa's experience in the next section. However, these views of Stace and Bharati are helpful in illustrating the possible distinction between experience and subsequent interpretations, the significance of a person's sociocultural interpretive framework in influencing the mystical experience itself, the sectarian tendencies of mysticism, and the religious and moral implications of mystical experience. In the view of Bharati and Stace, not only is mysticism connected with religion only subsequently and adventitiously, but it is also wholly disconnected from morality. Stace contradicts himself on this matter, claiming that mystical unity is the source of love and hence ethical action. Bharati is consistent: given that the intrinsic nature of the experience is an amoral and inactive oneness, he claims that the "mystic who was a stinker, socially speaking, before he had the zero experience remains a stinker, socially speaking, after the experience" (Bharati 1976, 53). R. C. Zaehner makes the same point in a more serious and troubling manner: "Once you have reached the stage of the eternal Now, all is One, as Parmenides taught in ancient Greece. 'After all,' [Charles] Manson said, 'we are all one.' Killing someone therefore is just like breaking off a piece of cooky" (Zaehner 1974, 67).

Questions Related to the Effects and Practices of Mystical Experiences

Some questions related to the subjective dynamics of mysticism are relevant also to a third major issue: the effects of mystical experience for the mystic and the community. What is the relevance of mysticism in responding to the problem of evil? Is mysticism pertinent to theodicy? Are some mystical experiences pathological? Is there a demonic mysticism? Can demonic possession be understood as a form of mysticism? What are the dangers associated with mysticism? Are some mystical experiences directly related or connected to sociomoral concerns and actions? What is the relationship of mysticism to sexuality? What is the relationship of mysticism to morality and ethics?

Mystics in some traditions claim to unite or identify with an ultimate Reality that transcends morality. The goal, then, is also understood to be beyond moral reference, and some mystics claim in their liberated state to exist in a condition that transcends good and evil and normal moral imperatives. How is morality related to the mystic path and ideals? Jeffrey Kripal and Bill Barnard recently edited an interesting volume that explores questions related to the morality of mysticism from various mystical traditions (Barnard and Kripal 2002). These issues have serious practical import because all spiritual traditions have authoritative figures who function as teachers or guides in relation to spiritual novices or adepts. Charles Manson is an example of a modern mystic figure who led his disciples on a killing rampage that he subsequently attempted to rationalize through reference to an amoral mystic ideal (Stoeber 2002, 387).

Zaehner's concerns about Charles Manson that I mentioned at the end of the last section are complicated by the fact that most mystics speak of difficulties and dangers along the mystical path. Michael Washburn (1995; 2003) attempts to give a theoretical context to such phenomena within the perspective of transpersonal psychology. This relates also to questions associated with the fourth major guiding issue, practices associated with mystical experience. In this case, what are the methods or practices or techniques of inducing or nourishing or inspiring mystical experiences? How do they affect the mystic psychologically and physically? Washburn and other writers distinguish between receptive and concentrative meditations, where the former includes mindfulness, insight, and sitting meditation in Buddhist traditions, as well as devotional prayer across religions, and the latter includes Hindu Yoga, Koan exercises, and Christian recollection and centering prayer. Washburn explores the way in which meditation and prayer act to disengage the ego from extraverted orientations. They tend to move mystics into introvertive contexts where they become more attentive to the structures that act normally to repress unconsciously embedded material, and the ego becomes demobilized as these structures are destabilized. The mystic thereby becomes aware of and more immediately influenced by personally unconscious materials as well as prepersonal phenomena of the collective unconscious.

The process is difficult because the ego naturally resists the movement, and it is hazardous because subconscious contents and energies can dominate and even overwhelm one's personality. Washburn's transpersonal model suggests spiritual transformation requires the regression into the personal and prepersonal unconscious, and the integration of their contents with the other facets of one's psyche. Relevant to the dangers inherent to spiritual transformation, he speaks of the instinctual-archetypal unconscious. Archetypes are collective and universal energy sources of the psyche that reveal themselves in symbols as figures, characters, events, or conditions. Archetypal energies can overwhelm one's consciousness and dominate one's personality in destructive ways. Similarly, survival and situational instincts that are normally under the control of the ego, especially those associated with sexuality, aggression, and fear, can come to overwhelm one's personality, as meditation acts to uncover aspects of the submerged unconscious. These practices associated with mystical experience can unhinge the normal checks and balances of very powerful primitive impulses. As unconscious contents surface in the transformative process, they can contribute to various degrees of ego inflation, perhaps even to diabolical mysticism, rather than to an overcoming of basic egoic tendencies (Washburn 1995, 2003).

Mysticism might also be related to more traditional theological ideas of demonic possession, where destructive sources of the experiences are thought to exist quite apart from a person's subjective unconscious. Current deliverance and exorcist ministries tend to distinguish between levels and degrees of demonic influence and propose systematic methods in responding to this phenomena (Cuneo 2001; Peck 1983; 2005; Kraft and Debord 2005). We explore some of this material in my course "Spirituality and Suffering." Traditionally, theorists have not tended to classify this phenomena as mystical, even if scholars such as William James spoke of "a *diabolical* mysticism, a sort of religious mysticism turned upside down" (James 1961, 334). However, if one accepts the possibility that people can become mystically open to and unite with positive spiritual realities or energies, then there seems no reason to think that one cannot become mystically open and influenced by evil spirits or energies, if these also exist. This latter phenomena has much scriptural support in Christianity and is significant traditionally in many other religions.

How does mysticism relate to the problem of evil? In my course "Spirituality and Suffering," we explore the ways in which certain kinds of suffering might contribute to spiritual transformation and how certain kinds of spiritual experience, including mysticism, might be significant in responding to suffering (Stoeber 2005, chaps. 2, 3). Although some sufferings are utterly destructive, mysticism involves an affective consolation that not only significantly reduces some suffering for some persons, but it can also support certain themes in *theodicy*—which means most generally, religious responses to the theological problems of pain and suffering. Mystic consolation provides a positive thrust to an enterprise that normally focuses on the defense of God's love, goodness, and power in the face of the great depth and pervasiveness of evil in the world. Some mystics espouse a religious ideal and claim intuitive realizations that have positive bearings on themes of theodicy (Stoeber 1992, chaps. 7–9). Moreover, in some religious traditions, mystics are thought to have special powers with respect to the charismatic healing of both humans and the cosmos (Idel 1988, chap. 8).

Despite these positive claims of mysticism in responding to the problem of evil, there seems a general tendency among mystics to deviate from traditional religious institutions and practices. Bharati might be mistaken in his claim that the essence of *all* mystical experience is a numerical oneness, which I describe in the last section, but he surely is correct in noting the unorthodox propensities of Christian and Islamic mysticism and the suspicion it attracts from religious and political authorities. As De Certeau observes, mysticism is spiritually divergent by nature and distances itself from traditional institutions and authorities (1992, 12–13). St. Teresa has already been mentioned in that regard. Given the fact that her grandfather was a Jewish convert who confessed and was punished publicly with his sons for practicing Judaism in secrecy, one is astonished that she garnered the influence that she did, in reforming the Carmelite order and as a spiritual teacher. Also, her possible connections to aspects of Jewish mysticism are intriguing (Green 1989). Her metaphor of a personal, interior journey through the seven mansions of an interior castle corresponds to the visionary journey in Jewish throne-chariot mysticism (*Merkavah*), through the seven heavenly mansions or palaces, to behold God in the center. Her spiritual theology creatively integrates a variety of religious practices and ideas, and a certain independent spirit runs throughout her writing. Note her admonishment to her sisters: "take your delight in this Interior Castle, for you can enter it and walk about in it at any time without asking leave from your superiors" (Teresa 1989, 234).

Teresa also helpfully brings into question the claims of Bharati and Stace about the fundamental monistic nature of mystical experience, simply through the wide variety of experiences she recounts in her *Life* and *The Interior Castle*. This brings us back to the first major guiding issue, the nature of mystical experience. Although Teresa warns against the delusionary nature of most voices and visions and claims that higher level experiences are nonsensory and nonintellectual, she nevertheless goes on to describe rapture at the level of the sixth mansion as clearly containing imaginative and vividly sensory and sensual features (1989, 126–203). I will begin to illustrate this point, when I briefly explore the question of sexuality and mysticism. Teresa's varied descriptive accounts appear to provide strong prima facie evidence against the claims of essentialist theorists, that theistic mystics always interpretively overlay a nonsensory, nonintellectual, and amoral experience of undifferentiated unity.

Related to this question, I have my students in my "Comparative Mystical Traditions" course read a short autobiographical account of the conversion experience of Charles Finney, a nineteenth-century Congregational Revivalist theologian. Over a period of a number of hours, Finney experienced a vision of Jesus that was initially very strikingly numinous in nature, but which shifted into interior feelings of unitive penetration. He writes that it was "like a wave of electricity, going through and through me. Indeed, it seemed to come in waves and waves of liquid love; for I could not express it in any other way" (Ellwood 1999, 11). The sense of union with a spiritual Reality that he describes has some strong sensory elements and is very embodied and sensual in orientation.

The typical reaction of students to this account is to regard it obviously as a mystical experience, despite the clearly sensual and sensory features, but not plausibly as a theistic overlay by Finney of an awareness of fundamental undifferentiated unity. The same applies in reading Teresa's descriptions of the various mansions of the Interior Castle, even if she tends to use some vivid monistic metaphors to describe the experiences of the highest mansions: two candle flames united as one, rain that falls into a spring or a river, and light that forms in a room from two different windows. Indeed, in reading these metaphors of Teresa and focusing on other aspects of her account of the sixth and seventh mansions, one can see why Stace and Bharati might be inclined to postulate for her a basically monistic experience within a theistic interpretive code. However, like certain other mystics from different traditions, the many various mystical descriptions she gives seem to support better the postulation of different kinds of mystical experiences, including nondualistic types, as well as those that have sensory, physical, and moral features (Stoeber 1994, chap. 3).

In reading Teresa, one cannot also fail to see a strong sexual component that surfaces in her mysticism. In some of her writings, she draws on the erotic imagery of the *Song of Songs*, especially in visualizing the object of her devotional intimacy as Jesus. We see this erotic element also in her experience of transverberation, vividly depicted in the famous sculpture by Bernini. She describes a vision of a very beautiful angel with a golden spear that was tipped at its endpoint with fire: "This he plunged into my heart several times so that it penetrated to my entrails. When he pulled it out, I felt that he took them with it, and left me utterly consumed by the great love of God. The pain was so severe that it made me utter several moans. The sweetness caused by this intense pain is so extreme that one cannot possibly wish it to cease, nor is one's soul then content with anything but God" (Teresa 1957, 210).

What is the relation of sexuality to mysticism? Until recently, theorists of mysticism have not paid much attention to this question. Freud, in postulating a neonatal condition of uninhibited sensual unity with all of life, provides a theoretical context by which mystics can be understood to be reexperiencing this oceanic bliss of primary infantile narcissism. In this view, vital sexual energy has become repressed and restricted to the genital area of the body, through the development of a person's differentiated ego. A mystic is able to override normal repressive mechanisms, in identifying with this underlying cosmic energy. Ken Wilber, a contemporary transpersonal theorist, adapts Freudian theory in understanding Kundalini Yoga as a process where one attempts to release and experience constricted sexual energy throughout one's whole body, through various postures, movements, and breath and visual meditations of yoga practice. Wilber writes: "The higher consciousness is being freed from its chronic restrictions in 'lower'—that is, limited and bounded— modes of awareness and energetics. God consciousness is not sublimated sexuality; sexuality is repressed God consciousness" (Wilber 1990, 130).

Jeffrey Kripal provocatively explores the erotic in some of his recent research, treating mystical texts, in his words, "as cultural sites of sexual and gender liminality, as semiotic openings to a more polymorphous erotic existence that would be impossible within the more orthodox parameters of the social register in question" (Kripal 2001, 17). In so doing, Kripal highlights an apparent homoerotic desire (and not necessarily, he points out, a homosexual practice) that has tended to predominate among male mystics in Western monotheistic traditions, given the exclusive focus on masculine symbolism in reference to the Divine. He insightfully raises an interesting and complex issue that has significant implications for other dimensions of religion. Even Evelyn Underhill was aware of this tendency in Christian mysticism, as illustrated in her qualifying remarks on the erotic symbolism of St. Bernard of Clairvaux drawn from the *Song of Songs*: "we find images which indeed have once been sensuous; but which are here anointed and ordained to a holy office, carried up, transmuted, and endowed with a radiant purity, an intense and spiritual life" (Underhill 1990, 137). So, Underhill goes on to remind her readers, it is the soul, and not the man, who speaks these words to the divine groom: "Let Him kiss me with the kisses of His mouth." It is interesting and telling that Underhill does not feel the need to make the same qualification in reference to the erotic passion of female mystics, such as Teresa's transverberation experience (Underhill 1990, 292–293).

Another important question related to sexuality and mysticism pertains to the way in which human sexual *relations* have been excluded from Christian mysticism. Virtually all the leading and influential Christian mystics have been celibate, or at least purportedly so, and more affective strands of the mystical tradition tended to advocate a redirecting or transmuting of sexual desire for other persons into passion for God. Although it seems clear that sexual desire is an essential stimulant in the movement of many Christian mystical experiences, traditionally it was thought that human sexual *relationships* could not possibly be mystical in character, given the negative perception of sexual desire and pleasure, as *always* spiritually distorting and corrupting. However, more positive, personalist understandings of sexuality in some contemporary Roman Catholic and other Christian theology allow for an interpretive framework that might draw certain sexual experiences into spiritual and mystical contexts, where lovers are able to surrender and transcend normal egoic-narcissistic orientations in the spiritual ecstasy of emotional and physical sexual union (Stoeber 2009, 21–24; Evans 1993, chap. 3). Traditionally, some Jewish theology has integrated sexuality with mysticism, though it is interpreted within a cosmology and view of divine attributes that differs somewhat from traditional Christian accounts (Laenen 2001, 138–139).

This relates to other questions pertaining to the subjective dynamics of mystical experience. Are there distinguishable *feminine* and *masculine* elements of mystical experience? In light of traditional male domination of the traditions of mystical theology, has there been a repression or persecution of women's mystical experience? In deconstructing the history of Christian mysticism, Grace Jantzen illustrates how the social construction of mysticism has been determined largely by privileged men in dominant positions of society. We explore her work especially in my course "Classics of Christian Spirituality" (Jantzen 1995; 1998). She argues that although there was some resistance historically by a few creative and sometimes influential women, these dominant male figures tended to ignore, marginalize, or even violently persecute women's religious experience that deviated from masculine norms. Patriarchal perspectives on mysticism tended to suppress women's more embodied and social-oriented experiences.

Jantzen provides an overview of the historical shifts that defined mysticism in terms of rituals of initiation into mystery religions, contemplative Platonist transcendence of the body, and experiences of sacred scripture and sacramental practices. She argues that contemporary philosophy of religion has tended to focus on issues of psychological epistemology in theorizing about mysticism, given the influence of the postenlightenment stress on the rational, individual subject. In modernity, mysticism comes to be defined as a private and personal psychological feeling-state distinct from social and political realities, and contemporary theorists tend to read its history within this limited framework. Modern theorists and theologians of mysticism tend to highlight a kind of "intellectual" mysticism—associated with an ideal of "infused contemplation"— one that aspires to a disembodied experience of God that is envisioned as a private psychological state achieved only in contemplative isolation.

Moreover, even in more "affective" mysticisms, where the accent is on love, the ideal seeks similarly to transcend the body. All other forms of religious experience are regarded as inferior, suspect, or spiritually dangerous. We see this clearly, for example, in Evelyn Underhill's critical disparagement of visionary experience—a critique that depends heavily on the teachings of Walter Hilton and St. John of the Cross (Underhill 1990, 266–297). The basic claim is that sensory and imaginative experiences cannot be trusted to be authentically mystical, and are only rarely so: "Vision…is recognised by the true contemplatives as at best an imperfect, oblique, and untrustworthy method of apprehension". It is not made clear why this should be the case, except to insist that sensory and imaginary experience contain "much danger and delusion" and that the reliability of authentic mystical experiences is correlative to their degree of introversion (Underhill 1990, 281). Jantzen would argue that such narrow views of mysticism unfairly preclude much religious experience from

being perceived to be spiritually transformative and genuinely
a pastoral context, this means certain genuine mystical ex
never be supported or nourished within one's own tradition
would not even be open to certain spiritually transformative
given the narrow understanding of authentic possibilities.

Conclusion

Jantzen focuses on women's experience in her concerns about distorted or
overly narrow definitions of mysticism that tend to exclude or even persecute
legitimate forms of spirituality. However, her critique applies also to the way in
which more embodied aspects of male spirituality have been neglected or suppressed historically through biased understandings of mystical experience.
I mentioned that sexuality has been excluded from traditional Christian mystical contexts and visionary experiences have been disparaged and downplayed.
An important question is if one should not regard certain depth, visionary, and
numinous experiences as various types of mystical experience, perhaps within
the context of a view of spiritual unfolding and growth, where all these experiences might play a significant role in the transformative dynamic. In such a
view, imageless contemplative mysticism need not be regarded as a form of
spirituality that is superior to more embodied kinds of religious experience, but
merely as one of different types within a mystical continuum.

The categories of spiritual experience that I introduce to students in my
courses are left open for adjustment or correction, and most students seem to
appreciate a dialogical approach that poses and reflects upon these various
questions associated with the four guiding issues that I began to illustrate in
this chapter. In the multidenominational context of Regis College and TST,
I have come to appreciate the benefits of maintaining a broad and open-ended
understanding of mysticism, as well as the importance of positive intention, in
enabling a person to participate creatively, constructively, and perhaps even
personally, within this field of study. By keeping the field as wide as possible,
the hope is not to preclude possibly authentic mystical experiences from the
collection of data or personal encounter. It also helps one to be open to the
continued evolution of mysticism, and perhaps even to contribute positively to
it, if only in some minor way, within the context of a rich religious multiplicity
that is becoming more and more tangible in our contemporary global world.

Notes

1. The mission statement can be found at the Regis College webpage: http://www.
regiscollege.ca/regis/mission.

2. These ecclesiastical degrees are the Bachelor of Sacred Theology, Licentiate of Sacred Theology, and Doctor of Sacred Theology.

3. Currently I focus or touch on the topic of mysticism in the following courses: "Comparative Mystical Traditions," "Classics of Christian Spirituality," "Themes in Hindu Spirituality," "The Spiritual Theology of Evelyn Underhill," "Spirituality and Suffering," "Issues in the Philosophy of Religion and *The Brothers Karamazov*," "Religious Experience in the World's Religions," "Theology and Spirituality of Dorothee Soelle," and "Prayer Through Pencil, Pastel and Ink Sketching."

4. The breakdown for students entering the seven member schools of TST in 2008 was 52% Roman Catholic, 17% Anglican, 10% United Church of Canada, 6% Presbyterian, and 15% from twenty-one other Christian denominations and one Jewish denomination. Students attending TST from the four affiliated colleges come largely from the Christian Reformed, Lutheran, Mennonite, and Anglican traditions. There were 1573 students registered at TST for 2008–2009, with 720 of these being full time. In terms of geographic origins, 19% of the students were other than Canadian, with 33% of these coming from the United States, 17% from India, 14% from South Korea, and 36% from at least twelve other countries. Statistics pertaining to the Christian denominations of students are from the Toronto School of Theology Entering Student Questionnaire 2008–2009, whereas all other statistics are from the Toronto School of Theology Enrolment Report 2008–2009.

5. Because there are ministry and spiritual formation programs at Regis College, I am able to assign in some of my "Pastoral Theology" courses short pastoral/theological reflection papers that are geared toward stimulating students affectively and spiritually. In these assignments, I ask students to reflect creatively and personally on issues or themes of the course: to summarize briefly key elements of specific course readings; to reflect on their attractions/resistances/aversions to aspects of these readings, and what might cause these; to relate this material to similar or contrasting ideas or practices; to explore the ways in which this material might or might not speak to a contemporary reader's sense of spiritual well-being and development; to discuss the questions or issues that it raises for the student; and to reflect on the possible pastoral/theological significance (or limitations) of the material. Typically, these assignments are quite thoughtful and interesting to read.

6. "Interview with Oprah Winfrey," *Larry King Live*, CNN Television, December 9, 2003.

7. Among other sources, this has included: G. William Barnard (1992), Agenanda Bharati (1976), Michel De Certeau (1992), Carolyn Franks Davis (1989), Louis Dupré (1989), Donald Evans (1989), Dierdre Green (1982), John Hick (1977; 1989), William James (1961), Steven Katz (1978), Rudolph Otto (1978), Karl Rahner (1983), Ninian Smart (1965, 1983), W. T. Stace (1960), Michael Stoeber (1994, 2001), Jeffrey Kripal (2001), Evelyn Underhill (1990), Michael Washburn (1995), R. C. Zaehner (1961).

References

Barnard, G. William. 1992. "Explaining the Unexplainable: Wayne Proudfoot's *Religious Experience*," *Journal of the American Academy of Religion* 60: 231–256.

Barnard, G. William, and Jeffrey J. Kripal, eds. 2002. *Crossing Boundaries: Essays on the Ethical Status of Mysticism*. New York: Seven Bridges Press.

Beauregard, Mario, and Denyse O'Leary. 2007. *The Spiritual Brain: A NeuroScientist's Case for the Existence of the Soul.* New York: HarperCollins.

Bharati, Agehananda. 1976. *The Light at the Center: Context and Pretext of Modern Mysticism.* Santa Barbara, CA: Ross-Erikson.

Callahan, Annice. 1989. "The Relationship between Spirituality and Theology," *Horizons* 16 (2): 266–274.

Cuneo, Michael. 2001. *American Exorcism: Expelling Demons in the Land of Plenty.* New York: Doubleday.

Davis, Caroline Franks. 1989. *The Evidential Force of Religious Experience.* Oxford: Clarendon Press.

De Certeau, Michel. (1968) 1992. "Mysticism," translated by Marsanne Brammer, *Diacritics* 22 (2): 11–25.

Dupré, Louis. 1989. "The Christian Experience of Mystical Union," *Journal of Religion* 26 (1): 1–13.

Ellwood, Robert. 1999. *Mysticism and Religion.* 2nd ed. New York: Seven Bridges Press.

Evans, Donald. 1989. "Can Philosophers Limit What Mystics Can Do? A Critique of Steven Katz," *Religious Studies* 25 (1): 53–60.

———. 1993. *Spirituality and Human Nature.* Albany: State University of New York Press.

Feuerstein, Georg. 1991. *Holy Madness: the Shock Tactics and Radical Teachings of Crazy-Wise Adepts, Holy Fools, and Rascal Gurus.* New York: Penguin Arkana.

Green, Deirdre. 1982. "Unity in Diversity," *Scottish Journal of Religious Studies* 3 (1): 46–58.

———. 1989. *Gold in the Crucible: Teresa of Avila and the Western Mystical Tradition.* Shaftesbury, Dorset: Element Books.

Hick, John. 1977. "Mystical Experience as Cognition." In *Mystics and Scholars: The Calgary Conference on Mysticism 1976*, edited by Harold Coward and Terence Penelhum. In *Studies in Religion*, Supplements 3, 41-56. Waterloo, Ontario: [Wilfred Laurier University Press] Canadian Corporation for Studies in Religion.

———. 1989. *An Interpretation of Religion.* London: Macmillan Press Ltd.

———. 2006. *The New Frontier of Religion and Science: Religious Experience, Neuroscience and the Transcendent.* Houndsmills, UK: Palgrave Macmillan.

Idel, Moshe. 1988. *Kabbalah: New Perspectives.* New Haven, CT: Yale University Press.

James, William. (1902) 1961. *The Varieties of Religious Experience: A Study in Human Nature.* Reprint, New York: Collier Books, Macmillan Pub. Co.

Jantzen, Grace M. 1995. *Power, Gender and Christian Mysticism.* Cambridge: Cambridge University Press.

———. 1998. *Becoming Divine: Towards a Feminist Philosophy of Religion.* Bloomington: Indiana University Press.

Johnston, William. 1989. *Being in Love: The Practice of Christian Prayer.* San Francisco: Harper & Row.

Katz, Steven, ed. 1978. *Mysticism and Philosophical Analysis.* London: Sheldon Press.

Kraft, Charles H., and David M. Debord. 2005. *The Rules of Engagement: Understanding the Principles that Govern the Spiritual Battles in Our Lives.* Eugene, OR: Wipf and Stock Publishers.

Kripal, Jeffrey J. 2001. *Roads of Excess, Palaces of Wisdom: Eroticism and Reflexivity in the Study of Mysticism.* Chicago: University of Chicago Press.

Laenen, J. H. 2001. *Jewish Mysticism: An Introduction*, translated by David Orton. Louisville, KY: Westminster John Knox Press.

Lewis, C. S. 1956. *The Problem of Pain*. London: Geoffrey Bles.

Lonergan, Bernard. 1979. *Method in Theology*. 2nd ed. New York: Seabury.

Newberg, Andrew, and Eugene D'Aquili. 2001. *Why God Won't Go Away: Brain Science and the Biology of Belief* . New York: Ballantine Books.

Otto, Rudolph. (1923) 1978. *The Idea of the Holy: An Inquiry into the Non-Rational Factor in the Idea of the Divine and Its Relation to the Rational*, translated by John W. Harvey. Reprint, New York: Oxford University Press.

Peck, M. Scott. 1983. *People of the Lie: The Hope for Healing Human Evil*. New York: Simon and Schuster.

———. 2005. *Glimpses of the Devil: A Psychiatrist's Personal Accounts of Possession, Exorcism, and Redemption*. New York: Free Press.

Price, James Robertson Price III. 1985. "Lonergan and the Foundation of a Contemporary Mystical Theology". In *Lonergan Workshop*. Vol. 5, edited by Fred Lawrence, 161–191. Chico, California: Scholars Press.

Principe, Walter. 1983. "Toward Defining Spirituality," *Studies in Religion* 12 (2): 127–141.

Rahner, Karl. 1981 "The Spirituality of the Church in the Future." In *Theological Investigations: Concern for the Church*, translated by Edward Quinn, Vol. 20, 143–153. New York: Crossroads.

———. 1983. *The Practice of Faith: A Handbook of Contemporary Spirituality*, edited by Karl Lehmann and Albert Raffelt. New York: Crossroad.

Smart, Ninian. 1958. *Reasons and Faiths*. London: Routledge and Kegan Paul.

———. 1965. "Interpretation and Mystical Experience," *Religious Studies* 1 (1): 75–87.

———. 1983. "The Purification of Consciousness and the Negative Path." In *Mysticism and Religious Traditions*, edited by Steven Katz, 117–129. Oxford: Oxford University Press.

———. 1989. *The World Religions*. Englewood Cliffs, NJ: Prentice Hall.

Stace, W. T. 1960. "What is Mysticism." In *The Teaching of the Mystics*. New York: New American Library.

Stoeber, Michael. 1992. *Evil and the Mystics' God: Towards a Mystical Theodicy*. Toronto and London: University of Toronto Press and Macmillan Press.

———. 1994. *Theo-Monistic Experience: A Hindu-Christian Comparison*. London and New York: Macmillan Press and St. Martin's Press.

———. 2001. "Mysticism and the Spiritual Life: Reflections on Karl Rahner's View of Mysticism," *Toronto Journal of Theology* 17 (2): 263–275.

———. 2002. "Amoral Trickster or Mystic Saint? Spiritual Teachers and the Transmoral Narrative." In *Crossing Boundaries: Essays on the Ethical Status of Mysticism*, edited by G. William Barnard and Jeffrey J. Kripal, 381–405. New York: Seven Bridges Press.

———. 2005. *Reclaiming Theodicy: Reflections on Suffering, Compassion and Spiritual Transformation*. Houndsmills, Basingstoke: Palgrave Macmillan.

———. 2009. "Reflections on the Virtues and Dangers of Sexuality and Celibacy in the Roman Catholic Tradition," *Journal of Inter-Religious Dialogue* 2: 11–32. http://irdialogue.org/journal/issue02/reflections-on-the-virtues-and-dangers-of-sexuality-and-celibacy-in-the-roman-catholic-tradition-by-michael-stoeber/.

Stoeber, Michael, and Hugo Meynell, eds. 1996. *Critical Reflections on the Paranormal*. Albany: State University of New York Press.

Teresa of Avila. 1957. *The Life of Saint Teresa of Avila, By Herself,* translated by J. M. Cohen. New York: Penguin.

————. 1989. *Interior Castle,* translated by E. Allison Peers. New York: Image Books.

Underhill, Evelyn. (1911) 1990. *Mysticism: The Preeminent Study in the Nature and Development of Spiritual Consciousness.* Reprint, New York: Doubleday.

————. (1914) 1942. *Practical Mysticism.* Reprint, Columbus, OH: Ariel Press.

Washburn, Michael. 1995. *The Ego and Dynamic Ground: A Transpersonal Theory of Human Development.* 2nd ed. rev. Albany: State University of New York Press.

————. 2003. *Embodied Spirituality in a Sacred World.* Albany: State University of New York Press.

Wilber, Ken. 1990. "Are the Chakras Real?" In *Kundalini: Evolution and Enlightenment,* rev. ed., edited by John White, 120–131. New York: Paragon House.

Wiseman, James, OSB. 1993. "'I Have Experienced God': Religious Experience in the Theology of Karl Rahner," *The American Benedictine Review* 44 (1): 22–57.

Zaehner, R. C. (1957) 1961. *Mysticism: Sacred and Profane.* Reprint, New York: Oxford University Press.

————. 1974. *Our Savage God: The Perverse Use of Eastern Thought.* New York: Sheed and Ward.

PART IV

Tracking Mysticism

PEDAGOGY AND CONTEMPORARY CULTURE

14

From "Comparative Mysticism" to "New Age Spirituality"

TEACHING NEW AGE AS RAW MATERIALS OF RELIGION

Steven J. Sutcliffe

The Pedagogical Potential of New Age in the Religious Studies Curriculum

"New age" has been both difficult to specify and tricky to theorize in the standard terms of the academic study of religion. *New age* or *holistic* or *alternative* phenomena have proved difficult in the first place to define (Chryssides 2007). A related difficulty is whether to classify the phenomena as *religion* or *spirituality*, an issue increasingly elided as *spirituality* acculturates in the academy as an adjunct descriptive category alongside *religion* without a clear analytical distinction between the two terms. Once the hurdle of definition has been negotiated, a fresh difficulty arises: how to locate teaching new age within a curriculum still dominated by the *world religions* taxonomy, which continues at least implicitly to reify and rank religious formations according to an antiquated Victorian prototype.[1] Persistent problems in data selection and analysis with respect to new age—what is to "count" as new age, and what is empirically and/or theoretically significant about "it" anyway—at least in part derive from the inferior position that the selected phenomena have been made to occupy in the historical taxonomy of "religion entities": those reified "things" we instinctively and precritically think religion "is." Thinking in terms of the *world religions* taxonomy renders the empirical data for new age residual by default. Its components come to signify what is left over after the "world" formations and their adjunct ("new") and surrogate ("global") classifications have taken their share of the substantive cake. New age data settle to the bottom of the pile of "religion entities," along with other apparently anomalous data going under names such as "paranormal," "mind body spirit," and "occult." The sum is that presenting new age in the classroom is to teach against the grain of students' assumptions about what counts as "proper religion."

This has been a problem both in terms of developing a sophisticated research program with respect to new age, but also in terms of teaching an undergraduate course in this area in the first place, as the historical bias in the
curriculum toward "world" models makes a course on "new age spirituality" a
luxury for departments on tight budgets—which means most of us. Partly in
response, perhaps, the study of new age has sought a niche within the wider
field of studies of "new religious movements," which have successfully established their presence as a bona fide subfield of the wider study of religion,
through ingenious efforts to make the shifting contours of new age count as a
special type of "new movement" (Sutcliffe 2003b, 21–30, 197–199).

New age is thus a contested subject matter in the study of religions. This
insight can be converted from negative to positive and put to productive pedagogical use if it is placed in the context of the multifaceted modern critique of
the category *religion* from W. C. Smith ([1962] 1991) to Fitzgerald (1997), among
others. The hermeneutic of suspicion applied to the category *mysticism* by Katz
(1978) and Penner (1983), for example, which is bound up with a critical turn
against the perceived theoretical emptiness of the concept of *experience* (Sharf
1998), is a case in point: the various accusations of reification, semantic indeterminacy, and disguised political interests (one way or another) with respect
to *religion* and *mysticism* also hold in the case of *new age*. In this sense, the
debate on specifying and demarcating new age can be made to connect to core
questions about category formation in the study of religion (Baird 1971).

A common concern in categorical debates is the various taxa's elision of
internal heterogeneity in favor of a static, biased, or otherwise artificial homogeneity. Not unlike *religion,* where any number of ideas and practices have
seemingly been folded into a catch-all category, some scholars have treated the
idea of a separate field called "The New Age" or "The New Age Movement" as
a construction that distracts attention from more interesting theoretical possibilities raised by analyzing the same data—but in different ways.[2] For example, Wood (2007) has recently argued that the seemingly endless debate about
how best to demarcate new age has distracted attention from more interesting
theoretical questions of how the exercise of power and authority is identified
and negotiated by practitioners in these less determinate regions of the religious field. Wood's model presents new age practitioners as subject to a spectrum of more-or-less authoritative institutions operating between what he
calls *formative* and *nonformative* poles (Wood 2007, 156–163). Formative authority tends to reproduce its forms and structures as recognized, effective
traditions. Nonformative authority is characterized by weakness of reproduction, seen in incomplete and episodic acknowledgment of authoritative sources
by practitioners, and tending to leave ambiguous and somewhat fragmented
effects on their lives. Although the *nonformativity* of new age institutions and
the relative weakness of new age *traditions* inevitably serves to destabilize the

phenomenon as a unified and boundaried field, Wood's approach shows how this becomes theoretically interesting for comparative studies of how religious formations are produced and maintained at a popular or grassroots level. The relative lack of formative new age authorities means not that no authority operates at all (which would be an attractive yet superficial conclusion) but rather that the failure of strong authority (its relative lack of formative power) tends to generate multiple weaker authorities, whose individual force and impact is relativized through their very proliferation. Wood's model helps to explain why *new age* identities, beliefs, and practices have had such a high turnover and why the scope of participation in a distinctive formation called *new age* has been so hard to specify.

Identification of nonformativity as the mechanism behind the proliferation of new age authorities and a major cause of its precarious corporate identity can be put to good use in classroom teaching. In addition to teasing out how authorities multiply with diminishing effects, but without ever entirely disappearing, it allows us to consider new age in the light of the popular-official dialectic in the study of religion, which posits a structural tension between local grassroots practice and centralized institutions (Vrijhof and Waardenburg 1979). New age as a popular formation might also serve as interesting testing ground for cognitive science treatments of religion by virtue of the lively "theological incorrectness" displayed by its practitioners (Slone 2004) and through the horizontal epidemiology (Sperber 1985) of its dissemination. Through these and other examples of popular features and mechanisms that are disguised when the same data are read through "world religion" lenses, new age can be thought of as a kind of laboratory or, better, creative playground in which certain "raw materials" for the production of religion stand revealed. The nonformativeness of new age, therefore, should not be considered a negative signal of "failure" or "irrelevance," but it can be interpreted as a positive signal of the aggregation and interaction of elements of "proto-religion": that is, religion before discursive "religion," or what we might call "religion-in-the-making."

In sum, as a local formation arising in the "backyard" of Anglo-American culture (Sutcliffe 2003a, 24), new age displays in a direct and accessible form elements of a very different model of *religion* compared with the implicit model of a rationalized bureaucratic organization supplied by the *world religions* taxonomy. New age data are not anomalous or residual, as must be deduced if new age is tackled from within this logic, but they can become central to rethinking the arrangement of forms within the religious field as a whole.

Furthermore, it is important that we explore the implications of this approach for research and teaching combined. Teaching is in some ways a bigger challenge because of the relatively underdeveloped analytical competence of many incoming undergraduate students, who will likely be alert and responsive to questions of religious diversity and pluralism, but who may

well show less appetite for theorizing the causes and structures of "religion."
The superficially "exotic" world of new age spirituality offers an unlikely but
potent opportunity to challenge this mindset.

Locating New Age in the Discursive Drift from *Mysticism* to *Spirituality*

Recently scholars have directed attention to a continuity of interests between
mysticism and (new age) spirituality. For example, Schmidt (2003, 276) claims
that

> The recovery of mysticism as a modern artefact is...important for
> making sense of how the catchall term *spirituality* has now spread itself
> so luxuriantly in contemporary Euro-American culture. Mysticism
> is...the great foundation upon which this revived love of spirituality has
> been built.

Schmidt points in particular to the "wide" and "expansive" sense of these
terms, identifying the "liberal circles" of the New England Transcendentalists
(284) as a key incubator for the notion of mysticism as "loosely spiritual, intuitive, emancipatory, and universal" (286), and as such constituting "the universal quintessence of religious experience" (276). He also identifies its key players
as "seekers," arguing that "it was a small step from...seekers of mysticism at
the turn of the twentieth century to...questors after spirituality a century
later" (295).[3]

Reinforcing the idea of a close connection between the discourses of *mysticism* and *spirituality*, King (2009) emphasizes the "rather woolly and ill-de-
fined manner" in which the terms are used in popular contexts:

> The adjective "mystical"...is commonly used to describe any object,
> person, event or belief which has a vaguely mysterious aspect to it. It is
> also applied to extraordinary experiences of union, whether religious or
> not, and to the supernatural, the magical and the occult in general
> (306).[4]

King contends that contemporary discourses on *spirituality* developed out of
earlier discourses on *mysticism* through a common focus on psychological experience. He presents this drift toward psychologization as being bound up
with claims of "ineffability" or "the indescribable nature of intense and private
experiences" (320). Unlike Schmidt, he links this to a perceived privatization
of religion that he finds in the increasing use of *spirituality* to "denote some
kind of interiorised experience," which is in turn "oriented towards the individual self rather than religious traditions as the source of...authority" (320).

These are interesting insights, but two important dimensions of the inter-relationship between mysticism and spirituality are missed that classroom teaching must address if it is to engage with wider theoretical debates. First, *mysticism* has tended to be a discourse preferred by social and cultural elites, whereas the distribution of *spirituality* has followed a more popular and de-motic route. Second, spirituality discourses have modern histories that predate recent patterns of use by new age and mind-body-spirit constituencies. These histories contain elements of collective tradition and authority that problema-tize the dichotomous claim that *spirituality* represents a "private" world of the "individual self" standing over against the "public" world of "religious tradi-tions." Heelas's model of "self-spirituality" (1996, 18–20), when read in the light of his earlier work on "socialising the subjective," which argues that subjectivi-ties are socially conditioned phenomena (Heelas 1982), suggests that spiritual-ity discourses are better understood as young or emergent traditions rather than as a field in which authority and tradition are absent altogether.

The discursive drift from *mysticism* to *spirituality* remarked by Schmidt and King can be given practical focus through conceiving the teaching of new age as an engagement with the many Jamesian varieties of religious, mystical, and now spiritual experience. My own interests began with *mysticism* but moved on to *new age* during my doctoral research in order to test my impression that the discursive drift from *mysticism* to *spirituality* was occurring through the medium of popular beliefs and practices in particular. This thesis is supported by the primary sources for new age, whose established "psychic" and "esoteric" content was increasingly supplemented by tropes of *spiritual* and *spirituality* between the mid-to-late 1960s and the mid-1980s. However, whereas typical sources on *mysticism* (both primary and secondary) concentrate upon the philosophical and aesthetic preoccupations of religious and artistic elites,[5] new age practitioners tend to be lay-people and self-appointed authorities operat-ing toward the popular end of the popular/official religious spectrum.[6]

In new age sources, appeal is made to the experiential and subjective quali-ties of a practice or a belief irrespective of the strength of its connection to a legitimating tradition. A new practice or idea typically circulates on the basis of trial and error. Its legitimacy or proof is tested by practitioners on the basis of "trying it out" within their own phenomenological experience. This demotic "turn to experience" challenges the linguistic turn in humanities scholarship. For practitioners, there is a manifold world of experience "beyond the text." Indeed, the realm of greatest value is represented as neither intellectual nor cognitive but imaginative, vital, and embodied. At the same time I also draw students' attention to the sociodemographic evidence base, which broadly pre-dicts participation in new age spirituality (Frisk 2007), in order to qualify emic claims concerning the radically unique or *sui generis* quality of the "experi-ence" of a particular individual.

History of a Syllabus I: Teaching "Comparative Mysticism" in Adult Education

I turn now to the twists and turns of my own syllabus. Superficially its shifts in content and theory reflect my own development from practitioner to student to researcher to teacher. But its changes are conditioned by wider debates and structural conditions that accompanied the cultural drift from mysticism to spirituality during this period. Simply put, my syllabus is itself a product of its time and place.

A general line of development can be traced: from presenting a phenomenological description and interpretation of, first, *comparative mysticism* and latterly *new age spirituality* based in biographies, practices, and beliefs, to an increasingly theoretical interest in accounting for the structure and production of *new age* formations as a contribution to comparative problems in the study of "religion." I would argue that teaching in all *religious traditions* should somehow connect with metatheoretical questions about *religion,* derived from my conviction that the study of religion must be a comparative theoretical enterprise if it is to fulfill its promise. Otherwise, it risks becoming simply a congeries of discrete, tradition-based hermeneutics that could feasibly be taught (and indeed in many places are taught) by separate centers in particular named *traditions,* or else within departments of social anthropology, history, or area studies. The increasing incorporation of theory in my syllabi is therefore also intended to point students toward questions about the overarching disciplinary purpose of the study of religion or Religious Studies as an academic enterprise.[7]

After ten years of personal "seeking" in British new age networks (Sutcliffe 2003b, 1–3), I returned to university specifically to study Buddhism and "alternative" religion. I was first exposed to the academic study of *mysticism* in the 1991–1992 academic year at the University of Stirling, where I wrote a short dissertation called "Mystical Experience, Language and Practice: a Comparative Philosophical Investigation."[8] Following graduation, and emboldened by my teacher's comparative approach, I began to teach a weekly two-hour class called "Comparative Mysticism" at the University of Glasgow Department of Adult and Continuing Education, which like many British universities offers a diverse program of extramural studies. This class ran for twenty weeks across the autumn and spring terms of 1992–1993, and I followed it up with a day school entitled "Common Ground in Mysticism? A Comparative Approach." This early stage in my intellectual career is reflected in the syllabus, which in part looked back to the enthusiasms of my earlier career as a "seeker" via its focus on "common ground" and universality of *experience,* but also in part anticipated the deconstructionist and poststructuralist interests that shaped the study of religion in the 1990s. So, for example, my advertisement for the course boldly begins:

> What do we mean by "mysticism" and "mystical experience"? Is there a universal thread running through religious experience, or can we only make sense of the world in our particular contexts of belief and practice?

The material we were to study ambitiously included:

> Western Christian Mystics, such as Meister Eckhart and St. John of the Cross; Mahayana Buddhist writings from the Prajnaparamita and Ch'an/ Zen traditions; the Chinese Tao-te-Ching; Sufism; Jewish mysticism; and the "New Age" movement.

Note that already new age was on the agenda, by implication as the latest manifestation of a putative "universal thread" of "mystical experience."

The following year, I developed my adult education teaching in two directions. First, I offered a Sunday afternoon discussion class at the newly opened St. Mungo Museum of Religious Life and Art in Glasgow, under the title "Issues in Religion." Nearly half the course drew from the mysticism/new age nexus, and Ninian Smart's "dimensions of religion" model supplied a wider disciplinary framework:

1. Religious Studies: the role of "faith" and "objectivity" in exploring issues in religions.
2. What is a religion?
3. Myth in religion
4. Practical/ritual and social/institutional dimensions of religion
5. Religious and mystical experience
6. Mysticism and the "perennial philosophy"
7. New age religion

Back at the Department of Adult and Continuing Education, I taught a short class in the spring term 1994 called "Quest and Vision: Literature and Religious Ideas." This represented a return to my earlier participatory interests, based on an eclectic selection of mid-twentieth-century literary writings. These included the canonical *Four Quartets* by T. S. Eliot as well as David Lindsay's Gnostic fantasy *A Voyage to Arcturus* and Rene Daumal's Gurdjieffian *Mount Analogue*. My rationale for this syllabus was the texts' common concern with what I called in the course descriptor "a personal quest for religious or 'spiritual' revelation." In this way I was effectively presenting a "high culture" model of the "seekership" that I had been practicing in the preceding decade. Thus the course content veered back toward the more elite aesthetic preoccupations of the *mysticism* debates even as it introduced—for the first time in my syllabi— the popular term *spiritual*.

Doctoral Interlude: From "Comparative Mysticism" to "Sociology of Mystical Experience"

The connection between *mysticism* and *new age* became explicit in my PhD proposal in February 1994. Entitled "A Sociology of Mystical Experience in Contemporary New Age Movements in Scotland: Self, Experience and Society in Redefinition," the key elements in the *mysticism* debate are present— "experience" (twice, for good measure!) and "self"—but set now within a less philosophical and altogether more empirical context. The new sociological emphasis in the words of the original proposal was designed to probe the relationship between "the mobility of individuals and religious ideas/practices" with the politico-economic symbol of the "free market." However my presumption of an underlying connection between *mysticism* and *new age* remained firmly in place through my claim that "New Age movements typically validate the self's 'quest' for (mystical) experience and present this as the contemporary religious task *par excellence*."[9]

In the event, the biggest changes I made over the next four years of research and writing were to drop the *mysticism* debate entirely, along with the philosophical and psychological focus on "the self," and to engage the metaproblem of defining the structure and impact of new age as a religious formation. This required both a sociological and especially a historical approach, as I discovered that the primary sources for popular debates on the meaning of the *new age* trope extended well before the standard post-counterculture periodization of the phenomena. Where this emphasized the late 1960s genesis of the so-called new age movement in the aftermath of the hippie counterculture and dawning "Age of Aquarius," my research found that the same period was in fact witnessing the high-water mark of a popular millennialistic discourse on the coming new age, which extended back into the 1930s (Sutcliffe 2003b, chap. 2). I submitted the thesis to the Open University in 1998 under the title "'New Age' in Britain: an Ethnographical and Historical Exploration," which indicates the clean break from comparative philosophy. The key elements of "self," "quest," and "mystical experience" had transformed into models of "seekership" and "spirituality," which I attempted to reposition as structuring elements within a history of a neglected popular religious formation. The analytical shift from (elite) *mysticism* to (popular) *spirituality* was complete. Now all I had to do was to convince my students that this made sense.

History of a Syllabus II: Teaching an Undergraduate Class on New Age

The latest and most substantial period in my teaching has now lasted a decade and has produced three versions of roughly the same syllabus.[10] I taught my first undergraduate class in 2000 at the University of Sunderland in northeast

England. This was a dense, detailed, and in retrospect overambitious class entitled "New Age and Paganism: The Return of Popular Religion." It foregrounded the motif of *popular religion* that has remained central to all subsequent versions of the course, as well as a comparative dimension that also persists. This first version used two course books written almost entirely by British-based scholars,[11] but I have since preferred to create a course reading pack based on an adjustable range of articles and chapters. This is in part because of the phenomenological fluidity of the field, which is not always captured in set texts, but it also reflects my intention to present the material within a wider theoretical framework.

The overall approach took the form of a descriptive mapping of practices, beliefs, identities, and themes. This kind of "phenomenological descriptivism" to a certain extent continues to underpin the syllabus. Although description has become something of a dirty word in recent theoretically driven critiques of the study of religion, I consider judicious empirical description (Sutcliffe 2004) justifiable and indeed essential, especially where the topic is not fully established or is likely to challenge expectations. At the same time, students need to be made aware that there can be no description without prior theoretical commitments, however vague or implicit. Indeed I would argue that the study of religion as an autonomous academic field can only finally be secured through theoretical and metatheoretical analysis. But this analysis must be evidence based.

What is immediately apparent from the syllabus is the almost complete absence of terms and referents from the *mysticism* debate. There remains some phenomenological mapping of material involving appeals to special kinds of *experiences*, such as channeling and shamanic activities (weeks 3 and 5) and expressive spirituality and "personal growth" (week 9), but the syllabus largely consolidates the shift made during the course of my doctoral research from philosophical debates (on *mysticism*) to historical sociology (of *new age spirituality*). Most of the new age material came from my PhD thesis, but for paganism, I was largely reliant on secondary sources.

Week 1. Mapping the field: defining *new age* and *paganism*; identifying popular religion in the modern world.

Week 2. New age I: contemporary profile and historical perspective; case study—the Findhorn Community, Scotland.

Week 3. New age II: case studies: channeling and alternative/holistic healing.

Week 4. Paganism I: contemporary profile and historical perspective; case study—Wicca.

Week 5. Paganism II: Case studies: Druids, Heathens, Shamans, Celts, Goddess spirituality.

Week 6. Structure and practices: How new age and pagan practitioners *do* religion. Structure: networks and groups, seekers and gurus. Practices: meditation, magic, healing.

Week 7. Ideas and beliefs: from numinous materialism to world-denying idealism—"this-worldly" and "other-worldly."
Week 8. The geography of new age and paganism: rural enclaves and urban refugees—the romance of landscape. Earth mysteries and urban settlements. Sacred sites—Glastonbury and Iona.
Week 9. Cultural affinities: environmentalism and "personal growth." From "nature spirits" to "Earth First!"; Humanistic and expressive spirituality—"personal growth."
Week 10. Gender in new age and paganism.
Week 11. Attitudes and values: Alternative or mainstream? Spiritual dissidence and countercultural values; marketization and the spiritual supermarket.
Week 12. Bricolage and innovation: making religion up. Innovation, invention, and institutionalization.

I offered this syllabus only once. For my second attempt, I sensibly dropped the paganism material to focus entirely on *new age*. I also introduced the term *spirituality* to better reflect emic discourses, although with some misgivings due to concern over its lack of analytical purchase. The result was called "New Age Spirituality in Cultural Context" and I taught it at the University of Stirling in central Scotland in 2002.

Week 1. Mapping the field: method and theory in new age studies. Studying *new age*: terms, definitions, theories, methods.
Week 2. Genealogy and contemporary profile: genealogies of *new age* from theosophy (Alice Bailey) to new age (the Findhorn community). Contemporary/ethnographic profile: beliefs, values, practices, institutions.
Week 3. Colonies and communities. The colony at Findhorn; a "sacred" site—Glastonbury.
Week 4. Practices I: Meditation and channeling. Varieties of meditation practice; channeling in action.
Week 5. Practices II: Healing: a spectrum of healing, alternative and holistic. Health and well-being in cultural context.
Week 6. The content and function of *new age* books. Case study: James Redfield, *The Celestine Prophecy* (1994).
Week 7. Popular religion in theory and practice. New age and comparative models of "popular religion"; *doing* religion—practice theory and new age.
Week 8. Practices III: "Personal growth." From apocalypse to self-realization: the hermeneutical shift in *new age*; spiritualities of bodies and feelings: "this-life" values and practices.
Week 9. The demography of new age. Gender and social class: significance and function. Ethnicity and age: impact and prospects.

on analyzing the operation of institutions and authority in new age in order better to explain its diffuse yet real societal presence, located midway between "private" and "public" domains as these have been traditionally represented. Following publication of *The Spiritual Revolution* (Heelas and Woodhead 2005), I have added a class in which we explore data on the "holistic milieu" and associated "subjective-life spiritualities" from this empirical research project in a small English town. This has helped to contextualize the final class in which we assess the overall salience of new age as a "spiritual turn" within Western (especially Anglo-American) religion, using project data to explore the attributes of *spirituality* and associated processes of "subjectivization."

> Week 1. Defining *new age*: demarcating the field. Context: "post-Christian" religious pluralization, secularization, and consumption. Distinguishing new age from related fields, especially spiritualism and neopaganism; the discursive construction of new age. Problems locating new age phenomena in the taxonomy of religion: Is it "a religion," a "world religion," a "new religious movement"? New age as a field of popular religious practice.
>
> Week 2. Modern history of new age. Roots I: romanticism and vitalism → a new age of subjective experience(s). Roots II: Christian millennialism and theosophy → the "coming new age" as a revelation. "Alternative" and "popular" aspects: new age as "culture criticism," but also as popular religiosity. Twentieth-century genealogy of uses of the term *new age*: from Alice Bailey to the Findhorn community.
>
> Week 3. Profile of practitioners: who, where, when, why? Qualitative data: models of self, subjectivity, relationship. Auto/biographical narratives of experience and "seeking"; "relationality" in new age religion. Quantitative data on sociodemographic profile, especially patterns in gender, social class, ethnicity. Sociodemographic constraints on new age participation?
>
> Week 4. Institutions and authority: *seekership,* group, network. The "cultic milieu" and *seekership*; the mobilization of seekers in groups and networks. Patterns in socialization and transmission: *seeker* as a social role, *seekership* as a social institution. Sources of authority and tradition in new age and the relativization of authority: new age as "nonformative" religion (Wood 2007). Case study: the Findhorn colony.
>
> Week 5. New age cosmology: case study, *The Celestine Prophecy* (book and film). The return of "animism": new age and the "reenchantment" of modernity. A differentiated cosmos: multiple levels of action; different entities and deities. Karma and reincarnation as building blocks of a new theodicy. The relationship between social group and cosmology in a religious formation.

Week 6. Practices I: possession. A spectrum of "possession" practices: from "intuition" to "guidance" to "channeling." The source of authority in possession practices: from a "supernatural" to a "natural" locus of power. Locating modern new age practices in wider history of "spirit possession."

Week 7. Practices II: healing. Continuities between new age and "folk" healing within popular religious formations. Epistemic and institutional context of new age/holistic healing: allopathic and nonallopathic medicine. The relationship between (gendered) new age bodies, healing anatomies, and cosmological ideas. Case study: Reiki.

Week 8. New age into "holistic milieu": the Kendal Project (Heelas and Woodhead 2005). Acculturation of new age beliefs and practices as the holistic milieu. Methodology and findings of the "Kendal project" in the context of comparative studies (eg. Glastonbury, Sedona). The "subjectivization" thesis. Testing the boundaries of the group.

Week 9. Consumption and capitalism in new age religion. Investigating affinities between new age beliefs and practices, cultural consumption, and neoliberal (global) capitalism. Religion and consumption in comparative perspective: Is new age really a special case? Countercultural, liberal and conservative positions in new age. "Capitalist" or "alternative" spirituality?

Week 10. Public impact: "spiritual revolution" or "religious failure"? New age as the "tip of the iceberg" of contemporary spirituality? Where is new age located on the spectrum between "private" and "public" religion (Casanova)? Is *new age spirituality* an emergent form of "public religion" in civil society?

Week 11. Review and revision. Discussion of course content and sources.

Discussion: Religion-in-the-Making? Teaching New Age as Raw Materials of Religion

A constant concern has been to balance the descriptive contribution of the course with adequate theoretical analysis. Because of the nature of the material, I need to provide accurate empirical data to keep classroom discussion on track. On the other hand, too much description coupled with the perennial problem of demarcating the field can disorient and even overwhelm students with exotic details and fuzzy boundaries. J. Z. Smith's adage "less is better" (1991) is a salutary reminder in this respect. My task remains to convince students that new age is no more and no less familiar or strange than any other religious formation.

Several issues recur. The first is the negative effect of prevailing taxonomies of "religion entities" on coming to terms with a formation such as new age. These typically issue in two interlinked questions (voiced or unvoiced): Is new age really *religion*? And if so, is it "proper" religion? These questions derive in part from the allure or repulsion exercised by the material through its representation by students as "exotic" and "other" on the one hand, or as "trivial" and only for the "gullible" on the other. As noted, the nonformativeness of new age supports theoretical probing of the relative absence of certain formal qualities of *religion,* such as authoritative *traditions* and legitimating institutions recognized by a wider community, as well as instability in collective identity derived from its permeable boundaries. I try to present this not as an occasion for consigning new age to the dustbin of "failed" religion[12] but as an opportunity to reevaluate approaches to apparently "marginal" or "anomalous" subject matter: in particular, to represent new age positively as displaying key "raw materials" of religion—for example, healing, vitality, comfort, insight, wealth, and friendship. Although the field lacks strong institutions, its energetic and vivid promotion of these and related elements allow us to think of new age as a form of "religion-in-the-making."

The perception of the triviality of new age and its suitability only for the gullible is linked to deep-rooted assumptions that religion and consumption are (or rather should be) mutually exclusive, and that the undisguised economic aspect of many new age transactions may signal an underlying venality that preys on insecure personalities. For some commentators, new age has become the epitome of the commercialization of contemporary religion. There may be an implicitly Protestant assumption at play here that is uneasy about popular material culture. Others—notably Heelas (2008)—seek to nuance the debate by pointing to the multifaceted nature of modern consumption and the serious motivations of new age practitioners, especially as revealed through ethnographic fieldwork, who are far from being the passive subjects implied by some critiques.[13] Perceptions of new age's "vulgar" consumerism may also fuel assessments of its sociological irrelevance, insofar as the proper goods of religion are represented as having been entirely reduced to naked market exchanges.

I think I have been more successful in fostering appreciation of how new age spirituality is located within a "high"/elite versus "low"/popular tension within both the practice and the study of religion. The changes in my syllabus show that this dialectic maps broadly onto the historical drift from *mysticism* to *spirituality.* For example, the literary texts of my adult education course, "Quest and Vision," including Eliot's *Four Quartets* and Daumal's *Mount Analogue,* contrast strikingly with my main new age exemplar: Redfield's *The Celestine Prophecy,* originally a self-published text. I now experience a tension between (passionately) wanting accurately to represent and defend the *popular* positions of new age and increasingly finding myself removed from simply "celebrating" them as a form of cultural populism, as has been the case in some celebratory or "fan" versions of cultural studies (see Ross 1992). While wanting to defend the status of new age within the academic study of religion, my own position depends on maintaining the critical distance necessary to making a fully comparative study of religion.

Thus I recognize a degree of tension between some students' continuing appetite for "experience(s)" and subjectivities and my increasing pull toward historicizing and theorizing the data in a more structuralist vein. I recognize that this also goes a little against the grain of the local and particularistic interests typical of what I have called the "second wave" of new age studies (Sutcliffe 2003a, 21), which succeeded the pioneering "big picture" monographs of the 1990s. The popularity of the field report suggests that many students identify with new age's celebration of subjectivities. The language of *experience* and *experiences* connotes an unmediated phenomenological intensity of engagement to which many students respond positively.

In contrast, the history of the phenomenon has not proved particularly attractive to students, despite the fact that cultural history provided me with the methodological key to unlock the definitional problem of whether there is or was a *new age movement* in the strict sense. One reason for disinterest is the relative difficulty of accessing the historical sources, whose popular, decentralized, and sometimes ephemeral production base has not often been to the taste of library special collections, or otherwise helped the archiving process. Another is the short period of time available: to teach the modern (twentieth-century) history of new age in just one session is an impossible undertaking except at the most rudimentary and schematic level. But it may also reflect a more general lack of interest in historical method in contemporary Religious Studies.

If history is the Achilles' heel of new age teaching, the comparative enterprise remains crucial. I would urge teachers to place new age on a comparative footing at every opportunity, asking the question: How does this particular structure or representation or mechanism connect or fail to connect with counterparts or analogs in other formations—both religious and nonreligious? In my view, the study and teaching of new age is ill-served by pursuing it as an end in itself.

In summary, the focus of my teaching has shifted from the intrinsic interest of *mystical* and later *spiritual* experiences, to structural interests in how to classify and explain these experiences and the people who "have" them within the wider study of religion. The theoretically interesting metaquestion is not "what do these experiences *feel like* and how can *I have them* too?" but "what *produces* the embodied sensations for which *mysticism* and *spirituality* are discursive tags, and how is this language used and how are its accompanying practices legitimated and disseminated in the wider population?"

My chief interest, therefore, lies in teaching new age as a local laboratory or playground (in the sense of a creative and spontaneous arena) for the production and dissemination of what Durkheim in a rather different context called "elementary forms of the religious life." This approach seeks to turn the unfinished and incomplete nature of the new age formation to positive theoretical advantage. New age can be approached as religion-in-the-making both at a discursive level—that is, in terms of examining the workings of the cultural politics of identity and representation mobilized in this field—and in terms of investigating the embodied sensations that underpin these sociocultural processes. These bodily sensations appear to be quite widely distributed, at least according to popular testimonies of *experience* (whatever exactly this term "placeholds," to use the terminology of Sharf [1998]). This entails emphasizing the tie-in of new age teaching with larger theories of religion and with the study of religion as a disciplinary field. Paradoxically, I have found that only through a critical teaching of the construction and deconstruction of new age spirituality can the vitality of the empirical data be noticed for what they are and their theoretical significance fully assessed.

Notes

1. C.P. Tiele's entry on "Religions" in the 9th edition of the *Encyclopaedia Britannica* (1884, 358–371) is the classic example: see Smith (1998) and compare Fitzgerald (1990) and Geaves (2005).

2. See Hess (1993), Klippenstein (2005), and Frisk (2005).

3. Further on seekers in the history of American liberal religion, see Schmidt (2005).

4. Cf. Bocking (2006, 1): "one colleague recently joked to me that a better spelling of Mysticism would be 'Mistycism,' reflecting a general scepticism about rational efforts to clarify such a topic." See King (1999) for an analysis of the emergence of interest in "the mystical" under the influence of Orientalist representations of Indian religion.

5. See Underhill ([1911] 1957) and Streng (1991) for typical examples of primary and secondary sources, respectively.

6. See Hanegraaff's extensive selection of new age sources (1996, 525–530) and the "holistic" representatives chosen by Bloom (2000).

7. See also Sutcliffe (forthcoming).

8. Supervised by Richard King, now Professor of Religious Studies in the University of Glasgow, to whom I am very grateful for introducing me to the comparative study of mysticism.

9. Original PhD research proposal, February 24, 1994.

10. The three (truncated) syllabi are edited and presented in increasing detail of content to indicate the main lines of theoretical development.

11. Sutcliffe and Bowman (2000) and Pearson, Roberts, and Samuel (1998).

12. As done, for example, by Bruce (2002, chap. 4).

13. See for example Lau (2000) and Carrette and King (2005).

References

Baird, R. D. 1971. *Category Formation and the History of Religions.* The Hague: Mouton.

Bloom, W., ed. 2000. *The Holistic Revolution: the Essential New Age Reader.* London: Allen Lane/The Penguin Press.

Bocking, B. 2006. "Mysticism: No Experience Necessary?," *DISKUS* 7: 1–18. www.basr. org.uk/diskus.html.

Bruce, S. 2002. *God is Dead: Secularization in the West*. Oxford: Blackwell.

Carrette, J., and R. King. 2005. *Selling Spirituality: the Silent Takeover of Religion*. London: Routledge.

Chryssides, G. 2007. "Defining the New Age." In *Handbook of New Age*, edited by D. Kemp and J. Lewis, 5–24. Leiden: Brill.

Fitzgerald, T. 1990. "Hinduism and the World Religion Fallacy," *Religion* 20: 101–118.

——. 1997. "A Critique of 'Religion' as a Cross-Cultural Category," *Method and Theory in the Study of Religion* 9: 91–110.

Frisk, L. 2005. "Is 'New Age' a Construction?" Paper delivered at the 2005 CESNUR International Conference, available online at *www.cesnur.org/2005/pa_frisk.htm*

——. 2007. "Quantitative Studies of New Age: A Summary and Discussion." In *Handbook of New Age*, edited by D. Kemp and J. Lewis, 103–121. Leiden: Brill.

Geaves, R. 2005. "The Dangers of Essentialism: South Asian Communities in Britain and the 'World Religions' Approach to the Study of Religions," *Contemporary South Asia* 14 (1): 75–90.

Hanegraaff, W. 1996. *New Age Religion and Western Culture: Esotericism in the Mirror of Secular Thought*. Leiden: Brill.

Heelas, P. 1982. "Californian Self-Religions and Socializing the Subjective." In *New Religious Movements: a Perspective for Understanding Society*, edited by E. Barker, 69–85. Lampeter: Edwin Mellen Press.

——. 1996. *The New Age Movement: the Celebration of the Self and the Sacralisation of Modernity*. Oxford: Blackwell.

——. 2008. *Spiritualities of Life: New Age Romanticism and Consumptive Capitalism*. Oxford: Blackwell.

Heelas, P., and L. Woodhead. 2005. *The Spiritual Revolution: Why Religion is Giving Way to Spirituality*. Oxford: Blackwell.

Hess, D. 1993. *Science in the New Age: The Paranormal, Its Defenders and Debunkers, and American Culture*. Madison: University of Wisconsin Press.

Katz, S. 1978. "Language, Epistemology and Mysticism." In *Mysticism and Philosophical Analysis*, edited by S. Katz, 22–74. London: Sheldon Press.

King, R. 1999. *Orientalism and Religion: Post-Colonial Theory, India and "The Mystic East."* London: Routledge.

——. 2009. "Mysticism and Spirituality." In *The Routledge Companion to the Study of Religion*, edited by John Hinnells, 306–322. London: Routledge.

Klippenstein, J. 2005. "Imagine No Religion: On Defining 'New Age,'" *Studies in Religion* 34 (3–4): 391–403.

Lau, K. 2000. *New Age Capitalism: Making Money East of Eden*. Philadelphia: University of Pennsylvania Press.

Pearson, J., R. Roberts, and G. Samuel, eds. 1998. *Nature Religion Today: Paganism in the Modern World*. Edinburgh: Edinburgh University Press.

Penner, H. 1983. "The Mystical Illusion." In *Mysticism and Religious Traditions*, edited by S. Katz, 89–116. Oxford: Oxford University Press.

Ross, A. 1992. "New Age Technoculture." In *Cultural Studies*, edited by L. Grossberg, C. Nelson, and P. Treichler, 531–555. London: Routledge.

Schmidt, L. E. 2003. "The Making of Modern 'Mysticism.'" *Journal of the American Academy of Religion* 71 (2): 273–302.

———. 2005. *Restless Souls: the Making of American Spirituality*. New York: HarperSanFrancisco.

Sharf, R. 1998. "Experience." In *Critical Terms for Religious Studies*, edited by M. Taylor, 94–116. Chicago: Chicago University Press.

Slone, D. J. 2004. *Theological Incorrectness: Why Religious People Believe What They Shouldn't*. New York: Oxford University Press.

Smith, J. Z. 1991. "The Introductory Course: Less is Better." In *Teaching the Introductory Course in Religious Studies*, edited by M. Juergensmeyer, 185–192. Atlanta: Scholars Press.

———. 1998. "Religion, Religions, Religious." In *Critical Terms for Religious Studies*, edited by M. Taylor, 269–284. Chicago: Chicago University Press.

Smith, W. C. [1962] 1991. *The Meaning and End of Religion*. Minneapolis: Fortress Press.

Sperber, D. 1985. "Anthropology and Psychology: Towards an Epidemiology of Representations," *Man* 20: 73–89.

Streng, F. 1991. "Mysticism: A Popular and Problematic Thematic Course." In *Tracing Common Themes: Comparative Courses in the Study of Religion*, edited by J. Carman and S. Hopkins, 127–138. Atlanta: Scholars Press.

Sutcliffe, S. 2003a. "Category Formation and the History of 'New Age,'" *Culture and Religion* 4 (1): 5–29.

———. 2003b. *Children of the New Age: A History of Spiritual Practices*. London: Routledge

———. 2004. "Introduction: Qualitative Empirical Methodologies—an Inductive Argument." In *Religion: Empirical Studies*, edited by S. Sutcliffe, xvii–xliii. Aldershot: Ashgate.

———., ed. Forthcoming. *What is Religious Studies? A Reader in Disciplinary Formation*. London: Equinox.

Sutcliffe, S., and M. Bowman, eds. 2000. *Beyond New Age: Exploring Alternative Spirituality*. Edinburgh: Edinburgh University Press.

Underhill, E. [1911] 1957. *Mysticism*. London: Methuen.

Vrijhof, P., and Waardenburg, J., eds. 1979. *Official and Popular Religion: Analysis of a Theme for Religious Studies*. The Hague: Mouton.

Wood, M. 2007. *Possession, Power and the New Age: Ambiguities of Authority in Neoliberal Societies*. Aldershot: Ashgate.

15

Mystical Education

SOCIAL THEORY AND PEDAGOGICAL PROSPECTS

Philip Wexler

Introduction: Mysticism, Sociology, and Education

My academic work occurs at the intersection of sociological theory and educational research and practice. Here, mysticism has almost no place. It is true that sociologists have written about mysticism, notably Weber (1978), whose sociology of religion is significantly influenced by the non-sociologist, Troeltsch ([1911; 1931] 1960). Durkheim (1995), considered the founder of sociology, expressly excludes magic and mysticism as not institutional religion and focuses on ritual and belief, in his sociology of religion. Collins (2008) offers a contemporary note on Weber's typology of religious action, and although he wants to resuscitate Weber's concept of "inner-worldly mysticism" as a topic for sociological research, he readily acknowledges that such research is part of an agenda for the future. But, Collins's oeuvre (2004) is Durkheimian, and as part of a current sociological tendency toward microsociology, he wants to write Durkheim small and not reverse the traditional Durkheimian positivist antipathy toward the mystical (see Strenski 1997).

The founding and central figure in the academic study of Jewish mysticism, Gershom Scholem (1967), who follows Weber, and Troeltsch even more closely, makes a point in his later work to decry the more general silence about society, among scholars of mysticism. Scholem writes (1–3):

> "If we wish to discuss mysticism and society in their mutual relationship there is one astonishing fact which should be pointed out from the outset. In the infinite welter of literature on mysticism, which especially during the last two generations, has taken on quite extraordinary proportions, *the problem of mysticism and society has received but scanty attention*" (emphasis added).

Though it should not be forgotten that the study of education, like that of mysticism, also has a deep and abiding blindness to the social—which has been set and reinforced by an originary and continuing preeminence of individual psychology in Educational Studies—there is an established and recognized *sociology* of education. But if the study of mysticism denies the social, then sociological analyses of education deny the mystical. Sociology of education operates on a horizontal, this-worldly, empiricist plane, whether in distancing from, or reconnecting its empirical researches to their paradigmatic beginnings and theoretical commitments (Hallinan 2002; Wexler 2008; 2009).

The same Durkheimian tradition begins in application to education, alongside religion, though here there is a countertradition, in Marxism and critical theory. Between them, and in various guises, they continue to divide and rule social analyses of education, and so, understandably, there is no opening toward the question of the relationship involving education, society, and mysticism.

Unless we consider Weber, who had something to say socially about mysticism, but little to say explicitly about education, particularly in a small note about "pedagogical ends and means" (in Gerth and Mills 1946, 426), to which I will want to add a bit, later on. Nevertheless, even with Weber's engaging hints (Wexler 2007), sociology of education remains within the ambit of modernist macrosociology and has almost nothing to say about the dynamics of a mystical education. It is this silence and perhaps, denial, which we appear to be on the verge of overcoming.

False Promises: Microsociologies and Spiritualities

We are getting beyond this so-called *classical,* modernist sociology of the turn of the late nineteenth and early twentieth century, which, among other things, has kept our conceptual eye on the structural, systematic nature of society, and, simultaneously, as key to modernity, on the evolutionary broad decline of religion and the rise of a secularized culture. There are many holes in this nonetheless enduring modern sociocultural container, but these two aspects— the structural and the secular—are particularly relevant for beginning to think about education in relation to mysticism.

Against the grain of the macrostructural emphasis of both Durkheimianism and Marxism, there is a renewal, revision, and emergence of interest in microsociology. The displacement of emphasis from large-scale, historical, systemic social structural "collective" phenomena to the study of social interactions and interpersonal relations should be more closely attuned to the subjectivity of mysticism, especially when it is understood as a "contextual," social process (Katz 1983; Wexler 2000). This move, too, redirects attention from the societal functions of education, which, with different valences, has preoccupied both macrostructural traditions of classical European sociology. Interest moves to the more immediate, smaller-scale dynamics of school and identity interactions (Wexler 1992), and to the consideration of pedagogy as a social relation (Bernstein 1996). We can begin to see how mysticism and education might intersect, analytically at least, in the everyday social interactions of microsociological understanding.

In sociological theory, as well as in social practice, a more porous modernist regime has been allowing the social world beneath social structure to appear. Social theory has begun to accept the only partial—if there ever was— success of secularization and the quasilegitimate appearance and reappearance not simply of traditional religious forms, but of less institutionalized religious expressions. These have come to be recognized as mysticism, and even more widely, are now referred to as *new age spirituality* (Forman 1998; Wexler 2000; Heelas and Woodhead 2005; Heelas 2008).

Yet, microsociology is only apparently congenial to a mystical interest. Indeed, even micro-Durkheimianism deflects again from mysticism, and the most vibrant microparadigms, though they trace their lineages to Simmel and James, are remarkably silent about religion at all, to say nothing of mysticism. Likewise, the emergent sociologies of spirituality are more aimed at explaining new age spirituality than at articulating contemporary versions of long-standing mystical traditions. They make sense of the new spirituality with the tools of classical, modernist sociology and eschew the possibility of developing a mystical analysis of society, a mystical sociology of interaction (Wexler 2007). If there is a "desublimation" of a repressed interactional and mystical field, it is quickly channeled and re-repressed, into a secular interactionism, on the one hand, and a modern *culture* of spirituality, on the other. A pedagogy of mystical interaction could not flourish easily under these historical conditions. For that we need a different social foundation and a different understanding of the contemporary expressions of microsociology and mysticism.

MICROSOCIOLOGIES

The three most powerful contemporary forms of microsociology, in their own ways, promise the possibility of seeing the mystical aspects of social interaction. Such a possibility would provide the social foundational context for conceptualizing and practicing mystical education. But, each of the microsociologies disappoints, in a different way.

Collins's "promise" (2004) is that he follows Durkheim by locating the energic core of society in collective rituals that are centered around representations of the sacred. His apparent difference form Durkheim is that he generalizes the energic core of ritual interaction as the nucleus of a society that is best understood as a chain or network of such interactions, rather than as a social structure, or as the Functionalist heirs of Dukheimianism put it, a social system. His theory is at once religion-centered and interactional. But sacred ritual interactions are an energy source, a "battery," and as with Durkheim, society—whether considered as chains in a network or a systemic social structure—moves *away* from the sacred, appropriates its force, or "emotional energy," as Collins calls it, into the secular collective representations that are the moral order of society. The sacred is a moment in the ritual production of the moral integration of societies. Its postmodern value, as it was for Durkheim the modern, is to create energy that can motivate society's members and integrate them within a shared cognitive, sustainable social order of moral solidarity. Whether at the level of ritual interactions or structures of social division of labor, the transcendental moment, which is first and foremost a *collective* ecstasy, operates as the renewable fuel of social order. Durkheim's early and continuing antipathy to the magical and noninstitutional dimensions of religion, such as mysticism, is retained in Collins's move toward microsociology.

A more radical promise to overturn the reified life of social structuralism and what it refers to as the "mechanized positivism" of the sociological mainstream (Blackman 2008, 23), "the stasis and mechanism of cultural inscription models that have emphasized being over becoming and structure over process" can be found in the neovitalist forms of microsociology. Although Blackman aims to restage James, and indeed, promises a "radical relationality," where there is a dissolution of boundaries between self and other, resonant with the heart of mysticism, neovitalist microsociology draws most prominently from the work of the more sociological modern, Simmel. Here, Scott Lash (2005; 2006) wants to reactivate vitalism, recalling Bergson and Leibnitz, but centrally relying on Simmel's sociology of forms as a way to bring sociology back to life. He emphasizes the "intersubjective pulsion" of Simmel's monadological/process/flux desire for "more Life." He wants to replace the contemporary global flows of capitalism with a Simmelian sort of flux that cannot be contained by social forms. If Durkheim is miniaturized by Collins, Lash carries Simmel's quest for the social élan vital into the structure of the information age. Lash works in the critical theory tradition, the "other" mainline of sociology, the Marxist counter to the varieties of Durkheimianism. Appropriating Simmel's life force beyond forms of sociology will enable "reflexivity," which becomes a critique of corporate capital's globalization in the age of globalized communication.

Yet, in this theoretical revitalization effort to create a contemporary microsociology, one modality is absent. Whereas Simmel (1997) wrote a series of essays on sociology of religion, including analyses of the replacement of religion by *religiosity*, in which he discusses the historically transitional importance of mysticism, Lash's otherwise scholarly treatment of Simmel is oddly silent about these analyses of religion and their relevance for a contemporary revival of spiritual power, or mysticism, in society. The secular modernity of sociology is reasserted, despite the potential of the sacred and the vital, in a strange commonality between American mainstream Durkheimianism and European Marxist critical theory.

Symbolic interactionism (Sandstrom, Martin, and Fine 2001, 217–232) is the archetypal microsociology and has always promised a sociology of "becoming," of "symbolically mediated realities," and social interactional processes, as opposed to the dominant traditions of sociological macrostructuralism. In their words—and Fine has been a leading proponent of contemporary symbolic interactionism, in a way paralleling Collins and Lash, for Durkheimianism and Marxist critical theory, respectively—symbolic interactionism (2001, 217) "challenged the mechanistic world view and dualistic assumptions of classical rationalism." Their current version of symbolic interactionism, heir of the so-called Chicago school of sociology, which traces its origins to the pragmatism of Mead, Dewey, and James, aims to reconnect the micro and the macro, but in the opposite direction, by showing how microsociology is not social structure writ small, but culture. Symbolic interactionism is the "anthill" of culture, the "doing of culture." According to Fine and Fields (2008), "emphasizing performance and practice, culture for the micro-sociologist is a matter of circumscribed agency…broader social forces, properties, and processes can be understood as constituted in practice" (p. 131). Microsociology is about the "connection between meaning, behavior, and structure" (p. 144).

The irony of this third microsociology as offering a potential grounding for understanding mysticism in everyday social life, and so better enabling us to think about mystical education, is not merely that it too replicates sociology's neglect of mysticism. Rather, the origins of symbolic interactionism, in the social philosophies of Mead and Dewey, are built upon the suppression of the importance of mysticism in the work of their common ancestor and teacher, William James. A mystical interactionism begins with the cosmic sociality that the tradition of symbolic interaction in sociology has ignored, forgotten, or denied. A number of commentators have asserted James's foundational importance for sociology (Petras 1968; Barbalet 2004), especially noting how this influence worked through Dewey and Mead to the Chicago school of an empirical "symbolic interactionism." But, it is the philosopher Richard Gale (1997) who shows how the intermediary influence, particularly through Dewey, silenced the mystical aspect of James's work, for philosophy, psychology, and, I suggest, also for sociology. Gale argues that over the course of fifty years in his work, Dewey diminished, or even denied the mystical aspect of James, in favor of his own instrumental scientism. According to Gale, Dewey "naturalized" James (1997, 49):

> While not calling into question the philosophical brilliance of these essays, it will be shown that they gave a blatantly distorted, self-serving account of James's philosophy, the basic aims of which were to despookify

and depersonalize it so that it would agree with Dewey
socialization of all things distinctly human.

Microsociologies, however close to offering a natural ground
ticism and education, on the field of social interaction, remain
ism, historicism, and materialism.

SPIRITUALITIES

Mysticism now appears to be less the "secondary" aspect of religion, as Troeltsch ([1911; 1930] 1960, 730–731) put it, for sociologists. A variety of empirical survey researches (Heelas 2008, 233–235) show how the inwardness and
direct experience of mysticism have become more socially prevalent. Wuthnow's (1998) social transition from a religion of dwelling to a spirituality of
seeking, Forman's "grassroots spirituality" (2004), and Heelas's (2008) "inner-life spirituality," all present evidence of the shift from "traditional," "institutional" aspects of religion to *spirituality*. Mysticism is beginning to be
recognized as a significant topic of study by sociologists, but it is under the
rubric of *spirituality*.

The term-shifting reflects, on the one hand, that inner-worldly mysticism
may not be the historically consistent minor aspect of religion, suggested by
Weber and Troeltsch. On the contrary, the evidence suggests that the opposite
of Weber's view is now the case. Yet, in the separation of the terms, along with
the recognition of mysticism, is its forgetting of long traditions, not of institutional religion, but of mysticism itself. Heelas (2008) makes an effort to see
in the contemporary "expressivist humanism" of "inner-life spiritualities" a
cultural continuity, but it is with British and German Romanticism. He fails
to take the further step, shown by M. H. Abrams (1971) and later, Suzanne
Kirschner (1996), who argue for not only the Romantic, but the historic religious origins of contemporary culture, from poetry to psychoanalysis.

The rediscovery of mysticism with a short memory, in practice and in
theory, as *spirituality*, is only part of the reason that it is a false start toward
rethinking contemporary social interaction as a mystical process. The analytical problem is that contemporary social analyses of new age spirituality, including those that are proudly sociological and anthropological, focus more
on ideas and culture than on social interactional processes that are the context
of pedagogy.

Heelas (1996; 2008; Heelas and Woodhead 2005), who is arguably the leading sociologist of the new age spirituality, employs social scientific research
methods, both in direct observational field studies and in interview and questionnaire surveys. In addition, he is particularly interested in identity questions and claims that the key to understanding movements in new age
spirituality is the "subjective turn" and "self-spirituality," which he sees as

ıging to "the assumptions and values of humanistic expressivism" (1996, 15). While he is sensitive to bringing what he refers to as "more general theorizing" (1996, 8) to new age phenomena, the way in which this is to be accomplished is through "the study of culture." Not only at the level of what aspect of general sociological and anthropological theory ought to be "applied" to the new age movement, but in his particular explanation of these movements, Heelas emphasizes their continuity with mainstream cultural tendencies, underlining that they are the "summation of long-standing cultural trajectories" (1996, 154). The reliance on "culture" and the "expressivist-humanist complex" as the explanation of spirituality reappears also in his later work (2008, 194).

This sociological theory of spirituality that Heelas has most consistently articulated is a cultural theory, abstracted from the historical dynamics of production, class, politics and sexuality. It operates with the framework of the present cultural imaginary, the taken-for-granted of materialist individualism—though it very much registers the Romantic protest, and reaches out, from its core of sociocultural continuity, to an alternative way of being in the world.

Sociology of new age spirituality still belongs, conceptually, to the modern age of classical social theory. Moving beyond structuralism and secularism, to focus on microsociologies and spiritualities certainly reveals a crack in the "iron cage" of modernist sociology. Yet, it is a long way from there to understanding social interaction as a mystical process, and from there, to thinking about education as a pedagogy of mystical interactions. This further step, comes, I think, from outside of sociology, from a new mood, that puts social interaction not into historical social structure, and education along with it, as an ancillary "function" or "reproduction" (Wexler 2009), but into a wider frame—that of an emergent cosmic renaissance. In the last century, it was James who heralded this larger field of social life, which is why forgetting this aspect of his work by the founders of American social science and their contemporary heirs is so telling.

Mystical Interaction in the Cosmic Renaissance

COSMIC RENAISSANCE

James wanted to define the social cosmically. In his last works, he moves beyond intrapersonal consciousness to the interpersonal. He uses the term *intimacy* to at once express philosophical congeniality, and also to talk about sociality. It is in this intimate sociality that we see how James has himself, "enlarged the nimbus," as he wrote about widening the margins of consciousness, and lowered the threshold of the individual self to include the field of social interaction. Defining the social cosmically means that not only is our private and expansive mystical consciousness cosmic, but also that our social interactions occur on an extended field, a much wider context. Our intimacy is a sociality of interactions in a field unlike that of symbolic interactionism's "Other," or the more openly bounded interpersonal other of sociological neovitalism, or Durkheim's collective effervescence writ small as socially created emotional energy that motivates the self. Rather, our interactional context is the cosmic field of the universe.

"From a pragmatic point of view," James wrote (2007, 14) in his last book, *A Pluralistic Universe*, "the difference between living against a background of foreignness and one of intimacy means the difference between a general habit of wariness and one of trust. One might call it a social difference, for after all the common *socius* of us all is the great universe whose children we are. If materialistic, we must be suspicious of this socius, cautious tense, on guard. If spiritualistic, we may give way, embrace and keep no ultimate fear."

He foresaw that any shift toward this way of thinking was not imminent, as he wrote in one of his final papers, published two years before his death in 1912, which he modestly called "A Suggestion about Mysticism" (1910, 92): "We shall not understand these alterations of consciousness either in this generation or in the next." Indeed, it was not until well into the twentieth century that the eminent philosopher of science, Stephen Toulmin would aim to systematically describe and understand what he called a "return to cosmology." Toulmin sees the "task of constructing a conception of the overall scheme of things" as part of the development of a "new cosmology" (1982, 17).

What is asserted, but undeveloped in James and Toulmin, is a redefinition of the meaning of social interaction, to include a wider, cosmic screen, reaching inward and outward, beyond the meaning that symbolic interaction in sociology has given to the symbolic. There, what is symbolic, what is "other," are the embodiments and ethical standards of a "community," the "generalized other," which is taken as an advance on individualist psychology. Likewise, in Durkheimian, Functionalist sociology, society is constituted by an integrative process that Wrong described in his famous phrase and critique of the model that links the individual and the collective through the internalization of shared norms and values, as the "oversocialized conception of man in modern sociology" (Wrong 1961).

Instead of either of these tacks—symbolic interactionism and functionalism—as the theoretical subject and, instead of either Durkheimian inner-life culture or Marxist technological deboundarying as the object of understanding, I want to take the cosmological perspectives of James and Toulmin as historical social facts and as bases for social explanation. Social interaction needs to now be understood as "cosmic interaction."

Weber, the classical sociologist of mysticism, offered a social historical explanation for the rise of religions generally, whether, as he put it, of either a "mystagogic or prophetic type" (1978, 503–504). He was particularly interested in the loss of power, in the demilitarization and depoliticization of ruling strata as an inducement to the development of salvation religions, which give meaning to everyday social life. I would add, however, that our present historical conjuncture includes, in addition to the depoliticization of "socially privileged groups," also a continuing intensification of what Durkheim called the "cult of the individual," and importantly, as empirical sociology of spirituality has shown, a reduction of the transcendental system of theistic belief in favor of inner-life spirituality (Heelas 2008).

My hypothesis is that under social conditions that combine a loss of power, a changing conception of divinity that detranscendentalizes divinity and makes power both personal and inward, and where, in addition, individualism has no limits, then premodern mysticism returns, though in detraditionalized and decontextualized forms. There is a "new mysticism," in which the divinization or self-deification of ancient models of the sacred again becomes possible, as a central component of social interaction. As Weber wrote (1963, 160), "self-deification was the prevalent goal of sanctification, from the beginning of the soma cult of intoxication in ancient Vedic times up through the development of sublime methods of intellectualist ecstasy and the elaboration of erotic orgies."

This primordial goal of religious action, as the focus of sacred practice namely self-deification, becomes displaced, both by the need for a more permanent state of sacred grace than is afforded by ephemeral orgiastic ecstasy—which is to say by the elementary, microcosmic form of the routinization of charisma, or rationalization—and by the changing conception of divinity. "But wherever there is a belief in a transcendental god all-powerful in contrast to his creatures, the goal of methodical sanctification can no longer be self-deification" (Weber 1978, 536). This bar is, however, increasingly removed, under present sociohistorical conditions, and divinization or self-deification, again becomes a goal of social practice.

MYSTICAL INTERACTION

Scholars of comparative mysticism are understandably distrustful of any attempts to transfer elements of their accounts of medieval mystical cosmologies to contemporary spiritual, especially, *new age*, practices. White is very clear about distancing his analyses of medieval Hindu Tantra from contemporary new age culture (2003, xiii): "New Age Tantra is to medieval Tantra what finger painting is to fine art," he observes. Flood, in his studies (2006) of medieval Hindu Tantrism, insists on the importance of entextualization in performative practice, and more gently asserts the incompatibility between such medieval Hindu cosmological views and contemporary spiritual quests (2006, 186).

Yet, it is the historical demand for these social technologies that presses for the adaptation and revision of traditional forms of mysticism and raises the level of interest in medieval cosmologies. A "cosmic renaissance" may be developing both at the level of mass social movement practices and quests for new social technologies of meaning and transformation in "the here and now," as Weber put it in his effort to explain the rise of salvation religion, and also among theorists—not of the sociology of spirituality, but of a new generation of textual scholars and theorists of mysticism.

Here, in the new mystical scholarship, one can find not simply sourcebooks for misappropriation by practitioners of new age spirituality, but also models of social interaction, of mystical interaction, that may again become analytically resonant, especially with the declining intuitive validity of modern sociological theory. Neither classical sociological secularizing structuralist modernism, nor recent microsociologies and sociologies of spirituality offer alternative models for making sense of social interaction that are consistent with a "return to cosmology," as a background assumption of contemporary efforts at making social sense of everyday life.

The academic new mysticism arrives at the sociohistorical conjuncture that I have alluded to, drawing here from the classical analyses of Weber and Durkheim: namely, an intersection of powerlessness, a limitless individualism, and an unintended detranscendentalization of theistic belief that drives "godliness" to inner-life spirituality, but also ends the forced, vertical separation of the human from the divine. Under these conditions, empowerment, self-deification, or divinization and a sexualization of interaction revitalizes the social field (not through assemblies of Durkheimian collective effervescence or, in Collins's revision, emotional energy produced by ritual performance) by recurrent, imaginative creative engenderment (Corbin 1969; Wolfson 1994; 2005; Mopsik 2005). The field and parameters of social interaction thus shift, as James predicted they would; or at least our understanding of this field has shifted. Empowerment, divinization, sexualization, and creativity become the core elements of social interaction, fearlessly adding what Steinbock (2007) refers to as "the vertical dimension" to the social field. If education, as all the sociological traditions argue, follows the societal paradigm, in practice and in theory, in modernity and in classical sociology, both macro and micro, then a mystical education can begin to be conceived of now on the basis of a changed model of social interaction.

In rethinking mysticism, Hollenback emphasizes the empowering dimension (1996, 26): "My third objective—and this is one of the most unusual aspects of this study—is to draw attention to the importance of *enthymesis*, or what I have termed 'empowerment' of thought will and imagination." Garb contextualizes the importance of empowerment in contemporary mysticism, reminiscent of Weber, at first, but clearly drawing on the historical cases of Jewish mystical movements (2009, 38, 43). The deep ascents and descents across worlds described by Idel (2005) are the expanded field of cosmic social interaction in an emergent new mysticism. New age "culture" is supplanted by more conscious borrowings from medieval cosmology and the social order is now an imaginal order, a symbolic interaction with "others" who are both supernal figures and potencies. Certainly, this is something different and more variegated than the symbolic community other of sociology or the internalization of shared values that derive from transcendental, ethical commands. A mystical "imaginal geography" (Corbin 1969; Wolfson 1994) now becomes popular channeling, angelology, and incredible corporealization of spiritual entities who appear in television series, films, and in literary fictional cosmologies. In his effort to move away from what he describes as Scholem's "theologization of Kabbalah," Idel, following Corbin, asserts an "imaginary faculty" (2005, 19).

Despite the differences and complexities of the paradigms of Kabbalah and Tantric Hinduism, they both offer models of human social interaction that are interactive with divine models of interaction, as well as with aspects of attributes of the divine. In both instances, it is the conjugal coupling of the feminine and masculine deities or aspects of the deity, which may be influenced by human interaction and influence it in turn, but are, in any case, exemplars of how integration occurs in the universe. This is an integration of forces, emanations, powers, or energies and not the sociological view of normative integration through value homogeneity. On the contrary, it is a dynamic, ongoing iconic reintegration based on the unification of difference. This may seem less far-fetched and distant from ordinary approaches to social interaction when we consider the similarity of these homologies and interactions between the human and divine cosmic actors and forces to the "postconventional" subjective dynamics of a critical psychoanalysis described by Whitebook (1995). Here, there is not only an integration of the sexual and the spiritual, a "reconciliation of sexuality and spirituality" (249–250), but, following Loewald (1988), a "new synthetic organization," a "differentiated as opposed to an undifferentiated unity."

Along with the reverse theurgic empowerment of kabbalistic ascents, as Wolfson has argued (1994; 2005), and as Abrams (2004) emphatically describes in an embodied reading of sexuality and the "Divine Feminine," sexualization as well as empowerment characterizes the cosmic interactional field of contemporary kabbalistic interpretation. We have already noted White's complaint about the fabricating Westernization and distortion of Hindu Tantra, and the same may become increasingly true of sexualized readings of Kabbalah. Yet, within Kabbalah scholarship, Mopsik (2005) makes explicit the connection between divine sexual dynamics and the emplacement of this-worldly relations, which are not only sexual, but more broadly social, within the ambit of divine dynamics. He writes, "the relationship within the couple is taken as the ideal type of social relationship" (20). Further: "The bisexual model of the world of emanation, the divine structure is reflected on the human level" (34). More specifically: "The divine world and the world of man is organized along fundamentally identical principles" (124).

In medieval Hindu Tantra, too, these cosmologies of divine coupling are about the much wider dynamics of cosmic forces and their constitutive power for human being. White (2003, 97) cites a medieval text: "Desire (kama) is the root of the universe. From desire all beings are born....Without Siva and Sakti creation would be nothing but imagination. Without the action of kama there would be no birth or death."

Flood (2006) reasserts the essential contextualization of Tantra within traditional scripture and ritual, arguing for the "entextualization" of the body in Hindu Tantra (here reminiscent of the role of the letters and the body in Hebrew Kabbalah). Here, too (2006, 53), "the Tantras are dialogues between the main deity of the tradition and his/her spouse or sage. Tantras focused on Siva are presented as dialogues between him and his Goddess of Sakti (83). There is an imaginative, cosmic, symbolic interaction (120): 'Inhaling the image, it pervades the adepts body from the thighs to the knees and is dissolved into its mantra, then into the energy of taste which he emits through the exhaled breath'" (2006, 113).

In both empowerment and sexualization, in the academic and popular domains, we can see the fulfillment and specification of James's and Toulmin's expansion of horizons and its implication for a much wider definition of the meaning of sociality. The social can be understood as interaction with imagined and corporealized supernal figures and the inclusion of the physical elements of the universe, along with the spiritual/mystical, in the interactive process.

What is revealed is also a different "mechanism" of social life. Mediating between individual and society is not the internalization of the "oversocialized conception of man," but a cosmic interactionism. Corbin's (1969) rendering of the Sufism of Ibn Arabi highlights both the broader cosmic field, and its interactional character. He anticipates key emotional, imaginative and creative elements of what we are calling *mystical interaction*, asserting without hesitation the inclusion of materialist interaction within this larger field of interactions, making social interaction into cosmic interaction (1969, 215): "Psychology is indistinguishable from cosmology; the theophanic Imagination joins them into a psycho-cosmology. Bearing this in mind, we can now investigate the human organs of visions, of transferences, and of the transmutation of all things into symbols." Corbin's mystical interactionism is a model of love, of "fedele d'amore," between the human lover and the divine Beloved, in which there is an ongoing sympathetic dialogue between them, and which is manifested through the mutual creative imagination: "the totality of our being is not only the part which we at present call your person, for this totality also includes another person, a transcendent counterpart which remains invisibile to us, what Ibn Arabi designates as our 'eternal individuality'—our divine Name" (1969, 173).

Here too, there is ascent and continuous creativity (1969, 207): "The ascent is then the Divine Epiphany in these forms, a perpetually recurrent Effusion, a twofold intradivine movement. That is why *the otherworld already exists in this world*; it exists in every moment, in relation to every being." This is a transmundane symbolic interactionism (243): "The symbolic exegesis that establishes typifications is thus creative in the sense that it transmutes things into symbols, into typical Images, and causes them to exist on another plane of being." The "Creative Feminine" is essential to the theophanic imagination, which is the creative of sympathy of loving relationality, across the materialistic divide, to the Active Imagination of the divine realm.

There is then an alternative to sociological positivism. My unusual suggestion here is that theories of mysticism, in diverse traditions, provide a model of social life that may be better able to grasp not only the life of the rare mystic, but of a much more general pattern of an expanded form of mystical interaction that is coming to typify contemporary society (Wexler 2000; Garb 2009). This multiworld, multidimensional sociality described by mystical traditions is a postsociological social theory. It is at least as elaborate as macro and micro, modern and postmodern sociologies, and if there is an empirical validity to claims of a new age spirituality, it may also be better able to provide a more valid interpretation of the present social reality.

It is on this social foundation that we can now ask about the prospects of a mystical education.

Mystical Education as a Pedagogical Type

PEDAGOGICAL TYPES

In these conditions, education may be seen as an effort to replicate the social ideal, which is now linked for us, however, to an imagined, or symbolic interactional divine process: divinization as potentially a socially constitutive process, replacing shared values as a social mechanism of mobilization and integration. Such a replication would not be a "reproduction," in the language of Marxist sociology of education (Wexler 2009), but an "engenderment," in the language of the new mystical scholarship, both gendered and recurrently creative. In this view, education becomes a process of sociocultural initiation. Indeed, here too, with pedagogy, as with a sociology of mysticism, I see Weber as the central forbearer, though again, one whom we wish to revise.

Weber's pedagogical typology is directly implied by his model of authority, which is the empirical specification of his more general theory of social action. Different types of social authority express different sorts of social action, and, historically, there are increasingly two main types, which, in pedagogy, as in social life, are in opposition to each other. The pedagogical opposition is the social opposition, between a society of the authority of the rationalized experts, the "specialists," whom Weber—despite all claims of neutrality—obviously detests; and their fierce, but sporadic opponents, the "charismatic" leaders, who burst forth onto the historical stage, to disrupt the earlier historical social orders of tradition, and the increasingly rationalized bureaucratic order, which evermore effectively supplants it, with the "iron cage" of modernity. Between rationalization and charisma there is tradition, and while not strictly parallel, Weber suggests, perhaps as an analytical catch-all, a "pedagogy of cultivation." There are then rational, charismatic, and cultivation pedagogies, as he writes (1946, 426–427): "finally, attempts to *educate* a cultivated type of man, whose nature depends on the decisive stratum's respective ideal of culture."

Here are, in his words, "the great types of education" (1946, 426): "Historically, the two polar opposites in the field of educational ends are: to awaken charisma, that is heroic qualities or magical gifts; and, to impart specialized training. The first type corresponds to the charismatic structure of domination; the latter type corresponds to the *rational* and bureaucratic (modern) structure of domination." These types are opposites, and Weber (1978, 1144) sees them as the basis for conflicts on the educational field. Weber is a critic of bureaucratic rationalism, no less than Marx is a critic of commodity capitalism, while recognizing its historical ascendance. Still, it is charisma which interests him, from the vantage point of social change, and as a type of pedagogy (1978, 426):

> The charismatic procedure of ancient magical asceticism and the hero trials, which sorcerers and warrior heroes have applied to boys, tried to aid the novice to acquire a 'new soul,' in the animist sense, and hence, to be reborn. Expressed in our language, this means that they merely wished to *awaken* and to test a capacity which was considered a purely personal gift of grace. For one can neither teach nor train for charisma. Either it exists *in nuce*, or it is infiltrated through a miracle of magical rebirth—otherwise it cannot be attained.

We can agree to follow Weber's lead in analyzing at least historically formative aspects of social action in terms of "methodologies of sanctification," without agreeing with his personalized view of charisma, or with the ascetic and militaristic coloration of the initiatory practices of charismatic education. Pedagogy can, however, be seen as initiatory and awakening, not for personal charisma, but for the capacity for interactive, imaginative divinization and as a method of social reempowerment. In this way, a mystical pedagogy becomes part of a political process, which is a radical one. Like charismatic education, a pedagogy that enacts the emergent social model of mystical interaction, represents taking a stand against the existing bureaucratic-rational order, and, against the socioeducational order that institutionalizes a hyper-rational, digitalized pedagogy of the specialists and experts—who now constitute the "privileged social groups" and the "decisive social stratum." These are the avatars of modernity and postmodernity, who Weber described as "without spirit" and "without heart" (Weber 1958). As it is historically the case, certainly in Weber's brief examples, pedagogies enact the social life conduct and interests, the "habitus," as he called it, of these groups, which defines the hegemonic education.

Yet, again, there are "polar opposites," and exemplary pedagogical alternatives, both historically and cross-culturally, which direct us toward the possibilities of still another pedagogical type, one based in the social varieties of mystical interaction.

PEDAGOGICAL PROSPECTS

One can find precursors of a mystical education and styles of pedagogy that better represent social forms of mystical interaction than the modern forms that we have come to take for granted as "normal" in society and education. Instrumental rationalism, commercialism and commodification, repressive traditionalism, and one-dimensional alienation have long been the "mainstream" targets of social and educational opposition. What is new, particularly for sociologists working in education, is that the educational opposition can be drawn not only from the traditions of Marxism, or even from a romanticism less known to social analysts, but from religious traditions, and especially from the minor chords of mysticism and spirituality. Critical sociologists of education are entirely unaccustomed to discovering the possibilities of an historical alternative in the precincts of comparative mysticism (Wexler 2008).

This is not surprising. Sociologists, as we have seen, have also ignored the mystical interests of their own forbearers. James, like Weber, had something to say about education as well as mysticism. In the "Talks to Teachers," which he first delivered in his hometown of Cambridge, Massachusetts, he off-handedly alludes to his favorable inclination toward Hinduism, and to what it implies for a different way of social life (James 1899, 74).

James goes on to show how his ideas about habit, thinking, action and attention, will, and memory can involve the teaching-learning process, pedagogy. As we know, he was interested in "streams of consciousness" and the associative aspect of thought as central for memory and learning. The practice of attention and free association, which he sees as salutary, is hindered not only by the worried and hurried character of American culture and social action, but by the ego-centered psychology that drives it (1899, 220).

Buber (1965) is the most well-known interpreter of Jewish mysticism, in its historically explicitly social aspect, as Hasidism, to write about education. Like James, he gave talks to teachers, though in Tel Aviv, rather than Cambridge. Buber takes the dialogical aspect that we can find even in the most transcendental of mysticisms, such as Corbin's "sympathetic" and "intimate dialogue," and applies it as a basic principle of teaching. Buber observed, "the relation of education is one of pure dialogue...that subterranean dialogic, that steady potential presence of the one to the other is established and endures, then there is reality *between* them, there is mutuality" (1965, 98). But, Buber's "longing for personal unity" is less directed in education toward the self-deifying and divinizing imaginative refiguration that we have been emphasizing in trying to outline a mystical interaction and the pedagogy that follows from it. Rather, he aims for an education for community. "Genuine education of character," he writes, "is genuine education for community." Buber does write of the transcendental dimension, of God and mystery, but Buber, who was a student of the early microsociologist Simmel, returns to a sociology of dialogue and community.

Within Hasidism, the more kabbalistically oriented attempt to bring mysticism to bear on education is the treatise of the Sixth Lubavitch Rebbe, Yossef Yitchak Schneersohn, who wrote *The Principles of Education and Guidance* at about the same time that James gave his talks to teachers, though it was not published as a small book until almost half a century later. Schneersohn's work ([1990] 2004) is elaborated and appears in an English language discourse on education by a contemporary (and controversial) teacher of Hasidism, Yitzchak Ginsburgh (2003), in his book *The Art of Education: Internalizing Ever-New Horizons.*

Similar to Weber's discussion of charismatic education in terms of initiation, Ginsburgh describes kabbalistic education as a process of initiation (2003, 26): "Conceptually, an act of initiation of inauguration draws down spiritual energy. It involves a ritual that awakens the recipients to a higher level of consciousness."

The Seventh, and perhaps the last, Lubavitch Rebbe was an educational activist and organizer. (For a full analysis of the mystical theory of "the Rebbe," see Elliot Wolfson's recently published, *Open Secret: Postmessianic Messianism and the Mystical Revision of Menahem Mendel Schneerson* [2009].) One effort to describe the practical, empirical, educational results of Rabbi Schneerson's educational work is Lowenthal's analysis of educational model of the Lubavitch yeshiva (in Etkes 2006, 369–395). Lowenthal's central point is that this sort of school is "a bridge." Here I translate his concluding observation from the Hebrew (2006, 394): "it bridges different worlds, the revealed and the hidden, the academic and the practical, and the lives of the religious and the secular."

Conclusion: From Charismatic to Mystical Education

Weber was clear that despite the ephemeral character of charisma and charismatic education, it was the pedagogical type that could best "stand in the face of the existing orders." He wrote, "however, genuine charismatic education is the radical opposite of specialized professional training as it is espoused by bureaucracy" (1978, 1144). Morevover, "therefore, the real purpose of charismatic education is *regeneration*, hence the development of the charismatic quality, and the testing, confirmation and selection of the qualified person" (emphasis added; 1978, 1143). He then goes on to describe, in a long parenthesis what he refers to as the "elements of charismatic education." These are in fact the elements of rites of initiation. In the various trials of initiation that he mentions, "the physical and psychic exercises of the most diverse forms" have as their ultimate purpose, "to awaken the capacity of ecstasy and regeneration."

In the contemporary social world of incessant rationalization and commodification, despite historical precursors and isolated current educational examples, "imparting training," the hallmark of the "specialist type of man" remains the prevailing type of pedagogy. Whether there will be a more popular return to premodern forms, not of charisma, but of mystical interaction, cannot be easily known. One is reminded of Gershom Scholem's closing to his path-breaking analysis of Jewish mysticism (1946, 350): "Under what aspects this invisible stream of Jewish mysticism will again come to the surface we cannot tell."

We can tell, however, that models of mystical interaction are currently being described across the range of comparative mystical scholarship. We can tell also, that however distorted or commericialized (Carrette and King 2005), new age spiritual movements represent incipient efforts toward the reconstitution not only of culture, but also, less prominently (see, for example, Garb 2009) of different forms of social relations, which draw on models of classical mysticism.

The educational work and the educational question that is before us now is twofold. Can mystical interaction become mystical education? Can this be accomplished within the commodity shell of the training-oriented, bureaucratic social organization of contemporary education?

References

Abrams, Daniel. 2004. *The Female Body of God in Kabbalistic Literature*. Jerusalem: The Hebrew University Magnes Press (in Hebrew).

Abrams, Meyer H. 1971. *Natural Supernaturalism*. New York: Norton.

Barbalet, Jack. 2004. "William James: Pragmatism, Social Psychology and Emotions," *European Journal of Social Theory* 7 (3): 337–355.

Bernstein, Basil. 1996. *Pedagogy, Symbolic Control and Identity*. London: Taylor and Francis Ltd.

Blackman, Lisa. 2008. "Affect, Relationality and the 'Problem of Personality,'" *Theory, Culture & Society* 25 (1): 23–47.

Buber, Martin. 1965. *Between Man and Man*. New York: Collier Books.

Carrette, Jeremy, and Richard King. 2005. *Selling Spirituality: The Silent Takeover of Religion*. Oxfordshire: Routledge.

Collins, Randall. 2004. *Interaction Ritual Chains*. Princeton, NJ: Princeton University Press.

———. 2008. "The Four M's of Religion: Magic, Membership, Morality and Mysticism," *Review of Religious Research* 50 (1): 5–15.

Corbin, Henry. 1969. *Creative Imagination in the Sufism of Ibn Arabi*. London: Routledge and K. Paul.

Durkheim, Emile. 1995. *The Elementary Forms of Religious Life*. New York: The Free Press.

Etkes, Immanuel, ed. 2006. *Yeshivot and Battei Midrash*. Jerusalem: Zalman Shazar Center (in Hebrew).

Fine, Gary A., and Corey D. Fields. 2008. "Culture and Microsociology: The Anthill and the Veldt," *Annals of the American Academy of Political and Social Science* 619: 130–148.

Flood, Gavin. 2006. *The Tantric Body: The Secret Tradition of Hindu Religion*. London: I. B. Tauris.

Forman, Robert K., ed. 1998. *The Innate Capacity: Mysticism, Psychology, and Philosophy*. New York: Oxford University Press.

———. 2004. *Grassroots Spirituality: What It Is, Why It Is Here, Where It Is Going*. Charlottesville, VA: Imprint Academic.

Gale, Richard. 1997. "John Dewey's Naturalization of William James." In *The Cambridge Companion to William James,* edited by Ruth Anna Putnam, 49–68. Cambridge: Cambridge University Press.

Garb, Jonathan. 2009. *The Chosen Will Become Herds: Studies in Twentieth Century Kabbalah*. New Haven, CT: Yale University Press.

Gerth, Hans H., and C. Wright Mills. 1946. *From Max Weber: Essays in Sociology*. New York: Oxford University Press.

Ginsburgh, Yitzchak. 2003. *The Art of Education: Internalizing Ever-New Horizons*. Kfar Chabad, Israel: Gal Einai.

Hallinan, Maureen T., ed. 2002. *Handbook of the Sociology of Education*. New York: Springer.

Heelas, Paul, and Linda Woodhead. 2005. *The Spiritual Revolution: Why Religion is Giving Way to Sprituality*. Oxford: Blackwell.

Heelas, Paul. 1996. *The New Age Movement*. Oxford: Blackwell.

———. 2008. *Spiritualities of Life: New Age Romanticism and Consumptive Capitalism*. Oxford: Blackwell Publishing.

Hollenback, Jess Byron. 1996. *Mysticism: Experience, Response and Empowerment*. University Park, PA: Pennsylvania State University Press.

Idel, Moshe. 2005. *Ascension on High in Jewish Mysticism: Pillars, Lines, Ladders*. Budapest: Central European University Press.

James, William. (1899) 1913. *Talks to Teachers: On Psychology: And to Students on Some of Life's Ideals*. London: Longmans, Green and Co.

———. 1910. "A Suggestion about Mysticism," *Journal of Philosophy, Psychology and Scientific Methods* 17 (Feb): 85–92.

———. 2007. *A Pluralistic Universe*. London: Tutis Digital Publishing Pvt. Ltd.

Katz, Steven, ed. 1983. *Mysticism and Religious Traditions*. New York: Oxford University Press.

Kirschner, Suzanne. 1996. *The Religious and Romantic Origins of Psychoanalysis: Individuation and Integration in Post-Freudian Theory*. Cambridge: Cambridge University Press.

Lash, Scott. 2005. "Lebenssoziologie: Georg Simmel in the Information Age," *Theory, Culture & Society* 22 (3): 1–23.

———. 2006. "Life (Vitalism)," *Theory, Culture & Society* 23 (2–3): 323–349.

Loewald, Hans W. 1988. *Sublimation: Inquiries into Theoretical Psycholanalysis*. New Haven, CT: Yale University Press.

Mopsik, Charles. 2005. *Sex of the Soul: The Vicissitudes of Sexual Difference in Kabbalah*. Los Angeles: Cherub Press.

Petras, John W. 1968. "Psychological Antecedents of Sociological Theory in America: William James and James Mark Baldwin," *Journal of the History of the Behavioral Sciences* 4 (Apr): 132–143.

Sandstrom, Kent, Dan Martin, and Gary Alan Fine. 2001. "Symbolic Interactionism at the End of the Century." In Handbook of Social Theory, edited by George Ritzer and Barry Smart, 217–231. London: Sage.

Schneersohn, Rabbi Yosef Yitzchak of Lubavitch. (1990) 2004. *The Principles of Education and Guidance*. New York: Kehot Publication Society.

Scholem, Gershom G. 1946. *Major Trends in Jewish Mysticism*. New York: Schocken Books.

———. 1967. "Mysticism and Society," *Diogenes* 58 (Summer): 1–24.

Simmel, George. 1997. *Essays on Religion*, edited by Horst Jurgen Helle in collaboration with Ludwig Nieder. New Haven, CT: Yale University Press.

Steinbock, Anthony J. 2007. *Phenomenology and Mysticism: The Veritcality of Religious Experience*. Bloomington: Indiana University Press.

Strenski, Ivan. 1997. *Durkheim and the Jews of France*. Chicago: University of Chicago Press.

Toulmin, Stephen. 1982. *The Return to Cosmology: Postmodern Science and the Theology of Nature*. Berkeley: University of California Press.

Troeltsch, Ernst. ([1911] 1931) 1960. *The Social Teachings of the Christian Churches*, translated by Olive Wyon. 2 vols. New York: Harper Torchbooks, Harper and Brothers.

Weber, Max. 1946. *From Max Weber: Essays in Sociology*, edited by Hans H. Gerth and C. Wright Mills, pp. 426–34. New York: Oxford University Press.

Weber, Max. 1958. *The Protestant Ethic and the Spirit of Capitalism*. New York: Charles Scribner's Sons.

———. 1963. *The Sociology of Religion*. Boston: Beacon Press.

———. 1978. *Economy and Society*. Vol.1. Berkeley: University of California Press.

Wexler, Philip. 1992. *Becoming Somebody: Toward a Social Psychology of School*. London: Falmer Press.

———. 2000. *Mystical Society: An Emerging Social Vision*. Boulder, CO: Westview.

———. 2007. *Mystical Interactions: Sociology, Jewish Mysticism and Education.* Los Angeles: Cherub Press.

———. 2008. *Symbolic Movement: Critique and Spirituality in Sociology of Education.* Rotterdam: Sense Publishing.

———. 2009. *Social Theory in Education.* New York: Peter Lang.

White, David Gordon. 2003. *Kiss of the Yogini: "Tantric Sex" In its South Asian Contexts.* Chicago: University of Chicago Press.

Whitebook, Joel. 1995. *Perversion and Utopia: A Study in Psychoanalysis and Critical Theory.* Cambridge, MA: The MIT Press.

Wolfson, Elliot R. 1994. *Through a Speculum That Shines: Vision and Imagination in Medieval Jewish Mysticism.* Princeton, NJ: Princeton University Press.

———. 2005. *Language, Eros, Being: Kabbalistic Hermeneutics and Poetic Imagination.* New York: Fordham University Press.

———. 2009. *Open Secret: Postmessianic Messianism and the Mystical Revision of Menahem Mendel Schneerson.* New York: Columbia University Press.

Wrong, Dennis. 1961. "The Oversocialized Conception of Man in Modern Sociology," *American Sociological Review* 26 (2): 183–193.

Wuthnow, Rober. 1998. *After Heaven: Spirituality in America since the 1950s.* Berkeley: University of California.

16

Secrets in the Seats

THE EROTIC, THE PARANORMAL, AND THE FREE SPIRIT

Jeffrey J. Kripal

[Let us take up] the question of Mysticism.

—RALPH WALDO EMERSON DURING A MEETING
OF THE TRANSCENDENTAL CLUB IN MEDFORD,
MASSACHUSETTS, MAY 20, 1838

...only in the perfect uncontamination and solitariness of
individuality may the spirituality of religion come forth at all.

—WALT WHITMAN, *DEMOCRATIC VISTAS*, *1871*

Introduction: The Pedagogy of Integrity and Honesty

The vast majority of my teaching, like almost any teacher's pedagogy in
the humanities, I gather, is absorbed with remedial matters and with the
close reading of both theoretical and historical primary source material. It
is common work. And it is most of my work. In more than a few rare moments in the classroom, however, something suddenly "clicks," a kind of
pedagogical magic happens, and a deeply human connection is made. I do
not want to pretend that these moments are particularly numerous or especially common, and I certainly do not want to leave the impression that
my teaching experience is a long and eventful series of these. It is not. But
they nevertheless do happen, and I do see these moments as reflective of
what I am trying to accomplish in my teaching, particularly around the
category of *mysticism,* or, as I much prefer to call it, *the mystical.*

Over the years—seventeen of them now—I have come to see that there are
three focal points around which this occasional pedagogical magic tends to
happen, that there are three sorts of characters in the classroom, sitting there
in those seats, who spark the most excitement and generate the deepest

teaching philosophy (handwritten)

discussions. I will call these characters the Erotic, the Paranormal, and the Free Spirit.

I have also noticed that in each of these cases, the excitement arises not simply from the topic itself (for each can be handled in atrocious and deadening ways), but from a certain pedagogical process that usually develops in two relatively seamless stages: (1) the creation of a kind of temporal and spatial "safe zone," an academic ritual space, if you will, within which students come to see that almost any question can be comfortably asked and treated with respect and care; and (2) a subsequent narrowing or even collapse of that psychosocial space between what an individual most deeply feels, thinks, intuits, or even knows "inside" and what he or she is willing to say in public on the "outside." We might give this latter narrowing or collapse a double moral name. Let us name it simply *integrity* and *honesty*. Let us also admit that in many cases, such an integrity or honesty is more or less transgressive or subversive. In extreme cases, it can even feel obscene or blasphemous (hence the importance of the safe space). All of these labels, it must be immediately noted, are relative ones. They make sense only in relationship to a social field that is attempting to hide or repress something, and probably a whole lot of things. What is patently plausible and possible in one social field is entirely outrageous and impossible in another. One woman gets very angry. Another giggles. One man's blasphemy is another man's joke.

This collapsible space between the inside and outside is policed and disciplined in multiple ways in the classroom, including by some of the academy's own reigning intellectual paradigms, or what I like to call, following William Blake, our contemporary mind forg'd manacles. Perhaps the most hardened and restrictive of all such manacles is the claim that there *is* no accessible inside; that assumed realities like the subject, mind, psyche, and soul are little more than psychological, social, or neurological froth; that all we really have to work with in our scholarship and teaching are completely public discourses, texts, social behaviors, physical artifacts, demographic statistics, and pretty computer screen images of brain states.

There is some measure of truth and a whole lot of usefulness in such a claim, and any methodology that dismisses such public objects of study and the overwhelming historical, cultural, and neurological shaping of human consciousness is woefully inadequate to the present state of the field. But taken as an absolute truth-claim free of its own profound, and profoundly questionable, ontological assumptions (read: materialism), such a claim borders on pure nonsense. It is nonsense, moreover, that conflicts, radically, with each and every person's own immediate sense as a free conscious agent or intimate expression of mind. Most of all, it conflicts, again radically, with the data of the history of mystical literature, which is filled with and defined by ontological realizations and "rogue" phenomena that simply cannot be fitted into any such materialist paradigm (Kelly et al. 2007).

What we really have at the end of the day are not discourses, texts, or behaviors, but our experiences of discourses, texts, and observable behaviors that are themselves expressions of other people's experiences. This oft-noted and much-maligned hermeneutical loop between our own experiences and other people's experiences is unavoidable in the study of mysticism, for that is what the study of mystical literature, or any other truly humanistic discipline, is largely about: consciousness encountering and analyzing consciousness indirectly through the prisms of cultural memory, language, text, art, and history. Which is all to say that we have much, much more to work with in the classroom than discourses, texts, and behaviors. We have forms of mind, states of consciousness, and extraordinary memories sitting in those seats. In short, we have our students' own mystical experiences (Kripal 2008).

And our own. There is that loop again.

As I have argued in detail elsewhere, these deeply personal, often socially anomalous, and cognitively dissonant experiences are precisely what constituted the category of *mysticism* as a scholarly subject (in both senses of that word) in the nineteenth and early twentieth centuries; what drove some of the most creative scholarship throughout the twentieth century; and what still, in the twenty-first century, create whatever draw a course or book on the subject still possesses (Kripal 2001; 2006a). We can ignore this experiential genealogy and proceed as if we only had discourses, texts, behaviors, and so on, but only, I would suggest, at very significant pedagogical and professional cost. Such a strategy, for example, more or less guarantees the utter irrelevance of the subject for any larger interested student body or reading public. If we want to doom our work into almost total solipsistic isolation and oblivion, this is a very good way to go. For my own part, I am tired of writing for fifty, maybe a hundred people in the world, half of whom hate me. I am also of the opinion that the robust study of religion is more relevant, more possible, and more potentially transformative today than it has been at any time in human history (yes, I believe that). The day is ours, if only we could stop thinking and arguing ourselves into smaller and smaller, more and more technical, and increasingly deadening and dehumanizing corners. We are practically disappearing, much like the sacred and the psyche that are supposed to have already disappeared (Kripal 2010). They did not disappear, of course. We just pretend that they have.

Intellectual correctness and current academic fashions are not the only sources of the incredible shrinkings at hand. There are other, much more powerful and much more traditional forms of disciplining taking place in our classrooms and worlds that prevent individuals from narrowing the space between the inside and the outside. Some are religious. Religions lie. Some are cultural. Cultures hide. Some are political. Political systems repress. Some are familial. Families deny. All, however, have the same effect—they create a gap or space between what an individual knows and what he or she can—in both senses of "is capable of" and "is allowed to"—speak in a public space.

No, they do more than this. It is hardly the case, after all, that there is always some sort of transparent or pure experience "inside" that is then "let out" into the classroom or public space. I am not so naïve or dualistic. Usually, it is not like that at all. Rather, it is more the case that all of these disciplinings and policings hide truths from the subject itself. In effect, they create what Freud called an unconscious. In the process, they render the most difficult, and most important, truths of the mind confused, inarticulate, distorted, and, most of all, anxious and fearful. I want to propose here that the task of at least some forms of scholarship and teaching on mysticism (by no means all) is to enable such relatively unconscious or repressed truths to come to some measure of expression and interpretation, however tentative. In other words, I want to explore the idea that it is the task of some forms of pedagogy to really and truly hear these voices and then speak them as transparently as possible in the world, or at least in that part of the world we call a classroom, until what is said on the outside more or less matches what is intuited or known on the inside.

The Erotic: Public Secrets, Private Confirmations

There are few features of mystical literature that are more well known to scholars and more vociferously denied by religious authorities than the incredible, really mind-blowing erotic dimensions of these texts and traditions. There are also few features of the history of mysticism that create more intolerable gaps—that is, more lies—between what people suspect on the inside and what they are willing to say on the outside. The reason for those gaps and lies is fairly simple: from the "right" perspective of "straight" religion and society, the human spirit is fundamentally and irrepressibly queer.

Thus the further we move into the history of mystical literature, the more fluid the erotic complexities become, as we encounter: posited heterosexual encounters within a bisexual Godhead in Teilhard de Chardin's (1975) remarkable essay, "The Evolution of Chastity"; male souls encouraged to abandon "lustful Venus" in order, secretly, to woo, kiss, marry, and experience spiritual coitus with the Virgin Sophia as the feminine aspect of the Logos or as the passive efflux of the Trinity within Boehmean Sophianic mysticism (Versluis 1999); cross-dressing, transgendered berdache figures and the homosexual proclivities of shamans in various Amerindian, African, and primal traditions (Baum 1993); male mystics uniting heterosexually with their wives in order to homoerotically arouse the divine male into activity within medieval Kabbalah (Wolfson 1994); subliminal pederastic encounters designed to enflame the soul's polymorphous sprouting of philosophical feathers and wings through the excitement of a homoerotic gaze in Plato's *Phaedrus*, or to give witness to the beauty, love, and existence of God within medieval Persian Sufism (Wafer 1997); third-gender returns back to a primordial infancy that is neither male nor female in the Gospel of Thomas; symbolic and literal sex-changes in ancient Christian Gnosticism and Chinese Mahayana (Paul 1979); legends explicitly (and positively) linking the cultural origins of esoteric Buddhism and the introduction of homosexual love in Japan (Schalow 1992 and Faure 1998); men imaginatively given spiritual breasts through textual interpretation and elaborate speculations on "French kissing" Christ in the writings of the medieval Catholic mystic Bernard of Clairvaux (Kripal 2003a); women given penises through magical means or—the more usual method—reincarnation within Chinese Mahayana; and eunuchs (who, by the way, were often assumed to engage in passive homosexual activity in the ancient Mediterranean world) "castrated" for the sake of the kingdom of heaven in the Gospel of Matthew. This is the usual stuff of mystical literature, the "open secret" for those with the proverbial ears to hear. And it goes on and on and on. And on.

It is not simply a matter of historical interest, though. The Erotic, I want to suggest, is also the first and most fundamental secret in the seats and one of the keys to teaching mysticism. Why? Because the subject of the erotic provides one of the surest and most natural "hooks" for students. Not everyone in the classroom, after all, has had a mystical experience, and no one has been a medieval bridal mystic, an eighth-century Theravāda Buddhist monk, or a nineteenth-century medium (that they can remember). But every single body sitting in our classrooms is, without a shadow of a doubt, a sexual body. And every single person, without a shadow of a doubt, is gendered. Sometimes, moreover, these sexualities and genders manifest in extremely complex and conflicted ways that generate tremendous levels of anxiety, reflexivity, and emergent criticism vis-à-vis the social and religious systems that have set up the conditions for this very sexual suffering. These individuals, it turns out, make some of the very best students. Need I point out the obvious? Blithe happiness and contentment do not produce deep thought or critical theory. Conflict, anxiety, and marginality do.

Alas, sometimes this anxiety and this sexual suffering can become quite extreme. The *eros* of the mystical as it has been developed and experienced within any number of religious systems seems to be, if we are to believe its many diverse witnesses, ontologically primordial, that is, rooted deeply and blissfully in (human) being, but its effective access usually requires strategies of sexual repression, moral condemnation, and social suffering that are, by many of our modern standards, ethically problematic. Put differently and perhaps too baldly, erotic mysticism as traditionally conceived is both religiously profound and morally unacceptable. Different versions of this thesis have been demonstrated, usually with a feminist, queer, or psychoanalytic methodology, with any number of traditional materials. Here I am thinking of texts such as Mark Jordan's (2000) subtle analysis of the ways Roman Catholic ecclesiology, sanctity, liturgical aesthetics, and institutional authority are generated through the tortured dialectic of a sublimated celebration of homoeroticism and a public moral condemnation of homosexuality; of Elliot Wolfson's (1994) nu anced work on the phallocentric and homoerotic dimensions of medieval Jewish Kabbalah that erase the very being of woman; of June Campbell's (1996) feminist analysis of the different institutional and ritual structures of Tibetan Buddhism and its Tantric sexual practices that work to remove, silence, even threaten female agency; and Grace Jantzen's (1995) Foucauldian deconstructions of medieval Christian mysticism.

Perhaps nowhere, however, are these paradoxical patterns more dramatically displayed than in those cases in which early psychosexual trauma appears to have resulted in a splitting of the psyche via processes akin to what we today call dissociation, but which in premodern or non-Western cultures was/is usually understood and experienced as possession. In some of these cases, when the traumatic context is long past and the individual has reached some level of healing, these same dissociative skills can be used for creative, cultural, even apparently transcendent functions. One is no longer "possessed" or "haunted" by one's past or multiple others. One is now "divinized," "empowered," or "enlightened," and one can enter ecstatic states of extreme freedom, charismatic power, religious beauty, and cultural creativity, paradoxically, through the very same psychological mechanisms that were once anxiously called on for defense and survival. I have speculated about these traumatic processes in the historical cases of the Hindu saint Ramakrishna, in Mother Anne of the Shakers, and in Jesus of the gospels (Kripal 1995; 2006a; 2006b; see also Davies 1995), but I suspect that it is in fact extremely widespread in the history of religions in general.

From my very first pages on this idea, I warned readers from the assumption that the early trauma somehow "causes" the later mystical states. I suggested rather that the original trauma and splitting "opens up" something in the psyche that allows already existent mystical states to manifest in consciousness. The mystical states, in other words, need not be reduced to the original traumatic contexts. Alternately, we might imagine the brain as a kind of stable filter, transmitter, or reducer of consciousness that is temporarily suppressed, traumatized, or damaged, so that expansive forms of Mind come rushing in, rather along the lines that Aldous Huxley (1954) argued with respect to mescaline and mystical states in *The Doors of Perception*. We might also imagine here the relationship between, say, a car accident or brain surgery and an out-of-body experience. The historical fact that many people experience themselves leaving their bodies immediately after horrific car wrecks or during radical surgeries does not necessarily entail that the accidents or surgeries caused the out-of-body experiences. It can just as well, and in my opinion probably does, imply that the physical trauma temporarily shuts down the brain-body and so "frees" consciousness or mind for other states and experiences. I recognize that such metaphors remain metaphors and are layered with all sorts of profound philosophical questions, but my basic point, I hope, is clear enough: causality and correlation are not the same thing, to observe the latter is by no means to prove the former, and there *are* ways to relate mystical states to traumatic contexts without naively conflating the two.

In any case, my purpose here is not to defend or further explain this particular thesis. It is to describe and comment on its pedagogical effects. The
simple truth is that no idea of mine has produced more dramatic and more
positive pedagogical responses than this one. For seventeen years now, I have
encountered students and correspondents who have confirmed—in incredibly
detailed and emotionally poignant ways—the truth of this thesis not through
any rational argument or learned essay on the history of mystical literature or
psychiatry, but through the painful, beautiful honesty and integrity of their
own life stories. Such individuals have approached me, always in private, with
powerful personal stories of early sexual abuse and later mystical experience.
One after another, they have told me their stories. And one after another, they
have told me that my writing and teaching were the first contexts that they had
encountered that (1) allowed them to articulate intellectually a connection between the trauma and the mystical states that took seriously *both* the horror of
the former *and* the beauty and power of the latter; and (2) provided them with
a safe ritual space—that is, the course or correspondence—in which they could
explore, articulate, and experiment with these impossible ideas. No readers or
students of my work have affected me more. No pedagogical experiences have
been more meaningful to me.

The irony here—which confirms for me how much mystical literature has
long been produced, transmitted, and repressed—is that I cannot in good con-
science tell a single completely accurate and truly detailed story here. I have
written, in generalities, about a few of these cases elsewhere, actually, in an earlier Oxford volume on *Teaching Freud in Religious Studies* (Kripal 2003b). And
I continue to hear dramatic confirmations from academic and psychiatric colleagues, such as the psychoanalyst who responded to a paper of mine on this
idea with the story of one of his female patients, who reported actually leaving
her body and floating to the ceiling while a family member raped her on the bed
below (the analogies with the out-of-body experience during the car wreck
could not be any more clear). But, for the most part, there is little I can say about
these private confirmations of my public ideas, as I must preserve these people's
privacy and trust in me. The result is less than intellectually satisfying: the stronger the evidence, the more likely is it that it cannot be spoken. So the secret, in
the end, is preserved. The mouth remains shut. As it perhaps always has been.

A final note here on the Erotic. Actually, it is really more of an elephant in the
living room. It is simply this: teaching anything related to human sexuality and
gender is a very delicate and intimate art, and such a practice must be entered
only after establishing firm professional boundaries and a very clear statement
of purpose and intent. I do many things here to prevent misunderstanding, to
set those boundaries, and to relieve the nervous pressures of the classroom.

One of them is to make it very clear that I am not a therapist, and that nothing I say or do in the classroom should be construed as such. When students
very rarely approach me with such needs, I recommend the college counselor's
office or a professional therapist. I should say that this does not always work. In

one extreme case, I literally had to walk the student to the therapist's office at her repeated, and obviously heartfelt plea. Another, very different, strategy that I use is humor. Like nothing else I know, humor melts tension. Humor opens people up. Humor is honesty posing as entertainment. Another technique I employ is to speak explicitly up front, preferably on the first day, about both the occasionally difficult nature of some of the material and the necessarily open nature of our future classroom discussions. Anyone, I counsel, who is not emotionally, religiously, or cognitively ready for such material and such discussions should drop the course immediately. Period. I also include in the syllabus what I call a "contract paragraph" that sets out in unequivocal terms the sexual subjects that will be covered. I then tell the students that by accepting and keeping the syllabus, they are acknowledging their awareness of the subject matter and are agreeing to take part in the discussions that follow, even if this taking part involves simply listening. This is a very simple, but very effective pedagogical tool, as it sets the tone immediately and makes it perfectly clear to the students that the moral choice and final responsibility to enter, or not to enter, this four-month experiment remains squarely and unequivocally with them.

The Paranormal: Answering Logos with Mythos

The figure of the Paranormal is a very different character, although, in historical truth, not entirely different. As anyone who has read far enough into the literature on the history of animal magnetism, mesmerism, spiritualism, and psychical research knows, this history is haunted, metaphorically and literally, by erotic desires and astonishing gender and sexual liberalisms. The nineteenth-century spiritualists preached about sex in heaven, did not worry too much about divorce, and were among the first to promote radical gender equity, on Earth as it is in heaven (Gutierrez 2009). Ectoplasm, moreover, did not just flow from mouths and noses. It also occasionally emerged from vaginas. And one of the most successful and colorful of all physical mediums in the literature, the Italian peasant Eusapia Palladino, was famous for her raunchy jokes and sexual aggressions. Indeed, she would often emerge from an altered state obviously horny and jump into the laps of her staid male observers. Which must have been quite a sight.

But it is not the paranormal as the erotic that I want to focus on here. It is simply the fact that, like human gender and sexuality, psychical and paranormal phenomena are ubiquitous. The Paranormal is sitting there in the seats right next to the Erotic. Indeed, I have come to realize that this second character is so omnipresent and so potentially important that I have penned one provocation, my "Mutant Marvels," that suggests that what our classrooms, and certainly our graduate schools, are really filled with is mutants, cultural and religious (and sometimes actual parapsychological) mutants who came into their powers at puberty (I told you the Paranormal was sitting next to the

Erotic) and are now trying to figure out how to name, nurture, and stabilize these abilities in ways that are constructive, creative, and, perhaps most difficult of all, professionally possible (Kripal 2006a). We are all Professor X.

Or at least can be. It took me many years to see and accept this, that is, to realize just how common the figure of the Paranormal is and choose to engage him and her pedagogically—about fourteen to be exact (I am a slow learner). The occasion of this particular lesson came in the form of a paper that I delivered at one of the national meetings of the American Academy of Religion. The paper, later published in a journal, was on the history and analysis of what we today call psychical or paranormal phenomena (Kripal 2007b). Such things are generally left out of courses and books on mysticism, with very few real exceptions (Hollenback 1996). Part of my paper's point was that this standard omission is a real mistake to the extent that it is little more than a reflection of the standard rejection, or even demonization, of these phenomena on the part of the orthodox religious authorities, who see, correctly, that such common things seriously challenge their own authority and mediation. Psychical and paranormal phenomena are famously democratic. They make no distinction between elite and popular culture, nor do they honor the distinctions between the traditional and the contemporary. They are as likely to happen to a sexually crude and thieving Italian peasant medium (Eusapia again) as to a saintly Tibetan lama, to a group of Appalachian teenagers dating in a black '57 Chevy (the Mothman phenomena of Point Pleasant, West Virginia, in 1966–1967) as to a medieval monk in a monastery.

My conference paper briefly delineated the history of the study of such phenomena and suggested, in passing, that these events are amenable to humanistic methods of study and analysis, that is, that at least some of these events appear to work remarkably like "living texts" that can be read and interpreted like any other text or story. The respondent, Ivan Strenski, was critical of my paper, but not so much because of anything I said or claimed. It was the phenomena to which, I gathered, Ivan was really objecting.

Then something really very interesting happened. During the question-and-answer session, which lasted almost an hour, person after person in the room raised a hand, stood up, and addressed himself or herself to the subject of my paper. But they were not really talking to me. They were talking to Ivan. What I found so fascinating, and so intellectually productive, here, was the fact that they did not answer his reason with more reason, for there was really nothing wrong with his reasoning. Rather, they answered his reasoning with personal stories that could not possibly be fit into anyone's reasoning. In short, *they addressed the limits of reason by enacting their own myths.* The latter amounted to story after story of this or that psychical or paranormal event in their personal lives. I do not honestly recall any of these stories, or how many of them there were, only that there were a number of them. What I do very distinctly remember is being very struck by the fact that *these were true stories coming into deep conflict with good reasons.*

Then something even more interesting happened. After about an hour of this, Ivan stood up and said something along the lines of how he knew that these things happen all the time. He was simply arguing, he explained, that he could not see how they could become reliable objects of academic discourse and analysis. Then he told what amounted to a family ghost story!

That was a key turning point for me, not because I was right and he was wrong. He was not wrong, and I am sure I was not entirely right. Rather, it was a turning point because it was at that moment (really, looking back on that moment) that I realized, *whatever* else they are, paranormal and psychical phenomena tend to work in ways that constitute narratives, texts, stories—basically, little mythologies. I realized, in short, that very often (not always) the primary function of paranormal events is a semiotic, hermeneutical, or narrative one, and, moreover, that there are very deep links between the mythical, the mystical, and the paranormal that we have not even begun to understand. It was out of this same conviction that I later wrote *Authors of the Impossible* (Kripal 2010).

And all of this had a profound effect in turn on my pedagogical practices, for I learned something more. I had long noticed that, as I traveled around the country and talked about my ideas about comparative mystical literature and sexual orientation in the abstract, people often found these ideas bizarre, even occasionally offensive. When, however, I just talked about my life, that is, my own personal narrative or *mythos,* and contextualized these ideas in the context of that life story, the ideas made almost immediate sense to people. Even if some, maybe many, individuals could not still accept these ideas, they could well see why I would think such things and want to talk and write about them so much. In short, I was beginning to realize that the key of whatever pedagogical success I could muster lies in the story and not just the abstract idea, in the *mythos,* not the *logos,* or perhaps best of all, in the *logos* expressed and transcended in the *mythos.*

The Free Spirit: Engaging Popular Sentiment as Emergent Critical Theory

Right between the Erotic and the Paranormal sits the Free Spirit. I got to know, and I mean really know, this final secret in the seats through a long historiographical project that I pursued in the first decade of this century around the American human potential movement (Kripal 2007a) and a subsequent course I developed around the same at my home institution. The book is entitled *Esalen: America and the Religion of No Religion,* and the course is called "American Metaphysical Religion." Both treat that broad historical sweep of highly individualistic, usually heterodox, often esoteric, and lately *mystical* or *occult* movements that writers such as Catherine Albanese (2006), Mitch Horowitz (2009), Christopher Partridge (2004), and Leigh Eric Schmidt (2005) have made the focus of their writing. Indeed, I named the course with Albanese's magnificent *magnum opus* in mind.

But it is the subtitle of my own book that really focuses my comments here—the religion of no religion. The phrase was originally created and used as a book title by a Stanford professor of comparative religion named Frederic Spiegelberg (Spiegelberg 1953). Spiegelberg was a friend of Martin Heidegger, Carl Jung, and Paul Tillich. Tillich's mature understanding of mysticism, it might be noted, comes very close to that of Spiegelberg. Tillich, after all, defined the "mystical element" of the history of religions as a "critical" one that "is not satisfied with any of the concrete expressions of the Ultimate, of the Holy," that represents—together with the "sacramental" and the "ethical/prophetic" dimensions—"the fight of God within religion against religion." It is in this spirit, Tillich suggested at the very end of his life, that, "we have to absorb the past history of religions, and annihilate it in this way" (Tillich 1966). In short, the religion of no religion.

It was Tillich who helped get Spiegelberg to the United States (Tillich had fled the Nazi thought police shortly before him). It was Tillich again who gave Spiegelberg his signature theological language of the astonishing Ground of Being beyond the gods. Spiegelberg fled Nazi Germany in 1937, shortly after he attended an academic conference about which he had been warned. He returned to his university to the news that he had been fired, after which he immediately fled to the United States, where he eventually taught Asian religions, comparative mysticism, and the history of religions with a classical comparative focus at Stanford. It was there, in the 1950s, that he happened to teach two young men, Michael Murphy and Richard Price, who would soon, in the fall of 1962 to be exact, found a little visionary community in Big Sur that would become the Esalen Institute. Spiegelberg's personal mentoring of Murphy was particularly profound and life-changing for the future founder.

Spiegelberg's "the religion of no religion" was no vacuous abstraction or simply clever turn of phrase. It was a lifelong *koan* fashioned from a deep and direct metaphysical experience. More specifically, the expression was based on a mystical encounter with nature that Spiegelberg had undergone as a seminary student in 1917. He had been reading, among other things, medieval Latin mystical theology. On this day, however, he was doing no reading. He was walking in a wheat field in the bright sun when, suddenly, his ego vanished and what he called "the Self" appeared. Through this altered perspective, he began to see that God was shining through everything in the world, that everything was divine, that there was nothing *but* holiness. As he reveled in this new realization, he came around a corner and found himself confronting a gray church. He was horrified. How, he asked himself, could such a building claim to hold something more sacred, more divine, than what he had just known in the poppies, birds, and sky? The little church seemed completely preposterous to him.

From the theological scandal of this initial altered state of history, Spiegelberg developed and theorized what was essentially (or nonessentially) an apophatic mystical theology that approaches religious language, symbol, and myth as nonliteral projections of some deeper metaphysical truth that is located, paradoxically, in both the immanent human and natural worlds and in the transcendent divine world—a kind of dialectical or mystical humanism through which Feuerbach and Freud meet Boehme, if you will (and Spiegelberg, by the way, cites Boehme to explicate and explain his own mystical revelation).

It was just such a learned comparative mystical theology grounded in the natural world and just such a critical but deep engagement with the religious traditions of the world that inspired Murphy, Price, and their colleagues in their new venture and what would become the human potential movement (the latter expression was coined in 1965 by George Leonard after the civil rights movement, which he had covered for *LOOK* magazine). It was this highly intellectualized human potential movement, moreover, that would in turn morph into the populist and increasingly commercialized new age movement of the 1980s and 1990s.

I mention all of this to make a number of points. The first, which I hope is already obvious enough, is that Prof. Spiegelberg's pedagogy did not just focus on mystical movements; it also played a major inspirational role in the founding of a modern one. Second, this pedagogy was partly derived from his own initiatory experience, which was then put into comparative conversation with both Western esoteric literature (hence the Boehme part) and Hindu mystical philosophy (hence the Self part). In other words, Spiegelberg did not just teach "comparative mysticism." He lived it (turns out that, *pace* the nay-sayers and traditionalists, this is perfectly possible, particularly for intellectuals).

Third, as this single example also makes clear, if one does the requisite digging, it can usually, if not always, be seen that contemporary metaphysical movements, however popular or commercialized, display deep and sophisticated theological roots in earlier movements and figures. Such contemporary movements may often express themselves in simple sound bites—like "I am spiritual, but not religious"—but such phrases by no means necessitate a kind of cultural rootlessness, spiritual narcissism, or apolitical irresponsibility. In historical fact, such phrases are popular expressions of elite, sophisticated, and often highly deconstructive, mystical forms of thought and experience that stretch back hundreds, if not thousands, of years and, at different points in history, have come into serious, even deadly political conflict with both orthodox religious authorities and highly authoritarian political systems (hence Spiegelberg's flight from Nazi fascism).

In the American context now, such contemporary movements almost certainly have their deepest and most obvious roots in what F. O. Matthiessen (1941) famously called the American Renaissance, that is, that astonishingly productive and definitive literary movement of the middle of the nineteenth century that sparked and spiked around figures such as Emerson, Thoreau, and Whitman. It is certainly no accident, as authors such as Leigh Eric Schmidt and Michael Robertson (2008) have shown in great detail, that the distinction between the *spiritual* and the *religious* is probably first found in Emerson's early essays, after which it blooms in Whitman's ecstatic poem-prophecy *Leaves of Grass* (1855) and is then explicitly articulated in the same poet's *Democratic Vistas* (1871), where "all religions" become "but temporary journeys." Nor is it insignificant that, as Schmidt again has demonstrated, the very first American occurrences of both *mysticism* and *spirituality* (used now in their modern senses) appear in Emerson (in 1838) and Whitman (in 1871), respectively (Schmidt 2005).

All of this deep historical and literary background appears to be lost on any number of elite critics of these modern spiritualities. To be frank (and a bit crabby), I have grown weary and impatient with highly abstract criticisms of such movements from intellectuals who have never done any serious ethnographic work among such communities and have never mastered the relevant literatures. Too many scholars of religion, it seems, can treat any practice or idea from the ancient or medieval world or from another culture, no matter how unusual or bizarre, with perfect seriousness and respect, and then turn around, encounter a similar idea or practice, and sometimes the very same idea or practice (now performed by people with the wrong color of skin), in California or Colorado and comfortably pronounce it "narcissistic," "capitalistic," "colonizing," or whatever. It is all very suspicious.

Most of all—and this is the important point in the present context—it is also pedagogically dysfunctional. I say this for three reasons. First, it is dysfunctional because such easy dismissals teach people, implicitly or explicitly, that the past is somehow utterly distinct and always "better" than the present. In this, such a move simply reproduces, again, the ideologies of the major religions, all of which locate revelation in the past and tend to see the present as fallen or corrupt. Second, it is dysfunctional because the experiences of modern peoples are uniquely productive for modern scholarship since (1) these experiences are often suffused with precisely the kinds of self-reflexivity and critical questions that scholars are and ask, and (2) these experiences are often far more accessible than pre-modern ones. Third, and perhaps most importantly, this attitude is dysfunctional because a phrase like "I am spiritual, but not religious" is a perfect starting-point to teach students critical theory with respect to religion. I would go further: such a phrase is *already* a form of critical theory, here expressed in popular sentiment.

These "spiritual" individuals, after all, seldom adopt such a phrase out of the blue or for no particular reason. They usually have very, very good reasons. More often than not, they were raised in traditional religious communities and with religious teachings that did serious personal harm to them—sexually, emotionally, and cognitively. Few leave a nurturing healthy community willingly. People leave communities because the latter have grown painful and dogmatic, or just stupid. People abandon religious traditions because religious traditions hurt them, or simply no longer make sense to them. People become "spiritual, but not religious," in other words, for what amount to perfectly understandable moral, intellectual, and philosophical reasons, few of which they can articulate as someone with a PhD in the study of religion might. But they know, or at least intuit, these things nonetheless. Why not take advantage of these emergent critical sensibilities in the classroom? Why not ground them historically, enrich them philosophically, and articulate them more beautifully by tracing them back to people such as Spiegelberg, Emerson, and Whitman? Why ignore these people's real religious questions and real sufferings and pretend that their convictions are superficial and without good reason, that they are just "shopping," when what they are really doing is "leaving," "giving up," and "seeking"?

I am even crabbier still, for I also have a historical point to make here. I would go as far as to say that much of the contemporary study of religion, and especially the comparative study of religion, can be thought of as a rationalized expression or secular sublimation of the kinds of social activisms and countercultural mysticisms that have flowed through American life in the last fifty years. It is not all Emerson and Whitman. It is also Huxley and Ginsberg. In effect, the altered states of the counterculture became the altered categories of the university. It is no accident, for example, that the explosion of "comparative religion" in American universities coincided *exactly* with the counterculture and its famous turn East. The American Academy of Religion was founded in 1964, two years after Esalen and just as the counterculture was getting off the ground. David Haberman has penned a powerful essay on this same idea (Haberman 1999). And Sanskritists have long noted the presence of "the seeker" students in their classrooms. Nor is it an accident that race, class, and gender have come to define much of the field. These, after all, were *precisely* the concerns of the 1960s via the civil rights movement, the sexual revolution, and the definitive birth of feminist and gay consciousness in that still reverberating decade. To the extent that intellectuals still insist on placing these forms of thought at the very heart of their critical thinking, they still inhabit what is essentially a countercultural state of consciousness and what were once "mere" popular sentiments.

My point? That we would do well to engage the popular "spiritual" sentiments we encounter in the classroom and in the public with a good deal more seriousness and historical consciousness. We would do well to sneer less and listen more to the Free Spirit. Such sentiments, after all, are most likely the seeds of the future.

Beyond the Secret

So we have the Erotic, the Paranormal, and the Free Spirit sitting in our seats. Whether we acknowledge them or not, they are there. I have suggested a common pedagogical strategy for engaging all three characters. I have suggested that the task of teaching mysticism (literally secretism) requires the courage to speak secrets and, occasionally, even to hear them. If all of this is done transparently enough, one often ends up creating what I have called a "safe zone" in one's books, in one's correspondence, and in one's classrooms in which other intellectuals, other readers, and other students can recognize their own anomalous experiences and their own difficult questions. I sometimes think of this speaking and hearing as the work of culture, as a kind of clearing of a dark forest (hints of Peter Berger's *The Sacred Canopy* and Gananath Obeyeskere's *The Work of Culture*?). One labors for years to clear just a few feet, but this gives a space for others to dwell in and make their own. They can then clear a bit more, and others a bit more, and still others still a bit more.

The goal of all this clearing, at least for me, is neither to speak nor to hear more secrets. It is to refuse being such secrets. It is to narrow or even collapse the space between the inside and the outside, which, I might add, sounds remarkably like a mystical experience.

References

Albanese, Catherine. 2006. *A Republic of Mind and Spirit: A Cultural History of American Metaphysical Religion*. New Haven, CT: Yale University Press.

Baum, Robert M. 1993. "Homosexuality in the Traditional Religions of the Americas and Africa." In *Homosexuality and World Religions*, edited by Arlene Swidler. Valley Forge, PA: Trinity Press International.

Campbell, June. 1996. *Traveller in Space: In Search of Female Identity in Tibetan Buddhism*. London: The Athlone Press.

Davies, Stevan L. 1995. *Jesus the Healer: Possession, Trance, and the Origins of Christianity*. New York: Continuum.

de Chardin, Teilhard. 1975. *Toward the Future*. New York: Harcourt Brace Jovanovich.

Faure, Bernard. 1998. *The Red Thread: Buddhist Approaches to Sexuality*. Princeton, NJ: Princeton University Press.

Gutierrez, Cathy. 2009. *Plato's Ghost: Spiritualism in the American Renaissance*. New York: Oxford University Press.

Haberman, David. 1999. "Religious Studies 2000." The Lester Lecture on the Study of Religion, Department of Religious Studies, University of Colorado, Boulder, Month day(s).

Hollenback, Jess Byron. 1996. *Mysticism: Experience, Response, and Empowerment*. University Park, PA: Pennsylvania State University Press.

Horowitz, Mitch. 2009. *Occult America: The Secret History of How Mysticism Shaped Our Nation*. New York: Tarcher/Penguin.

Huxley, Aldous. 1954. *The Doors of Perception*. New York: Harper and Brothers.

Jantzen, Grace M. 1995. *Power, Gender and Christian Mysticism*. Cambridge: Cambridge University Press.

Jordan, Mark. 2000. *The Silence of Sodom: Homosexuality in Modern Catholicism*. Chicago: University of Chicago Press.

Kelly, Edward F., Emily Williams Kelly, Adam Crabtree, Alan Gauld, Michael Grosso, and Bruce Greyson. 2007. *Irreducible Mind: Toward a Psychology for the 21st Century*. Lanham, MD: Rowman and Littlefield.

Kripal, Jeffrey J. 1995. *Kali's Child: The Mystical and the Erotic in the Life and Teachings of Ramakrishna*. Chicago: University of Chicago Press.

———. 2001. *Roads of Excess, Palaces of Wisdom: Eroticism and Reflexivity in the Study of Mysticism*. Chicago: University of Chicago Press, 2001.

——— 2003a. "The Christology and Psychology of the Kiss: Re-reading Bernard of Clairvaux's *Sermones Super Cantica Canticorum*." In *Mysticism: A Variety of Psychological Perspectives*, edited by J. A. Belzen and A. Geels, 125–149. Amsterdam: Rodopi.

——— 2003b. "Teaching Hindu Tantrism With Freud: Psychoanalysis as Critical Theory and Mystical Technique." In *Teaching Freud in Religious Studies*, edited by Diane Jonte-Pace, 213–237. New York: Oxford University Press.

——— 2006a. *The Serpent's Gift: Gnostic Reflections on the Study of Religion*. Chicago: University of Chicago Press.

——— 2006b. "Sexuality and Eroticism." In *Handbook of Religion and the Emotions*, edited by John Corrigan, 162–180. New York: Oxford University Press.

——— 2007a. *Esalen: America and the Religion of No Religion*. Chicago: University of Chicago Press.

——— 2007b. "The Rise of the Imaginal: Psychical Phenomena on the Horizon of Theory (Again)," *Religious Studies Review* 33 (3): 179–191.

——— 2008. "Taking the Purple Pill: On the Paradoxical Pedagogy of Mysticism." Blackwell Compass website. http://religion-compass.com/2008/03/06/taking-the-purple-pill-on-the-paradoxical-pedagogy-of-mysticism/.

——— 2010. *Authors of the Impossible: The Sacred and the Paranormal*. Chicago: University of Chicago Press.

Matthiessen, F. O. 1941. *American Renaissance: Art and Expression in the Age of Emerson and Whitman*. New York: Oxford University Press.

Partridge, Christopher. 2004. *The Re-Enchantment of the West*. Vol. 1. London: T & T Clark.

Paul, Diana. 1979. *Women in Buddhism: Images of the Feminine in Mahayana Tradition*. Berkeley: University of California Press.

Robertson, Michael. 2008. *Worshipping Walt: The Whitman Disciples*. Princeton, NJ: Princeton University Press.

Schalow, Paul Gordon. 1992. "Kukai and the Tradition of Male Love in Japanese Buddhism." In *Buddhism, Sexuality, and Gender*, edited by José Cabezon, 215–230. Albany: State University of New York Press.

Schmidt, Leigh Eric. 2005. *Restless Souls: The Making of American Spirituality, From Emerson to Oprah*. New York: HarperCollins.

Spiegelberg, Frederic. 1953. *The Religion of No Religion*. Stanford, CA: James Ladd Delkin.

Tillich, Paul. 1966. *The Future of Religions*. New York: Harper and Row, 87–88.

Versluis, Arthur. 1999. *Wisdom's Children: A Christian Esoteric Tradition*. Albany: State University of New York Press.

Wafer, Jim. 1997. "Vision and Passion: The Symbolism of Male Love in Islamic Mystical Literature." In *Islamic Homosexualities: Culture, History, and Literature*, edited by Stephen O. Murray and Will Roscoe. New York: New York University Press.

Wolfson, Elliot R. 1994. *Through a Speculum that Shines: Vision and Imagination in Medieval Jewish Mysticism*. Princeton, NJ: Princeton University Press.

{ INDEX }